THE
MAN WHO SAW
A GHOST

ALSO BY DEVIN McKINNEY

∽

Magic Circles:
The Beatles in Dream and History

THE
MAN WHO SAW
A GHOST

The Life *and* Work of
HENRY FONDA

Devin McKinney

ST. MARTIN'S PRESS

NEW YORK

www.stmartins.com

Design by Kathryn Parise

LIBRARY OF CONGRESS CATALOGING-IN-PUBLICATION DATA

McKinney, Devin.
   The man who saw a ghost : the life and work of Henry Fonda / Devin McKinney.—1st ed.
        p. cm.
   ISBN 978-1-250-00841-1 (hardcover)
   ISBN 978-1-250-01776-5 (e-book)
   1. Fonda, Henry, 1905–1982.   2. Motion picture actors and actresses—United States—Biography.   I. Title.
   PN2287.F558M35 2012
   791.43'028'0924—dc23
   [B]

                                                        2012028274

                    First Edition: October 2012

              10 9 8 7 6 5 4 3 2 1

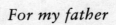

For my father

Contents

List of Illustrations

Great men, great nations, have not been boasters and buffoons, but perceivers of the terror of life, and have manned themselves to face it.

—Ralph Waldo Emerson, "Fate" (1860)

I now have a theory that our existence is a phantom—that it died, long ago, probably of old age—that the thing is a ghost. So the unreality of its composition—its phantom justice and make-believe juries and incredible judges.

—Charles Fort, *Wild Talents* (1932)

THE
MAN WHO SAW
A GHOST

Prologue

The Return of Frank James

Once upon a time, he strode through meadows, was chased by Mohawks, buried the ax in the stump, and read from the law book as if it were the Bible. In all eras, he ran, galloped, slouched, and rounded into and out of the Hollywood dream of American history.

As the prairie town's tin star, he was hard but clean, proficient but haunted. As the comic victim of romantic love, he took pratfalls for lustful females. In war, he led armies and studied his thoughts while other men whacked maps with sticks. Other times, he was the loner, drifter, killer—the dark shape cornered with a gun, or the parolee flattened by sunlight against a scorched expanse of heartland. Even when falsely charged, he was the criminal of his own imagination, because he could so easily have done what they accused him of—robbed the bank, or committed the murder.

He would appear in different places, looking familiar but never quite the same, sometimes leading the crowd, sometimes off to the side, an American artist caught up in representing his country's history—the history of centuries or of hours ago—sometimes its forceful subject, sometimes its mere object. At his noblest, he embodied the highest promises of democracy. At his darkest, he was the quiet, antisocial, anti-*pluribus* American, the American whose "Don't tread on me" meant just that: *Leave me alone, or I might kill you.*

∽

You find Henry Fonda in every corner of the mythic history and imaginative geography mapped by the movies. Like any star of such duration, he puts his name to many bad movies along the way; the career in total recalls John Berryman's remark about the collected works of Stephen Crane: "majesty and trash scrambled together." But in the fullness of time, he creates an image of the national man that is kaleidoscopic, frightening, and wildly improbable.

His best performances—*You Only Live Once, Young Mr. Lincoln, The Grapes of Wrath, The Ox-Bow Incident, My Darling Clementine, Fort Apache, The Wrong Man, Fail-Safe, Once Upon a Time in the West,* even *The Lady Eve*—are animated by the dark energy of contradiction. Viewers sense a man living in public and private dimensions at once, and recognize a continuity of mysteries in the actor. Fonda becomes the body and voice of the satisfied man's paranoia, the good man's bad urge, the hero's despairing shade, and the patriot's doubting conscience. In him and through him, the hidden becomes visible, specters are raised, and shadows begin to move on their own.

∽

"I suppose one human being never really knows much about another." Asked in 1966 to characterize Fonda, his friend of almost three decades, John Steinbeck offered this shrugging axiom. But read on: "My impressions of Hank are of a man reaching but unreachable, gentle but capable of sudden wild and dangerous violence, sharply critical of others but equally self-critical, caged and fighting the bars but timid of the light, viciously opposed to external restraint, imposing an iron slavery on himself. His face is a picture of opposites in conflict."

Everything that matters about Fonda is in those words, and we want to get behind them—seek the sources of those conflicts, that violence, the imprisoned aura; to watch the face as opposites collide, the eyes as they search; to apprehend, finally, the truth of such a tribute. Our hunch is that Fonda, like any artist who leaves a line of clues across many years and a vast collection of works, can be read—if we devise a language to read him.

∽

This is a critical biography, in that it does not find its subject to be either saint or simpleton; a psychological biography, in that it finds many things to have been acted out rather than plainly spoken; a straight biography, in that it observes decent constraints on how far one may veer from fact in pursuit of a hot surmise; a crooked biography, in that many interesting data, anecdotes, postulates, and possibilities have been left out because they contributed insufficiently to the whole—that being, we hope, a broad, deep, comprehensible sense of Fonda, the essence of his life and the weight of his work.

As I see it, I've gone after the story. Every life makes its own kind of sense, and a book like this is useless unless it sifts fact and perception for the themes of a life formed by character—unless it goes after the story.

The story being, perhaps, this: that Fonda was a solitary man who distinguished himself in the most public of arts; that therein lay his tension and his style; that his conflicts made him a vital artist and emotional mystery, a rather baffling and altogether fascinating man. And that repeatedly over the course of a long and lauded career, he pulled off the amazing feat of being not only what he appeared to be but also what he didn't appear to be.

His solitude was deep and his style glamorous enough to constitute one ideal of the American character. The audience embraced it because it was strong, appealing, and reducible to its most favorable qualities.

Yet Fonda's best portraits not only hold up but grow richer because the years reveal a pentimento of sorrow and anger beneath their surfaces. Like great novels, his great performances yield themselves to time, to contexts of national and personal history.

All of which is to say that if Americans opened their doors to Fonda for his virtue and sincerity, they kept his company for a deeper reason— the suspicion that, wherever he'd come from, wherever he might go, he traveled with ghosts.

Part 1

1

Springfield, 1839

Young Mr. Lincoln

It is a basic American scene. Torches, a rope, a jailhouse, a crowd; darkness lit by fire, smashed windows, vulnerable door. A basic, terrifying scene. No American can fail to recognize it.

Someone was murdered earlier tonight. Two men are in custody, and the crowd wants them. In front are elderly drunks who at another time might be lovable. "We've gone to a heap of trouble not to have at least one hangin'," one drawls.

Only Abe Lincoln, lawyer for the accused, is there to oppose them. He pushes through the crowd and defends the door of the law. Dressed in black, face glowing white, he screams at the crowd to listen.

He allows that, had they lives to spare, the prisoners inside could stand some hanging. "But the sort of hanging you boys'd give 'em would be so—so *permanent*. Trouble is, when men start takin' the law into their own hands, they're just as apt, in all the confusion and fun, to start hangin' somebody who's not a murderer as somebody who is."

Lincoln knows that only the surrender of identity and responsibility makes the mob event possible. So as he speaks, he looks the lynchers in the face, becoming the mirror that reflects and judges them. He says their names, and shrewdly throws in a bit of Bible so they may walk away reassured of their morality.

"This scene," writes the German novelist Peter Handke, "embodied every possibility of human behavior. In the end not only the drunks, but also the actors playing the drunks, were listening intently to Lincoln, and when he had finished they dispersed, changed forever." That's lovely to imagine. But it doesn't last two seconds. We know these same men will be back in a month, a decade, a century to hang someone else. We know they'll succeed, because Abe won't be there to stop them. Lincoln has risked his life to forestall what he knows to be inevitable—that in this world, mobs kill.

It's Springfield, Illinois, circa 1839. So much of the worst is still to come.

∽

"A jack-legged young lawyer from Springfield": That was John Ford's Lincoln. He'd drawn this Lincoln from daguerreotype, the narratives of schoolbooks, the mythology of martyrdom. He'd fashioned a noble, humorous, cagey man with a reverence for law and an instinctive sense of right. This was the Lincoln photographed by Mathew Brady and chronicled by William B. Herndon, yet he was barely a historical figure. He was something both simpler and stranger: a product of the national imagination. Facts could be arranged as needed.

Now this was a hero. Courageous, articulate, visionary, yet a common man, respected from mansion to shack. He'd been through pain of his own, and knew what other people suffered. Ford's Lincoln had wit, love, and a sense of loss. Ford's Lincoln was heartbreaking. It broke the heart to know that no leader so ideal had ever walked our country's roads, in any century; and it broke the heart to imagine—as Ford imagined, and would have his audience imagine—that that ideal just might, this one time, have been the truth.

To play his Lincoln, Ford wants that jack-legged young actor from Omaha. Henry Fonda has spent the last few years in Hollywood quietly making himself remarkable. Career-advancing intervals of romantic comedy and rural hokum have been cut with a handful of harsh performances: a mountaineer in *The Trail of the Lonesome Pine* (1936); an ex-con in *You Only Live Once* (1937), first of the Bonnie and Clyde movies; an aristocrat in the plantation weeper *Jezebel* (1938), sweating feverishly as he carried Bette Davis to an Oscar; and brother Frank in *Jesse James* (1939), in which all Fonda had to do to steal the picture from Tyrone Power was spit a stream of tobacco juice and glare over his mustache.

Fonda has leaped past his competition, and past himself. He's one of Hollywood's biggest near-stars and most protean support players; he's shown tensile strength on the screen, and a gift for charismatic silence. He's handsome and healthy, but when the climax comes, he dies eloquently, memorably.

So he seems fated to play the sixteenth president. The two have had a long association: At the age of twenty, Fonda toured the Midwest with a Lincoln impersonator, portraying Lincoln's secretary in a sketch he wrote himself. He estimates he has already read most of the Lincoln books that exist. And there was that scene in his very first film, *The Farmer Takes a Wife*—a brief encounter between the Fonda character and a prepubescent John Wilkes Booth. In terms of the story, the meeting between Booth and Fonda's river rat in an 1850s canal town had no function. But in the context created by *Young Mr. Lincoln* four years later, it was a clear case of foreshadowing.

Fonda cannot claim surprise at being asked to play Lincoln: As early as 1935, he was named in Hollywood columns as the next Abe of the screen. But when John Ford calls, rational Fonda resists. Playing Lincoln's secretary is one thing, but the man himself? "It's like playing Jesus," he says.

Ford, a stout, fleshy, hard-drinking Irish-American, is already famed for his dark glasses and floppy hat, his briar pipe and profanity. He is keenly aware of his personal power and developing legend, and he wields them as weapons of fear. He cows Fonda with a four-letter aria: "What the fuck is all this shit about you not wanting to play this picture? You think Lincoln's a great fucking Emancipator, huh? He's a young jack-legged lawyer from Springfield, for Christ sake."

Heroes come of humble beginnings, and artists are humbled to become great.

Henry sits for the laborious application of prosthetics and pancake. Photos and screen tests are taken, and all are stunned with the result. The great man's gravity is there: The nose is soft putty, but the brow ridge is as hard and dark as a log.

The film, shot mostly around Sacramento, is completed in time for its world premiere, in Springfield, on March 30, 1939—exactly a century from the point the events it portrays took place. Soon it goes into broad release and is recognized as a profound piece of American popular art, warm and earthy as bread from a cabin stove.

From the Soviet director Sergei Eisenstein it will draw, in 1945, one of the most poignant appreciations ever written of a movie. "I first saw this film on the eve of the world war," Eisenstein will recall, a crucial detail that directs him to *Young Mr. Lincoln*'s "womb of popular and national spirit." He will extol "its unity, its artistry, its genuine beauty," and, with a poet's yearning tugging at his technician's mask, describe how "the rhythm of the montage corresponds to the timbre of the photography, and where the cries of the waxwings echo over the turbid flow of muddy water and through the steady gait of the little mule that lanky Abe rides along the Sangamon River."

Eisenstein cares only so much about the rhythm of the montage. For this moment, he wants nothing but to ride along that river, see that beautiful country.

∽

The archetypal Hollywood director, D. W. Griffith, released his first masterpiece, *The Birth of a Nation*, in 1915. It was based on *The Clansman*, Thomas Dixon, Jr.'s best-selling novel of ten years before—an exhortatory romance meant to illustrate how, in "one of the most dramatic chapters in the history of the Aryan race," an "'Invisible Empire' had risen from the field of Death and challenged the Visible to mortal combat . . . and saved the life of a people."

That "Invisible Empire" was, of course, the Ku Klux Klan. Dixon painted the postbellum night riders as heroes, protecting the South from carpetbaggers, and magnolia belles from black rapists. Griffith disclaimed any personal racism, yet he inflated Dixon's theses with thunder, pageantry, and innovative technique. Made to sweep history in its wake, and granted a famous endorsement by President Woodrow Wilson— "Like writing history with lightning"—*The Birth of a Nation* grossed over sixty million dollars and was viewed by more Americans than any film yet made.

The National Association for the Advancement of Colored People succeeded in getting it banned in many cities but could not prevent its seep into the American mind. On leaving a theater in Lafayette, Indiana, that was screening the Griffith film, a man named Henry Brocj shot and killed Edward Manson, a black high school student. Bosley Crowther, later film critic of the *New York Times,* was a boy in North Carolina in 1915. "If the people coming out [of the theater] did no more than abuse the Negroes they saw in the street," he recalled, "it was fortunate. Actually, a lot of people would throw rocks at them and do things of that sort." In his novel *Appointment in Samarra,* John O'Hara flashes back to the Pennsylvania boyhood of his protagonist, describing how his street gang "would play Ku Klux Klan, after having seen *The Birth of a Nation.*"

Historians concur that Griffith's film played a significant role in the surge of race violence that marked the late teens and early twenties. Certainly it was instrumental in the revival of the Klan: It became a recruiting tool for the terror group, and well into the 1960s, Klan chapters throughout the South were known to screen private prints in chamber of commerce basements and Masonic lodges whenever blood courage and race inspiration were called for.

Appearing as one of Griffith's Klan riders—a nearsighted White Knight holding up his hood to see through black-rimmed spectacles—was a young Hollywood hang-about named John Martin Feeney. Feeney had yet to assume the professional name of John Ford, and he was years away from beginning to become one of the great American directors, and the camera poet behind *Young Mr. Lincoln.*

Sometimes histories meet to make chaos. Sometimes they weave a shapely braid: the new strand unfurls from the last.

∽

As mythic narrative and secret history, *The Birth of a Nation* is actually about the birth of a nation *within* a nation—that is, the Invisible Empire itself: a violent conspiracy to enforce a supremacist doctrine through rape, murder, and fear. Its countermyth, *Young Mr. Lincoln,* is about the birth of a different America, whose progress is driven instead by compassion, objectivity, and respect for truth: a shadow utopia, a conspiracy of kindness. Both are fantasies woven from chosen bits of American history; which one is closer to the truth may depend on who is looking.

Yet the young man who rode in D. W. Griffith's Invisible Empire is also the older man who brings the countermyth to life. It's as if the director is discovering his subject, his medium, and his country in every scene. Serenely assured, Ford dissolves his scenes to black as they are performed, by stopping down his lens to close out the light; he prints only one take of each scene, ordering all others destroyed. Thus, myth springs complete and articulate from his eye, no rough draft flapping in its wake. He strolls through an Independence Day fair, not so much following Abe as encountering him at every turn—as rail-splitter, judge of pies, anchorman in a tug-of-war. Ford turns to watch a parade of war veterans roll past in buggies, the only witnesses left to the War of 1812 and the Revolution; and he can only stare, amazed that he is so close to the origins of his country.

Never again will Ford's patriotism be so affirmative. It's not the patriotism of an old man clutching a flag and cursing dissenters, but that of a much younger man entranced by the *possibility* of goodness in

America. Ages later, we hear a muffled dialogue behind it, questions the film can't ask itself but which we can scarcely avoid: Could these patriotic clichés and Americanist homilies ever be true? Despite the massacres, slave ships, burnings, lynchings?

Young Mr. Lincoln is an act of empathy and of imagining. It is also a myth, or even a fairy tale. Let us imagine, it asks, that these homilies *are* true, that this man is just that good, and that America once offered such a man the opportunity to steer it. Let us imagine that Lincoln's goodness will enable him to save the innocents and expose the truth. Let us imagine that, by placing a complex character at the center of simple events, we can imply the complexity of this country and its history. Let us imagine that we can raise a few bloodied specters of the American past, and, in the realm of myth, if nowhere else, purify them.

Let us imagine: That's the process that enables myth, and it's the mythic hero that enables the process. In *Young Mr. Lincoln*'s act of imagining, all the unspoken truths of our bloody history will flow through Lincoln, as mud through a river. He will take in the poison of violence, absorb hatred and pain, die for our sins, and live in our myths forever as a ghost of righteousness and rebuke.

And as Ford and Fonda portray him, he'll walk, talk, sit, think, speak, and spit with the resolve of one who has seen it all coming—one who *knows,* as other men and women simply do not.

∞

Fonda carries these details in every gesture and expression, his bearing as elemental as the film's lowering skies. There is something about how he lures the Lincoln out of himself that enables him to speak and move like an unseen watcher, an omnipotent witness. That something is the deep silence of one who will never surrender that last part of himself—the part that digests information and emotion, and produces empathetic vision from a private place.

Everything in *Young Mr. Lincoln* depends on this tension between the public figure and the private man, the servant who offers everything and the individual who relinquishes nothing. It all depends on this tension being felt but not discussed, and being felt immediately, at Lincoln's first appearance on a clapboard porch on a dusty afternoon. A pompous attorney addresses a cluster of earnest countrymen. Someone named Abe, familiar to the locals, is introduced as a candidate for the legislature. The attorney steps aside with a flourish. Cut to a figure reclining in the shade—a man with a private smile and a gift for dramatic timing, who eases himself to fullness and steps into the sun.

"Gentlemen—and fellow citizens . . . I presume y'all know who I am."

It's dizzying. How often does myth take flesh before our eyes? Seldom have movies achieved, through makeup or miracle, so arresting a combination of attributes as this, so bizarre and fixating a meld of physical actor and imaginative essence. The face is Lincoln's; the voice is Fonda's. The body moves with the proper languid resolve, looking just as Lincoln's would have, had it ever been caught on moving film.

We witness a fusing of faces, and of fates. Lincoln starts to speak; Fonda starts to exist. The one steps into destiny, the other into movie myth. And to both we can only say, Yes, this is how it was supposed to be.

∽

Part of the magic of Fonda's portrayal is that at the same time he speaks for Lincoln, he asks Lincoln to speak for him. Each uses the other to express his own sadness and conflict; two spirits war within the imperturbable costume that to us appears filled out by one integrated body.

What is the sadness? What is the conflict? Primal scenes are both inadequate and irresistible; myth couldn't do without them. So the Lamar Trotti screenplay founds itself on not just one primal scene, but two—the near lynching on the prison stairs, and a young woman's death.

That woman was Ann Rutledge, Abe's first love, whom he met upon moving to New Salem, Illinois, in 1831. Her father, a tavern owner, was young Lincoln's employer; one of her forefathers had signed the Declaration of Independence. Ann had ambitions beyond New Salem, and planned to attend a women's college. She saw Lincoln's potential and encouraged him toward the law. Abe was besotted with her, and they were engaged. Then, in August of 1835, she took sick and died from what was called "brain fever" but was probably typhoid.

The story was first embellished by Herndon, Lincoln's law partner and first important biographer, and has been a wrangling point of historians. "He mourned her loss with such intensity of grief that his friends feared for his reason," Carl Schurz wrote in 1905. "A highly dubious business," Gore Vidal called the story some eighty years later. Melodramatics aside, there is sufficient evidence that Ann's death left a deep void in Lincoln. He was already given to long despondencies, not surprising given the poverty of his childhood and the deaths he'd witnessed, starting with both parents and an older sister.

In *Young Mr. Lincoln,* Abe and Ann have just one scene together. Fonda presents Lincoln as a serious young man, though callow in his coonskin cap, and Ann is Ford's model of supportive American womanhood. The two stroll beside the flowing Sangamon, nearly bursting with anticipation of the future and each other, but the exchange is infused with sadness. Already we have the sense of things too fine and fleeting to last.

Abe tosses a stone in the river. A dissolve turns the concentric ripples of springtime water into jagged pieces of ice dragging past the Sangamon's banks in deepest winter. Ann Rutledge is dead—gone, just that fast—and Abe lays flowers at her grave. From the natural world of springtime, we go to a studio set of simulated winter. The transition from love, youth, and yearning to chill, death, and snowy ground is pure instinctive mysticism. It's what religion tries to make sense of, and what art, in its highest moments, may capture.

Douglas L. Wilson writes of the "symbolic significance" that Ann's sudden death had for Lincoln. That symbol was the grave. A Lincoln neighbor told Herndon, "I never seen a man mourn for a companion more than he did for her he made a remark one day when it was raining that he could not bare the idea of its raining on her Grave that was the time the community said he was crazy he was not crazy but he was very disponding a long time." Wilson finds this convincing evidence of "Lincoln's emotional fixation on Ann's grave."

Not just the grave but also what it represents: the obligations left by the dead upon the living. In *Young Mr. Lincoln,* Abe stands a stick on the frozen ground over Ann's grave and offers a proposition. He will let the stick fall, and if in falling it points to the grave, he will fulfill Ann's dream of his destiny and become a lawyer. If it points away, he will stay a shop clerk.

Abe wonders, when the stick points to the grave, if it was more he or Ann who influenced its direction. It doesn't matter: The stick has two ends, and Abe knows that if one points at the grave, the other points back at him. He and the ghost are one.

∽

Fonda knows he's not impersonating Lincoln, but collaborating with a specter. His eyes are sunken and haunted, as if Abe were half man and already half spirit. He lives in two worlds—a sunlit world of elections and baking contests and political calculations, and another of stark elements, apprehensions, omens. The icy river running past Ann's graveyard; the forest clearing where a stabbing occurs; the rainy hilltop where Lincoln sees his country's future. Light and dark, day and night; material world and ghost world.

A. Alvarez describes how Freud "showed that in mourning and its pathological equivalent, melancholia, the ego tries to restore to life whatever has been lost by identifying with it, and then incorporating, or introjecting, the lost object in itself." *Young Mr. Lincoln* shows the steps by which Abe absorbs Ann's ghost and becomes a different man. He feels humble, special, responsible; he thinks and speaks with uncommon deliberation. This is the weight we sense in people who seem to have more than the usual portions of sadness, gravity, and modesty. It's the sense Lincoln carried that the dead required something of him, that the stick pointed at the grave and at him, and that there was a ghostly determinant to human events.

It's a sense he never shook, and died trying to fulfill.

∽

Back on the prison steps, Lincoln addresses the lynching party: "We do things together that we'd be mighty ashamed to do by ourselves."

His words go right to the heart of democracy. In the film, Lincoln is always suspicious of that brutal togetherness: He is a thoughtful watcher, where his neighbors are impulsive doers; a loner, where they are joiners. Often—as when the townspeople besiege the Clay brothers in the clearing, or when Mary Todd coquettishly lavishes attention on Lincoln's rival—Abe stands back, observing the display from a shadow or an upper floor. Eisenstein sensed Lincoln's sunken watchfulness structuring the film, calling it "a gaze of cosmic reproaches to worldly vanities."

But Fonda's Lincoln doesn't just observe democracy; he participates in it, jokes and dances with it. Henry is a stiff, inhibited dancer, but he *knows* how he looks, and from stiffness comes style. He's so bad, he's charming: Directors persist in making him dance. Ford's dancing scenes in particular are ways of making democracy itself dynamic and physical. Springfield's town dance is the daylight counterpart to its after-dark lynching party, the community showing its best face and allowing Abe to relinquish all his tragic suspicions of his neighbors, if only for the moments it takes him to reel about the square with Mary Todd and incarnate the great man as deadpan physical comedian.

As a lawyer, Abe is master of the folksy shim-sham, and Ford and Fonda plant and detonate some of the biggest courtroom laughs since *The Pickwick Papers*. But throughout, the mob is a testy presence. So easily excited, so stupidly passionate, it is as ready to tear down a building as it is to roar with laughter. Abe is right not to trust it. And, with the guilty man finally exposed, he knows when to step out of its way. Having affirmed law and order, probity and logic, Lincoln replaces his hat as if restoring the lid to democracy's boiling pot, while offscreen, the mob howls again, as it had at the prison steps.

During the trial, Fonda sits to hear a witness. Ford poses him in shadow and profile, so that Abe looms upon the scene as a spirit in the foreground, a history-book silhouette. The film has such somberness and weight that the image, while contrived, doesn't register as anything less than justified and true. At that moment—and at Ann's graveside, and at the march of the war veterans, and at the prison steps—*Young Mr. Lincoln*'s countermyth is redeemed. The revisioning of history comes emotionally alive, and rings with a profound clarity of conception and belief. Again and again, the film achieves this pure sense, not just of a national ideal expressed in composed and harmonious drama but also of the sadness and fear such an ideal would conceal.

Fear of what? Of people and their prejudices, as implacable, seemingly, as mountains and rivers; of the violent mass; of America itself. *Young Mr. Lincoln*—in its deep night, its grave, its noose, its observant Lincoln certain the worst is to come—is rich with that fear. Ford and Fonda know it and feel it. They will offer a mythology of purity, an idealized imagining of the American past, but their fantasy will tremble with the falling of night.

∽

Joseph McBride believes the film's central metaphor "is that of Lincoln as a symbolic reconciler of opposing forces in American life." But we're unable to view the events of Ford's film without realizing the disjunctions between Lincoln's aspiration and America's reality. If McBride is correct, this Lincoln symbolizes nothing so much as failure—his, and ours.

But a great popular artwork yields metaphor as Midwestern soil produces food. So other metaphors present themselves, ones containing other parts of the truth. Two, to be exact: the noose and the grave. Abe at the prison, facing down the mob; and Abe at the graveside, talking to Ann's ghost. The first symbolizes public fear; the second, private sorrow. Both symbolize loss, and a lifelong condition of yearning for the unattainable. Both imply that essential opposing forces—the man's private life, the American's public life—cannot be reconciled.

John Ford needs Henry Fonda to make these metaphors breathe. He knows Fonda will bring Abe down from the monument and make him a man. Fonda is the essential counterweight to the pro-American tone, both nostalgic and progressive, to which Ford aspires. He needs Fonda to step into the American story, to embody its tragedy and its memory.

Fonda knows enough about Lincoln, America, and himself to play

Abe as a haunted man aware of what is in store for him, who moves and speaks carefully because of the burden such foreboding places on him, and who spends the film, in Graham Greene's words, "preparing himself for his last defeat at the hands of a violent world."

∞

The ending gives us this: Lincoln has saved the innocent men from the mob, justice from the noose, democracy from itself. The Clay family's wagon climbs a hill into thunderclouds, and Lincoln follows. He reaches the hill; pauses. Thunder, lightning, wind, rain. All elements converge on his lean outline. Lincoln, holding his hat, walks into the storm.

Historians have always fancied, following the man's own writings, that Lincoln foresaw his destiny, and walked into the storm freely. So it is fair to interpret Lincoln symbolically, given that he lived that way; and fair to conclude of *Young Mr. Lincoln* that its judgment on both his character and our history is formed by the elements of destruction and loss, the noose and the grave.

If Fonda tells us anything about America, it's important that *Young Mr. Lincoln* tells us something about Fonda. Like the young jackleg lawyer from Springfield, Fonda feared the closeness of the crowd even as he sought its soul. He was an artist of democracy and a man of sorrows. He knew about the noose, and about the grave. And like Lincoln, he acted as though there were a certain kind of life he was obliged to live: some long-ago death he was bound to honor.

2

The Elephant and the Black Dog

Henry Fonda, age 14

B e ashamed, an old man like you."
These are the first words Fonda speaks on film. The year is 1935. The picture is *The Farmer Takes a Wife*, the setting the main street of an Erie Canal town in the 1850s. A senior citizen is bursting with spunk and spoiling for a fight. Suddenly, a young man appears in the street like a luminescent totem pole; he holds the geezer back, makes the old man seem a boy.

Up to now, the film has been quaint and clattering, a cacophony of stage actors bellowing their lines at a wincing camera. Now it settles somewhat, and grows quiet around Fonda. His physical being is unusual, but the twang in his voice is like rust on a nail. The voice pierces the unearthliness of the body and pins it to reality.

There's little else to recall about the film, which is defeated by cuteness and contrivance. The female lead, Janet Gaynor, has charm, and the director, Victor Fleming, gives a nice sun-blasted sense of the hot outdoors; but otherwise, Fonda's first has minimal claim on history's attention, or ours.

Finally there is only the man at the center of it—observant, radiant, sad.

And sincere. "One of Mr. Fonda's most outstanding assets," wrote Eileen Creelman of the New York *Sun,* reviewing *The Farmer Takes a Wife* in 1935, "is his appearance of sincerity."

⸎

Fonda, from the Latin, means "foundation" or "base." It is also the name of a valley in the Apennines, near Genoa, where the family's origins lie. There was at least one troublemaker back along the line: In the fourteenth century, the marquis de Fonda was chased out of Italy under ambiguous circumstances. In *Early American Families* (1916), the Reverend William Asbury Williams claimed the marquis "was one of the leaders of a revolution in Genoa, having for its object the overturning of the aristocratic government, and putting the election of the Doge [chief magistrate] and Senate, into the hands of the people at large." The marquis is described as "an early republican."

He and his family fled to Amsterdam. There they intermarried with the Dutch, and were assimilated into the Dutch Reformed Church. This Protestant branch, rooted in Calvinism, proclaimed humanity's inherent depravity and placed salvation at the sole discretion of a capricious God, irrespective of any good works or repentant acts. A tense way to live, but for the Fondas it became ordinary life over several generations. Then, as the Dutch Reform movement grew in the wake of Luther's challenge to Roman Catholic hegemony, its adherents were subject to all manner of papist persecution. Again, panic and flight.

This time, all the way to the New World. Jellis Douw Fonda was the first of his line to lay eyes on North America. Henry placed his forebear's arrival in the Mohawk Valley of upstate New York at around 1628—though it was probably closer to midcentury, since Jellis's only son, Douw Jellis, is recorded as having been born in Amsterdam in 1641.

This son fathered nine children and became the ancestor of all American Fondas.

In 1751, Jellis's great-grandson, Douw Jellis (stingy with names, these people) decamped from Schenectady to settle at a site called Caughnawaga—Iroquois for "on the rapids"—between the Mohawk River and the foot of the Adirondacks. He purchased many acres and grew very wealthy. Several children were raised, two wives loved, lost, and mourned. Douw settled in for his twilight years as a squire, respected and comfortable.

But by then the Revolution had begun, and war found Douw in his rural fastness. Sir John Johnson, British Loyalist and son of the superintendent of Indian Affairs, commanded a brigade of Crown-serving Iroquois. In May 1780, as Johnson's armies campaigned to regain the Mohawk Valley for George III, immigrants, colonists, and Indians friendly to either side were massacred, and the land torched. Among the dead lay Douw Fonda—mutilated, according to accounts, by a Mohawk named One-Armed Peter. It is remarked by one source that "venerable old David [sic] Fonda was killed and scalped by an Indian party . . . [and] cut in several parts of his head with a tomahawk."

A Fonda family historian records that Douw's "house was plundered and burned," and that although he "had always been on good terms with the Indians . . . his life was taken as 'heartlessly' as though he were an active enemy. He was seventy-nine years old." He was buried in a local graveyard, with other casualties of the War of Independence. Caughnawaga was later renamed Fonda in Douw's honor.

∽

Some eight decades hence, shots were fired on Fort Sumter, and a new war was on. Henry's grandfather, Ten Eyck Hilton Fonda—born in his family's namesake village in 1838, and nicknamed "Nike"—volunteered for the Union army and was made a telegrapher. In this capacity, he helped turn the course of history. "At midnight June 30, 1863," ran a newspaper report fifty years later, Ten Eyck "personally delivered the telegram transcription from Secretary of War Edwin Stanton to General George Meade of the Union Army warning him of the advancing Confederate Army under Robert E. Lee toward Gettysburg and commanding Meade to assume the offensive. Fonda is credited with delivering this important warning, which allowed the Union armies to prepare for the approaching Confederates."

In a letter to his brother, scribbled on telegraph blanks on the Independence Day after his ride, Henry's grandfather wrote, "I had orders to spare nothing, horseflesh and money was of no account if I would only deliver the message. I tell you I made the old horse get."

How does a man go from that to being a ticket agent on the New York Central Railroad? We can guess that, like many a veteran, Ten Eyck sought in the hole-punching regularity of his unvarying job an escape from violence. Imagine a man who has sped through the night, confident that his failure to do his job means thousands on his own side dead. Imagine his special peace when the victory is, in small and secret part, his alone. He must breathe every breath feeling justified; must feel he can take the rest of his life slowly.

∽

Take it slowly, and see some of the country "out there." In 1869, the Burlington & Missouri River Railroad was completed, connecting the markets of Chicago and Omaha on a route through southern Iowa. Ten Eyck moved his family from the New York valley the Fondas had helped settle more than two centuries before, and took a telegrapher's job in Omaha. His fourth child, William Brace—Henry's father—was born there in 1879.

William married a local girl, Herberta Lamphear Jaynes, in July 1903. They began to plan a family, and by the time evolution and event, travel and tumult had done their work to achieve the Fondas of Omaha, they were, as a friend called them, "ordinary American people." Mainstreamers, with little or no Italian seasoning left, the harsh Calvinism as much a psychological disposition as a spiritual inheritance. Trade Dutch Reformed for Christian Science, Colonial buckles for sensible buttons, and the change was all but complete. Out of Europe, America; out of defiance, rectitude; out of many, one.

But nothing is really forgotten. Family fears come down through generations and settle in the minds of the young. Something of those ancestral troublemakers and frightened runners came down to Henry, even through centuries of migration and assimilation, of ethnic melt-down, of submission to snow and cold as the Fondas forged westward . to their latest settling point, far on the plains of Nebraska.

Is the settler ever truly settled? Looking at Henry, we would have to say no.

∞

Fonda's second picture, *Way Down East* (1935)—based on a play first filmed by D. W. Griffith in 1920—is situated, like *The Farmer Takes a Wife,* in a bucolic niche of mid-nineteenth-century New England coun-tryside and is likewise a grand opera for Middle America: broad jokes, narrow rescues, happy harvests. Familiar players make a community of comic stereotypes, a heartland village set in the movie mind of another time.

Fonda is the community's straight man, its spokesman for "human kindness" against "self-righteous bigotry" (his character uses those words). Everyone else flies over the top, leaving only Henry to speak slowly, act seemly, and plant his feet on the earth. He's first spotted, as he was last seen in *The Farmer,* at one with the land—guiding a horse team and thresher across a picturesque piece of farmland. Even when interacting, he is a private person, with a slightly dissociated quality; even in his youth, he is graver than the old men around him.

And even in a paltry movie, he cuts an amazing image. He is an American out of frontier storybooks, worthy of paintings, who yet stands apart from the community that looks to him to find its ideal.

∞

Say "Nebraska," and most Americans think of a rectangle somewhere in the middle of the map. In the early nineteenth century, when American Indians lived there, it was a vast prairie with unsettled borders. When California gold was found in the 1840s, wagons came through in such numbers as to carve ruts in the ground; upon these, the pioneer trails were established.

Nebraska was almost the precise midpoint of the continent, heart of the heart of the country, and the "great highway" of westward migration passed right through it. Its major arteries were the Oregon, California, and Mormon trails—collectively, the Great Platte River Road, a corridor running along either side of the Platte River through its namesake valley.* The estimate is that some 350,000 passed through in the years between 1841 and 1866.

The adventurers suffered from hunger and the elements on their journey west, and there was no reason for them to come but one: the promised land. That meant California, Nevada, Utah. It didn't mean Nebraska. Glory was found in the Far West; misery and death stayed in the heart of the country. Between 1842 and 1859, an estimated thirty thousand people died along the Platte River Road from exhaustion, malnutrition, cholera, wasting. At first, the departed were buried decently, with orations and prayers. Then deaths grew too common and burials too arduous. Some left the bodies of their dead in shallow graves; others "simply abandoned hopeless cases by the roadside."

These immigrants took almost nothing from the land as they passed through, because the land had almost nothing to give to those unwilling to settle on it. If they left anything, it was their belongings, their bones, and the crosses marking their graves—ten graves, it's believed, for each mile of the trail west.

∽∾

Not long after Henry Fonda was born, so was "the Middle West"—the term and the idea.

The myth of the Middle West was built upon those abandoned bones and lonesome crosses. The myth reaches back to the founding of the

---

* Platte: derived from the French word for flat. Nebraska: "flat water" to the Otoe Indians.

country, and something called "the pastoral ideal." Thomas Jefferson had emphasized the agrarian above all sectors of society; "he believed deeply," Richard Hofstadter wrote, "that rural living and rural people are the wellspring of civic virtue and individual vitality, that farmers are the best social base of a democratic republic." By "farmers," Jefferson meant a landed elite, men who were educated and owned slaves. But he also meant farmers: men whose lives depended upon the dirt.

Long ago, the ideal turned to myth, and like all myths it served a psychological necessity. James R. Shortridge describes this as "a general need for Americans to regionalize—that is, compartmentalize—national myths in order to avoid a confrontation with the contradictions inherent in these myths." Though increasingly cracked by reality (urbanization in villages and industrialization in cities; decimation of the Indians; oppression of blacks and immigrants), the myth of rural purity thrived in the popular mind. As America entered the twentieth century, with much violence to be forgotten and much money to be made, it was in the national interest to preserve, by unspoken consensus, a locus of moral propriety, political conservatism, and natural bounty.

Thus was the Middle West born: a state of mind, a definition of patriotic character. "This is America uncontaminated," John Gunther could write of the heartland as late as the mid-1940s. "Here sounds the most spontaneous natural note in the nation." Or as Garry Wills has written more recently, "To curse a farm is like desecrating the flag."

∞

As Dave Tolliver, upholder of a feud between Kentucky hill clans in *The Trail of the Lonesome Pine* (1936), Fonda is a watcher, and a mean son of a bitch. A Louisville engineer (Fred MacMurray) has come to mark coal mines and plot railroad lines; from start to finish, Dave looks at the city slicker with nothing but hatred. Fonda puts his sharp profile to the camera, keeps his shoulders back, and pierces the screen with burning blue eyes.

Yet the film as a whole—the first ever to be shot outdoors in three-strip Technicolor—is of great pastel prettiness, and the odd scene will show unrepentant Dave Tolliver as a jovial, whistling country boy. Proving two things: that Henry goes vacant-faced and mechanical when asked to be jovial; and that the suicidal tribalism of our native communities is nothing a pretty piece of Americana can't whistle away.

The term *Americana* describes works embodying a nostalgic sense of what the country once was, or ought to have been, in some pellucid past. *The Trail of the Lonesome Pine* idealizes a rustic life while welcoming brutal machinery. Americana is another species of myth, directed at suppressing rather than expressing contradiction, and here the contradiction lies in all that will come with the coal company's arrival: mining disasters, indentured economy, strikes, reprisals. It lies in the battles of "bloody Harlan," shoot-outs between miners and thugs in Kentucky that had occurred just a few years before the film was made.

Of all its characters, only Dave Tolliver acts as though he knows such events lie in wait. Only his body resists; only his eyes burn as they see the future in Fred MacMurray's unassuming form. But his is, finally, a small resistance. In this onward-and-upward proposition, there's no suggestion that communities should doubt the good intentions of whatever corporation approaches with its glad hand out. *Progress comes at a price,* Hollywood says to all the Dave Tollivers in the land; *but the price is worth paying. See for yourself—the wonders of three-strip Technicolor!*

∾

On Independence Day, 1854, the city of Omaha was established, and made the commercial heart of the Nebraska Territory. Like every great American city, it was founded on civic ideals and noble visions by pious, clean-minded businessmen—and by blackguards, scavengers, and bribe passers out to make a killing.

"Omaha was, from the very start," historian David Bristow writes, "a scheme." Specifically, a scheme conceived by a group of Council Bluffs, Iowa, businessmen to exploit the railroad they knew would be crossing the Missouri River on its way west. The town quickly became a vortex of vice, a crossroads of corruption. Lacking public works, it was also a bitter, disgusting place to live. In wet weather, streets turned to bogs of manure and mud, and in dry times, dust storms were blinding. Pedestrians were chased by packs of stray dogs, animal carcasses rotted in the streets, and water supplies were infected by runoff from private outhouses.

The Omaha encountered by Ten Eyck Fonda and his family, circa 1870, was post–frontier America in the raw. "On Saturday nights," a historian wrote of Omaha as it was in that year, "the town was alive with open carriages occupied by questionable women, from the sixty-one houses of ill fame. Squaws and papooses begged for money and drinks on the streets. Strangers and fortune seekers swarmed in the hotels and grog shops." Omaha was on its way to being, as John Gunther would call it, "a great place for aggressive hijinks on Saturday night [with] more night clubs, so-called, than any city between Chicago and San Francisco except, perhaps, Kansas City, Missouri. . . .

"It is full of dust, guts, noise, and pith; what it lacks mostly," Gunther noted—without going into the grimmer corners of Omaha history— "is effective civic leadership."

∽

In 1904, William and Herberta Fonda moved from Omaha to Grand Island, 150 miles to the southwest. From a banker named George Bell, they rented the tiny six-room house where Henry was born on May 16, 1905. The next day's *Grand Island Daily Independent* carried the announcement: "Dr. Roeder reports Uneeda Biscuits for sale at any old price from salesman William Brace Fonda this morning, a bright baby boy having arrived at the home of Mr. and Mrs. Fonda on West Division Street yesterday."

When Henry was just months old, the Fondas returned to Omaha, and William gave up baked goods to work as a print jobber. Herberta gave birth to two daughters—Harriet McNeill in 1907; Herberta Jayne two years later—and the family moved to a larger house in the suburb of Dundee. William would soon be running his own print shop downtown, and suburban life fit the family's ascending fortunes. Set at the city's western edge along Happy Hollow Boulevard (what a lovely name), Dundee was developed as a residential suburb and annexed by the city in 1915. The contemporary description notes its "ornamental shade trees, shrubbery of various kinds, paved streets, electric lights, and sewers [that] have made Dundee an ideal city of homes."

For entertainment, there was the nickelodeon across from William's print shop, where Henry watched the two-reelers of William S. Hart and Charlie Chaplin. At Harney and Sixteenth streets, also a short walk from the shop, was the Orpheum Theatre—a grand stop on the Orpheum vaudeville circuit—where Harry Houdini did his magic act and a prepubescent Omahan named Fred Astaire danced with his sister, Adele. There were country clubs close to the Fonda home, and summertime activities in Krug Park—plays, concerts, hot-air balloons, ball games, circus acts, picnics.

It was the lemonade dream of American childhood, but Omaha was undergoing the radical, convulsive processes of urbanization. Henry Fonda had a close view of the heartland as it underwent these changes, albeit a view from a cushion: The Fondas had money, and even, for a period, a live-in servant—a white girl from Iowa named Minnie Stout. Dundee, though annexed to Omaha, was also its own world, miles from the rough and salty riverfront, the burgeoning city center, and South Omaha, with its stockyards, packing plants, and immigrant cemeteries.

For all that urban expansion lay before Henry's eye, the enormous spaces and silences of the heartland offered hints of the unseen. People out there had a different way of seeing—both more practical and more mystical. Middle Western practicality was founded in the uncertainties of soil, weather, money, movement. But mysticism—as is often the case in unsettled cultures—was practicality's hopeful ghost: Faith in the unseen meant life might not be reducible to the dirt in one's hand.

Legends of the Pawnee, Otoe, Sioux, and the decimated Ponca Nation were still on the plains around Omaha, while white mysticism went back to the pioneer trails and something called "seeing the elephant." Diaries, letters, and other reports of the day include references to this apparition, a Great Plains Moby-Dick invented by folk talk and journalese. "To have seen *the elephant*," explains an 1889 dictionary of slang, "is to have had a full experience of life or of a certain subject or object." Merrill J. Mattes calls the elephant "the popular symbol of the Great Adventure, all the wonder and the glory and the shivering thrill of the plunge into the ocean of prairie and plains. . . . This creature seldom appeared except on the fringes of danger, and then it was only a fleeting glimpse."

As trails gave way to rails and towns expanded, the elephant grew dimmer. But Omaha in the early twentieth century was not far from those days when the diverse amazements of a pioneering life could be mythicized in the form of an exotic, towering beast. Henry Fonda's boyhood views were not bound by factory and billboard. The unseen and undiscovered were still there, all around him: soil, sky, space. The elephant.

∽

The Fondas were Christian Scientists. Mary Baker Eddy's doctrine of self-healing, first espoused in *Science and Health with Key to the Scriptures* (1875), prohibited all medical intervention, claiming that bodily illness was soluble by faith. Theological Darwinism: Implicitly, the healthiest Christian was the most pious, while the pained and infirm were suffering nothing but a deficit of spiritual will. Eddy was a controversial figure: Mark Twain attacked Christian Science at length in a 1907 polemic, and Willa Cather coauthored a scathing biography of the church's founder two years later.

Undoubtedly, this religion had a deep influence on Fonda's ways of thinking and feeling. Eddy's doctrine was all about denying weakness and putting mysticism to a purpose, with nothing bloody or sexy to its sense of sin. Though he didn't pursue Christian Science as an adult, Henry's values were molded by its precepts. Peter Fonda writes that his father, far from rushing to succor his children's everyday wounds and viruses, tended to respond "as if they were caused by some sort of sin in our soul," and that this "must have been due to the whisperings of Christian Scientist influences in his youth."

There is also something Fondian about the contradictions of the faith. Christian Science, for all its plainness, presumed the existence of miracle and magic. It taught not merely that disease could be allayed by prayer and wounds healed by hand but also that, through sufficient investments of effort and belief, the dead could be raised. The emblem of the faith was a gold seal depicting a crown and a crucifix, the whole circled with an inscribed creed. The words of the creed remain unchanged, and to this day they are seen emblazoned on the windows of Christian Science reading rooms around the world:

> *CAST OUT DEMONS*
> *CLEANSE THE LEPERS*
> *HEAL THE SICK*
> *RAISE THE DEAD*

∽

Whenever Henry spoke of his parents, it was with reverence, not insight. His mother, he said, was "an angelic woman." As for Fonda senior, "Everything he did was wonderful."

Henry remembered flying, at the age of four, a kite built by his father. The wind was strong and threatening, but William took control, and his son looked up in awe. As well as toys for the children, Fonda senior constructed amateur radio sets in the basement; he was a skilled handyman. He was also, Henry would learn, remarkable in ways not so obvious to a boy's eyes. "Only when I grew up and moved away did I realize exactly how much I loved him, how much he meant to me and what an unusual man he was."

Fonda's third wife remembered wondering about the nature of parental discipline and emotional authority in the Fonda house. "I was always trying to find out but he said he didn't remember a lot. . . . Perhaps he didn't want to remember." That "perhaps" opens a door, behind which there might be nothing at all. Or something: Daughter Jane refers to the "biological vulnerability to depression" that runs in her family, and her own suspicion that William Fonda was afflicted with chronic melancholy—trailed by what Winston Churchill, a depressive, called his "black dog."

In a family snapshot contained in Henry's autobiography, five Fondas are arranged informally before a garden trellis. Chubby, smiling Henry sits between his sisters, Harriet and Jayne. His eyes and face are soft; he is perhaps twelve. Nearby, William, about to say something, glances back at Harriet. His eyes are tired, the sockets dark. The impression is one of premature age and a collapsing center.

The dark around the father's eyes is the dark behind the son, a place that we cannot fully penetrate—and a place where his identity begins. A child is formed by everything that touches him, but there's only so much that tangible influences will tell us about an artist. The map of creative imagination begins and ends where the individual ceases to be shaped and begins shaping; where the story becomes not what the world has made of the boy, but what he makes of the world.

Henry's teenage years are mostly unremarkable. Mostly. We'll leave him for a while in that vague region—private, innocent, an ordinary American boy living the lemonade dream while it lasts.

∽

Playing Gil Martin, hero of *Drums Along the Mohawk*—the second teaming with John Ford, released at the other end of 1939—Fonda makes the man earnest, courageous, tenacious, and a little dull. Ford wants that of him, reasoning that it will mean more to an audience to see the brave man frightened, the unmovable man moved.

The source is a historical best-seller, adapted by four screenwriters, but it could have been mounted with Fonda in mind, for it encompasses a broad swath of his own family's history. New York's Mohawk Valley, 1776: Newlyweds Gil and Magdalena (Claudette Colbert) are at work on their American dream—field, forest, cabin; at night, a stuffed pipe and soft pillow. Skirmishes have occurred lately among colonists, Indians, and British. But for now, the Martins' vista vibrates with peace.

The rural landscape, infused with color on the verge of oversaturation, is quite beautiful to look at. There are burnished wood interiors, miles of sky, and towering forests. Even the shadows are midnight blue. But the picture is deformed by reactionary coarseness: The Mohawks are a monstrous swarm projecting arrows and fire, and the sexual politics are barely more tolerable. All that ties the film to a pioneer's pain is Fonda. He redeems Gil's dullness as the flat surface of a deep man, and haunting tones fall from his performance like droplets from a placid sky.

Two scenes stand out. In the first, a battle-bloodied Gil rests among the dead and dying; as Magdalena dresses his wound, he relates the battle. Others hurry in and out of the frame, but Ford holds on Fonda, who moves his face this way or that to avoid seeing the things he describes: an Indian impaled on a spear; a comrade's revel in the slaughter; a friend—named Ten Eyck—"with his head blown half off."

The other high point is a chase. The settlers are under attack; Gil flees for the military fort, miles away. Pursued by three Mohawks through the night, across an astounding variety of terrain, Gil might be running the breadth of the continent—from flatland to forest, through streams and stands of pine, the sky changing from black and purple to blue and white. The color deepens, the image broadens, and nature swallows the minuscule runners in a succession of monumental vistas.

You wonder what enacting the chase means to Henry. Whether he thinks of grandfather Ten Eyck, messenger of war, chased by the howl of history down his neck; whether he savors the presence of Ten Eyck's name in the story. Henry's run for his life carries us clear back to the marquis, the first runner—finding trouble, fleeing trouble, running toward safety, toward danger, an open sky, a new world.

∽

Fonda could have been safe for life in Omaha, if he hadn't drifted. In fact he was a drifter before he was an artist.

"I had no ambition to be an actor," he will later say. "But it was summer, and I had nothing else to do . . ."

Coming from conventional people, Henry drifts to conventional options. His first steps into the world are those of one trying to follow a design for living. First, he studies journalism at the University of Minnesota—a creative, active occupation, nominally stable—but his grades are only average, and the deeper itch is not scratched. He drops out in the summer of 1925, at the end of his sophomore year, and moves back to Omaha.

There follow two years of sideways drift, in and out of transient jobs: iceman, mechanic, window dresser. But between punches of the clock, he keeps an option open—the Omaha Community Playhouse, where he acts for the first time in that first summer after leaving college, and where he continues to work, part-time, performing odd jobs, from stage dressing to janitorial tasks.

"It was a nightmare": So Fonda will describe his first experience of acting. He's all of twenty, and has been invited to audition by a family friend, Dorothy "Do" Brando, who is active in the Community Playhouse. To kill time in the Omaha summer, he reads for the juvenile lead in Philip Barry's recent comedy *You and I*. To his surprise, and even dismay, he's cast by the director, Gregory Foley.

Hank steps onto the boards at first rehearsal, and—"It was a nightmare." He will one day characterize the nightmare specifically in terms of witnessing: "I didn't dare look up. I was the kind of guy who thinks everybody is looking at *him*."

Eventually, he does look up, and he sees that, indeed, everybody *is* looking at him. Somewhere between his two great fears, and the great fears of the Middle America he will one day represent—the fear of seeing, the fear of being seen—he's caught forever.

∽

All the conventions of his upbringing remind Henry that the theater is no life for a man. Acting is not exactly a respectable profession today; it certainly was less so in bourgeois Omaha in the mid-1920s. Only a few generations before, actors on tour were told by saloonkeepers to eat their dinner out back, with the pigs. The call of convention induces Fonda to take an entry-level position with the Retail Credit Company of Omaha. He is only filing papers at first, but his efficiency and dedication stand out and soon they are grooming him for the managerial track.

The journey thus far has been entirely ordinary. Most members of the middle class go through these uncertainties of identity, and most take a straight path. But Henry—typical though he is in so many ways—is not "most." So he preserves that opening, that stage door, back of which lie the nightmare and the desire.

The Omaha Community Playhouse is only a year old when Fonda joins, but in its genome are decades of history, theory, aspiration. It grows out of the Progressive Era, a period of political reform and social experiment lasting from the 1890s to the 1920s. A group of Omaha benefactors joins in the Little Theatre movement—what Dorothy Chansky terms a concerted effort by "writers, various kinds of activists, university professors and other educators, clubwomen, settlement workers, artists, and social elites" to bolster local playhouses against the onslaught of Hollywood, whose growing popularity is transforming many stage theaters into movie houses. The Community Playhouse is founded in 1924, and its first president, Omaha architect Alan McDonald, avows its purpose: "To raise the drama from a purely amusement enterprise into an educational, cultural force."

Little Theatre was a middle-class phenomenon with progressive intentions and a conservative agenda. "Like other reform activities in the era," Chansky writes, it "had contradictory strains; it included forward-looking activism and modernist aesthetics as well as skepticism, nativism, elitism, and nostalgia, sometimes within the same production company or publication." Certainly the movement took for granted the cultural supremacy of those who drove and financed it: "Most Little Theatre workers assumed that their middle-class, Protestant heritage was a standard by which all culture could be measured."

But in the context of middle-class, suburban Omaha in the 1920s, the Community Playhouse does not do badly. Under Foley, it cops to light Broadway fare but also stages naturalism, futurism, high farce—Shaw, Wilde, Molnár, O'Neill, Capek. Audiences are kept alive to past classics and modern currents, and the ideological limitations of Little Theatre are perhaps pushed out a few inches. The contradictions noted by Chansky provide the ideal opening into acting for a young man whose exteriors and values are conventional but whose ambitions and perceptions are extraordinary. Little Theatre allows Henry Fonda to experiment with states of safety and expressiveness, diverting him from aimlessness and the Omaha blues while giving him access to another world—that torturing, tantalizing state of watching and being watched.

The key turns in the fall of 1926, when Henry plays the lead in *Merton of the Movies*, a George S. Kaufman–Marc Connelly comedy about a Middle Westerner who stumbles into Hollywood stardom. Omaha's theatergoers give Henry a standing ovation, and later, in the Fonda parlor, the family eagerly dissect the show: Henry, mother Herberta, sisters Harriet and Jayne—all but William, who has been skeptical of his son's stage ambitions from the first, and who, at this moment of triumph, hides himself behind a newspaper.

Feminine praise pours over Prince Henry, while the elder remains hidden, judging all by his silence. Then a sister begins to speak in merest mitigation of the praise, suggesting how Henry might better have crafted his performance this way or that.

"Shut up," the father says. "He was perfect."

And just that fast, he is back behind the newspaper.

Henry's life is decided that night. In quick order, bourgeois distractions will be traded for a new mode of existence, one that for several years will be all rail and no station, all fall and no net. In a few months, he will quit the credit office and become Foley's assistant director at the Community Playhouse.

First, though, he will hit the road with a hard-drinking Abe Lincoln impersonator, playing to farm families along the heartland circuit.

Beyond that waits the itinerant life of an unemployed actor in hungry days. Soon Henry will be toiling in repertory up and down the coasts of New England; living on rice in a Manhattan garret; pioneering a course eastward, whence the Fondas had first come. Tracking the elephant, the black dog at his side.

∽

As he moves, Fonda keeps an eye on the terrain—observes his fellow citizens, judges and sometimes condemns them. But because he has the "appearance of sincerity," he is accepted; and because he has more than that, he is admired, elevated.

He represents our best ideals. He also represents much that we do not like to talk about. Fonda breaks with the mass of Americans on a basic point: He has a compulsion toward remembrance. Not nostalgia, but recall—true, deep, and clear. It's this that makes him a critic at the same time he is leader and representative. As a nation, we seldom allow ourselves to remember too vividly the bad we've done. Yet always Fonda seems to ask: What does it mean to remember it as it happened, to remember it all?

It's an eminently American quality to live as if history didn't exist. We're encouraged, by our cultural heritage as much as our leaders, to forget the past. But Henry Fonda acts as if he has never forgotten anything.

3

A Time of Living Violently

Fonda's first head shot

The Henry Fonda who left Omaha was raw youth, an actor with ambition but without a persona, willing to hurl himself at any challenge. He was a leaper, a laugher, a fighter; he played characters with exotic accents; he sang, danced, walked on his hands. There was nothing his arms and legs, face and voice wouldn't try.

As a lover, too, he was eager for all-or-nothing bets. So he fell for another actor, a starlet of imperial breeding, impossible demands, and unstoppable talent. When it came crashing down, the noise stunned the boy into silence. He drew back, guarded his obsessions and fears, and began vouchsafing his talent through an opening that, for both good and bad, could seem the narrowest point of emotional entry a screen star ever presented to an audience.

Fonda knew disillusion long before the audience's eyes met him in

The Farmer Takes a Wife. He was experienced in varieties of loss. That—and the inborn Nebraska austerity—must be why, from the start, he made such a grave impression; why he had a rare feel for anger and sadness; and why, at the other end of things, he could seem closed off, unreachable, an enemy of feeling.

∽

Wearing a Union army uniform, slick hair sliced in the center, young Henry squints into the sun. Hands clutched at his back, he embodies the military posture of Maj. John Hay, presidential secretary. Beside him, much taller, wrapped in a shawl and black raiment, eyes shaded by a stovepipe hat, is the Lincoln impersonator, George Billings.

A crack runs through the photograph like a vein in old skin, a score in marble, a divide in time. It's the spring of 1926. At one hundred dollars a week, Fonda has been hired by Billings—once a Hollywood carpenter, now the star of a silent film called *The Dramatic Life of Abraham Lincoln*—to write a show-length sketch out of famed Lincoln speeches. Additionally, Henry is to act the part of Major Hay, which mainly requires his paying rapt attention to the great man's orations.

Billings and Fonda ride the circuit of little theaters and picture palaces across Nebraska, Iowa, and Illinois. Thanks to the intensity of the star's portrayal, they are a success. "Lincoln of Stage Sinks All of Self in Soul He Plays," reads the *Evening Courier* of Waterloo, Iowa, where they play the Strand Theater. "I pride myself that when I am acting, no one can see Billings," the star says, using words Fonda will paraphrase many times in the course of his own career. "The audience . . . see only the character I am living for that moment."

A scene from the show is described. Major Hay tenders Lincoln the death warrant of a Union soldier prosecuted for desertion. Hay then reads a letter from the man's wife, explaining that she had called her husband away "in a time of great need" and pleading with Lincoln to spare his life. "As the long-fingered hands gripped the death warrant and tore it in two and two again," the witness records, "many eyes watching

Lincoln were wet with tears. And Lincoln's own eyes streamed tears into the shawl."

George Billings is a drinker. Some nights he fails to appear, and Fonda is onstage alone, gamely reading Lincoln's letters. Finally, after one such night, Henry leaves the theater and doesn't return.

But picture him sitting at the side of the stage, witnessing, as Billings declaims the second inaugural address: "With malice toward none, with charity for all, with firmness in the right as God gives us to see the right . . ." At the exact melodramatic point, the theater's modest orchestra keens the melody of "Hearts and Flowers." And Fonda watches this aged woodworker, drunkard, and ham actor believe in himself, in Lincoln, perhaps even in the promise of his country.

Maybe that is how it went, nights when George Billings's eyes "streamed tears into the shawl." Those who would know are long dead now.

∽

The prairie road offers no spectacle, and meager reward. So you leave. You dream of elsewhere: New York City, cradle of the real American theater.

Henry gets his first taste of it in the early spring of 1927. An Omaha woman asks if Henry might travel to Princeton, New Jersey, and drive back with her son, who has purchased a new Packard. Henry grabs the chance and practically lives for a week on Theatre Row. He sees, by his account, such eminences as Helen Hayes in *Coquette*, Otis Skinner in *The Front Page*, Ethel Barrymore in *The Constant Wife*, Charles Bickford in *Gods of the Lightning*, Glenn Hunter in *Tommy*, and Humphrey Bogart in *Saturday's Children*.*

From this trip comes an anecdote so unlikely, it stands a chance of being true. Henry double-dates with his friend and two sisters named Bobbi and Bette. Sitting in the twilight behind Princeton Stadium, he plants a nervous peck on his debutante—seventeen-year-old Bette Davis,

---

* In fact, not all of these happened to be on Broadway in the spring of 1927. Suffice it to say that Henry saw many shows in a short time.

who notifies Henry the next day that her mother will soon announce her daughter's engagement to the young man from Omaha. Gasping, Henry flees the scene—only to bump into Davis a decade later, by which point she is an Oscar winner and they are costars in a comedy called *That Certain Woman.*

The trip east is a head spinner. In a week, Henry has discovered Manhattan, Broadway, and the desire of a wealthy, sophisticated young woman. Each is a net that catches him forever.

After that, Omaha must seem a gentle suffocation. Fonda accepts Gregory Foley's offer of an assistant directorship at the Community Playhouse, and in the next year he squeezes all opportunity out of it. He acts in productions of *The Potters, Secrets, The School for Scandal, The Enemy, Rip Van Winkle, Seventeen,* and, opposite Do Brando, O'Neill's *Beyond the Horizon.* He is biding his time, keeping the stage beneath his feet and the fantasy alive.

∽

Nineteen twenty-eight is the summer of his leaving. With a family friend, he drives east to the gnarled arm of Cape Cod. He's heard of the summer-stock theaters that dot the island, servicing the entertainment needs of weekend commuters, maiden aunts, antique dealers, and sailors on liberty. The Cape is an outpost of Little Theatrism, and in the late 1920s, idealistic Ivy League drama graduates are as common as sand crabs on the beaches.

Henry auditions first at the Cape Playhouse in Dennis, and straight off he is playing a lead, in Kenyon Nicholson's *The Barker,* a Broadway hit of the previous year. Then he moves down to the armpit of the Cape—to Falmouth, where he tries out for a troupe called the University Players Guild.

He enters laughing. Joshua Logan, a Princeton undergraduate, is onstage in a comedy. He begins to speak, and "a high, strangulated sob came from the darkness," Logan will later write. "I thought someone was having an asthma attack." Logan imagines the sound issuing from "some odd human animal."

Begun by two Harvard students, Bretaigne Windust and Charles Leatherbee, the UPG is, like the Omaha Community Playhouse, powered by Progressive sentiment and populist ideals, presenting a repertory of recent Broadway hits, murder mysteries, and melodrama. There is also an aspect of pioneering to the venture: The group is in the process of constructing its theater on the outskirts of West Falmouth, and Henry is put to work painting walls, hammering nails, and wiring spotlights. Soon he will be making theater on a stage he has helped build.

A gangly gawker hailing from regions most of the Princeton boys and Vassar girls have never seen, Fonda draws their fascination at once. Logan, eventually to become Henry's close friend and collaborator, notes his oddly "concave chest" and "protruding abdomen," his "extraordinarily handsome, almost beautiful face and huge innocent eyes."

Fonda's parts at the UPG are a mix of whatever comes his way. He is first seen in *The Jest,* an Italian Renaissance costume piece; Fonda plays, of all things, an elderly count. Despite his intelligence and lack of upper-body muscle, Fonda is next cast as a brainless boxer in a sporting comedy, *Is Zat So?* At this, he does better: Young Henry is gifted at embodying subverbal man-beasts. In improvisation with Logan, he even transforms himself into ten-year-old Elmer, a small boy who mimics fish and birds.

Henry is also in touch with his darker aspects. Though popular and convivial, he shows an innate seriousness and a tendency to stormy moods. In Sutton Vane's *Outward Bound,* he incarnates a dead man adrift in the afterlife. "Several years ago in a New York theatre," writes the Falmouth reviewer, "when Alfred Lunt found himself aboard a ghost ship outward bound for heaven or hell, he cast over his audience an eerie spell which we thought could never be repeated. But Henry Fonda repeated that experience for us in his excellent interpretation of the same role in the same play."

A key lesson in Fonda's creative education comes when he reprises his hometown success, *Merton of the Movies.* "[N]ow he was aware," stage manager and set designer Norris Houghton writes, "of the presence of the audience and its response to him, of which he had had no consciousness in Omaha." As Fonda is less Merton, he is more himself embodying Merton in a self-aware process—mastering the actor's ability to distance himself from the action so as to achieve control over character and affect, while each time believing in the act sufficiently to appear spontaneous. Fonda was "learning the technique of acting without realizing it . . . learning for himself such elements of what is known in the 'Stanislavsky System of acting' as 'emotion memory.' "

For these summer months, Fonda eats well, sleeps well, lives and laughs in camaraderie. The rest of the year is hard. There are jobs here and there. Charlie Leatherbee, in the off-season a stage manager for the prestigious Theatre Guild, gets Fonda a bit in Romain Rolland's *The Game of Love and Death,* filling space behind stars Claude Rains and Alice Brady. The show, which opens November 25, 1929, is, in hindsight, an event of some moment—Henry Fonda's Broadway debut—but its run is short.

He spends the winter months of 1928–1929 and 1930–1931 in Washington, D.C., as a dance pantomimist with the National Junior Theatre, a troupe that performs for children. In March 1930, he returns to Omaha to star in a Community Playhouse production of *A Kiss for Cinderella.* This is the young actor's life—rejection, retrenchment, scrambling for lines and bits; winters in the cold mazes of Manhattan, sleeping on other people's divans, haunting casting offices and coffee shops.

He leaves Famouth, finally, in early 1932. The company has one more summer of repertory, after which it will cease to exist in its original form. It will mutate into something called the Theatre Unit, then into Stage Associates, a cooperative of producers and actors whose aim, as of January 1935, is to bring to Broadway "stimulating plays in the most professionally competent manner and with the most efficiency." Among the Stage Associates are Falmouth veterans Fonda, Logan, Houghton, and Leatherbee, as well as James Stewart, Mildred Natwick, Burgess Meredith, and Aleta Freel, wife of Fonda's close friend, actor Ross Alexander.

But Stage Associates is another sweet ideal in a time full of them. Leading light Charlie Leatherbee will die later in 1935, at the age of twenty-seven. A year after that, fire will destroy the theater he, Logan, Fonda, and the others built.

By then, Henry is in Hollywood, nearly a star. But the Falmouth years are the most constructive of his theatrical life—a workshop, with himself as the project. He hammers sets and constructs the frame of an identity; makes lifelong friends, tastes freedoms, tries the limits of his voice and body. Seasoning himself in the safety of a community, he stocks memories of great nights on the boards, love in the dunes, theater in the sun.

∽

And a fair amount of pain.

Henry meets Margaret Sullavan in Cambridge, Massachusetts, in April 1929, when they both appear in a musical comedy revue and she, as part of a synchronized production number, slaps him silly. "She intrigued me," he says.

That summer, Sullavan—whom friends call Peggy—appears in Falmouth at Leatherbee's invitation, and joins the University Players. She and Fonda costar in the opening production of the 1929 season, *The Devil in the Cheese*. It is a debacle for the ages. A live, spiky fish displaces water from an onstage tank; a loose turtle swims off the stage and crawls up the aisle; attempts at thunder, fire, and hurricane turn the stage into a wet, chaotic smear; a monkey urinates on Sullavan's shoulder. And at the end, the audience stands in ovation to see disaster so heartily engaged.

The two are next costarred in *The Constant Nymph*, a tale of love and obsession in the Tyrol, whose tragic climax arrives when Sullavan dies in Fonda's arms. All present are spellbound by the combined spectacle of her dying and his suffering—an omen of their performing futures.

Hank and Peggy go on to costar in a dozen or so regional stage productions, one marriage, one divorce, one Hollywood movie, and innumerable offstage tumults. Margaret Sullavan, a society belle from Virginia—small in stature, delicate in inflection, with a voice always described as "husky"—blows across the plain of Fonda's emotional life like a little twister, devastating the house of his mind.

Her face is made for the soft dazzle of a movie camera—small, round, charmlike, with hints of sadness to the sloping eyes. Her body is compact, agile, a tomboy's body, yet certain of every stance and movement; even tall, strong men appear timorous beside her. She enjoys acting and does it with apparent ease, while showing a blithe disdain for show business in her career calculations. "By the time I am thirty-five," she is recorded as saying, "I will have a million dollars, five children, and I will have starred on Broadway." At which point, she will set aside childish things and get on with the business of living. And that is pretty much what she does.

Henry describes her as "cream and sugar on a dish of hot ashes." At Falmouth, she becomes the third point in romantic triangles that hadn't existed before, and her presence brings out tensions and truths. Charlie Leatherbee is in love with Peggy, while the sexually or at least sensually ambiguous Logan has an undeclared crush on Henry. (Desire informs his every description of Fonda's body and face.) But their unrequited likes can only stand by and watch as Fonda and Sullavan become infatuated. The two even discover they share the same birthday.

Their dynamics are in place immediately, Fonda alternately brooding and admiring, Sullavan whimsically following her mood of the moment. He is openly love-struck, more exposed in his devotion; Sullavan, the coquette, wields more power. "Hank was much in love with Peggy," Houghton recalls, summing up the imbalance, "and Peggy thought she might be in love with Hank." Where Fonda, like everyone else, calls her "Peggy," Sullavan addresses him as "Fonda."

As they share their Falmouth triumphs, Sullavan is the only one to achieve success in the outside world. Where Henry returns to Omaha for a prodigal-son performance at the Community Playhouse, she returns to the family manse in Norfolk, Virginia, for her society debut. Where he gets a bit part in a short run, she understudies the lead in the southern road-company production of Preston Sturges's *Strictly Dishonorable,* a big hit. Where he works odd jobs, cadges meals, and hunts for work, she gets the lead role and sparkling reviews in *A Modern*

Virgin. By late 1931, Sullavan's name buzzes on Broadway, and the movies come sniffing.

During these years, she and Henry split and reunite multiple times. On June 2, 1931, they go as far as obtaining a marriage license from the New York State Department of Health. (Under "Occupation," Henry puts "Artist"; Sullavan enters a dash, as if waving off a silly question.)

When the University Players are invited to Baltimore for a nine-week season of repertory in the fall of 1931, Sullavan—fresh from the road company—rejoins as a minor star. Fonda initially objects to Sullavan's return but soon the two are, to no one's surprise, again a hot item. They are noted by gossip columnists and become minor Baltimore celebrities. But Henry has grown more combative and self-protective, and their battles are epic: "They fought so terribly," says one witness, "that you'd have to get out of the room."

And so, following the logic of doomed couples throughout history, they decide to get married. They apply for a new license, this time at Baltimore City Hall, and then lie about it: When the application is exposed in a local gossip column, Sullavan denies it exists. But the lie is revealed soon enough, and the two marry in the dining room of the Kernan Hotel on Christmas Day, 1931.

H. W. B. Donegan of Christ Episcopal Church officiates, and the Falmouth gang is in attendance. But it's a glum affair, with no blissful effusions from the couple. Nothing is said about eternity—they know themselves at least that well.

∞

If the young, raw Henry can be found anywhere on film, it is in his romantic comedies of the later 1930s. They are themselves malformed, irrational, stupefying, full of pratfalls and low comedy. Fonda's strangled voicings and desperate gestures are often less hysterically funny than simply hysterical.

Conceived as a gilded chariot for French opera star Lily Pons, touted by RKO as a high-line import item, the musical-comedy romance *I Dream Too Much* (1935) has a proto-Cassavetes scenario about a volatile marriage capped by an elaborately wacko musical climax. As a struggling composer whose wife becomes a singing sensation, Henry is intense, controlling, and dangerously jealous. It's not all script, either: The character as written is insane, but Henry makes him more so. His mood swings are out of balance with the air of triviality, and they are not eased by a climax that turns the composer's wretched opera into an orgy of Deco production, leaving behind scenes from marital hell and memories of emotional violence bobbing like body parts.

Often a Fonda comedy's only tension comes from what is repressed. *That Certain Woman* (1937) is, as well as a comedy, a morbid soap opera highlighted by premature death, an illegitimate child, and a crippled wife named Flip. Yet it's dull for all that, except in flashes, here and there, of Fonda playing one of his very few weak-willed characters. What he represses, and therefore expresses, are doubts about himself—about his power. Is he a match for Bette Davis? Is he a match for any woman, let alone her master? Henry is most endearing when the butch Davis teases him for not being rugged enough, and the Fonda voice, that classically placid and soothing instrument, tightens to a near shriek.

A better-worse example is *The Mad Miss Manton* (1938)—a terrible movie, but one in which gremlins of repression and expression run rampant. "You are a nasty creature, aren't you?" Fonda asks Barbara Stanwyck. "But in time I'll beat it out of you." Tremble, temptresses! But Henry's efforts at masculine dominance are only funny. In one scene, he is bound, gagged, and stuffed in a bed next to a pop-eyed China doll; elsewhere, he plays a comic death scene as a cop warbles "Home on the Range." *The Mad Miss Manton* is broken at intervals by piercing screams; they might represent the cri de coeur of Fonda's hapless man in a world of willful women who force him into silence, a suffocating bed, a dishonorable grave.

These films are painful, but they are in varying degrees alive, because they draw on the tension between Fonda's challenged manliness and the effortless dominance of his costars. Each one is a woman; each woman is a challenge; and each challenge is a mirror cast on Fonda. Every movie he makes is a piece of an ongoing account—that of Henry

Fonda's responses to life, to experience, to the country around him, to the woman before him.

∽

After a brief cohabitation in a Greenwich Village flat, Fonda and Sullavan separate in March 1932. The fighting has been constant, and the professional inequality gnaws at the young husband.

He moves to a fleabag hotel. Even before the divorce comes through, Sullavan is found to be dallying with theatrical producer Jed Harris, who, it is said, is intent on making her into a star. Peggy, for her part, may love Harris, or hope to use him, or both. The Vienna-born producer is exotic, dashing, and powerful. Before the age of thirty, he's had a half-dozen Broadway hits, been on the cover of *Time,* and become known as a diabolical consumer of people.

Harris lives with, and has a son by, the stage actress Ruth Gordon; jolted by the Sullavan development, Gordon leaves him, writes plays, and goes on to be even more successful. But Fonda's world comes down around him. Sullavan soon leaves New York, en route to Hollywood; she stops in Chicago to initiate divorce proceedings, and wires Fonda the news on May 16—their shared birthday.

Fonda tells of being spiritually rescued at this dire point by a stranger in a Christian Science reading room. He doesn't detail the substance of this counsel, but we know the Eddy doctrine advises self-sufficiency and self-succor. Rather than show his pain, Henry will swallow it. Rather than act it, he will repress it.

∽

Sullavan and Fonda will stay in each other's lives; webs of celebrity inbreeding will continue to connect them. In the summer of 1933, they will work together at the Westchester Playhouse in Mount Kisco, New York, where Sullavan is the company's designated leading lady and Fonda is a set designer. Soon after, when both are in Hollywood, there will be a single screen pairing, followed by brief talk of remarriage. Sullavan will wed Fonda's agent (and her own), Leland Hayward, in 1936; soon the couple will be living less than a block away from the Fondas in the Hollywood suburbs. When the Fondas move to Connecticut thirteen years later, Sullavan and her fourth husband will be found living nearby. Jane Fonda will become best friends with Margaret's older daughter, Brooke, while Peter will suffer an agonizing schoolboy's love for her younger daughter, Bridget.

Margaret Sullavan will have a dark final decade. Partly from fear that she is losing her looks, she withdraws from the screen; her final appearance is as a terminally ill woman in 1950's *No Sad Songs for Me*. Six years later, she drops out of a hit stage comedy, claiming illness; and soon after, set to star in an installment of the live CBS drama series *Studio One*, Sullavan disappears from the set, having decided that she would be "unable to give the role 'the kind of performance' it deserved."

Her depressions grow more frequent. She starts to lose hearing in her right ear, which makes her anxious about missing dialogue cues. There is a retreat to a sanitarium; in 1958, she undergoes ear surgery. Meanwhile, she stays attentive to her children, her husband, her gardens—and ultimately, she plans her return to the stage in a play entitled *Sweet Love Remember'd*.

She's in New Haven, Connecticut, performing in previews, when her body is found in a hotel room on January 1, 1960. Death comes in a handful of barbiturates. Though the medical examiner reckons it an accident, with signs of acid poisoning, not everyone is convinced—especially when it's learned that the outcome of her ear surgery was still in doubt, and that she had bequeathed her remains for deafness research.*

The curse continues beyond her. During and after her days of crisis, Sullavan's three children—Brooke, Bridget, and Bill—undergo numerous breakdowns and crack-ups. Bill survives mental institutions and drugs to become a successful film producer; Brooke, an actress, outlasts

---

* Sullavan's otologist, Dr. Julius Lempert, believed she had "deliberately developed for her work what I should call a cello voice, which was not her natural voice, because she could hear low tones better than high ones." Sullavan's donation of both her outer and middle ears for research, Lempert said, would be a great boon to science. See *New York Times*, January 9, 1960.

daytime soap opera, drink, drugs, and a disastrous marriage to come out with *Haywire,* an unnerving memoir of growing up in a brocaded fantasyland of wealth and mental illness. It's Bridget, the middle child, who doesn't come through. She dies only nine months after her mother. It is likewise a pill overdose, and unmistakably a suicide.

Peter Fonda is devastated by the loss. When his daughter is born three years later, he names her Bridget. Bridget Fonda will do fine in movies— sometimes better than fine. She'll be appreciated by viewers and critics for her wit, grace, and gravity, and the assumption will be that she has her head screwed on.

End of curse.

∞

Henry Fonda was young, cruelly so, when he met and married Sullavan. He had no experience, romantic or sexual, against which to gauge her drama or her moods. His first sex had been with an Omaha prostitute, probably in the early summer of 1925, and his first romances were fleeting affairs. Sullavan was the first woman to get all of him, and the first to take some of him when she left.

The Moon's Our Home (1936)—the couple's sole film together— was created well after they'd played out their personal drama. In act 1, we meet a movie star, Cherry Chester, and an adventure novelist, Anthony Amberton, who hate each other despite having never met. In act 2, the combatants, in flight from the burdens of fame, hide out under their real names; anonymous to each other, they meet and fall in love. In act 3, the facts reveal themselves, and our stunned deceivers, evenly matched in love and loathing, finally square off.

The screenplay, embellished by Dorothy Parker and Alan Campbell, was fashioned to showcase its battling stars; many lines suggest awareness of their offscreen history. But does the movie's pulse come entirely from our knowledge of the Fonda-Sullavan drama, or partly from the screen's ability to translate their intimate vibrations into erotic energy? The movie itself—that third mind that comes alive when film egos interact—senses the history of intimacies in play: The air between the stars crackles with the camera's suspicion that something is up.

Fonda had compared Sullavan to "cream and sugar on a dish of hot ashes," and *The Moon's Our Home* is layered that way: sweet frivolity covering bitter sediments. There are delicious moments of innocence, bits of silliness, and Sullavan's glamour and sporting self-mockery. She looks beautiful in a black turtleneck or sledding togs, and she does funny things with her small body—like striding across a broad foyer in such a way that all locomotion seems to derive from the piston swivel of her hips. Henry contributes his totem-pole elegance, matchless profile, and dangling Byronic forelock.

Some scenes could only have been written by Algonquin cynics who were also true romantic believers. Take the wedding scene: Anthony has purchased a marriage license days in advance, knowing Cherry will accept his proposal. She is inflamed to discover this. The couple exchange sotto voce curses while Walter Brennan, as a deaf registrar, reads the marriage ritual.

"Do you want to call the whole thing off?" Anthony asks.

"I certainly *do*."

"Do you really mean that?"

"I most certainly *do*!"

Deaf Brennan hears only a bride confirming her vow. By the end of their first fight, Cherry and Anthony are married; and the fight is forgotten the next instant, as they are bathed in congratulations and each other's kisses.

Hot ash is the movie's other taste. The tension generated by the stars culminates near the end, when Sullavan throws a pillow at Fonda—and he throws it back, knocking her into a chair. You nearly flinch: The pillow hits her like a fist. Soon, they will be wrestling on the floor, and the camera will have to look away as another actor enters—less to acknowledge the actor than to avoid the indecent spectacle of Sullavan and Fonda ripping each other apart.

The story ends with Cherry and Anthony nuzzling in the rear of an ambulance, she stuffed in a degrading straitjacket. Critic Molly Haskell tastes the hot ash in this: Sullavan "is made to look delighted at being so conclusively overpowered, but after the spirit she has shown through-out, the ending leaves a bad taste." Yes, but—it's Cherry who has been the force of nature, Anthony merely her intrepid explorer. This surrender is only a mood between moods: Soon the jacket will come off, and this twister will fly again.

The Moon's Our Home does justice to Sullavan's charm—that mix of sex and madness, wit and vulnerability that made Henry and so many others go mad for her. It's the charm that radiates from those rare people who carry no taint of dull normalcy, whose nature it is to soar over others, picking them up and letting them fall. Sullavan cursed and gifted Fonda with decades of experience in a few short years. Without her, a man like him might never have known what it meant, in the raw-est terms of his own soul, to crash, or to fly.

∽

The period from 1931 to 1932 is a dim time in our chronicle. We don't quite know where Henry is, or what he is doing—though a stunning head shot from this period, Henry's face swathed in shadows, a sailor's striped jersey lining his collarbone, is marked with a Brooklyn address (5 Prospect Place), which might have been his temporary residence.

All is transience and struggle. Henry becomes a familiar face in cast-ing offices and audition lines, and he grows bitterly accustomed to being turned away. On the bum in the autumn of 1932, he settles in one corner of an apartment on West Sixty-fourth Street. His roommates are two Falmouth friends—Joshua Logan and Myron McCormick—and a long-boned youth, James Stewart, whose time with the University Players just missed overlapping with Fonda's. The building, dubbed "Casa Gangrene," is full of prostitutes; shady characters in fedoras lurk in the hallways. Word is that a famous mobster—Jack "Legs" Diamond, just lately assassinated by gangland enemies—had his headquarters two doors away. Fonda will remember these as some of his lowest days: Of the starvelings of Casa Gangrene, he is the one most consistently out of work.

Jobs do come along. An office girl with pity will, it seems, always fix him with a job in some theatrical backwater, chauffeuring actors, stagehanding, carting supplies, rustling props—"stooging," it's called. The summer of 1932 finds Fonda at a theater in Surry, Maine, occasionally acting (he plays Inspector Enderby in A. A. Milne's *Michael and Mary*), but mostly stooging. Back in New York in October, he appears— then disappears—in *I Loved You Wednesday,* a play described by one reviewer as "a sentimental romance with a fairly fantastic tinge." The star is Humphrey Bogart; Henry plays a bar patron and speaks no lines.

Then down to East Orange, New Jersey, for winter stock. Early in 1933, he is chosen by the already-legendary actress Tallulah Bankhead to understudy her male lead in the comedy *Forsaking All Others*; though the show runs from March to June, Henry never hits the stage. Come summer, he is at the Westchester Playhouse, in Mount Kisco, designing sets and avoiding his ex-wife. In December, he scores a small role as Tevvy in S. N. Behrman's *Love Story,* starring Frank Conroy and Jane Wyatt; the show aspires to Broadway but dies after four nights in Philadelphia. Fonda then, by his recollection, gets a part in S. J. Perelman's *All Good Americans,* possibly through the intercession of Jimmy Stewart, also a cast member.

About this time, back in Manhattan, Henry applies for a job at a West Side flower shop. Conceiving of this as an acting exercise, Henry fixes the proprietor, one Mr. Goldfarb, in an earnest gaze and says something like: *I have come all the way to your fine city of New York, Mr. Goldfarb, to be an actor. It hasn't worked out for me. So now I have decided that it's time for me to grow up. To put away childish things and become—yes, what I always wanted to be—a florist.*

Fonda is acting, but part of him must be telling the truth, because he gets the job. Now he is hauling flowerpots up and down a staircase, scaling an endless ladder in a tiresome dream. What keeps the body pressing against failure, the spirit against rejection? It must be the sense that there is no alternative to perseverance—or that the alternative is unthinkable.

∽

Then, out of nowhere, the *thing* happens. Anyone who storms or steals past fame's first forbidden gate gets through on a *thing*: a break of breaks, the moment of being seen.

Fonda is cast in *New Faces,* a musical-comedy revue conceived by a fledgling impresario, Leonard Sillman. It's conceived as a performance showcase for unknown stage talent, a collection of sketches, dances, songs, parodies of pop culture—"a potpourri, a bouillabaisse," in the words of composer Arthur Siegel, "in which there was something for everyone." Sketch will follow sketch in rapid order, with music covering the cracks and blackout routines fronting the set shifts. For Sillman, Siegel says, pace "was very important. He didn't want to give an audience a chance to think about what it just saw."

Fonda snags an audition. He admits he can't sing, dance, or tell jokes; instead, he does his impression of a man changing a baby's diaper while driving a car. Sillman—who is even younger than Fonda, and a hearty laugher—signs him. Henry becomes one new face in a troupe of twenty-two.

The band of outsiders rehearses in whatever space is found (apartments, a church, a restaurant, unheated lofts) and runs performances for selected "angels" (investors). "Finances had to be pooled so that quarters could be doled out for lunch money," runs a contemporary account. "Collections were taken to buy shoes for two penniless performers. Watches and jewels were in pawn . . ." Finally the balance is tipped when a producer places a call to Hollywood, and America's Sweetheart herself, Mary Pickford, agrees to foot half the bill.

The show goes on. Fonda is not at first prominent; he and a few others, including a classical dancer named Imogene Coca, do a deadpan group dance during blackouts. But later, Fonda will stand in for an ailing singer to deliver the show's hit song, "She's Resting in the Gutter and She Loves It."

New Faces imparts welcome silliness to an uneasy springtime, and a cool breeze to a few thousand souls stewing in the cauldron of the Great

Depression. Critics and playgoers turn out to root for the underdogs; reviews are encouraging. *Time*'s critic believes the show "lacks pace and polish, [but] contains enough wit to make it good entertainment of its type." The Associated Press says it is "a fairly witty and pseudo-sophisticated revue and, more important, is a box office sell-out." Staged at the Fulton Theatre and running for 149 performances, from March through July 1934, *New Faces* is a small hit.

And Fonda is a hit in it. His song and dance routines are enough to convince at least one spectator that he could be the next idol of musical comedy. Tractor mogul and part-time producer Dwight Deere Wiman says he would like to place Fonda under contract for one year, during which time he'll receive instruction as a singer and dancer. The dangling carrots are one hundred dollars a week and Henry's vision of himself in a tuxedo, spinning into the night.

Funny that he was first noticed and pursued not for his moody magnificence or wholesome mug, but for talents—singing and dancing—that in his hands would have been the blunt tools of low comedy. His entire career shows that when walking, running, riding, or gesturing, Fonda was an instinctive artist of the body; and that as a dancer, he was either comical (when well used) or merely stiff (when not). We can only conceive of young Henry as a limited musical comedian, a gangly clown and piercing crooner, Ray Bolger crossed with Alfalfa.

A lethal notion—but here, in nearly its last manifestation, is that raw youth who is lost to time. Henry the jackal, loose, limber, and laughing hysterically, partnered with the divinely silly Coca, convincing two men of high standards and great foresight—agent Leland Hayward and film producer Walter Wanger—not only of his star power but the wisdom of getting him under contract and allowing him to grow.

∽

Hayward is an independent talent spotter with an impressive client list, a high-powered mentor in Myron Selznick—older brother of producer David, and first of the Hollywood superagents—and a job résumé that touches every scroungy corner of the publicity racket. Slightly older than Fonda, likewise a son of Nebraska, he is always on the hunt for clients. He and Henry, passing each other in the theatrical agencies, have a vague acquaintanceship. Henry introduces Hayward to Margaret Sullavan, who first becomes his client and later his wife, but Hayward expresses no interest in representing Fonda.

That is, until he attends *New Faces* and sees Fonda doing whatever our lost Fonda does: lamenting his gutter princess, flapping his arms, popping his eyes at the pop-eyed Coca. (Long, tall Henry is having a backstage fling with his gamine costar, a light, jocular affair, and surely that translates into charm in the performance.) Hayward goes backstage and expresses his interest in obtaining Fonda as a client. Fonda informs Hayward of the offer already before him.

The agent urinates, metaphorically, on the Wiman deal. One hundred a week is nothing; seven hundred and fifty! Hayward promises in thunder. ("Hayward has the agent's habit of thinking about money in big figures," according to a 1936 profile, "and encourages his clients to do the same, even when they are broke.")

When *New Faces* finishes its run, there is a telegram from Hayward, telling Henry to get on the next plane to Hollywood. Fonda—as he has a tendency to do—reacts as if trying to sidetrack his own success. He says no, he'd rather not: "It wasn't my ambition," he'll say one day, "to be in the movies." Nor had it been his ambition, back in Omaha, to be an actor; nor will it be his ambition, a few years from now, to play Lincoln. In Fonda, there is clearly a pressing, though no less absurd, desire to somehow go unnoticed as he practices his very public art.

Fate, though, with strong hands steering—Do Brando's, John Ford's, Leland Hayward's—holds its track. Hayward has seen something in Fonda's silly routine: a magnetic apparition, an odd human animal, a rising star.

But as the star rises, the animal recedes. The blackout ends, the revue rolls on, and that Fonda is gone.

Good-bye, my fancy! Farewell, jackal.

∽

Somewhere beneath the Hollywood palms waits an independent producer with the odd name of Walter Wanger—rhymes with *ranger*. Fonda, at Hayward's insistence, meets him in the Beverly Hills Hotel in the summer of 1934.

Insulated by the theater, Henry has not heard of the producer. Rather than a cigar-chewing vulgarian, he encounters a high-talking New Dealer, a cravat-wearing, ideal-spouting archetype of the Hollywood liberal whose dogma is that movies should uplift and edify "the masses," cleanse the great unwashed in wellsprings of knowledge and quality production design. Fonda refuses to be awestruck. But he listens to the deal, because Wanger has a history to go with his grandiloquence.

Born Walter Feuchtwanger, he'd been a stage producer at the dawn of the Little Theatre movement, then protégé to pioneer movie mogul Jesse L. Lasky, whose company, Famous Players–Lasky, formed with Samuel Goldwyn, was the forerunner of Paramount Pictures. In the silent era, Wanger had helped bring early classics like *The Sheik* (1921) and *Beau Geste* (1926) to the screen; later, he would lure to the movies many writers and directors whose careers had been made on the stage (Cukor, Sturges, Mamoulian). Wanger had gone on to work for both Harry Cohn at Columbia and Irving G. Thalberg at MGM; in the latter post, he was William Randolph Hearst's studio liaison on properties starring Hearst's mistress, Marion Davies. By 1933, when he struck out on his own, he'd become famous for infusing his productions with leftist political content.

As an independent, he would produce classics by Ford, Hitchcock, Lang, and Ophuls. He would marry actress Joan Bennett, and, in 1951, bestow a legend on Hollywood by shooting her lover, agent Jennings Lang, in the groin. After serving four months on an honor farm near Los Angeles, Wanger would seek out director Don Siegel to make the prison drama *Riot in Cell Block 11* (1954). The two would then collaborate on *Invasion of the Body Snatchers,* during which Wanger would introduce Siegel to an aspiring actor-writer named Sam Peckinpah, thus providing the latter with his entry into movies. Wanger's main labor in late years would be hauling the disastrously expensive Elizabeth Taylor–Richard

Burton remake of *Cleopatra* to the screen. He would die in 1968, his achievements little noted, an exile in the land he helped make.

But now it is the summer of 1934, and Wanger is a prince of Hollywood. Stars like Sylvia Sidney and Charles Boyer are in his stable; he's conquered the industry on his way to becoming its resident champion of "problem films," the man who is called "a fine and daring producer" (Fritz Lang), "a daring experimenter" (*Time*), and a purveyor of "one of the fanciest shell games even this industry has seen" (Otis Ferguson).

He has been tipped to Fonda by Hayward. Wanger comes from Broadway, and he still has spies reporting to him from Forty-second Street. (He is, in fact, a close friend of Fonda's nemesis, Jed Harris.) Hollywood has fairly recently discovered sound, and the miraculous or mortifying effect of the human voice on the screen image. The movies are hungry for actors who can *talk,* and that means actors from the stage: already, erstwhile Broadway players like Fred Astaire, Edward G. Robinson, Katharine Hepburn, James Cagney, Humphrey Bogart, and the Marx Brothers are building movie careers that will far outclass their collected achievements in the theater.

In Fonda's summary, Wanger's deal is this: "I could go back to my beloved theatre in the winter and come out the next summer to do two pictures for one thousand dollars a week." A remarkable offer, by any standard; it speaks of Wanger's visionary eagerness to invest faith and dollars in the unknown. But Henry resists: "I turned to [Hayward] and said, 'There's something fishy.' I just couldn't believe it. And he laughed and laughed."

Wanger is one of the half dozen key people in Fonda's professional life. But Henry will not recall him warmly, seeming to blame him for the cornpone quality of his early parts. He's being unfair. Wanger convinces Fox to cast the unknown stage actor in *The Farmer Takes a Wife,* though the executives desire Joel McCrea or Gary Cooper (both unavailable). Wanger takes half of Fonda's five-thousand-dollar-a-week loan-out fee, but by far the greater profit, in the long run, is Henry's. Wanger produces six of his first thirteen films, and lends him for the others, but part of Wanger's contract is that the star gets approval on loan-outs. And if Fonda's pickings are initially slim, they improve immensely once the producer places him in two key properties—*The Trail of the Lonesome Pine* and *You Only Live Once.*

Wanger positions Fonda to come over as both a star and an actor. He helps him to cultivate an image appealing to both sexes, free of binding assumptions about social class or hypervirility, and applicable to a wider range of parts than is plausible for almost any other male star. Through Wanger, he'll get into comedies, tearjerkers, social dramas, and even a Technicolor innovation or two. From 1935 to 1938, there is seldom a Fonda film on show that isn't in some way special or topical, or that lacks some hook to lodge it in the public's mind.

But the Fonda-Wanger partnership begins on a blank space—the movie that would have been Fonda's first but wasn't. On August 14, 1934, gossip queen Louella Parsons reports that Wanger has placed Fonda in a property called *The President Vanishes.* The producer's notion of debuting Fonda in this politicized version of a Rex Stout mystery indicates that, from the start, Fonda's handlers feel compelled to place him in proximity to politics, stand him next to flags.

The picture will be made without Fonda. He has either declined or been vetoed by the studio. Either way, Henry and Hollywood have not had the smoothest of meetings. He finds Hayward intimidating in his bluff assurance of every success, while Wanger is offering something suspiciously close to the moon and stars.

Henry returns to New York. What does he want? What does he not want? From the man comes a familiar shrug: "I had no ambition to be a movie actor." *I had no ambition*—yet again. But we know by now that he does have ambition. We know, too, that his peculiar self-protecting tendency is to let himself be drawn along, lured into emotional and professional places he will not go on his own. We know that he needs men like Hayward and Wanger, as he has needed men and women before and will need them again, to push, convince, and inspire him to be himself.

We also know that *The President Vanishes* is scripted and shot, under Wanger's production and William Wellman's direction, in the fall of 1934; that it is released early the next year, to indifferent response; and that, at the time it is filming, Fonda is back in New York, onstage at the 46th Street Theatre, starring in his first Broadway lead, in a play titled *The Farmer Takes a Wife.*

∽

Distracted by the Wanger offer, Henry fulfills his summer obligation to the Westchester Playhouse. There, he is cast in a production of Molnár's *The Swan,* alongside actor Geoffrey Kerr. Kerr is the husband of June Walker, then among the foremost ladies of the American stage, peer of Hayes and Bankhead, already on Broadway when Henry Fonda was shooting marbles in Omaha. Walker, in her turn, is set to star in a new play coauthored by Frank B. Elser and Marc Connelly—the latter, coauthor of *Merton of the Movies,* and Broadway's chief nostalgia merchant since the enormous 1930–1931 success of his Deep South comedy *The Green Pastures.*

Walker goes to Westchester to see Kerr in *The Swan*, and takes notice of Fonda. Henry overhears her whisper, "Wouldn't he be wonderful as the farmer?" Walker then passes his name to Connelly, who requests Fonda's presence in his suite at the Gotham Hotel on Fifth Avenue. There, Henry learns that he is under consideration for the male lead.

The farmer of the play is Dan Harrow, a roughneck on the shipping barges that crawl the Erie Canal in 1853, after the canal had connected the Atlantic Ocean to the Great Lakes, and the eastern seaboard to the rest of America. Dan wants to get off the barges and onto a farm, and he tries to pull his feisty love interest, the cook Molly, with him. Thin stuff—though perhaps at the time, anything that hinted at the existence of blisters, sunburn, and labor was bound to give a whiff of realism.

The Gotham Hotel meeting goes happily. According to Connelly, who plans to direct the play, Fonda is awarded the hero's role for his note-perfect reading of the boyish, calloused rough-and-ready hero: "He was patently ideal for the character, completely convincing, totally real." According to Fonda, he is never asked to read a word. Rather, he gets the part because he has the good sense to compliment Connelly on *his* animated performance of the entire script.

After tryouts in Washington, D.C., the play returns to New York, where it opens October 30, 1934. Something about it connects; something in the mood of the Broadway audience is succored by the play's return to simplicity. It is a prevailing American wish in late 1934, as at nearly every other time: Give us the simple of it. Stage our national past in a diorama of period costume and antique activity; show us a day when there were still dreams undiscovered, vistas unseen. Take us back; take us *away*.

To judge by the critical response, Fonda understands and delivers on that wish. In the *New York Times,* Brooks Atkinson calls Fonda's Dan Harrow "a manly, modest performance in a style of captivating simplicity." For the *Brooklyn Eagle* reviewer, it is "an extraordinarily simple and lustrous characterization." Another critic is sure Henry "will be transferred to the movie colony in jig time to become the newest of the leading men for Norma Shearer, Constance Bennett or Miriam Hopkins."

The Farmer Takes a Wife runs for over a hundred performances and is a success for all—another ruby in June Walker's tiara, another divan in Connelly's parlor, and Fonda's second Broadway triumph in a row. Henry will gain more than anyone from the play. The other principals have already arrived at the summit of their fame; the unknown Fonda—so appealing and free of airs, presenting a new, sharp-lined, dark-haired definition of our country's natural man—is seized on as the one whose star may rise on the Americana the production typifies and exploits.

∽

The part of Dan Harrow gives Henry a chance to toss cargo, have a fistfight, leap, lunge. But it is his gentleness that audiences respond to— his combination of the physical and melancholy, the manly and phantasmal: the Fonda we see in the film version of *Farmer.*

Probably the stage performance is less controlled than its filmed counterpart. Shooting the movie in Hollywood, Fonda, performing his first scene, will be warned by director Victor Fleming that he needs to pull back a bit. Henry is horrified to realize he's hurling his voice at a sensitive microphone, moving his body in ways that seem overscaled so close to the lens—that Cyclops that represents the eye of the nearest viewer. So he retracts the gesturing, reins in the voice, and internalizes forever the one major piece of direction he will ever require as a screen actor.

Even magnifying the film performance by several degrees, it's not difficult to imagine Fonda's appeal as Dan Harrow on the stage, his sweetness and sadness. It is also easy to imagine that the sadness is real. On October 5, 1934, after Henry has returned from Hollywood but before he opens in *The Farmer Takes a Wife,* his mother, Herberta Jaynes Fonda, dies in Omaha. She suffers a coronary thrombosis, brought on by a blood clot developed after breaking a leg. Christian Science is not able to save her, nor prayer sufficient to raise her from the dead.

Not for the last time, Henry goes onstage immediately after the death of a loved one and does his job. Embodies sweetness, simplicity, the manliness of an American man, and, along with those qualities, conceivably, something else not so easily named.

∽

Our young man goes west—more or less for good—in March 1935, two months after *Farmer* closes. Though he will spend more years residing in Hollywood than anywhere else, something never quite gels between Fonda and the town that makes him a star. He is pulled there by a contract, but he insists it carry a clause releasing him for summers on Broadway.

However much Henry wants Hollywood, it's clear that Hollywood in 1935 wants him—or, more exactly, wants the qualities embodied by those who represent the screen's new wholesomeness. This trend to the nostalgic, chaste, and rural is indicative of a movie industry still in the process of recuperating its image—an image marred during the previous decade by a run of scandals appalling to both the newspapers' ink-stained moralists and a public addicted to movie-star gossip.* By the

---

* There had been, in 1921, the manslaughter trial of Fatty Arbuckle; in 1922, the unsolved murder of director William Desmond Taylor; in 1923, the asylum death of drug-addicted action star Wallace Reid; in 1924, Charlie Chaplin's marriage to a fifteen-year-old girl, and their sensational divorce trial three years later.

early 1930s, Hollywood is losing money to this perception of sin and scandal, and to the Depression. Every business forms its own response to fear and crisis; if Hollywood is known as "the dream factory," and if the factory is beset by blown fuses, defective belts, clogged lines, and leaky moldings, surely another dream—newer, happier, healthier—is the prescribed repair.

Rather than necessarily making better films in the mid-1930s, Hollywood will make *nicer* ones. It will scramble to regain virility, and shake off the taint of decadence. And that is where Henry Fonda fits. He is fresh, boyish, "simple." His true blood—along with that of Spencer Tracy, Joel McCrea, Gary Cooper, Claudette Colbert, Jean Arthur, James Stewart, and a clutch of others—will cleanse Hollywood. He will become one of the town's favored sons, a spearhead in his industry's move toward respectability and higher purpose.

∽

He eases himself into his contract, and into the monotonous flow of publicity. Glossies are taken, and interviews awarded to columnists eager to print a studio's PR. Many quotes are dispensed, and juicy items planted about handsome Henry vis-à-vis some starlet with equal need of exposure. Fonda tests out his interview mien—eagerly unexciting, candidly unrevealing—and begins accumulating his store of personal anecdotes, highlights of his career and development, to be honed over many years and many tellings.

After a few months, Henry rents a bungalow with Jimmy Stewart, his comrade from Casa Gangrene, and another stage veteran recruited for pictures. The two live, briefly, like boys whose pockets bulge with candy money. They double-date with Lucille Ball and Ginger Rogers, have nights out at the Cocoanut Grove, drive Henry's Ford roadster into the hills. They fly a large model plane made of balsa wood in their backyard—a Martin bomber they've built themselves, whose construction was begun back in New York, and which Stewart transports to Hollywood by Pullman car.

It is a strange place, a strange life. The skeins of connection and coincidence between professionals in Henry's new, suddenly smaller world can seem unending. Still new in town, he lunches, costars, and house-hunts with ex-wife Sullavan. By this time, she has already been married to and divorced from the director William Wyler. Wyler will soon be directing Fonda in *Jezebel*—alongside Bette Davis, whom Fonda kissed behind the Princeton Stadium in 1927. Leland Hayward, Sullavan's next husband, is agent to them all.

Then there is the brief, brutal saga of Ross Alexander and Aleta Freel. Henry knows them from Falmouth and Mount Kisco, and he stood as best man at their wedding; soon after, Freel's name would follow Fonda's on the roll of the short-lived Stage Associates. The couple have left for Hollywood in advance of Henry, and both are under studio contract. Alexander, costar of the Errol Flynn actioner *Captain Blood,* is even approaching a certain level of stardom. But on December 7, 1935, Freel shoots herself in the head. Her husband, rushing toward the sound, discovers her body by stumbling over it. He claims his wife had been despondent over the failure of a recent screen test.

Within days, Alexander is back at work. Louella Parsons writes admiringly, "The day following the suicide of Mrs. Alexander, Ross, knowing that Warner Brothers needed him in an important scene that called for many extras, astonished everybody by appearing on the set and insisting on going on." Yet barely more than a year later, Alexander will kill himself at his home, during a gathering of friends but out of their sight, also with a bullet to the head.

The one known outcome of the suicides—the first of many to strike close to Henry Fonda—is that a young radio announcer, hailing from Illinois by way of Iowa, receives his Hollywood break. A Warner Brothers casting director places Ronald Reagan in a western role meant for Alexander, feeling the actors' voices are similar.

If Aleta Freel had not killed herself, would Ross Alexander have lived? If Ross Alexander had lived, would Ronald Reagan have gotten into the movies? If Ronald Reagan hadn't gotten into the movies, would he have become president?

∽

There's another thing to be pointed out about Hollywood and Henry Fonda, the same thing that accounts for Ronald Reagan's entry into film: the sound of the voice. By 1935, the movies had talked for eight years, and it was accepted that voice as much as body defined the actor, that one could not become a star without distinctive tones. There is not an icon of the Hollywood 1930s whose voice is not central to his or her legend: Tracy's gruffness, Hepburn's clenched jaw, Grant's suave cadence, Cagney's bullet phrasing.

Fonda and his contemporaries moved into the space left by the stars whose mystique was built solely on movement and expression, and who now found they were unable to seduce an audience with its ears wide open. David Thomson notes the paradox that the coming of sound placed an unprecedented emphasis on silence—that is, on the trade-off between a voice and the silence that might precede or follow it, or the silence sounded in the timbre of the voice itself. He writes of how "a generation of favorites slipped away because they did not have access to that emotional quietness, and the allure that attaches to any mystery or reticence in a medium that seems to be giving you all the visual evidence."

Fonda has that access, that allure. It's partly the voice that leaves people at a loss for how to describe him. Here is a young man of uncommon reserve, so much of whom is implied in silence, lack of show. He seems smarter than Cooper, more virtuous than Gable, more melancholy than McCrea, more elusive than Tracy. Viewers who haven't seen anything quite like him before, who lack better words to describe it, call it "modest," "honest," "simple." But how do we describe simplicity in a way that does justice to its complexity? How do we prove the existence of the invisible, or translate a message in vanishing ink? Words like *simple* fall short when applied to Fonda, because they are asked to describe something not at all obvious—something that is there to be felt, yet is not there to be seen.

∽

So Henry has made it inside the gate. The future begins here. The next few years will fly past, and parts will accumulate. It will be determined by the pooled wisdom of Hollywood that he is to be taken seriously. He'll earn high regard for professional principle and integrity in performance. He'll begin the process of defining himself as a screen actor of rare and troubling depth, an American institution, a worthy bore.

His talent has barely begun to be tapped. Greatness lies ahead. But our theme to this point has been a sad one: that by the time Fonda reaches the screen and is for the first time widely seen—by our ancestors and proxies in the American movie houses of 1935, those encountering a complete unknown named Henry Fonda—basic parts of the man have already flowered and withered.

"Youth is a time of living violently," Henry's Falmouth colleague Norris Houghton writes, "and tears belong as much to violent living as do laughter and shouting." As a man, Fonda has been outgunned in love; as an actor, he's gone from dusty Omaha to sandy Cape Cod, dour Manhattan to pixilated Hollywood. He's been near enough to the edge of personal despair and professional failure to have come within spotting distance of his own abyss. He's had other losses—deep, personal ones. Extremities of emotion have been exposed, and now are hidden. So Fonda's subsequent career will be an expression less of discovery and attainment, the all-American pleasure in having and being, than of loss and wonder—qualities of estrangement and searching seeming to sound from a distant, different America that lurks somewhere inside the country, and inside ourselves. With the passage of a few years and a few key parts, we, the audience, begin to engage deeply with Henry Fonda.

This is the moment before that begins to happen. His first movie audiences have to wonder if they are seeing in this young actor a new face, or an old apparition; a fresh persona, or a glowing plainsman who, both young and old, straddles ages with those first words cast into the future by an old man's younger self, the wild boy now vanished:

"Be ashamed, an old man like you."

4

The Big Soul

Let Us Live

The only actor of the era with whom I identified was Henry Fonda,"
James Baldwin wrote, recalling the Hollywood movies he saw as a
youth in the 1930s and 1940s. "I was not alone. A black friend of mine,
after seeing Henry Fonda in *The Grapes of Wrath*, swore that Fonda
had colored blood. You could tell, he said, by the way Fonda walked
down the road at the end of the film: *white men don't walk like that!*
and he imitated Fonda's stubborn, patient, wide-legged hike away from
the camera."

Why *couldn't* a black adolescent in a big eastern city see something
of himself in white, middle western Henry Fonda? Fonda, as Baldwin
saw it, was not just walking away; he was showing us his ass. Baldwin
was writing of the few small, useful things he'd been able to derive as a
child from his country's movies, those images of defiance that contributed
to his "first conscious calculation as to how to go about defeating the
world's intentions for me." For Fonda to show us his ass, using the walk

that to Baldwin and his friend identified him as a fellow outcast, meant he was making a small refusal that was recognizable to them alone.

Fonda might have smiled to hear such talk. Yet metaphor, the possibility of many meanings—colored blood, small refusals—arises from a great actor as organically and unconsciously as it does from a rich novel or a suggestive painting.

Emerging from the heart of the country as one talented American—really, no more than that—he reemerges on its movie screen as one version of the perfected American man. But Fonda spends these years focusing inward, on his own dilemma, as well as outward to find his place in the greater context of politics, mass movements, wars; and the processes are interlocked. What is remarkable is how far his personal journey becomes one in which millions of Americans feel they can share, an open road along which they see their country passing and an image of themselves approaching, wearing Henry Fonda's face.

Fonda's men are antiheroes who decide they must commit to a common cause—less because the cause is right than because isolation of the kind they feel natural with implies, finally, surrender and death. Fonda's hero must realize the degree to which he is not just the *unum* in the American equation but also one of the *pluribus;* realize, though it galls him, that he is—truly, dreadfully, awesomely—an American.

∽

By mid-1936, Fonda is a watched man, almost famous, a recognizable presence and replaceable head in the Hollywood arcade. Handsome, unattached, he goes out often and is linked to various women.

No doubt some of the links are real, albeit temporary, while others are the conjurings of publicity wizards. The gossips have gone so far as to announce in October 1935 that he is engaged—to Shirley Ross, an Omaha-born starlet who has appeared in *Bombshell, Hollywood Party, What Price Jazz,* and other musical comedies (as well as *Manhattan Melodrama,* the picture Dillinger was leaving when G-men plugged him in a Chicago alley). The affair is brief and insignificant, and the engagement talk vanishes like smoke.

Henry is still a boy in many ways, and he has his fun. He may be lonesome nonetheless, and crave stability over variety. In early 1936, he—or his PR team—begins advertising for a wife. "Henry Fonda says it is all right with him if he gets married by next Christmas," claims an article syndicated in May. "He has just bought a home in Beverly Hills, and although he admits there is no immediate prospect of a Mrs. Henry Fonda, the house is already [*sic*] for her."

On July 10, he boards a boat bound for England, in execution of a Walter Wanger loan-out. *Wings of the Morning* is to be filmed at the brand-new Denham Studios of UK film mogul Alexander Korda, and on locations from Surrey to Killarney. A love story with a horse-racing backdrop, it pivots on Gypsy curses, mistaken identities, and a beautiful lead actress in male drag—she being Annabella, sexy and French, who spends the first part of the film flirting with Fonda while disguised as an adolescent duke.

Though it's the first Technicolor picture produced in Europe, *Wings* will be received without excitement; Henry will collect more of the wan plaudits to which he is growing accustomed. ("One of the most personable, sincere, and able of our young leading men," says one critic; you could fall asleep reading Fonda's good reviews.) He has taken the job only because it offers him his first chance to go overseas. He lodges at the Savoy Hotel, then moves to a cottage in Buckinghamshire.

One day, Henry is introduced to a group of wealthy female American tourists who have been invited to the set. In their number is a striking young woman of patrician bearing. Introduced as Frances Seymour Brokaw, she is a friend of the producer's wife, currently touring Europe with a chaperone. She's twenty-eight, with a lithe outline, penetrating countenance, and confident manners. Her blue eyes, though large and candid, are also veiled, as if they focus on some farther, sadder reality.

∽

Born in Brockville, Ontario, on April 14, 1908, Frances comes from a family well placed in eastern society. She is related by marriage to such New York dynasties as the Pells, Stuyvesants, and Fishes; her father,

Eugene Ford Seymour, descends from English royalty of the Tudor era; and her mother, the former Sophie Bower, has ancestry tracing back to Samuel Adams and the Revolutionary War.

There's money, glamour, and influence behind the Seymours, but Frances rides the caboose of the gravy train, for her father has squandered most of the family's capital. Frances's mother is a gentle, long-suffering woman for whom no one has an ill word, but there is disagreement on the nature of the father. One biographer characterizes Ford Seymour as "an alcoholic with a violent temper," while another calls him "a part-time poet, with delicate, refined features . . . reserved and rather shy." Jane Fonda remembers her grandfather as "an exceedingly charming, devilish gentleman," while noting the suggestion of Frances's psychiatrists that he may have been a paranoid schizophrenic. To her doctors, Frances described an increasingly impoverished Seymour home, barred windows, and rooms wired shut by a patriarch slowly going mad. She claimed to have been molested at the age of eight by the one visitor allowed to enter the house—a piano tuner.

Like Henry, Frances has been married before; she has a daughter, Frances de Villers, nicknamed "Pan." Frances's husband is dead. George Tuttle Brokaw was a Wall Street lawyer, heir to a clothing dynasty, and a bully-bully sportsman in the Teddy Roosevelt mold. He was a multimillionaire with a mansion at Fifth Avenue and Seventy-ninth Street, and, presumably, many animal heads on his walls. He was also, like Ford Seymour, an alcoholic and abuser of women. His first wife, the future playwright and politician Clare Boothe, had miscarried four times before escaping to marry media magnate Henry Luce. It was said that each miscarriage was due to a Brokaw beating.

Frances was just twenty-two when they met, Brokaw nearly three decades older. She was working on Wall Street, fresh from the Katharine Gibbs Secretarial School in Boston—renowned as a training camp for ambitious girls seeking wealthy husbands—and she went after Brokaw with the same focus she would apply to Henry Fonda a few years later. A childhood of fear and genteel poverty had given her a strong will and a mercenary survival instinct; her chief ambition, she told a friend, was to "descend on Wall Street and marry a millionaire." The relevant anecdote has an impatient Frances suggesting to Brokaw that it's time he propose—whereupon the bully-bully type, caught off guard, accedes, meekly asking the future Mrs. Brokaw when the wedding will be.

So, in January 1931, Frances, with every calculation, married a man much like her father, whose notoriety as a husband was despicable. Whether her pursuit of Brokaw suggests a malformed kind of love, a cold-eyed acquisition of capital, the need to be chained to a violent master, or all of these, may be debated. What is agreed is that George Tuttle Brokaw spent his last year in a sanitarium, the Hartford Retreat in Connecticut; that sometime in the overnight hours of May 28, 1935, he died; and that he left a cash bequest of approximately one million dollars to his wife, and to his four-year-old daughter, a yearly income in excess of $31,000 and property worth more than five million dollars.*

∽

This, in harsh outline, has been the course of Frances's twenty-eight years. She has been dominated and often terrorized by men. Incredibly strong and incredibly fearful, she knows what she wants, and what she wants is the worst thing for her. When she spots Fonda at Denham Studios under placid English skies, something clicks in her mind, and she decides that he will be her next husband.

Like Henry's, Frances's self-presentation conceals a complex set of strengths and weaknesses. She overwhelms a goal once it is set; it's her talent to place things in order, balance credits and debits, and act upon desire in the most deliberate way. That applies to money and to men. "When a woman really wants a man," she is supposed to have said, "she should be the one who pursues and gets him." Daughter Jane quotes her even more frankly: "I've always gotten every man I've ever wanted."

First, a potential rival must be dealt with. Henry is rumored to be involved with his costar, the provocative, fun-loving Annabella. But

---

* The official cause of Brokaw's death was heart attack, but others believe he drowned, by intention or alcoholic accident, in the sanitarium's pool. See *FML*, 119.

Frances satisfies herself that it is only gossip, and soon she and Henry are socializing in glamour spots along the Thames. Frances is gay and charming, yet her aura of control is a universe removed from Margaret Sullavan's unpredictability. In fact, she seems an escape from drama and tempest: She evinces no particular interest in movies, and claims never to have seen Fonda on-screen.

Henry, for his part, is still involved with Sullavan. They have only recently finished *The Moon's Our Home*; the reunion has led to renewed romance and Hollywood house hunting. The day before shooting begins on *Wings of the Morning*, Hank writes "Dearest Peggy" a letter from the Savoy, extolling the English crew and "charming" Annabella, and noting it has been six years since he last wrote Sullavan a letter. Signing off, he expresses doubt that Peggy will visit him in England—evidently, she has hinted she might—along with hopefulness that she will.

But very soon after, Henry meets Frances, and she makes quick work of him. We can imagine he is tugged by her assurance, dazzled by her command, refreshed by her alienness. But more vengeful motives may also be at work. He recalls Sullavan's betrayal—hasn't his suffering earned him the right to a fling?

For Frances, though, it is no fling. She invites Henry to join her on the remaining stops of her European journey. He accepts the invitation. *Wings of the Morning* is wrapped, posted for Hollywood and historical oblivion, and the two depart England for Germany. The Sullavan complication is discreetly tabled; the chaperone is dismissed.

∽

Whirlwind is the word for their courtship: The gust of Frances's energy carries Fonda along like a grain of sand. They find themselves in Adolf Hitler's Berlin for the opening of the Summer Olympics on August 1, but they leave quickly, alarmed by the spectacle of fascist muscle. From there, the lovers travel to Munich, Austria, Budapest (where Fonda proposes), Paris (where Frances accepts), and finally homeward to New York. The news of their engagement travels fast—so fast, we have to wonder who cabled the press agents, and when. As early as August 24, headlines appear in stateside papers: "THEY'LL BE MARRIED—WIREPHOTO!"

On September 8, a reception, sponsored by a Chrysler heir, is held for the couple at the Waldorf-Astoria. In a letter to Sullavan, posted the following day from the Gotham Hotel, Henry suggests he was less than forthcoming about meeting Frances, let alone their now-public wedding plans. Has he let Peggy discover the fact for herself, in black and white in the *New York Times,* or, worse, from a gossiping friend? He apologizes to Sullavan for having been such a "blundering fool" in his handling of the matter; his concurrent lovers have barely missed scraping each other's shoulders in passing. Perhaps he privately enjoys bringing the once-dominant Sullavan up short. It would be a human thing to enjoy, and Henry is nothing if not human.

The wedding, on September 16 at Christ Church on Park Avenue, affords ritual splendor and maximum pomp. The bride wears blue taffeta, the groom a silk hat and swallow-tailed tuxedo. Frances's maid of honor is her sister, Margery; Josh Logan is Henry's best man; ushers are Leland Hayward and Frances's brother, Roger. There are hundreds of guests, enough flowers for a Rose Bowl float, sidewalks lined with fans and photographers. The arches of the Methodist shrine shelter the couple; the streets outside part for them. Henry can only feel dazed as bells chime over his head; it has been just two months since he and Frances were introduced.

∽

They are so much alike—but in the wrong ways. Each is a stoic, an absorber and hoarder of pain; each is confident that fear and weakness can be bolstered by rigidity. They share behaviors but not dreams, repressions but not freedoms, and their battle will be conducted in a thousand grim silences and gnashings of teeth between two people whose need for control is like anyone else's need for air.

Frances has gotten Henry to the church on time. If their marriage is a power battle, she has won the first round. But Henry takes the next.

The day after they are married, they return to Hollywood so that he may begin shooting his next movie. Frances has been thrust out of her world and into Henry's, and she will have to adjust to the climate, codes, and facades of a new way of life.

In a typical story, Louella Parsons asks the couple how they met. They giggle like children.

> "Mrs. Robert Kane asked me to meet the American leading man who was playing in Bob's picture," said Mrs. Fonda who has a very fair skin, big blue eyes and is much prettier than any of her pictures indicate. "I really like motion pictures, so I said, 'Oh, I'd love to. What's his name?' Mrs. Kane replied, 'Henry Fonda.'"
>
> "Just think, she had never even heard of me!" interrupted Henry with mock chagrin.

It's a con, on the public and on themselves. Frances's "I really like motion pictures" is contradicted by other sources, and Fonda admits that he has begun to secede from the union almost immediately.

The marriage will produce some good times and happy results, but Frances and Henry have struck a dark bargain. She will get the worst of it.

∽

As he constructs a simulacrum of domestic happiness, Fonda begins to cultivate anger in his acting. As he achieves stardom, his protagonists seek anonymity. The more materially comfortable he becomes, the more his characters are defined by class conflict. Fonda's acting continues to grow, mainly through a commitment to showing pain and doubt on-screen. It can't be accidental that, with few exceptions, all of Fonda's greatest work comes in the years he is married to Frances—or the years just after, as he deals with her specter.

His persona splits in the late 1930s into two modes: that of the wanted man and the workingman. In the first group are films like *You*

Only Live Once, Let Us Live, Jesse James, and *The Return of Frank James;* in the second, films such as *Slim, Blockade, Spawn of the North, Drums Along the Mohawk,* and *The Grapes of Wrath.* In either mode, Fonda projects anger over affirmation. Even playing Watson, assistant to the inventor in *The Story of Alexander Graham Bell* (1939), Henry pours a little acid on the refined sugar of costars Don Ameche and Loretta Young, implying the existence of another, realer world outside the frame.

He is almost always more convincing, attractive, and memorable when at odds with something—the situation, the community, himself. Witness his pivotal success in *Jesse James*: As brother Frank, Henry injects the prestige Western of 1939 with the unstintingly mean style of a man born to hate. *The Return of Frank James* (1940), an inert and pointless sequel, opportunistically apes the ambience and even the plot of the recent *Young Mr. Lincoln,* contriving Frank's rescue of an innocent man from lynching. Directed by an uninspired Fritz Lang, *Frank James* sacrifices the *Jesse James* sensation of Fonda as a bracingly bitter taste in a bowl of corn mush—which was all that gave the first film its savor and surprise.

Two other films of this period—*You Only Live Once* (1937) and *Let Us Live* (1939)—star Fonda as the luckless modern man before the bar of justice, in whom simplicities of guilt and innocence are blurred. The character is wrongly accused, but he troubles the narrative and the audience by always *seeming* guilty: he wears a cloak of existential shame, and his redemption is deflated by feelings of futility.

We are well out of Zane Gray country here, and brushing up against Kafka. In these two films—made prior to World War II but containing some of what that war was about—Fonda's nervous, acidulous persona interacts with a modernist sense of defeat, and lays blocks in the foundation of film noir. Look at the era: The aftermath of the Depression wearies America, as do recurrent clashes among Communists, capitalists, and socialists. War brews overseas: Henry Fonda has seen Hitler's Reich up close and made his hasty escape, as millions of Europeans in these years will not have the luxury of doing. The world pulses with horrors happening and waiting to happen. So *You Only Live Once* and *Let Us Live*—listen to those titles—have, whatever their flaws and evasions, a new urgency to press on their audiences, a new conviction about the value of life.

The new dramatic setup, and the new popular fear it answers, force from Fonda new effects. The contrasts are exciting as the farmer goes to the city and turns fugitive, and the actor escapes Americana to emerge in the here and now of an explosive and terrifying time.

Set in a nameless, sunless American city, *Let Us Live* centers on Fonda's Brick, a hard-boiled cabbie with a devoted sweetheart (Maureen O'Sullivan), middle-class dreams, and a "representative" face. Brick and his friend Joe—whose pinko talk of social injustice affiliates him with John Steinbeck's radical Okies—are erroneously fingered as the perpetrators of a fatal holdup. They're marched through the legal system, past trial and conviction to the point of execution, before being rescued by chance. But rather than redeemed, Brick is made more cynical: The process of justice has been one of scarification, of bad luck canceled by dumb luck.

Directed by German emigré John Brahm and shot by Lucien Ballard, *Let Us Live* packs a lot of movie; peer into its darkness and you may see a dozen later films—*Detour* or *White Heat, Cabaret* or *Eraserhead*—hiding inside. Only two scenes leaven the gloom with the conspicuous use of light. The first has Brick and Joe exposed under blinding light as their accusers bear false witness from enveloping shadows. The second has Brick in his cell, eyes cast upward as he says:

When I was just a kid I was standing on a street corner with my old man . . . watching a parade go by. Band's playin' . . . He hoisted me up on his shoulders so I could see the flag. He said to me, "You know, son, that's not just a flag, it's a symbol. It's a symbol for millions of people all over the world. It's all their hopes and beliefs. It's freedom and justice, all the things men fight for. Think all those people are wrong?"

The bottom of Fonda's face is in shadow, mouth hidden, eyes the focus. It's as if the words were coming from elsewhere, Fonda's eyes searching out the picture the words struggle to draw.

Let Us Live culminates Fonda's move from the pasture to the town, daydreams to night terrors. But it is also a calculation meant to ride the memory of another movie—*You Only Live Once*. Appearing in early 1937, it's loosely inspired by the story of Clyde Barrow and Bonnie Parker, Texas bank robbers who tore a swath through six states before dying, less than three years earlier, under machine guns in a Louisiana field. They are turned into young lovers Eddie and Joan, an ex-con and a receptionist who dream of home and happiness but wind up running for their lives.

Produced by Walter Wanger and directed by Fritz Lang, Fonda's eighth film is the first to become a socially resonant hit. Pauline Kael will later write that it "expressed certain feelings of its time," and place it among the best American movies of the 1930s. It may be that, but it is also ravaged by age and convention: Too much of the screenplay is dull homily, and there is insufficient charge in the filmmaking. What charge there is comes in nighttime exteriors that are unnaturally beautiful and vibrant with symbol.

You Only Live Once comes alive in the dark. Walking with Joan in a lushly overgrown garden of night, Eddie describes his first arrest—for beating up a kid he caught torturing a frog. The lovers are shown upside down in a pool of water. A frog crouches on a pad. Suddenly it jumps—exploding the water, the reflection, the moment, the future. Of course, it is the frog Eddie once tried to save, come up in time to prophesy doom. Fairy-tale elements are at work, as if Lang could revisit in his mind and conjure with his camera the Grimm-fabled forests of his lost Germany. The moment is just as corny, poetic, and touching as John Ford's fade from the Sangamon in spring to the ice of winter, from a girl's lovely face to her snowy grave.

But unlike Ford, Lang cannot find an equivalent poetry for his more functional scenes; the movie stiffens when aiming for the topical feel of social drama. It is up to Fonda to inject the necessary sense of pain and failure. His Eddie has the incipient ghostliness of a man under a death sentence, but Fonda grounds his life and death in prosaic agony. Observe the scene in which Eddie, who has been driving a truck, is fired for making a late delivery. Eddie begs the boss for a second chance. The scene is as pathetic as life, because Fonda doesn't stint: He squirms as a man must sometimes squirm. He martyrs himself to the dumb humiliation of the scene, the wretched office, the dead-eyed man behind the desk.

Most stars avoid portraying this kind of pain—the unglamorous, unviolent pain inflicted by power. How does it redound to a star's glory to remind us too much of ourselves, especially ourselves as we squirm? Fonda's offering is not to mime this scene, but to squirm it. And though we resent the absence of glamour, we can't fail to accept that offering as a gift of the soul.

Later, Eddie is on death row. To set up an escape, he cuts his wrists. They are hidden behind his back as he bends a tin cup and cuts himself on the crease. Lang shoots it as a staring match between caged man and jailer. The guard leans back, smugly smoking a pipe; Eddie faces him, sweating and trembling. A vein rises in his forehead; his jaw grinds; his eyes fix on those of the guard as if he were cutting the man's throat. And what is he doing with his hands? Fonda has found the *look* of murder, and it is all about presence as absence: the power of what is not seen.

The bravery and bitter clarity of this performance are striking next to its descendant of thirty years later, Warren Beatty in *Bonnie and Clyde*. The bank robbers of the 1967 Arthur Penn film are, in the bodies of Beatty and Faye Dunaway, pure creatures of pop, and when they are shot up at the end, the styling of the mayhem has enormous glamour. But Eddie's end is only the release of a miserable creature from the curse of life. He is a loser, whereas Beatty's Clyde is a winner, right down to his blazing exit: Clyde dies the kind of explosive death children imagine themselves dying.

But no child ever imagined dying like Eddie, nor any adult: sobbing, holding his dead lover, seeking an angel in the trees. Eddie dies quietly, pathetically. No one will remember him.

∽

Fonda is a watcher, a skeptic; he loves America and often hates what it does to people, or what people do in its name. His ascension in the late 1930s as angry man and antihero suggests a through-line to the audience, an understanding of subtleties and of the swelling waves of bad feeling in the land. His performances of these years do not come from nothing.

Asked how the Great Depression affected him, Henry said, "I was barely aware of it. We were in a depression as actors all the time." But he would have been in New York on October 29, 1929, near enough to the epicenter to hear the howls of alarm thrown up from the Financial District as the stock market crashed on Black Tuesday. Most likely, he was in glum rehearsal for his nonspeaking Broadway debut in *The Game of Love and Death,* which would open on November 25 to an audience with suddenly weightier preoccupations.

The crash is not the cause of the Depression, only the harbinger of an impending collision—namely, the collapse of the enduring American myth that anyone with sufficient nerve can be a millionaire overnight. That collapse results in the anger of the 1930s, and in new forms of unity and awareness. People now have to figure out what they owe one another, what they are owed by their government, and how the present system will or will not allow them to live justly. The thirties are extraordinary in modern American history for being a time of sustained debate about capitalism, and of daily doubt about the assumptions and goals of the republic.

Franklin Roosevelt's New Deal is a response to this. Within months of taking office in 1932, Roosevelt initiates a broad battery of social programs and agencies—from the Civilian Conservation Corps to the Soil Conservation Service, from the Social Security Administration to the Farm Security Administration—with short-term goals and long-term aspirations. There are successes and failures in the execution, inequities and flaws built into the New Deal, but it is a reformation in ideas of how American government can and should influence citizens' lives. It tries to do what the government of a republic is meant to do—use the mechanisms and resources of bureaucracy to extend the democratic promise to those most in need of it.

Those most in need number in the millions. Miserable and disquieted, forced onto the open road of a doubtful future, they are searching, listening, asking, thinking—and meeting each other. In the mid- and late 1930s, a phantom allegiance of the dispossessed grows from the enforced proximity of divergent lives. As James Baldwin puts it, "In a way, we were all niggers in the thirties. . . . [I]t was harder then, and riskier, to attempt a separate peace, and benign neglect was not among our possibilities."

Many Americans are recognizing themselves for the first time as part of a larger body, a mass of desperation and displacement. "And because they were lonely and perplexed," John Steinbeck writes, "because they had all come from a place of sadness and worry and defeat, and because they were all going to a new mysterious place, they huddled together; they talked together; they shared their lives, their food, and the things they hoped for in the new country."

∽

But there have always been those Americans who decline to pose for the family portrait, or march in the patriotic pageant. These are the "Don't tread on me" Americans, the loners whose lives are none of your business. Their desire is to live outside the apple-pie order—in a sense, to vanish—and the civil right they prize above all is the one Samuel Warren and Louis Brandeis called "the right to be left alone." They're found on the margins of eccentric artworks arising from the dust of the 1930s: Woody Guthrie's *Bound for Glory*; Edward Hopper's paintings; the novels of James M. Cain, Horace McCoy, Nathanael West, and Tom Kromer; the music of Appalachia and the Mississippi Delta—all of them drawn again and again to murder, flight, homelessness, the open road as romantic dream or dangerous reality.

The best prewar performances of Henry Fonda belong in that class. The loner represents his darker aspect, as it does that of the American

character—as, in Edmund Wilson's words, "the America of the murders and rapes that fill the Los Angeles papers is only the obverse side
of the America of the inanities of the movies." Fonda offers two truths,
sometimes at once: the grudging recognitions of souls on the open
road, and the social revulsion of the born outsider. He alternates between self-reliant American and cooperative American, between forsaking the community and taking his place within it. Doing either, he
embodies a critique of a foundering system, a new sense of what is absent in the public life of the nation.

∞

As Depression deprivation gives the wage earner a thirst for economic
alternatives, it gives the American moviegoer (often, of course, they are
the same person) a desire for aesthetic alternatives—for escapist spectacle on the one hand and, on the other, for a granular simplicity and
attention to something resembling ordinary working life.

Slim (1937) is a drama about the new breed of electrical linemen
engaged by the New Deal to rig live wires across the country. Though
it's not a hit, its attitudes are of the moment, and it exploits the associations an audience brings to Fonda: Evoking Dan Harrow, he appears,
in the first scene, as a farmer with a horse team and plow. But *Slim's*
ambition is to get off the plow and scale the pole, hang wires and jolt
America into its new age. Fonda goes electric! The choreography of
man and technology incarnates the mechanical romanticism of the thirties: There is less feeling in *Slim's* saccharine romance than in the single
hair-raising shot of two WPA daredevils climbing poles in symmetry as
a train shrieks across the limitless landscape behind them.

The 1938 Henry Hathaway actioner *Spawn of the North*, about
salmon fishermen, likewise belongs to the now-dormant tradition of
films about men engaged in dangerous, important work in out-of-the-
way areas. Second-billed to George Raft, Fonda is convincing when
throwing ropes and pulling nets; his body is made for controlled, efficient action. He is less adept at macho boisterousness: Shouting is unnatural to his fine voice, and his roaring laughter sounds false. But

Spawn of the North, while not political, is prole-sympathetic by virtue of being work-centered; it's a stage in Fonda's movement from laborer to labor organizer, working man to union man.

Out of the apolitical worker develops, in due course, the radical. *Blockade* (1938) begins as a collaboration between playwright Clifford Odets and director Lewis Milestone. It's a drama of the Spanish Civil War—a war begun in 1936 between Republican Loyalists on the left and the Falangist forces of the dictatorial Francisco Franco on the right. There is significant Franco support in the United States, most of it Catholic; meanwhile, the Loyalist cause has become a preoccupation of engagé artists and intellectuals like Ernest Hemingway, Jean Renoir, and *Blockade*'s producer, Walter Wanger—still a social-climbing liberal crusader, and still Henry Fonda's putative owner.

Worried about offending the Catholic moviegoer and the spirit of U.S. neutrality, the Hays Office, which administers the Motion Picture Production Code, instructs Wanger to remove any direct references to the Spanish war. Milestone and Odets drop out, to be replaced by William Dieterle, a director with more passion in his heart than in his eye, and screenwriter John Howard Lawson. Identifying detail is expunged, until the screenplay is as potted and inert as the dwarf palm in an executive's office. "The story does not attempt to favor any cause in the present conflict," a studio disclaimer assures the public.

As it happens, the message comes through plainly enough—but no one cares. Fonda, cast as a Spanish farmer who becomes a guerilla leader, makes a peculiarly stringy revolutionary hero, lacking virility in movement or nobility in speech. "We're a part of something, something greater than we are," runs his closing exhortation. "Those people out there— we've given them hope again—you and I." Then a pompous cymbal crash, and Fonda's cry: "Where's the conscience of the world?"

That speech is not so different from the parting words of Tom Joad. Yet we regard the one blankly and are held rapt by the other. *The Grapes of Wrath* will be an infinitely better film than *Blockade,* largely because it has men like John Steinbeck, John Ford, and Gregg Toland behind it, but also because everything strong and true in it—its socialism, humanism, and skepticism—will come to us through Fonda. As Tom Joad, he can express that part of himself that wishes to be an engaged American, a part of the big soul, as well as that other part, the one that would like to vanish.

∽

No American novel quite like *The Grapes of Wrath* had been written before, its style freighting newspaper headlines with the grandeur of eternal odysseys. Its protagonists, the Joads—a family of Oklahoma sharecroppers displaced by exhausted soil and bank foreclosure, driven west to California—were a clan of homeless hicks; they were also the Israelites. Tom Joad, oldest son and defiant soul of the family, freshly paroled on a manslaughter charge, was a mythic avenger, purified by hunger and politicized by the raw deal. There was color, poetry, and panorama to the Joads' long story, and that sense common to all ambitious popular fictions that an entire society had been put in orbit around a set of recognizable but remarkable figures.

The dust bowl resulted from western soil that had been parched and depleted over decades by a market demanding overcultivation of cash crops, particularly cotton. Croppers went so deep in debt to banks that they became tenants on land they'd once owned. When the Depression came, the banks sold the land, tractors flattened homes, and the exodus began: Approximately one million people headed west, drawn by handbills claiming a shortage of fruit pickers in the California valleys. At journey's end, most of the Okies—the migrants' collective name, no matter where they came from—were greeted only with the usurious practices of migrant camp operators, deputized thugs, and the resentments of pickers already in place.

The Grapes of Wrath was published in April 1939, when the Depression was already considered, prematurely, to be over and rumors of war in Europe were the new focus of mass worry. But the book rang chords of controversy. Some dismissed it as Soviet propaganda, while others were convinced the nation had its great novel at last. The book's impact reached the highest level of American influence. "I have read a book," President Roosevelt told a White House conference in January 1940. "It is called *The Grapes of Wrath* and there are five hundred thousand Americans that live in the covers of that book." It became a bestseller, won the Pulitzer Prize, and was sold, days after publication, to Twentieth Century–Fox for $100,000.

Steinbeck's novel helped a significant number of Americans feel conscious of the life of their country: It showed what that country looked like to other Americans, bringing them into new awareness, and even a bit closer to consensus. In so doing, it joined the short list of American books that had drawn lines and forced eyes open—that seemed to have turned the country inside out and left it revealed before itself.

∽

Grandpa Joad lies dying in a tent pitched at the roadside. Bodies pass in and out, folks tending the old man in his last hours. Then, in the flow of coming and going: "The shadow of someone walking between the tent and the sun crossed the canvas."

The author inserts the random detail as stealthily as a concealed blade. Only a second later do we realize, with the suddenness of blood, that the shadow of Death is circling the tent, moving among the destitute, here in a desert off Route 66.

Steinbeck's novel is an organism, based on a conception of life as the interplay of organisms—a large and unitary vision of existence wherein all substances and things are connected in a spiritual and biological flow. Things die throughout the book, and every death is answered by a suggestion of regeneration.

People, animals, earth, even machines—all share a oneness. Shades of the dead and the living dead are all around, and the abandoned shacks are haunted houses. The dust is the fine grain of this ghost world, its repository of blood, money, and dung, both earthly and unearthly: It precedes people when they arrive, and lingers after they depart. The theme of oneness is extended to the novel's politics, which argue a middle ground between New Deal liberalism and Communist collectivism. The story's conscience, Casy—an ex-preacher, half-cracked wanderer, and budding socialist prophet—makes the theme of oneness explicit: "Maybe all men got one big soul ever'body's a part of."

More mystical yet is Steinbeck's supposition that the migrant mass constitutes a shifting community of understanding and human sympathies—"an organization of the unconscious." He makes the mystical practical by applying it to the movements that are occurring all over the country, but particularly between the plains and the western states: "They's stuff goin' on and they's folks doin' things," Casy tells Tom Joad. "Them people layin' one foot down in front of the other, like you says, they ain't thinkin' where they're goin', like you says—but they're all layin' 'em down the same direction, jus' the same. An' if ya listen, you'll hear a movin', an' a sneakin', an' a rustlin', an'—an' a res'lessness."

The Joads never stop moving, malevolent strangers and temporary allies never stop crossing their path, and the dust never ceases to twist around them all. It's the story of people whose determination is to stay alive, to resist becoming ghosts. These are "people in flight from the terror behind"—from death, that shadow on the tent flap. The Okies take their flight on Route 66, the Oregon Trail of the automotive century, turned by the dust bowl into an infinite strip of mechanical graveyard, dead cars marking the miles as white crosses once marked the graves of pioneers.

Oneness, unending flow. A farm wife's infant is eaten by a pig. A dog is crushed by a car. A dead tractor is likened to a corpse. Rosasharn, Tom's pregnant sister, makes love to her husband in the Joad truck as her grandmother lies dying inches away. Rosasharn produces a dead baby, and ends the story by offering the milk in her breast to a starving old man in a barn as a rainstorm rages. It is the final transfusion of life into death, organism into organism, and anyone who would claim Steinbeck was not possessed of a poet's instinct for the inexplicable should look again.

The novel, like its characters, is half-starved yet broad with life, delirious yet gravid with the necessity of following an impossible journey to its unknown end. Clearly, it was written by an author whose feeling of oneness with his time demanded that he either write exactly the book he wrote or die from having failed to do so.

∽

The popular fatalism of the 1930s—the "hard-boiled" sensibility— comes from World War I; the Depression; Hollywood's celebration of gangsters; the terse, brutal prose of Hemingway and Hammett; and per- haps the fear drifting over from Europe, where large numbers of people are beginning to vanish. Doom consciousness tends to be a by-product of times when life makes no sense.

The Grapes of Wrath expresses this, but Steinbeck straddles two worlds—the dry wastes of the doom school and the socialist hypothesis of WPA liberalism. So he places his hero in a situation that tests his desire to remain cynical and self-serving; puts him squarely in the press of family, the necessities of a society and a point in history. We look at these divides, these tendencies and transformations personified in a single fig- ure, and we see Henry Fonda. He understands Tom Joad's conflict, and we understand the need in Fonda to express this phenomenon of solitude softened by community, self-interest remade as common purpose.

In the film, Tom Joad approaches from the sunbaked vortex of a high- way crossroads—a narrow body off center in a proscenium of telephone poles, wearing an ill-fitting suit and walking sideways. He hitches a ride with a gabby trucker; warding off the man's idle curiosities, Tom shows no need to be liked. But then, alighting from the cab, Fonda grins at the trucker, taunting him with a conciliation that is actually a threat—and the smile radiates charisma, charm, sexiness. This man could be in movies. This man could strike you dead.

From the start, Fonda's body stance is nervous but composed, tense and ready. Skinny body in its black suit with high-water cuffs, arms angled outward to stick hands in pockets, pelvis jutting slightly; lots of sunlight between the bony elbows and narrow hips. Watchful eyes in a rectangular head, topped by a huge cloth cap shadowing the eyes throughout the story.

Fonda's acting is close to the bone, and John Ford is in complete command of the early scenes. Tom leaves the highway for the overland trail and—walking uphill and away, like Lincoln—heads for the Joad place, along the way meeting Casy (John Carradine). Ford catches the novel's drawing of dust-bowl country as a spirit-ridden flatland, its dust thick with the matter of vanished things and people. He shoots in high-contrast light and rough-hewn settings, pruning Steinbeck's flowers of prose to leave only stalk and stem. Fonda and Carradine walk a darkening road; their voices echo against the landscape. The echo is an effect of the soundstage upon which the scene plays, but under the darkness and the wind, it sounds more like a reverberation in a corridor of time.

The image is active, the performing excitingly terse, director and star in tight sync. We feel we're watching a great movie. The confrontation with Muley may be its best passage—it is certainly its high point of horror, just from John Qualen's bug-eyed ferocity, and Fonda's and Carradine's awed regard of it. Muley materializes from shadows, and cinematographer Gregg Toland gives the illusion of lighting the pitch-dark cabin with a single blazing candle, floating Muley's ghost face in a flat black depth.

These are brilliant scenes, brilliant in the framing, lighting, and acting, with raw emotion enflaming pious dialogue. Their intensity has to do with movement, less of the camera than of the image itself—the willow branches that undulate as Tom and Casy talk in the foreground, the clothes waving on a line as the Graves family is evicted. The frame is vibrant with shifting darkness, scuttling bodies, sinister weather. In the committed deliveries of Fonda, Carradine, and Qualen, the talk sounds timeless, and the interactions have the gravity of encounters in ancient plays.

When Ford pulls out of Muley's first flashback, the camera is on Tom's watching, listening face; as significant as Muley's defeat is Joad's role as witness to it. Something like the enormity of what has been happening during his imprisonment begins to dawn on our hero. Muley asks Tom where his people are. "They're all gone 'r dead," Tom says, as if it were not a guess, but a decision.

But Ford shoots Fonda's back, not his face, as he says the line. Joad will witness others' devastations, but his own will stay hidden.

∽

The picture's first movement ends with Tom spitting into the weeds as government agents search the Joad place. The next begins when we jump from Tom to his family, as it prepares to leave for California. And here, the film slackens—becomes too much a conventional John Ford celebration of the clan. The old men are too cantankerous, the postadolescents too pretty, the children too manic. Jane Darwell hauls into view as Ma Joad, mother of mothers, ladling the thin soup of homily, and we feel the sag into compromise.

The movie has peaked too soon. John Ford will need Fonda, as he needed him in *Young Mr. Lincoln*, to hold things together—to put flesh on metaphors, to give scale to the overacting of other performers. It is a huge act of Fonda's will to be this encompassing presence, because *The Grapes of Wrath* doesn't always seem to have been shot with the same eyes, or felt with the same nervous system. It goes from nighttime Gothic to daylight realism, easing into studio-bound New Deal idyll before compelling itself toward an optimistic ending that imparts the illusion of unity to what has actually been a very mixed bag.

Yet the movie pulls through. Like the Joad jalopy, it threatens to break down when overheated by bad acting or false framing. Then it will be steadied by a scene of direct and heartrending sentiment, an image of perfect composition and absolute subtlety: Ma burning her mementos, holding earrings to her reflection in a smoky mirror; gusts of wind sweeping Uncle John's shack after the Joads drive away.

If *The Grapes of Wrath* is the story of one family's struggle and survival, it is equally the story of Henry Fonda's face and the changes it goes through. His look goes from hostility as he hitches with the trucker to shock and mystification at hearing Muley's tale. Riding west, the face is baked by sun, labor, and relentlessness into an attitude of hunger—dry eyes squinting, chapped face craning forward on skinny neck. In the dark scenes, the face is repeatedly caught in lamplight, flashlight, moonlight,

Ford fascinated by the emotional secrets exposed by illumination and shadow.

The family takes refuge in a government encampment over the California border. In Ford's New Deal view, the place is a utopia, with clean cabins and sanitary toilets; you can smell the fresh lumber. It is an outpost of hope, and Fonda's face honors hope as it honors Joad's other grudging shows of warm feeling. Passing a communal well, Fonda lets water course through his fingers and, per the posted sign, turns off the tap. Then he smiles, his face slightly away from the camera. It is Tom's first smile in ages, and so small that we wonder whether it registers hope of an equitable social system, or only shows us a man sharing a joke with himself—smiling to think that a stream of water could represent anything so large and impossible as life.

The government camp sponsors a community dance. The dance is Ford's delight, his happy obverse to the war scene or gunfight, an expression of cooperation; it's also a place for tensions to be expressed, or dispersed in the air. In this dance sequence, we see not only the migrants stifling an attempt by fruit-company thugs to incite a riot and bring martial law down on the camp but also Tom's sole moment of lightheartedness—waltzing with Ma while singing "Red River Valley." It is nothing much: a boxy, vertical back-and-forth movement, a rasping, tuneless voice. Yet there is beauty in the rasp, grace in these awkward bodies. Ma looks up with speechless joy; Tom beams down. His look is suddenly clear and content, and we realize that this is a man in whom love exists. The movie has realized a moment of perfect escape, a moment to defer farewells, a moment to stop time.

∽

In fact, two strands of time, of progress, have been brought together. As the story has progressed from dust bowl to peach valley, devastation to exile, it has taken Tom Joad back—back to what he was before prison, or perhaps never was at all: an innocent man.

Tom's final scene with Ma is prefaced with a lovely shot of Fonda rising in silhouette before the low-lit canvas of the tent flap and looking down at Ma with a cigarette in his mouth. Tom whispers to go out-side. He leans to kiss sleeping Pa on the forehead. Then follows Tom's farewell, a speech that not so many years ago was shared culture and common language. The speech exists in Steinbeck's novel, but not as summation or climax, only as one significant leave-taking among many. Here, it is the capstone of the story: Tom Joad's acceptance of a destiny.

Watch, and realize that Ford does little to prime the speech—does not wreathe the actors in filtered light, or cue violins from behind. Even less does Fonda act out an actor's big moment. He edges up to the words, feels forward into the frame of mind that produces them. He delivers not a speech, but a string of thoughts and impressions leading to a natural climax.

He's been thinking about Casy, Tom says, "about what he said, what he done, about how he died . . . I remember all of it." Fonda's poise, sit-ting at the edge of the dance floor with Ma, is to hold in his elbows and knees like a small boy, cold and nervous, cradling his tramp bag. Tom tells Ma he must leave so he can "find out somethin' . . . scrounge around." He can't say what it might be, but he has a feeling Casy was right: "A fella ain't got a soul of his own, just a little piece of a big soul. The one big soul that belongs to everybody."

"What'll happen to you then?" Ma asks, and Tom replies:

I'll be all around in the dark. I'll be everywhere . . . Wherever there's a fight so hungry people can eat, I'll be there. Wherever there's a cop beatin' up a guy, I'll be there. I'll be in the way guys yell when they're mad. I'll be in the way kids laugh when they're hungry and they know supper's ready. And when people are eatin' the stuff they raise and livin' in the houses they build, I'll be there, too.

Fonda creates the suggestion of stress around the eyes, as of tears that won't surface. He conjures the openness of a face that despite its scar and stubble, its years of hurt and humiliation, suddenly looks youthful. We remember the hard, hooded face we first saw, and realize that, by stages, the face has spread open before us and grown younger, been reborn into something like innocence, something like terror.

Tom's farewell affects us because Fonda neither accedes to heroism nor resists it. He merely gives the words their less obvious meaning—that accepting one's complicity in the fate of the whole race might be far more terrifying than exhilarating. We must, if we are to feel anything, feel the curse that has fallen on Tom, the burden he has decided to accept. So Fonda won't smile serenely as he says "I'll be there." His eyes won't mist over, nor his chest expand and sinews stretch as they reach for their moral purpose. Instead, he will suggest fear with the slope of his eyebrows, the downward curve of his mouth—as if the man inside were melting with dread at the choice he faces.

It's easy to feel distance from the words Tom speaks because they sound so damnably literary. They are an idea, and people tend not to express themselves in terms of ideas. But this film is a product of a time when Americans were forced by calamity and hunger to reconfigure their lives and their ethics. One had either to commit to something new, reinvest thin hope in failed systems, or renounce the idea of community and drop out. One's life had to become the expression of that choice, and therefore of an idea. Tom Joad's last words are literary, but they are fair. They are even accurate. But they could so easily have been botched by a bad intonation, a moment's puffery or tainting streak of ego. Fonda walks the line. He reads past the social moment that produces the words, to express the burden of a man trapped and transformed by American history.

Our last view of Tom is of a tiny figure walking away over a far hill in early morning, with "Red River Valley" sounding on a sad accordion. The figure could be anyone—Tom Joad, or another anonymous soul on the open road. To become someone, he has chosen to be no one. To enter America, he has chosen to disappear into it.

∽

Is Tom Joad striding on ahead, leading us to glory, or is he only walking away, showing us his ass? Well—say he is doing both. Say both are part of a flow, a oneness. In doing both—refusing and committing, striding on and walking away—Tom has already become what Casy imagined. So has Fonda.

"The one big soul that belongs to everybody": Much is contained in that line. "The big soul" means that community exists, that there is a group identity greater than the many single identities within it. But for anyone with Fonda's suspicions of the crowd, it also means taking into account how easily, when people join in a mass, health turns into sickness, moral people into mere fingers of the lynch mob or fascist army.

"The big soul" means, too, that one person can leave a Henry Fonda film feeling affirmed in the rightness of things as they appear, while another leaves the same film convinced that Fonda has colored blood—that hidden relationships and murky continuities function in him. It means that those truths are fused in a body and a face, a pair of eyes, a mind and a memory; and that the contradictions of community and country flow, for one revelatory stretch of film, through one man.

Whether or not we believe in "the big soul," Fonda shows that he believes in it. And we feel that his belief comes through layers of experience, empathy, and uncertainty that his own soul can ever begin to relinquish the cold strength of solitude. Somehow we know that Fonda has always believed in the big soul, and wondered of its claim on him long before Tom Joad appeared to give him the words he would have chosen for himself, were words and not action his manner of expressing his sorrow to the world:

"I remember all of it."

5

Ways of Escape

The Lady Eve

D eath in the guise of the new life in California is not going to prevail over me," says the main character in Walker Percy's novel *The Second Coming*. "Death in the guise of marriage and family and children is not going to prevail over me."

Family and domesticity are, for many, an irresistible lure, and a hook in the mouth. The lures are warmth, security, familiarity, legacy. The hook is a feeling of entrapment, that one's own needs and desires are forever subordinate to those of others. As that hook pierces and digs deeper with every year, resentment grows. *Who are these people? Why do they believe they have the right to all that I am? Can't they leave me alone?*

Fear that in the bosom of the family hides the death of the individual may be irrational. It may be a sane person's best defense against the crushing effects of mismatched parents and incomprehensible children. Or it may be a certain kind of person's natural recoil from closeness and community.

Some who feel the resentment express it, while others hold it inside. They play at being spouse and parent, meeting what they feel are the reasonable requirements of an unwritten contract. Bad feelings collect near the surface of life, and fester there. Quiet and stoicism become an especially unpleasant form of aggression as the violent act is replaced by the roaring silence. The hook digs deeper, but the blood stays on the inside, flowing backward, down the throat.

∽

Henry and Frances now have two children: Lady Jayne Seymour Fonda, born December 21, 1937, and Peter Henry Fonda, born February 23, 1940. Both are delivered in New York City by cesarean section.

Frances learns of her and Henry's first conception not long after Ross Alexander's suicide, and just as *You Only Live Once* is reaching theaters. The news makes her happy—she especially wants a boy—and Henry claims to be leaping with excitement. Then one day, like all fathers-to-be, he wakes up, blinks his eyes, and realizes the limits that are about to constrict him. At which point, like many fathers-to-be, he begins to spend as much time out of the house as he can manage.

Always a workhorse, he increases his pace, filming *That Certain Woman* with Bette Davis as Frances readies the nest. Henry then fancies a return to the stage—first at the Westchester Playhouse for a summer-stock rendition of *The Virginian,* then at the 46th Street Theatre, site of his Dan Harrow triumph, for Valentine Davies's *Blow Ye Winds,* a romantic comedy with a seaside setting and, as critics see it, insufficient salt in the talk.* Why would Fonda choose this summer to return east—for the privilege of acting in two mediocre plays, or to evade the gathering realities of fatherhood?

Blow Ye Winds wheezes to a close after only thirty-six performances. By this point, Frances has come to New York, first to oversee the auctioning of George Brokaw's furniture, and, second, to have the baby

---

*Brooks Atkinson wrote, "Although Henry Fonda is a pleasant actor with an engaging emotional sincerity, he is not the chap to pick a placid script out of the doldrums." See *New York Times,* 9/24/1937.

delivered by her personal obstetrician at the exclusive Doctors Hospital on the Upper East Side. Completing the missed connections of people who seem to be avoiding each other, Frances settles into her maternity bed just as Henry flies back to Hollywood to begin shooting *Jezebel*, the final film on his three-picture contract with Warner Bros.

But Henry is a decent man as well as a selfish one: He has had a provision written into his *Jezebel* contract that requires director William Wyler to release him from the production when the baby's birth becomes imminent. When Jane arrives, Henry is at Frances's bedside. After a brief visit, he returns to Hollywood; it is another two weeks before Frances follows him, Jane in her arms.

Henry goes almost directly from the set of *Jezebel* to the set of his next movie, *Blockade*, while Frances arranges the family's move to a new house on Monaco Drive in the Pacific Palisades area of Los Angeles. (Margaret Sullavan and Leland Hayward—Henry's ex-wife and his agent, now married and starting their own family—move in a few doors away.) There's much crisscrossing activity in these weeks; the couple continue to be conspicuously separated.

"Dad was so emotionally distant," Jane says, "with a coldness Mother was not equipped to breach." Contrasted to that are what she calls his "Protestant rages." Henry is absent much of the time, work being his chief concern: He has the male intentness on production and utility, and family exhausts his patience for nonsense. If the silence is a passive withdrawal from the burden of others' emotional needs, the rage runs deeper—too deep to be considered anything but a basic component of Henry's character. "We were all afraid of Jane's father in those days," says a friend. "We always felt he was a time bomb ready to explode."

Frances has her own preoccupations, which Joshua Logan identifies as "children, operations, jewelry, [and] the stock market." She is a hypochondriac, and visitors note that she seems excessively fearful that germs will get at the baby. Henry will later complain that he is not allowed to be as affectionate with his daughter as he wishes—that baby Jane is effectively "quarantined," and that Frances makes him wear a mask when nuzzling her.

Frances lavishes her attentions on Peter, who will grow into a sickly, neurotic child, a melancholy charge of private schools and relatives, with a destructive streak and penchant for violent games. There is also a half sibling in the house—Pan, Frances's daughter by Brokaw, six years older than Jane. There is gender ambiguity: Jane plays the tomboy to ape the masculinity of her adored father, and to be the son her mother wanted; while sensitive Peter is a constant source of perplexity to manly Dad.

In 1938, soon after Jane's birth, the Fondas move to a large family cottage on South Chadbourne Avenue in Brentwood. (Again, the Haywards follow them to a nearby house on Evanston Street.) Then, in early 1940, Henry and Frances discover a nine-acre property at 600 Tigertail Road in Beverly Hills, overlooking the Pacific, with views of the Santa Monica Mountains. Though the land is costly, this verdant suburb is not yet the exclusive domain of the Hollywood elite. In Henry's recollection, the landholder, Bell Telephone, is uncertain whether to sell or retain the thousands of acres. Selling would mean installing many miles of wire for phone service and utilities, and no one knows if such investment is justified. But by liquidating some of Henry's holdings and pooling them with her own, Frances is able to purchase the property for $27,000. Peter remembers the family moving there "in increments" between 1942 and 1944.

Tigertail is at first, Henry says, "a bare hill. Not even trees." With his own hands, he plants groves of citrus and pine. The wilds of Beverly Hills in the predevelopment 1940s are unspoiled but treacherous. "In those days," Brooke Hayward writes, "the sky belonged to patrols of turkey buzzards circling it leisurely, the hills swarmed with jackrabbits and deer, and at night packs of coyotes gathered on our lawn to howl at the moon." The tall grasses are alive with king snakes and rattlers.

The Fondas design and build a main house, with a number of outbuildings dotting the property. "Probably the most carefully planned home in these United States," it's called in a 1948 *House Beautiful* pictorial. "Before even the cement was mixed, trees were moved and transplanted on the grounds, flower beds were set out, a citrus grove was planted, and gardens were mapped." There are Mohawk Valley touches in the styling of the house, with its artificially distressed shingling and colonial furnishings.

For the kids, Tigertail is a pastoral wonderland, with horse stables, a two-story playhouse, and unlimited space. Brother and sister remember these as the happiest days of their childhood. In retrospect, they will understand their parents' unhappiness, signs missed or ignored at the time; but for now, there are sufficient sun, grass, and animals to divert them from the mysterious doings of the adults.

Henry works steadily during the construction, either at Twentieth Century–Fox—to which he is now contracted—or on the land. Frances's task and distraction is to take over the household finances, including the buying and selling of stocks and real estate. She grows more withdrawn, eats less, and begins to hoard pills.

At the same time, she multiplies her own money, while losing a good deal of Henry's in a series of bad investments. The implications are plain: As Henry withdraws attention and affection from Frances, so she withdraws a portion of his solvency and independence. The emotional constriction of the situation, the time-bomb silences and secret retributions, mean that Frances's manner and habits grow more institutional, as of one living in a prison, with herself as both inmate and jailer: She carries a ring around, with keys to every lock in Tigertail.

Or maybe she simply misses the hospital—any hospital. In 1940, suffering headaches and weight loss, she retreats for three weeks to the Scripps Clinic near La Jolla. It is her first confinement for nervous symptoms.

∞

Like many harried young husbands, Henry has stress at the office, and a boss he despises. Darryl F. Zanuck, head of Twentieth Century–Fox, is also from Nebraska—little Wahoo is a mere thirty miles west of Omaha. Zanuck is only three years older, and, like Fonda, he left his virginity in one of Omaha's many brothels. We don't know if the two ever compared notes on their first sexual experiences, or, indeed, if they might have chanced to share the same initiator.

But their common ground ends there. Unlike Fonda, Zanuck is a braggart who believes his own publicity. He is also an executive of raw brilliance who not only shepherds many daring projects to estimable ends but also manages to do little enough damage to others in the process. He becomes Henry's necessary antagonist during his finest decade on the screen, enabling or obstructing some of his most important films.

Zanuck's credits reach back to the silent era. He's risen from writing gags for dog star Rin Tin Tin to heading production at Warner Bros., where in 1931 he initiates that studio's cycle of archetypal gangster films. After that, he forms a production company, Twentieth Century, with Joe Schenck, president of United Artists; the company merges with the failing Fox Film Corporation in 1935, and Twentieth Century–Fox is created. There, Zanuck produces a body of cinema whose elements are, as Mel Gussow puts it, "a little melodrama, a big musical, a lot of spectacle, and a preponderance of fictionalized history." With plenty of Shirley Temple thrown in.

Zanuck is among the few who know instantly that talking pictures are not a fad. He has a sixth sense about story values, personally supervises the script construction and final edits on many pictures, and often takes a pseudonymous writing credit. For these skills he is genuinely, if grudgingly, admired by his directors—the likes of John Ford, Otto Preminger, Elia Kazan, Jean Renoir, and Joseph L. Mankiewicz.

In the 1940s, Fox becomes the top studio in Hollywood, and Zanuck, writes biographer George F. Custen, "would transform himself from a purveyor of colorful but basically escapist entertainment into the industry's preeminent serious producer." The phrase "serious producer" is like the phrase "great American"—we would do well to be wary of it. Zanuck wins Best Picture Oscars with *How Green Was My Valley* (1941), *Gentlemen's Agreement* (1947), and *All About Eve* (1950), and scores only slightly less exalted hits with *Song of Bernadette* (1943), *A Tree Grows in Brooklyn* (1945), *Miracle on 34th Street* (1947), and *The Snake Pit* (1948). If some of the Zanuck "classics" are insufferably trite today, and others oafishly sensational, a few retain shreds of what we can only call power.

By 1940, Zanuck has collected a stable of reusable stars: not only the Temple phenomenon, but also Tyrone Power, Alice Faye, Don Ameche, Loretta Young, and the skater Sonja Henie. They are mediocre actors and soft idols, however affable and reliable. None commands the actorly weight to confer real prestige on a studio—and Zanuck has the self-made, ill-educated man's thirst for prestige. Meanwhile, Henry Fonda is turning into one of the most prestigious items in pictures. He carries the library whiff of literature, the noble dust of history, and it is largely through Zanuck productions like *Young Mr. Lincoln, Jesse James,* and *Drums Along the Mohawk* that Fonda has achieved such stature.

Yet each man regards the other with hostility. There is something about Fonda—a refusal to buy all the way in, to become a contract player—that must look to Zanuck very much like a presumption of superiority. It may be that he dislikes watching Fonda reap the reward of prestige projects without showing due fealty to the producer whose sweat and aggression make them possible.

The actor, for his part, may resent the producer on matters of fundamental difference. Where Fonda is tall, lean, and quiet, Zanuck is squat, bullish, and loud. Where Fonda projects modesty, Zanuck is an inveterate attention grabber. Where Fonda is wreathed in public and critical esteem, Zanuck hears only the hosannas of yes-men. Where Fonda suffers, Zanuck revels—in women, parties, opulence, pushing patriotic product and homespun values while indulging what Gussow terms a "divided allegiance in matters of morality."

∽

But none of that matters to Fonda, so long as he remains his own man. In 1938, his contract with Wanger expires; offers fly at him, and in the following year he does some of his best acting. His commercial draw is increasing: "Henry Fonda is fast becoming a matinee idol in spite of himself," says a contemporary report. From a distance, Zanuck watches Fonda develop; he counts his profit and waits for his moment.

The Grapes of Wrath comes into play. Though it seems made for the screen, most producers shy away from its suggestion that something may be broken in the American system. Only Zanuck seems interested in taking up the novel's challenge, or exploiting its dollar value. "We intend to follow the exact book," he assures John Steinbeck, while allowing that some content will have to be sacrificed to the censors. Steinbeck, though less than easy with Zanuck's promises, takes his deal.

Ford is evidently not the producer's first choice as director, nor are all the actors in place from the outset. But as Custen writes, "one casting decision was never questioned: Henry Fonda was always Zanuck's choice to play Tom." Perhaps, but Custen doesn't say what Zanuck does to get Fonda—and to get him where he wants him.

In recounting their meeting, Fonda will note a single salient detail: Zanuck, an avid polo player, has the affectation of swinging a polo mallet—*whoosh, whoosh*—while talking.

Zanuck lays it on the line. Tom Joad is an epochal part, and Fonda is ideal for it. *Whoosh, whoosh.* But to get it, he will have to sign a contract tying him to Fox and Zanuck for seven years. *Whoosh.*

Inside, our hero curses. Out loud, he asks for the pen, and signs.

The deal will force Fonda to bite the bullet as an actor for most of the next decade, getting his shot at Joad in return for seven years of whatever contract trash is handed him. So Henry learns something new and bitter about the nature of necessity in Hollywood: No whore gets to shine without finally being reminded he is a whore. He will loathe Darryl Zanuck until the day he dies.

∽

If we linger over this stretch of mediocrity, it is only to note the varieties of abjection Fonda puts his back to—and the miracles of art that can occur in a commercial medium, no matter the impediments. So, following a nonchronological course from worst to best, we stroll through an unhappy Fonda phase that, if it isn't quite a season in hell, is surely a fortnight in purgatory.

Lillian Russell (1940). A musical, with Alice Faye as the once-famed Broadway singer. Fonda is third-billed as one of her many suitors, slack-shouldered in a role that forces him back to the boyish ardor of earlier films. Asked about it at the time, Fonda says he hasn't seen it: "I know I'm bad, and I don't intend to find out how bad."

Chad Hanna (1940). Jane Darwell, John Carradine, and screenwriter-producer Nunnally Johnson return from *The Grapes of Wrath* to mount a story of traveling circus performers. Henry is palpably disagreeable to playing, at thirty-five, another clod-kicking juvenile, mouthing phony hillbillyisms and carrying slop to pigs. Zanuck released this misery on Christmas Day.

Immortal Sergeant (1943). In August 1942, Fonda enlists in the United States Navy, and neglects to inform anyone at Fox of the fact. Though it is unprofessional of him, no one will criticize a screen star who selflessly surrenders his career for the duties and dangers of a common sailor in wartime.

But Zanuck will again prove himself Henry's master as gamesman and mallet swinger. The instant Fonda arrives at boot camp, Zanuck has him recalled on the pretext that he is needed to star in a piece of propaganda. This is *Immortal Sergeant,* a dreary story of heroics in the Libyan desert, whose script combines *The Lost Patrol* with a dire romantic plot. While the film has no measurable impact on morale, it does dampen Fonda's crisp escape from Hollywood, his perfect "fuck you" to Zanuck—and that must have placed a sweet taste behind the producer's smile.

The Magnificent Dope (1942). Henry is the bumpkin exploited by an adman in this Capraesque monkeyshines, which renews the great American myth of the honest man's triumph over cynicism and slickery. Fonda gamely applies himself to the thousand small, sour tasks of professionalism.

The Big Street (1942). Based on a Damon Runyon story, its every inhabitant has an inexhaustible line of colorful crapola, and a heart softer than a circus peanut. Fonda plays Pinks, a nightclub busboy inexplicably devoted to a woman he calls "Highness" (Lucille Ball), a gangster's moll who disdains and exploits him.

The movie is too bad to watch, the plot too good to resist. Highness, hit by a car and crippled, decides she must go to Florida, never mind why. Pinks wheels her all the way from Broadway to Miami Beach. When she starts acting cuckoo, Pinks consults a shrink, who asks, "Didja ever hear of a thing called paranoia?" He explains that paranoids are fine people, so long as their fantasy is preserved; contradict it, though, and they collapse—"Unless it's restored." ("He ain't a very good doctor, Pinks," says costar Agnes Moorehead, in the understatement of the 1940s.)

Pinks goes to elaborate lengths to reconstruct Highness's illusion, finally dragging his paraplegic love around a nightclub floor. Then, having induced her to hallucinate that she is both glamorous and self-ambulating, he carries her to the veranda, where she dies in his embrace beneath the stars. Strange. Very, very strange.

Tales of Manhattan (1942). An omnibus, directed by Julien Duvivier. Fonda's partner is Ginger Rogers, and their segment is the least interesting in the picture. In its single funny moment, Rogers does something to prompt a roar (yes, a roar) from Fonda. Hard to remember what.

Wild Geese Calling (1941). Our space- and time-traveling star is now a lumberjack in the Pacific Northwest, 1895, climbing a tree as cleverly as lineman Slim will scale an electrical pole forty years later. Back from *Let Us Live* are director John Brahm and cameraman Lucien Ballard; the screenplay is by pulp novelist Horace McCoy. The film is not wretched. Narrative contrivance is met by an overall impression of human bustle, some spirited make-believe, and the perennial tension to be wrung from a childbirthing climax set in a remote cabin on a stormy night.

You Belong to Me (1941). In which Fonda is paired for the final time with Barbara Stanwyck. The movie trades on Henry's image, inherited from *The Lady Eve* (still to come), as the passive player in *l'amour fou*, and, as in *The Mad Miss Manton,* he is feminized: Stanwyck as the husband-wife works; Fonda as the wife-husband sulks and shops. But with Stanwyck's support, he makes an exceptionally appealing romantic-comedy lead—likable even when self-centered or pathetic.

Rings on Her Fingers (1942). Fonda's movements have spring and flex, and he spends much of the picture lounging, leaning, pivoting, or angling in unfamiliar ways. In the dance scene, he and Gene Tierney start out moving like bread sticks, then break hilariously into an explosive jitterbug. The film is directed by Rouben Mamoulian, who may remember

Fonda from years before, having directed him in *The Game of Love and Death,* his Broadway debut.

The Male Animal (1942). Elliott Nugent and James Thurber contrive a hit play from the politics of the wartime college campus and prevailing American codes of manliness. Fonda seems at first almost too tailor-made for the part of Tommy Turner, bespectacled professor and scrawny, fuddled idealist. At the climax, as Tommy reads the jailhouse prose of Bartolomeo Vanzetti, the star removes his glasses, combs his hair, and becomes Henry Fonda—and the scene has the smell of an actor doing his specialty. But it's a fine picture from stellar material, directed at stage speed by cowriter Nugent. Fonda is given one of his finest romantic partners in Olivia de Havilland, who combines glamour, common sense, and a winning lack of neuroticism.

The Lady Eve (1941). It's either the genius of the system or the cretinism of chance that gives Fonda one of his career triumphs at a time when his work is virtually devoid of pleasure. But it is solely the genius of writer-director Preston Sturges that sees earnest Fonda as a timeless hero of screwball comedy.

Casting him as Charles "Hopsie" Pike—explorer of tropical interiors, student of snake life, and patsy to con woman Barbara Stanwyck—Sturges locates in Fonda fine grades of innocence that have been elusive to other directors. From his first appearance in white dinner jacket, we sense we're watching not a new Fonda, but a Fonda detailed and sharpened, made comedically exact and brought newly alive. He is beautiful as he sits and reads his book, with humor in his beauty, precision in the lines of his body: Fonda's physical discipline produces a funniness of *being.* Yet his face is magnificently solemn, impervious to the flutterings of the avaricious debs at surrounding tables, sweet predators who want his body, his money, his mouth, and perhaps even a bit of his strange, private mind.

Then Stanwyck's Eve catches his face in her hand mirror. She extends a leg, and Hopsie trips and crashes like a small skyscraper. There is nothing in Hollywood comedy like Fonda's fall, or Stanwyck's smile at the moment Eve knows Hopsie is hooked. From that point, Fonda's face alternates fear, a revolted turn-on, and the blanks of a man worrying every question to death in his head; his body lines go berserk as Stanwyck folds and crunches him into the director's frame like a stuffed animal into a trunk.

"You're certainly a funny girl to meet for anyone who's been up the Amazon for a year," Hopsie tells Eve, and in this sexy, absurd context, phrases like "funny girl" and "up the Amazon" tickle us in odd places. We get the most erotic scene in any Henry Fonda picture—a long, sustained shot of Hopsie and Eve clinching faces, she sensuously stroking his hair and whispering, he looking terrified and tumescent, his eyes cast upward in ecstatic martyrdom, a Joan of Arc burning at the stake of sex.

This is only the beginning of *The Lady Eve*. It goes on to be a perfect immersion in the Sturges world, with all its well-defined yet constantly recombinant elements—a world dominated by actors and chance, in which jungle beasts and a cruise-ship steam whistle, a rainstorm and a locomotive conspire to make life joyful. *The Lady Eve* is a sexy machine, a witty snake, a gift. And proof again that, whatever Henry's self-isolating tendencies as a man, as an actor he needs friends around him, artists of sympathy, in order not just to emerge but to take his fullest, most inspiriting shapes.

∽

There must be times when Fonda's career is incoherent to him. He is the actor as artist as craftsman, focusing on a narrow but deep range of expression and investigation, a certain class and cadre of American man. But the Zanuck regime blasts his focus, and Fonda hates it because he, more than most of his contemporaries, is ravenous for focus.

He thrives under directors who know just what they are doing, with scripts that are suggestive but solidly built. The Fox contract forces Fonda into swamps of inanity, attempts at populism that—as drama, comedy, or even fantasy—make no sense. And Fonda, craftsman and conventional man, wants to make sense.

That is both virtue and limitation. Making sense is a way of dealing with reality but also of denying it. As the sensible man belittles the chaos of emotion, the sensible artwork belies the complexity of *things*. The narrative that is too focused and coherent to admit ambiguity in life or character will leave an audience renewed in its certitudes and empty of curiosities; communicate a point of view, but bring nothing to life.

We're reluctant to apply these disclaimers to *The Ox-Bow Incident* (1943), for it is one of the few films from Fonda's Zanuck era that holds our interest now. And the project clearly means much to Fonda personally. He is instrumental in getting it made, and gives it some of his strongest, edgiest acting. Directed by action-film pioneer William A. Wellman and scripted by Lamar Trotti, it is not a work anyone will forget having seen. But at its core is a moral simplicity, a desire to make sense that reduces it. It shows Fonda as the too-conscious craftsman, too-justified liberal, and too-sensible artist, with all the limitations and virtues of the Nebraska son and Christian Scientist.

Walter Van Tilburg Clark's novel is set in the imaginary Bridger's Wells, Nevada, in 1885. Two freelance cowpokes hear that a recent spate of cattle rustlings has climaxed in a rancher's murder. A lynch mob finds three men who are implicated by circumstantial evidence. Despite protesting their innocence throughout a long night, the three are hanged at dawn by the vigilantes. It will be learned too late that they were innocent.

The book is highly praised and a best-seller, but its lack of any positive resolution makes it a near-impossible piece of movie material. Antilynching dramas are not conducive to American self-esteem as the nation heads into the hardest phase of World War II, and Darryl Zanuck is against the project from the outset. While he perceives the prestige value of a film done right, he feels an open indictment of lynching is "certainly not entertainment for these times."

The others involved disagree. Clark asserts the film wouldn't have been made but for the "high pressure salesmanship" of Wellman and Fonda. "Together," he says, "they went to bat for the work."

As an antilynching statement, *Ox-Bow* is a strong dose. It is brave in implying a relation between manliness and sadism, and its energy is bracingly modern: The frames breathe realism, toughness, cool. Indeed, with its high-contrast lighting, hard-boiled dialogue, volatile characters, and sense of fate, *Ox-Bow* may be the first noir Western.

The opening sequence, full of macho face-offs between itchy, horny cowboys, is an exhilarating buildup of tension. Fonda is again the strong center—terse, humorless, considered in his movements but always with a violent capability—and he plays the cowboy Gil Carter through the eyes as much as the mouth. *"Make that clear,"* he says in response to a taunt: the purity of Gil's danger is his expanding eye sockets and narrowing pupils. Those eyes will become the center of consciousness and judgment in *The Ox-Bow Incident*—the eyes of the cynic, the man at the edge of the group.

Yet the film still feels small and tinny. It is simple-minded, with a slick sense of despair, where the novel is messy and multidimensional. The movie trims Clark's slow, lurching scenario, making a straightforward indictment of mob violence and lynch law at a time when that is a crucial but unpopular thing to do. In social terms, that's quite a bit; in artistic terms, it's simply not enough.

Fonda is afraid of mess, but only, perhaps, because he knows it too well. There's an exchange in Clark's novel about the fear of the mess inside each of us. "Did you ever hear a man tell another man," the narrator is asked, "about the dreams he's had that have made him sweat and run his legs in the bed and wake up moaning with fear?" The narrator doesn't respond, but he is listening. "We've all had those dreams. In our hearts we know they're true, truer than anything we ever tell; truer than anything we ever do, even. But nothing could make us tell them, show our weakness . . .

"We're afraid our own eyes will give us away," the narrator is told—or warned. "That's what makes us sick to hear fear admitted."

Those are words Fonda would understand. They are the revelation of a strong man's panicked inner life. Fear is the motor of his acts: He cannot live without feeling, yet he can never let himself feel too nakedly, and so he is trapped with dreams of fleeing—fleeing himself, the exposed and vulnerable thing that he is.

∞

The Ox-Bow Incident has the same nocturnal preoccupation as *Young Mr. Lincoln*: The director of photography is Arthur Miller, who'd shot that film's key scene of Abe and Ann at the riverside. One of the three hanging victims is played by Francis Ford, John Ford's brother; he played a juror in *Lincoln,* the citizen who never spoke but nodded eagerly at the prospect of hanging someone. And crucially, *Ox-Bow* reverses the rescue fantasy of *Lincoln* by showing a hanging that is *not* averted. It's as if Fonda wants to show all the things *Lincoln* only insinuated: the scapegoating reflex in our public life, the evil capability of the mass, the malignance in the American night.

The Grapes of Wrath is evoked even more strongly, chiefly by Fonda's presence as a man recoiling from the vengeful community toward the isolation of a moral position forced on him by circumstance. There is also the presence of Jane Darwell, soulful as Ma Joad, here a cackling sadist (also called "Ma"). There is the use, in both films, of "Red River Valley" as a melancholy motif. *Ox-Bow*'s closing shot, with the cowpokes ascending the hill out of Bridger's Wells, recalls Lincoln and Joad climbing their hills at story's end. Wellman's direction throughout is keenly Ford-conscious, and this ponderous ascension has the feel of homage.

Finally, the letter read by Fonda at the end of the film—a message from one of the hanged men to his wife—paraphrases some of Tom Joad's last words. ("What is the conscience of any man save his little fragment of the conscience of all men in all time?") But see how Wellman shoots it: Fonda turns to stand in profile, and the camera's focus inches forth so that his eyes are obscured by the brim of another man's hat. Except for a single close-up at the very end, Fonda reads the entire letter with his main center of expressiveness unavailable to us.

As a Fonda moment—one directed and determined partly by his presence within it—the scene is another thread in a theme running through his career: hiddenness—presence as absence, the power of what is not seen. Wellman complements the way in which Fonda's illuminated eyes and shadowed mouth were shot in *Let Us Live*; returns us to the hidden cutting of the wrists in *You Only Live Once*; reminds us of the darkened Lincoln silhouette taking over the foreground of the Springfield courtroom; calls up Tom Joad, whose aloneness is shown in his strong, stooped back.

In Clark's novel, the cowpokes leave town and don't look back: "'I'll be glad to get out of here,' Gil said, as if he'd let it all go." They won't forget, but their responsibility now is to live as if one day they might. Fonda's drama runs the other way. His sense of obligation is deeper than the normal person's; his character can't "let it all go." He insists on riding out to the dead man's widow and children with his letter and effects, as if in payment of a debt only he believes he owes.

Fonda—like the characters he plays in those stories that mean the most to him—cannot imagine living without a responsibility to the dead.

∽

"I was a typical eager beaver who wanted to shoot at Japanese," Fonda will say as an old man.

When the Imperial Japanese Navy Air Service attacks the U.S. Pacific Fleet at Pearl Harbor on December 7, 1941, Fonda is in Hollywood, shooting *The Male Animal*. Only two days before, the movie columns have carried a facetious account of a staged fight between him and costar Jack Carson.

President Roosevelt, while appeasing the isolationists who oppose American involvement in the European war, has been sending arms and supplies to aid Britain's campaign against Hitler. Secretly eager that the United States should join the battle, he has issued a series of veiled threats designed to draw fire from Japan, Germany's military ally. Whether Roosevelt foresaw or indeed intended a response on the scale of Pearl Harbor is a question that those on both sides feel they have answered. But in the realm of the certain, nearly 2,500 Americans are dead and another 2,000 wounded, casualties of a strike whose forebodings were ignored either because of strategy or what war historian John Costello calls a "shared disbelief" among the bureaucratic elites "that the Japanese would make a strategically 'illogical' attack on Pearl Harbor."

The Third Reich threatens to turn Europe into a fascist rally-cum-beer garden. America's Great Depression will finally be dissolved by the cash flowing into and out of the war machine. Roosevelt will imprison thousands of Japanese-Americans in Nisei internment camps. The defense of freedom from fascism will engender destructive capabilities unprecedented in history. World War II will give us radar, mass-produced penicillin, napalm, the national-security state, and *Catch-22*.

Illogical? The world has entered a new age of illogic.

For all his uniqueness, we can't forget that Fonda is also a common man with common motivations, "a typical eager beaver." When the United States goes to war, he is like millions of others: He wants in. Wants to test his mettle in situations demanding competence and courage; wants to defend democracy against its enemies. Doubtless recalling the Revolutionary War death of great-great-grandfather Douw Jellis and the Civil War heroism of grandfather Ten Eyck, he wants to extend the family history of distinguished sacrifice in wartime.

He also wants to escape the life he has built for himself—to escape "Death in the guise of the new life in California . . . Death in the guise of marriage and family and children . . ." There has never been a shortage of men willing to risk quick death in foreign lands to avoid slow death by domesticity.

The prospect of mobilization, camaraderie, and hierarchy must seem to Fonda like an exhilarating expulsion of pent-up energy. Not to mention the persistent male desire for the absolutes of life and death. William Wyler—Fonda's director on *Jezebel*, and his successor as husband to Margaret Sullavan—will shoot combat documentaries with the Eighth Air Force, come back deaf in one ear, and articulate the impulse this way: The war, he said, was "an escape to reality. The only things that mattered were human relationships; not money, not position, not even family. . . . Only relationships with people who might be dead tomorrow were important."

Though a small child when her father goes to war, the adult Jane will sense this motivation in Henry: "He was genuinely patriotic and hated Fascism, but I think it was also about him wanting to get away."

∽

Some of Fonda's friends have already left. James Stewart is commanding bombing missions with the air force; John Ford is directing a field photography unit for the navy. In late June or July of 1942, Fonda contributes voice-overs to Ford's chronicle of the just-fought Battle of Midway—a three-day defense of a tiny atoll between Hawaii and Japan, in which American marines and B-17s have dealt the Japanese their first significant naval defeat of the war. Garish, grainy, jolting, *The Battle of Midway* gives us a glimpse of the extremity that pulls men into war and keeps them there.

Fonda's contribution quickens his urge to get out of Brentwood and into battle. It's only a few weeks later, on August 24, 1942—the day after wrapping *The Ox-Bow Incident*—that he volunteers for military service. Fonda informs his family of what he has in mind but, pointedly and remarkably, tells no one at Fox. He drives himself to naval headquarters in Los Angeles and requests active duty: "I'd like to be with the fellows who handle the guns," he says.

He tries to switch from movie star to navy recruit as quietly as possible; but the papers love it and give it prominent play. It confirms for them not only Henry's personal modesty but also that of the American character, the readiness of even the privileged to surrender safety for duty. "Without the usual Hollywood fanfare," runs one story, "Fonda waited in line with other prospective recruits, took his medical examination and was sworn in. [Recruiting officer] Lt. Blanchard said Fonda will be sent to San Diego within a few days and can realize his wish to 'handle the guns' by competing for a rating in the gunner's mate's school."

"It has been my desire to join the service for a long time," Henry tells the press, "and I am glad that I am able to get in and do a little pitching." To accept a family deferment never occurs to him. Unlike other stars who sign up in the months after Pearl Harbor, he won't jump the enlisted ranks to officer status, or, an even viler option, wear a uniform while staying out of the fight—whether by making propaganda films, touring with the USO, or hosting bond rallies at the Hollywood Canteen. Instead, he signs on as an apprentice seaman, the lowest rank available.

That means eight weeks of boot camp with a horde of postadolescents. He is thirty-seven years old.

It is, as well as a patriotic impulse, a Joad-like vanishing act, both altruistic and egotistical, self-sacrificing and self-serving—one man's need, superceding all other claims, to become an anonymous American; to see what he is made of; to serve his country and his time; and to get free of his family.

∽

On August 25, Fonda goes from the induction center to the boot camp in San Diego; upon arrival, he is detained by the Shore Patrol and sent back to Hollywood. It transpires that Zanuck has pulled strings to get Fonda's service deferred so he can star in *Immortal Sergeant*. Patriotism or retribution? It hardly matters. Henry will spend the end of the summer in Imperial Valley, California, making a movie in which, he later sneers, "I won World War II single-handed."

He returns to boot camp on November 18, and after eight weeks, he graduates as an ordinary seaman, third class, service number 562 62 35. This is followed by sixteen weeks of specialized training as a quartermaster—Henry finishes third in the class—and then his first assignment: quartermaster, third class, on the USS *Satterlee*, a destroyer docked in Seattle. After several weeks, he is told to report to naval HQ in New York for reassignment to an officer training program. Docking in Norfolk, Virginia, on August 26, 1943, Fonda takes the train to New York, and on September 15, he is sworn in as a lieutenant, junior grade (j.g.).

From there, he is sent to Washington, D.C., to report for his duty assignment. The navy brass present Fonda with an offer—an inevitable one, given his civilian status: He may serve out the duration by making training films and other vehicles for the War Office. He declines, saying he would prefer to work in intelligence.

It is the navy's Office of Strategic Services, created during World War II under the direction of renegade admiral William "Wild Bill" Donovan, that becomes the first organization in the United States designed for the gathering of foreign intelligence, and precursor to the Central Intelligence Agency. Fonda becomes an accidental pioneer: In 1943, military intelligence is being transformed by new communications technologies and an emphasis on joint intelligence among the service branches. Henry does not say why he is set on this aspect of naval operations, but the work of intelligence is profoundly congruent with his character, style, and inclinations.

He could have been a spy—a great one. Intelligence is about the hidden, and Fonda realizes that his natural reticence will harmonize with the hush-hush nature of the work. His job will call on his fortes of reading, listening, and absorbing to form raw units of fact and conjecture into justified predictions. There is, as well, a sensation of control: Marshaling predictions into coherent patterns to make prophecies of success or disaster confers a magisterial perspective.

Speculation is nearly all we have to go on here, since Fonda remained evasive or silent on his motivations for choosing intelligence work, his feelings about it, and, to a great degree, its nature. Speculation is a limited instrument, but it lets us suppose why he sought to make this particular contribution to the war, and why that contribution may finally have left him hollow.

∽

On October 4, Fonda reports to the school for officer candidates at Quonset Point, Rhode Island. There, he'll receive indoctrination instruction—that is, training for the newly created Air Combat Intelligence (ACI) section, whose graduates will be required to synthesize vast amounts of information, including aerial photographs, encoded intercepts, captured documents, POW interrogations, and daily bulletins, and use them in the planning of bombing missions.

An ACI candidate "should have had experience in dealing with people and have been successful in his chosen profession," and "be of good physical appearance, have a quick alert mind and a large measure of self-confidence, have a positive and pleasant personality and be free from nervousness." F. S. Crosley, the retired navy commander who recom-

Henry Fonda's birth home, Grand Island, Nebraska. *(Photo by the author)*

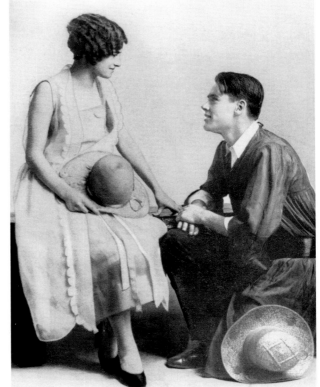

As "Peter" in *The Poet's Well*, Omaha Community Playhouse, February 1927. Costar Wenonah La Boisseaux went on to be an Omaha correspondent to the Associated Press. *(Photofest)*

Margaret Sullavan, c. 1934. "Her voice was exquisite and far away," said silent film star Louise Brooks, "almost like an echo." *(Photofest)*

Fonda and Sullavan in the University Players production of *Holiday*, Baltimore, January 1932. Here, the two are just married; weeks later, they are kaput. Left to right: Fonda, Myron McCormick, Sullavan, Joshua Logan, Barbara O'Neil. *(Photofest)*

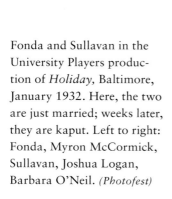

First Broadway lead: with June Walker in *The Farmer Takes a Wife*, October 1934. *(Photofest)*

Leland Hayward, mid-1930s. *(Photofest)*

Walter Wanger in 1934. *(Photofest)*

"His appearance of sincerity." Fonda and Janet Gaynor in *The Farmer Takes a Wife* (1935). *(Photofest)*

Henry in the Beverly Hills bungalow he shared with Jimmy Stewart, early 1936. *(Jerry Ohlinger's)*

Fonda and Sullavan rest between rounds in *The Moon's Our Home* (1936). "When they fight," Pauline Kael wrote, "you feel you're hearing their real battling rhythms." *(Photofest)*

She said she'd never heard of him. Henry and Frances in late 1936, weeks after their marriage. *(Photofest)*

One angry man: making *You Only Live Once* (1937, with Sylvia Sidney), Fonda incurred bruises and lacerations in fight scenes, and "jokingly" fired a prop gun at director Fritz Lang. *(Photofest)*

"I presume y'all know who I am." The opening of *Young Mr. Lincoln* (1939), with John Ford (in beret) directing. *(Photofest)*

"I never saw a man mourn for a companion more than he did for her." *(Photofest)*

Fonda with Frances and stepdaughter Pan on the set of *Blockade* (1938). Her father's bequest made Pan one of the wealthiest heiresses in America. *(Photofest)*

With Peter and Jane, before they started talking back. *(Photofest)*

Darryl F. Zanuck, c. 1940, minus cigar and polo mallet. *(Photofest)*

Shooting *The Grapes of Wrath* with John Ford, late 1939. Fellow Fox star Alice Faye visits. *(Photofest)*

"They're all gone 'r dead." Fonda, John Carradine, and John Qualen in *The Grapes of Wrath* (1940). *(Jerry Ohlinger's)*

Preston Sturges shows Fonda how to take a flying leap for *The Lady Eve* (1941). *(Photofest)*

With Harry Morgan in *The Ox-Bow Incident* (1943). Director William A. Wellman's instruction to Fonda: "Don't shave." *(Photofest)*

Receiving the Bronze Star from Vice-Admiral G. D. Murray, Marianas Islands, August 1945. Fonda will soon go home to a depressed wife, needy children, Darryl Zanuck, and a paternity suit. He can't wait. *(Photofest)*

Frances and Henry at the Hollywood premiere of Alfred Hitchcock's *Spellbound*, a love story set in a mental hospital. Late 1945. *(Photofest)*

The real Wyatt Earp was a pimp and a killer. But John Ford printed the legend, and made a classic. Fonda dances with Cathy Downs in *My Darling Clementine* (1946). *(Jerry Ohlinger's)*

Two manic-depressives writing a comedy: Tom Heggen and Josh Logan, 1947. *(Photofest)*

Onstage with Jocelyn Brando and David Wayne in *Mister Roberts* (1948). Note the false tropical sweat. *(Photofest)*

Susan Blanchard, late 1940s. *(Photofest)*

Henry and Susan on the town, c. 1954. "She was very young herself," Jane said, "and I often think of the sacrifices she must have made for us." *(Photofest)*

"Death in the guise of marriage and family": onstage with Leora Dana in *Point of No Return* (1951). *(Photofest)*

Fonda (onstage with Lloyd Nolan) declined the role of Norman Maine in the remake of *A Star Is Born* to play Lt. Barney Greenwald in *The Caine Mutiny Court-Martial* (1953). *(Photofest)*

In John Ford's film of *Mister Roberts* (1955), with William Powell and Jack Lemmon. The director was drunk, the star miserable, the movie a huge hit. *(Photofest)*

Fonda, Bogart, and Bacall in *The Petrified Forest* for television, 1955. *(Photofest)*

mends Henry for duty in the ACI section, believes he "demonstrates officer-like qualities of leadership, military bearing, loyalty, judgment and intelligence." Being an actor doesn't hurt: "[I]t has been determined," Crosley notes, "that individuals with acting, broadcasting and moving picture experience have made the best progress at [the ACI] school."

Indeed, Henry thrives in this world of quadrants and bearings, where there are no unruly children, neurotic wives, or mallet-swinging moguls—only head-down, fact-based work, and plenty of it. Throughout the ACI school, writes Melville C. Branch, "there was a favorable atmosphere of educational and behavioral maturity, intelligence, energy, and thoughtful patriotism. . . . Discipline was definite, but consensual rather than conspicuously enforced." Fonda is made the company's drill instructor, and the officer in charge of indoctrination remarks on his fitness report, "Lieutenant (junior grade) Fonda is outstandly [*sic*] sincere and loyal. He is intelligent and an indefatigable worker."

Henry graduates fourth out of forty-four officer candidates. "That impressed the shit out of people," he will recall.

He has a brief furlough, which will end just after New Year's, 1944, during which he sees Frances and the children. Then, from Quonset Point, he is reassigned to Kaneohe, Hawaii, across the island of Oahu from Pearl Harbor, for a two-week intensified course at the navy's anti-submarine school.* Fonda requests duty on an aircraft carrier in the Atlantic Fleet; instead, he is sent to the navy's Marshall Islands command in the central Pacific. Arriving April 11, he is appointed to the staff of Vice Adm. John H. Hoover—subordinate to Adm. Chester Nimitz, commander of Pacific forces—and given his second and final ship assignment, as officer courier on the USS *Curtiss*.

---

* A vignette of Fonda at this juncture appears in Henry Somers's 2004 novel *A Subway Ride to the Pacific*, about two New York buddies who enter the army in 1943. One of them is stunned to see, among the students in a Hawaii classroom, Henry Fonda.

"Some of the guys found it hard to believe that he was there, in person. They asked if he was really in the class or just visiting. 'I'm just another student,' Fonda replied, 'and I don't expect to be treated any different.' . . . Here was Fonda. His shirt opened at the neck, sleeves rolled up and wearing wrinkled khakis. He was just another serviceman and that was the way he wanted it." See Somers, 84.

Named after the designer of the navy's first flying boats, the *Curtiss* is a proud, rusty bucket with a seasoned crew and its share of scars. It was at Pearl Harbor on December 7, and returned fire, despite being exploded and burned belowdecks by a dive-bomber's load. Nineteen crew members died, and many others were wounded, but in little more than a month, the ship was back in service, "ferrying men and supplies to forward bases at Samoa, Suva, and Noumea."

At the time Fonda comes aboard in February 1944, the *Curtiss* is based at Kwajalein Atoll in the Marshalls, dead center of the Pacific theater. Flagship to the South Pacific Air Command, she is functioning as a seaplane tender—a repair and supply point for destroyers and small aircraft engaged in the great sea battles of 1943–1945 taking place in the Solomons and the Marianas. The *Curtiss* is also helping to carve a route of safe passage from San Francisco to Tokyo; in the later months of the war, as the Pacific campaign climaxes, the ship draws fire while nearing the home islands of Japan behind the ground troops who are battling for Guam, Iwo Jima, and Okinawa.

∽

Fonda's job as ACI officer, however fulfilling, is stressful and unpleasant. In the heat of the Pacific, perpetually drenched, bracing himself against waves and nausea, sardined with a dozen others into a tiny radio room with the noise of bombardment all around, Henry clings to focus and fact. Action alternates with boredom; hours and days are ground down in rituals of consumption—liquor, coffee, tobacco—reading, waiting, surrendering to exhaustion in a swaying, sweating metal bunk.

When action happens and an operation is called for, Fonda knows the intensest hours of his life. Operations demand of coordinating officers an ongoing mastery of the elements of chaos, of situations that have every potential for tragic failure. Evan Thomas paints a picture of the commotion in a shipboard radio room during such an operation—actually, it is the nerve center of Adm. William Halsey's command in the leadup to the October 1944 Battle of Leyte Gulf in the Philippines, but the room in which Fonda works can't feel much different.

Officers pored over a large chart table while sailors wrote on clear plastic plotting boards with grease pencils and relayed orders over a cluster of voice tubes. Airless, windowless, stuffed with men and machinery, [the room] reeked of a strange stew of smells: the acrid odor of radio tubes; the ever present, bittersweet warship smell of paint, lubricants, and a sealing solution called Cosmoline mingled with tobacco smoke and male sweat. Radio transmitters filled the stuffy room with the excited chatter of pilots on their bombing and strafing missions.

To appearances, though, Fonda in his downtime is affable. In a March 1945 dispatch, Henry, on liberty after many weeks of duty, is seen drinking and singing with other officers. Though he enjoys relaxing, he is never less than an obsessively hard worker; one shipmate claims that "our doctor has had to order him to take it easier."

At worst, he suffers a hangover from excesses of tension, tedium, and drink. Writer Robert Ruark will recall sitting with Fonda on the day after Christmas, 1944. The *Curtiss,* anchored at Saipan, has just come through a bombing raid.

> Lieutenant Fonda was listless as he faced me across the mess table at lunch. He looked at his Spam and looked away again, quickly. He was a little green around the gills. . . . The Japs could come, and the Japs could go, but Mr. Fonda had his hangover to take his mind off the war.

Gallows humor aside, these days death is coming closer to Henry than it has before or will again. During operations, he is one of death's dealers; as a combatant in an open theater of war, he is among its vulnerable targets.

In *"The Good War,"* his oral history of World War II, Studs Terkel speaks to Robert Rasmus, a business executive who as a young infantryman survived some of the worst battles of the European theater. Barely in his twenties, he has seen unspeakable things. Then, as he is being retrained stateside for the projected invasion of Japan, the atomic bomb is dropped. "How many of us would have been killed on the mainland if there had been no bomb?" is Rasmus's question. "Someone like me has this specter," he says.

Those words could echo forever. How many men found themselves walking, marching, crawling with some version of that specter beside them? Was the specter every question never asked about the horror they had to swallow? Was it the man of feeling that had to be separated from the man of action? How many men left their specter behind in the war, and how many came home feeling the specter was now them?

∽

Fonda describes a kamikaze striking the *Curtiss* in early 1945, after the Americans have captured Iwo Jima and firebombed Tokyo. The plane, damaged by gunfire, misses its target and crashes in the ocean near the ship. Fonda and a partner volunteer as divers to see if documents may be recovered. The two descend, and thirty feet below the surface, they encounter a tableau from a Surrealist painting, or a uniquely disturbing dream: the wrecked plane, and floating upside down, the strapped-in corpses of the pilot and bombardier. "It was an eerie sight," Fonda will recall. The hidden man remembers what he sees; the man of action cancels the feeling, recovers the documents, and retreats from the floating, inverted tomb.

There are—according to his account—three outstanding events in Fonda's war career. Each is an encounter with death, each a confrontation with his specter.

The first is an antisubmarine operation staged sometime in early 1945. Navy cryptanalysts are intercepting and decoding a high percentage of Japanese cipher traffic; as intelligence man on the *Curtiss*, Fonda has received many of these intercepts, mainly detailing enemy sub movements. He plots an attack area based on an estimate of the sub's position at a safe distance from its target; American search planes and patrol ships will swarm the designated area.

He has performed this function several times, passing on the information to higher-ups, then leaving the loop and hearing no more about it. But this engagement occurs close enough to the *Curtiss* for Fonda to feel the depth charges as the targeted subs are hit. It is the first time he feels a sense of aftermath sticking to an attack he has directed.

His autobiography presents the consequence flatly and factually: submarine parts bobbing on the surface of the sea. Among the things omitted is whether Fonda felt any elation at this deadly success—the elation that men in war zones are said to feel. Fonda will receive a Bronze Star for his part in this and similar engagements. The citation lauds his "keen intelligence, untiring energy, and conscientious application to duty. . . . His conduct and performance of duty throughout were outstanding and in keeping with the highest traditions of the Naval Service."

The second event occurs at dusk on June 21, 1945. According to the navy's Office of Public Information, the *Curtiss* is "operating in the Southern Ryukyus Islands, near Okinawa," when lookouts report a kamikaze at eight hundred yards. It strikes the *Curtiss*'s starboard side seconds later and explodes a half-ton bomb. "The engine, part of the tail assembly and the heavy bomb ripped through the skin of the ship, opening two gaping holes and exploding on the third deck," the OPI report reads. The sick bay, officers' mess, pantry, library, and other areas are destroyed; fires threaten to detonate the ship's own bomb- and ammunition-storage magazines. It takes the crew an hour to extinguish the blaze, with the help of nearby salvage vessels. In the end, twenty-eight men have been killed and twenty-one wounded.

Among the areas destroyed on impact is the stateroom occupied by Fonda and his bunk mate. But on the night of June 21, the two happen to have been on shore leave on Guam. Here, in the final weeks of the war—midway between V-E and V-J days—Fonda is nearly claimed by the death he has thus far been able to evade.

The third event is Hiroshima. Fonda accompanies his intelligence superior to Tinian, where they brief the crew of the bomber *Enola Gay* on weather conditions. The B-29 that carries the atomic bomb is, like Henry, a product of Omaha, where its captain, Col. Paul Tibbets, Jr., has personally selected it from the Martin Aircraft assembly line. The meeting itself is brief and businesslike, barely worthy of remembrance beyond being a tick mark on the agenda of the long-planned dropping of the bomb.

Fonda knows, though not clearly or completely, what the mission is really about—that the planes will drop something extraordinary, and that many will die. He probably hears the word Hiroshima. But he does not know enough to be prepared for the resultant blast and its human toll and moral aftereffects. The reality, when it dawns, "sort of took me back," he remembers.

By the end of 1945, an estimated 140,000 people have been killed by the bomb, either at the moment or during the aftermath. Robert Rasmus and thousands of others are spared an invasion and get to return home, with or without their specters.

From there, the latest battle for the fate of the free world winds down fairly quickly. On August 13, American papers carry a picture of Henry receiving the Bronze Star from Vice Adm. G. D. Murray. August 14 is V-J Day. Fonda learns of the Japanese surrender the next day, and he is ordered to report at once to Washington, D.C.

On August 16, Fonda steps off the *Curtiss* and begins his journey back to the States. Five days later, he stars in the first of four live weekly installments of a radio show, *The Navy Hour;* in addition to hosting, he narrates and performs in war sketches and battle dramatizations. September 11, he is detached from the Office of Public Information and sent to the naval station in Los Angeles; November 10, he receives his Certificate of Satisfactory Service from the navy—the reserve officer's equivalent of a discharge—and the next day is officially released to inactive duty.

But Henry Fonda will remain a lieutenant in the U.S. Navy until 1953, when he resigns his commission on the grounds that he is "over-age in rank." The resignation is accepted.

∽∾

One of Fonda's essences as actor and man is the contrast between his emotional being and what appears on the surface, his hidden and public

faces. When he is most turbulent inside, he may be most immobile outside; as the hidden man screams, the visible man grows inhumanly quiet.
His greatest acting comes when the hidden and the visible are forced into
contact and the cracks and stresses in the controlled facade come close to
breaking the man, the story, the image. It's then that the specter shows
itself, and long moments of doubt and fear are left graven on the eyes
and minds of an audience.

Everything about Fonda suggests he is cut out for success in wartime.
He has extraordinary self-control, a mind of unique finesse and subtlety,
a family military history as spur and incentive, and a belief in America,
or his personal version of it. Yet large parts of the man can do nothing
but recoil from the spectacle before him. Clearly, to be a success in war,
he has—like the other men around him—to exist as much as possible in
one aspect of himself: the aspect that is useful, controlled, amoral. He
must live as a wholly visible man. The moral residue of his actions is
submerged, to resurface in its varied and enigmatic forms as what we
have called the hidden.

That is how Fonda the civilian is *accustomed* to living—in repression,
denial, control. But seldom has civilian life presented to his senses anything as extreme as war. So in suggesting what war did to Fonda, we
have to wonder if he reached his limit—a point where hidden and visible
were no longer manageably separate and where an accumulation of
the deaths dealt and witnessed overtook his ability to make sense of it.

A silencing of horror has surrounded America's memory of World
War II. The mandate hanging over the men who came back was simple:
Hold it in. Therefore, historian Michael Sturma says, "Reactions to
combat stress among World War II veterans were most often characterized by emotional reticence and depression." Apply this to Fonda,
who spoke of his military past in dim generalities and lighthearted
anecdotes. His intimations of trauma were more than stoic; they were
benumbed. His war experience was brought down to dry sarcasm
("impressed the shit out of people"), querulous witnessing ("an eerie
sight"), and shallow wonderment ("sort of took me back").

It's apparent that Fonda was, in the middle western manner, simply declining to probe his feelings. On the whole, he clearly preferred to leave the subject alone. That is another reason Fonda was "ideal" for this work, for this war: He was inclined to the exact repression of horror that was one of the war's chief necessities and signal legacies.

When the war ended, he may have looked back and known that he'd played an important role in it. But it's unclear whether he felt pride or achievement at having done what he sought to do—"to be with the fellows who handle the guns," "to shoot at Japanese." We don't know if war was a trauma Fonda would have preferred to forget, or if it was merely an experience he'd once desired and then, having acquired it, locked it away, as so many others did with their own memories, those horrors experienced by silent men expected to remain silent.

Fonda was, above and beneath all else, a man who remembered. Repression, denial, deflection, and numbness are not erasers of memory, but ways of coping with its persistence; and often the stoic copes with experience that means too much by denying it means anything. Shortly before his death, Fonda was asked by Lawrence Grobel where he kept his Bronze Star.

"Peter lost it," he said.

Grobel asked if he'd been upset by that.

"No," Fonda replied. "It meant nothing to me."

∽

On November 10, 1944, Frances is the subject of a brief line in Dorothy Manners's Hollywood column: "Mrs. Henry Fonda is off to New York for a spell and has rented an apartment." On December 18, Louella Parsons picks up the ball: "Mrs. Henry Fonda, who had been desperately ill with flu in New York, arrives in Hollywood tomorrow morning to spend Christmas with her children."

The five-week sojourn in New York—Jane and Peter back at Tigertail with nannies, husband hunched in a radio room somewhere in the Pacific—may be accounted for by a hospital stay, a reunion with friends, or a romantic assignation. Each of her survivors will agree that Frances had affairs while Henry was at war.

At least one of her lovers becomes known to her children. Jane recalls being told by a friend of her mother's about a man named Joe, a musician. Frances, the friend says, "was crazy about him." True to pattern, though, he sounds like bad news—a drinker and "loose cannon." The friend says Joe brought a gun to Tigertail and shot a hole in the ceiling. Joe may also be the man recalled by Peter as an itinerant artist who briefly occupied the children's playhouse at Tigertail. Peter says the man taught him to play the harmonica; he doesn't mention a gun.

Touchingly, both children are pleased at the thought of their mother having an affair. But the liaison ceases, in all probability, when Henry comes home in August 1945. It's equally probable that Frances and Henry never manage to renew whatever physical relationship they had before the war.

It is always dispiriting to speculate about the sex lives of others, but less so if we accept that sex has something to do with patterns of behavior and the course of lives. Fonda's autobiography records that, sometime late in 1946, Frances begins administering the household—paying bills, following stocks, answering letters—from the couple's bed, leaving no room for Henry among the stacks of bills and receipts.

Frances gives no reason. Does she need to? She is pushing Henry out of the sack.

∽

The reason for the expulsion—and Fonda's reluctance to delve into it—might be found in a forgotten episode stemming from the weeks Henry spent in Imperial Valley, California, in September 1942, filming *Immortal Sergeant*. Almost a year later, in July 1943, Henry found himself the subject of a paternity suit brought by one Barbara Thompson, described in the press as a "twenty-five-year-old brunette divorcée" from Hollywood with four children—the latest of whom, a girl named Sharon, born June 21, was, if the mother could be believed, Fonda's.

Thompson claimed to have met him at an Imperial Valley nightclub the previous September, introduced by a man from the studio. "I accepted Fonda's invitation to have a drink," she said. "We had several of them." The actor then invited her to his room, where, according to Thompson, he seduced her. "I stayed with him during the remainder of his stay in the Imperial Valley—some two or three weeks." Thompson's suit demanded $2,000 a month in child support, $5,000 for medical bills, $10,000 for attorney's fees, and $2,500 for court costs.

Fonda, of whom the navy would say only that he was "somewhere on the ocean," issued no statement at first. But Frances did. She was adamant in supporting her husband. "It's not true," she said; "I know it's not true." Further: "Henry told me he didn't know the girl, and had never met her. . . . He denied the charges emphatically and said the suit was ridiculous." Did she believe him? "Of course I believe him." A spokesman for Twentieth Century–Fox revealed that Thompson had been in touch with the studio several months before, asking for a fifty-thousand-dollar settlement (later reduced to ten thousand). Only after these demands were refused did Thompson threaten legal action; Fonda, on leave in Hollywood at the time, had said she could "go ahead and sue."

It then surfaced that Thompson was wanted on a warrant stemming from an incident in Long Beach the previous July 23, just weeks before her alleged meeting with Fonda; the warrant charged her with "failure to appear for trial on disorderly conduct and vagrancy charges." As this was announced, Thompson's attorney said his client was "being removed to a hospital because of a nervous condition." And still more: sometime in 1942, Thompson had wed a serviceman in Honolulu while still legally married to her first husband, and was presently suing to annul the earlier union.

A lull in the case lasted through early October, by which time Fonda had been transferred to the naval air station at Quonset Point. Through his attorneys, he stated that he planned to "exercise the rights given him by the soldier's and sailor's civil relief act," which would allow him to defer any legal action until two months following the end of his service. His commanding officer affirmed Fonda would be unable to leave the base for another three months; Los Angeles judge John Gee Clark said he would not compel Fonda to appear in court for that period of time.

For more than three years, nothing was heard of the case. Then, on December 3, 1946—Fonda had been home for more than a year—it was reported that Thompson had dropped her suit. Lawyers for both parties agreed to make no public disclosure of the details, but papers printed Fonda's incensed statement. The suit, he claims, "was filed maliciously and without probable cause with the intent to injure me in the esteem of the public. . . . I certainly rue the day I decided to become an actor. I would have been better off as a farmer."

And with that, the mysterious Barbara Thompson collected her infant and walked into the Hollywood mist—another ghost, carrying a ghost in its arms.

What truly happened back in Imperial Valley? One would be more than inclined to credit Henry's enraged denials and dismiss Barbara Thompson as a scheming opportunist were it not for a passing comment in Jane Fonda's memoir. Several years into his marriage, Jane writes, "my father began having affairs." Frances, she feels, was ignorant of these until the highly publicized paternity suit; confronted with Barbara Thompson's claims, she paid the woman to abandon her suit and keep quiet.*

If Jane's assertion is true, Henry not only had the affair, but he excoriated his mistress in public, then expected Frances to second his lie while paying to suppress the truth of the betrayal. It rankles now to recall how, in his autobiography, Fonda referenced Frances's wartime affairs while implying he had none of his own; registered dazed bafflement at being ousted from the conjugal bed—coincidentally, at just the time Barbara Thompson dropped her suit; assumed a martyr's stance in declining to protest this expulsion; and quoted an anonymous friend to the effect that Henry, despite many amorous invitations, displayed a canine faithfulness to Frances throughout their marriage.

∽

---

* Jane never uses Barbara Thompson's name, but hers was the only paternity action ever brought against Fonda.

Money may purchase the silence of unwed mothers, but truths will come out in other ways. Before Fonda is even back in mufti, the gossips flash rumors of his divorce. "They say his domestic affairs are not too happy," concludes a report on Fonda's Bronze Star; soon after, columnist Harrison Carroll quotes Fonda "angrily [denying] the divorce rumors." On November 10, Louella Parsons says Frances is in a hospital near Los Angeles, "getting herself a good rest"; the affected casualness cannot fool readers into believing the hospital is anything but a sanitarium.

As for Henry's latest escape, it may fairly be brought down to an obsession with manure. In the *House Beautiful* pictorial on Tigertail, he claims that the secret to his plentiful produce "'lies in the fertilizer. You've got to spread it around.' And Hank Fonda, with an acre under cultivation, with a greenhouse to care for, with berry bushes, vegetable gardens, fruit trees and citrus groves to supervise, needs plenty to spread." Peter recalls that in this period, Henry "was seriously into making the best and the most compost in the greater Los Angeles area."

Much of Fonda's publicity just after the war focuses on his devotion to farming, model airplane building, and other escapist pursuits. One journalist claims that "the hottest 'news' that came out of our comprehensive hour-and-a-half conversation was that the speedy, gasoline-powered model monoplane which he and [Jimmy] Stewart are building in Henry's workshop will soon be ready for flight."

As Henry toils in the sun, devoting himself to the sciences of manure and monoplanes, Frances sits in a dark bedroom, with her key ring and her bills, growing more obsessed with her looks. That is, with losing them; that is, with losing Hank. Grimly preoccupied with the body and all that can be wrong with it, she continues her inculcation of neuroses in Jane and Peter.

At a certain point, Frances's doctors recommend a hysterectomy. She books a room at Johns Hopkins Hospital in Baltimore. But when Henry goes off on location for John Ford's *My Darling Clementine*—filmed in Arizona and Utah, April through June of 1946—she doesn't tell him of her plans. Instead, she takes Peter and flies to Baltimore on the pretext of visiting daughter Pan at boarding school. Peter recounts that, without his knowledge, Frances authorized the Hopkins doctors to check her son for a tapeworm as the possible cause of his persistent thinness. The six-year-old was restrained and a probe was inserted in his anus. "I screamed and yelled and cried and struggled," Peter writes, "but they only gripped me harder and became angry with me, like my father."

He seems not to have told anyone about the incident until years later. As for Frances, she is back in bed at Tigertail before Henry knows she has gone.

"In those days," Jane says of her father, "his major emotion was rage." Peter tells stories of routine transgressions being answered with hairbrush beatings and kicked-in doors. Henry's rage was no doubt a rage at failure—his own failure to be what his family needed him to be, and his family's failure to be as controlled and self-sufficient as he—their failure, in effect, to live as if they didn't need him. But it is insanity to expect young children to have the same controls against fear and pain that an adult like Henry had spent years building. And Henry—though he was, in Peter's words, "a very difficult man"—was assuredly not insane.

So there must have been more to his rage. It must have been, finally, the rage of the confined: the man who rages at his chains.

∽

"Death in the guise of the new life in California is not going to prevail over me."

How is Walker Percy's character able to speak Henry Fonda's mind so precisely? To articulate the fear in all these escapes from home and hearth, wife and children, the dream of success and nightmare of contentment?

"Death in the guise of marriage and family and children is not going to prevail over me. What happened to marriage and family that it should have become a travail and a sadness, marriage till death do us part yes but long dead before the parting, home and fireside and kiddies such a travail and a deadliness as to make a man run out into the night with his hands over his head?"

Is it only the successful middle-aged man's malaise that is being expressed? Self-pity, nostalgia, ego chasing its own youth? And if so, is that any less a human condition than another?

The nature of our man is to look always at the emptiness before him—not at the fullness or the bounty. To go toward the thing that is missing, vanished, hidden; because whatever that thing is, wherever it hides, that is where the ghosts are and the truth lies.

"What is this sadness here? Why do folks put up with it? The truth seeker does not. Instead of joining hands with the folks and bowing his head in prayer, the truth seeker sits in an empty chair as invisible as Banquo's ghost, yelling at the top of his voice: *Where is it? What is missing? Where did it go?*"

The mind of the man whirls in its self-made tempest, this suddenly visible world of Shakespearean specters: ghosts, thieves, phantom justice, make-believe juries, incredible judges. And finally, Percy's character calls back the name and suicide of an old friend—he who was found dead in a barn, years ago, somewhere in the land of fantasy and youth:

"Ross Alexander left his happy home in Beverly Hills, saying: I'm going outside and shoot a duck."

Death is the curse on all living things. It is also answer to all problems, mediator of all fears, and master of all unknowns. And if, like Henry Fonda, you are an artist with an art to apply, maybe you can make death your friend. Maybe you can know the many names of death yet go on living. If, like Frances Fonda, you do not have that escape; if you lack the means to manage fear; and if you feel you are being swallowed by the unknown, you may have no course but to choose death as answer, mediator, master.

But that's not me, says the stoic, he whose soul on one side is soft with every regret ever felt and on the other is caked hard as dry Nebraska earth by suppression, religion, convention, ego, sensibleness, manliness, Americanness.

"To know the many names of death," says Percy's man, and ours, "is also to know there is life. I choose life."

6

A Sort of Suicide

Henry and Frances

Doom is the dark shape in Henry Fonda's screen life, a compulsion toward it the spur to many of the performances we remember—Dave Tolliver, Eddie, Lincoln, others to come. Not fatalistic but fated, brought to his doom by an inability to be other than what he is, this version of the Fonda hero is wired by instinct to the absolute, the final.

Henry plays this man with the subtlest of magics. He plays him with understanding. How does he understand?

To get answers, we seek patterns. The suspicion of pattern in this next, pivotal phase is that he is carrying out in life the compulsion we identify in these characters, acting in ways that will force confrontation and hasten fate.

The core of compulsion, personality, and experience that yields the artist's creations also produces the man's cruelties. The sadness is that the doom to come is not truly his, but another's. This is life, the supporting players are made of flesh, and the flawed hero Fonda portrays is himself.

∽

The war, raw and recent, is present in the trilogy of films Fonda makes with John Ford after coming home: *My Darling Clementine* (1946), *The Fugitive* (1947), and *Fort Apache* (1948). These movies are very far from World War II in time and place, but it's hard to imagine them coming from artists who hadn't seen death up close. They are about other wars, other men facing deadly responsibility; they are studies in heroism, how it shapes and destroys men; and they are Fonda's first mature engagement with the evolving, troubling aspects of his own heroic persona.

Based on Graham Greene's novel *The Power and the Glory, The Fugitive* follows a priest's flight through an unnamed Latin American country, a newly Marxist state, whose clergy are being purged. Greene's priest is a man of dubious purity—alcoholic, father of a bastard—but also a believer who meets his ending with a martyr's open eyes. Ford (via the Dudley Nichols screenplay, which he supervised) gives the illegitimate child and ethical torment to the priest's pursuer, a fanatical army officer (Pedro Armendáriz), thereby rendering the hero absurd: He is tested against bad luck and persecution, but not, as a hero must be, against himself.

Transplanted to Mexico, Ford trades his native assurance for a tourist's reverence, reaching for art like a supplicant at a shrine, and he gaffs the nervous excitement that makes Greene's world sweat and vibrate. Fonda looks waxen, with eyes mascaraed for the Christly effect; his motifs are to appear always on the edge of tears, and to speak in a slightly deepened, denasalized register.

There's hotter fever and truer delirium in the dust pools of Monument Valley, where Ford and Fonda make *Fort Apache,* an epic of the U.S. Cavalry. A fictionalization of Custer's last stand, it is in some ways a traditional Western; in other ways, it is not one at all. Fonda plays Lt. Col. Owen Thursday, an aristocratic commander who detests Fort Apache and all the "uncivilized" land around it. Upon learning that the Apache Nation has removed from its government reservation to Mexico, Thursday makes it his all-absorbing goal to return them—violently.

Though his second in command, Captain York (John Wayne), warns that all-out attack will be suicidal, Thursday carries it through, and is slaughtered along with most of his regiment.

In the final scene, York, the new commander, approves a heroic painting of Thursday, along with the official narrative that he died nobly. The delirium of *Fort Apache,* its deep confusion of ideology and image, resides in this cover-up—which some take as Ford's endorsement of the Cold War mentality, others as evidence of a more conflicted agenda. York consecrates his lie while gazing through a window at a line of cavalrymen, many of whom will perish under his command: a double exposure of ghosts at the instant truth becomes myth.

Twenty years later, in the midst of another war, correspondent Michael Herr will recall *Fort Apache* as a "mythopathic moment": "More a war movie than a Western," Herr calls it in *Dispatches,* "Nam paradigm, Vietnam, not a movie, no jive cartoon either where the characters get smacked around and electrocuted and dropped from heights, flatted out and frizzed black and broken like a dish, then up again and whole and back in the game, 'Nobody dies,' as someone said in another war movie."

Call it delirium or mythopathy, but there is a virus of doubt in *Fort Apache.* Henry Fonda carries it, by paradoxically seeming absolutely certain of himself—by never undercutting Thursday's arrogance with softness, his vanity with romance, or his madness with flamboyance. Rigid with the character's contempt for all things, Fonda experiences physical freedom only with Thursday's death—a woozy, crumpling spiral, a pitiable dissolve on a sun-drenched rock. It's scientifically faithful to a soulless man's way of dying, as if every suppressed emotion has been channeled into a body confused at its failure to perform. Fonda's acting is impressive in its armored monotony: A kind of death has been caught here, and a kind of life.

As Marshall Wyatt Earp in *My Darling Clementine*—Ford's retelling of the O.K. Corral shoot-out in Tombstone, Arizona, in 1881—Fonda is again the emotional enigma around which other characters function and the story evolves. He constructs Earp through a variety of subtle moves and obfuscating expressions, yet he achieves a constancy of character whether playing against a more transparently showy actor or simply enjoying a joke with himself. That constancy comes partly from the changes wrought by time upon Fonda's body, which looks as able as ever but now moves more carefully, as if not every lunge or embrace can be taken for granted.

Withal, he radiates professionalism, mastery—and age. The hairline is higher, the eyes less avid. The classic late voice settles in. Fonda's Wyatt is like wine aged in oaken vats of experience; his projection of depth, toughness, and warmth makes his prewar performances seem callower than they were. This is a movie star coming into his maturity, and an actor-craftsman achieving complete control over his tools.

Yet Fonda's Wyatt is also dynamic and surprising, a self-made man always in the process of making himself up. A straight shooter who seldom smiles, Wyatt nonetheless has a humor laced with perversity. We see it when he teases the theater proprietor by suggesting he might not prevent an angry crowd from tying him to a rail. But when Wyatt watches the tubercular Doc Holliday recite lines from *Hamlet,* and we sense his emotional grasp of the poetry, it is not the least bit maudlin. Fonda's face shows tenderness, pity, empathy: Wyatt watches Doc sideways, as if straight on would hurt too much.

That face—what spirits of lightness and solemnity pass through it as the muscles and skin seem scarcely to move. At Ford's community dance, when Wyatt grudgingly invites Clementine to waltz, competing miseries and anticipations play in the face; like Sturges in *The Lady Eve,* Ford uses his star's apparent indifference to womanly charms for purposes of comic discomfort. Indeed, director and actor kid masculinity throughout the story, as Earp undergoes a process of hygienic and tonsorial dandification.

We cannot say whether Wyatt is a total square or the ultimate hipster, because Fonda uses his stiffness as a form of innate American poise— leveling his hat in the hotel window, sky and buttes reflected behind him; escorting Clem down Main Street with long, courtly strides; spinning the heroine on the dance floor with a rich smile. And the famous bit of leg business, Fonda balancing on a chair by dancing his feet on a post as Linda Darnell taunts him from behind. But just as nice is the grin Fonda tosses to the side after Darnell has left: so subtle, this flash of private humor from a man most alive within himself.

Ford takes Fonda's measure and directs from a complementary depth. After Wyatt meets Old Man Clanton, he rides on toward his brothers in the valley ahead, and flames seem to rise inside his body. It is the queerest illusion—until Ford dissolves to the brothers around a campfire and visual metaphor becomes practical reality. Elsewhere, there is Darnell wiping away tears on the hem of her skirt; the ghostly stagecoach that rides through the shoot-out at a key moment, coming from nowhere, going nowhere; a Clanton boy falling dead, gunshots exploding in a water trough an instant later—a novel twist on the "dead man's echo."* Clementine sounds the bell in an empty hotel lobby; it rings hollowly and fades—the pathos of that emptiness; Wyatt enters, and two lonesome people share a lonesome moment.

Clementine is winsome and easy, somber and strange, self-concealing and self-revealing. Feeling itself through Fonda, working its way forward on the rails of his nerves, it takes on every humane quality the star can give it through the openings in a part that seems all but unplayable. The film and its star express the knowledge, hard won in life and little observed in movies, that a man's real heroism is found in his response to the convergence of irresistible forces—the events to which he must react, the people to whom he feels obligated.

∽

Henry and Frances cannot be speaking much these days; the marriage is a mausoleum for their youth. The family lacks unity, each member taking a separate path to an isolated sadness. Jane rides horses and discovers boys, not yet beset by the eating disorders that will gnaw at her through adolescence and beyond. Peter gets into mischief, destructive escapades

---

* An effect memorable for its use in Tay Garnett's *The Postman Always Rings Twice*, released earlier the same year.

that signal his future. In one of the worst, he and Billy Hayward, son of Leland and Margaret, come upon a book of matches in a field of haystacks, and a vast piece of Tigertail pasture is destroyed.

Fonda knows it is coming apart. But most of his warmth goes into his performances, while wife and children are granted patterns of silence and selfishness. It must seem to him that his is a life of dire and depressing limits. So he escapes into a performance given for an appreciative director, a job that makes sense. His eye is out for specters—other people to be, other lives and deaths to imagine, ways to replace illness, alienation, and failure with the precisions of craft and the resolutions of drama.

He misses feeling free in the company of men. Making movies with Ford is as close as he can come. Nearly every man on the set is a veteran of one war or another, and the western locations are male domains where poker is played, guns are spun, and bullshit flies. That must be why Fonda shoots three Ford pictures in less than a year after returning home—not to mention the combination fishing trip/bacchanalia he enjoys in Mexico with Ford, Ward Bond, and John Wayne immediately after wrapping *The Fugitive*.* The other postwar jobs are less satisfying, just as their results are thinner. The movie career itself has become a set of shackles, a mere economic-legal imperative.

As a commodity, though, Henry sits prettier than ever. He's a titan in a town where faint bells toll the death of the old order. The Zanuck contract expires in 1947, and Fonda has put Fox on notice that it will not be renewed, though he will continue to work with them on a per-picture basis. In fact, his new agent, Lew Wasserman—heir to Leland Hayward as the powerhouse deal maker of the next generation—has gotten Fox to increase his weekly salary to six thousand dollars, all on the promise of one movie a year.†

---

* After describing the fishing trip (including a whorehouse jaunt) in salacious detail in his autobiography, Fonda records, with some wonderment, that Frances had chosen not to go along—begging the question of why any wife *would* accompany her husband on what was clearly planned as an all-male spree. See *FML*, 176–77; *Syracuse Herald-American*, 1/4/1948.

† In 1945, Hayward had sold the Hayward-Deverich Agency and its client list to Wasserman.

But success in the contract wars means—what? Perhaps what Fonda has dreaded, and his risk-taking ancestors avoided: a future of peace and security, sheltering trees and blue skies. Fonda feels that old need for a change of scene. Word goes out that he is interested in Broadway again.

The Tigertail farmer looks around at his citrus groves and scorched pasture and dying family. What will deliver him? It is the crisis an artist needs to stay alive.

∽

What to say about the remaining pictures of this postwar interregnum? None is important; none is utterly without interest. In Anatole Litvak's *The Long Night* (1947), Fonda is a steelworker driven to murder, who recalls the events of his ordeal while facing cops in an overnight stand-off. This remake of Marcel Carné's *Le Jour se Lève* (1939) labors to rebuild its French model virtually scene by scene; but where Carné directed the original in some kind of mystic trance, Litvak is a literalist whose gauge on rooms and props beats his feel for human behavior.

On Our Merry Way (1948) is a star-studded omnibus, and less laborious than *Tales of Manhattan*, thanks to the slapstick inspirations Fonda finds with his partner, Jimmy Stewart. As jazz hipsters in a talent contest, Henry works gymnastic wonders with his long legs and a pair of diverging rowboats, and Stewart has a diabolically funny way of sucking a lemon.

More interesting is *Daisy Kenyon* (1947), which brings together some eccentric types for a drama that ranks as slightly more than a classy soap bubble. A vehicle for Joan Crawford in her Kabuki prime, it puts Henry and costar Dana Andrews back at Fox, under the dark eye of director Otto Preminger—at this point, not the puffed-up Prussian of later fame, but master of small, atmospheric "mellers" with perversity and punch.

Among *Daisy Kenyon*'s pleasures are an unusual number of thoughtful, unhurried scenes, and some piquant dialogue. (Fonda: "Were you ever carried over your own threshold before?" Crawford: "Not sober, darling.") Henry plays in a style of wounded gravitas that contrasts profitably with Crawford's lipsticky exertions and Andrews's cool arrogance.

It's as if, swathed in Preminger's shadows, he can expose a little more pain than usual; as if, placed in an unfamiliar genre under a domineering director and star, he can wear a new mask, while generating enough torment and sexiness to suggest that the mask is not something he was handed, but a face he brought with him.

∽

Majesty and trash scrambled together: That is any good actor's Hollywood career. But it's too scattershot for Fonda. Moviemaking has gone dead for him, as dead as "the good life in California." As much as pride or ego, it is the desire to dismantle the circumstances of his life that makes him seek independence as an actor, and test the leverage of his fame. His real goal is not to be happier in Hollywood, but to be rid of it.

Through Fonda's press coverage in these months, we trace the confusions of a man uncertain of what image he wishes to project, certain only that he is in the wrong place. "I look forward to Sundays," he's quoted in October 1946, "when I can put on my khakis and get out and irrigate, and plow, and pull off the vines that creep up over the window screens." The next January, a piece calls him "the Burbank of Brentwood" and claims he grows most of the food his family eats. Columnist Jimmie Fidler eavesdrops on Fonda's interview with a magazine correspondent: "Deftly, she tried to turn the conversation to things glamorous; persistently, Fonda insisted on giving out about a new fertilizer he's using."

From promoting himself as the suburban farmer, Fonda goes in the opposite direction, insisting in September 1947 that he is "a city slicker, right off the sidewalks of Omaha," and that he prefers the city: "Out in the country . . . the crickets bother me and the roosters crow too early in the morning." Two months later, a story notes that Fonda "would like to do a stage play—and Broadway wants him back—but Hollywood has the hooks in for a long time to come."

But something is happening, by chance, on the other coast.

Late in 1947, Fonda flies to New York to talk to Joshua Logan, his old friend from the University Players. Logan has had both better times and worse times since the group split, from Stanislavskian study to Hollywood failure and nervous breakdown. Now he is the most successful director on Broadway, a man whose magic touch makes killer hits. Among his war-era smashes are *Charley's Aunt, By Jupiter, Annie Get Your Gun,* and *John Loves Mary.* Each has been an unceasing tap releasing cash to its backers. Logan's shows don't merely have legs; they have arms, breasts, and great rounded rumps. Brooks Atkinson, eminence gris of the *New York Times* drama desk, calls him "the wonderman of the musical stage."

Physically and psychically, Logan has always been Fonda's virtual opposite: tall and broad of frame yet given to softness and paunch, with ironic eyes, a delicate mustache, southern manners, and, above all, an emotionalism manifesting in frequent tantrums and collapses. Still, Henry has an idea for a film, and he hopes to interest Logan in directing it. But Josh demurs: his new play is just going into casting. Here it is, he says, and here's Tom Heggen, who wrote it with me. As long as you're here, too, why don't you sit down and let us read it to you?

It's a coy proposal, offered in a spirit of what the hell. But in fact, the coauthors have envisioned Fonda as their star all along—at least since they wrote the play's last words, and lowered the curtain on the death of their hero.

∽

The play is *Mister Roberts*; Logan and Heggen have adapted it from Heggen's novel. It's a comedy-drama set on the USS *Reluctant,* a supply ship in the Pacific near the end of World War II. Lt. (j.g.) Doug Roberts is beloved of the crewmen whom he defends against the tyrannies of the ship's captain. Despite being befriended by medical officer Doc and hyperactive Ensign Pulver, he is lonesome and unhappy. His sole desire is to get into combat, a transfer the captain won't allow; a bargain between the two alienates Roberts from the crew. After a forged signature secures the transfer, news arrives that Roberts has died in a kamikaze strike while awaiting transport to the war's last battle zone.

Henry has never been in a major stage hit, but he knows one when it is read to him. Something in the impromptu performance of the fervent, melodramatic Logan and his chain-smoking, rather dissolute partner Heggen; something in the arc of the character this odd couple have constructed; something in the *whole* of the thing tells Fonda to jump on it.

Published in 1946, Heggen's was among the earliest American novels of the war. Logan was alerted to it by Leland Hayward, then a fledgling Broadway producer; he and Heggen met, clicked, and wrote the play in a series of marathon sessions. The partnership was fraught—"I was a corpulent manic depressive," Logan recalled, "and Heggen was a thin manic depressive"—but the coauthors' complementary crazies preserved the downbeat in material that could easily have gone mawkish. The novel's content is the raw business of service comedy, yet its pace is too grave for slapstick, its prose too precise for easy consumption; there is something spooky and mournful to it. The play catches that. Rich in grown-up laughs, with a judicious spray of low clowning, it is informed by the persistence of sadness as chronically sad people feel it.

Fonda is willing to give up almost everything to do *Mister Roberts*. His commitment to it is an act of hope, will, nerve, and barreling brutality to the family that will be uprooted by his decision. Most important for Fonda, though, it is an *act*—a move away from decay and illness toward growth and health. He has been waiting for the thing that will enter his life with the force and suddenness of a Sullavan or a Ford, a Lincoln or a Joad: the thing that will take him from safety to a new frontier of freedom.

Most look at *Roberts* and see a hit. Fonda sees his deliverance.

∽

He has already signed the contract on his next picture, but contracts can be voided: That's why God created agents like Lew Wasserman. Henry returns to California with roughly a month to learn his part; then comes a lightning round of rehearsals back east, followed by out-of-town previews. Things fall into place with incredible speed. These are men with jobs to do, war veterans in a military mind-set, and matters like family will not be allowed to slow the boat.

Henry will take an apartment in New York until *Roberts* is on its feet; only then will the family join him. If divorce is on his mind, he doesn't press the point. Frances, typically for her, is acquiescent, even helping her husband run his lines. Maybe she is excited by his excitement; maybe she feels there is nothing else she can do; maybe, like Henry, she is biding her time.

Mister Roberts previews at the Shubert Theater in New Haven in early January 1948, and then has practice runs in Philadelphia and Baltimore. Fonda can only be elated at getting back to the theater. The work of a unified company toward a presentation in live time is what Henry has been missing in movies; his instincts snap to life under white lights and dark watchers. He even experiences some of the fun of old theater days. In Philadelphia, a goat led up the *Reluctant* gangway in one scene makes an unscheduled deposit on the stage—and Henry may just recall the urinating monkey of Falmouth.

The show comes together as a winner, and preview audiences reel before it. Just before the Broadway opening at the Alvin Theatre on February 18, Walter Winchell writes that *Roberts* appears to be "a gilt-edged investment. It is being hounded by censors in the stix [*sic*] and serenaded by reviewers, a surefire combination."

No one projects a small, respectable success. The expectation is that audiences will stagger out sore from laughter, choked with sobs; that theater history will be made. In a period that has seen the innovative pageantry of *Oklahoma!* and *Carousel*, and the new drama of *The Glass Menagerie* and *All My Sons*—with others like *A Streetcar Named Desire*, *Death of a Salesman*, and *South Pacific* soon to arrive—*Mister Roberts* must make its claim for Broadway event of the decade.

It does. From the cheer that greets Fonda's first stage appearance in more than a decade to the burst of sorrow and joy that erupts at the final curtain, opening night is a sustained thunderclap. The ensuing ovation lasts hours, it seems. "There were too many curtain calls to count," says Logan, deprived of his onstage bow by the neurotic Heggen, who refuses to leave the wings. The audience, Henry will recall, were "standing on their seats, hollering, whistling." Called out to speak, he offers to do the play again from the beginning. "And they went into convulsions all over again."

The next day's critical acclaim is universal, or near enough to dwarf any doubters. The *Post*'s Earl Wilson calls *Roberts* "one of the greatest plays of the decade." In the *New York Times,* Atkinson thanks Logan and Heggen for "a royal good time." "Noel Coward sat next to me and weeped [*sic*] in turn from the laughter and pathos," writes Jack O'Brian of the Associated Press, extolling the show's "brilliant detail, its deep human insight." "Pretty wonderful," John Lardner of *The New Yorker* writes. Logan and Heggen "have written the best comedy, the best war play—to come right down to it, the best new play of any kind—that has been seen this season."

Roberts is a smash of rare proportions, a cultural happening. The play's hero becomes a household name, and its creators achieve new levels of eminence: Heggen will be featured in the *Saturday Review of Literature,* Logan will be given a spread in *Life,* and Fonda will radiate heroism from the cover of *Newsweek.* Henry in particular is the man of the moment. For the next year, he will race between theater, radio studio, and TV soundstage, performing scenes and transmitting the Roberts mystique.

At its height, *Roberts* pulls in $35,000 a week—"bettering by several thousand," John Leggett notes, "the receipts of its nearest rival, Tennessee Williams's *A Streetcar Named Desire.*" On March 29, little more than a month after opening, *Mister Roberts* receives the Antoinette Perry Award as the Best Play of the 1947–1948 season. Joshua Logan is named Best Director, and Henry receives the Tony for Best Male Performance.

Two years on, the play is still running. Atkinson will estimate it has been seen by 1.3 million people on Broadway, and another 85,000 at road-tour stops across the country. By then, Doug Roberts will have joined Abe Lincoln, Tom Joad, and Wyatt Earp in the public mind as a classic Henry Fonda role, a patriotic paradigm, an American hero.

∽

For all that, *Mister Roberts* has not survived as a great play. It is high middlebrow: better than slick, but without the depth to provoke revision. Still, it's not difficult to guess why, in 1948, people responded to it intensely.

Roberts is a rousing entertainment, with momentum and payoff; Logan's showmanship keeps things active and dimensional. By spraying his actors with artificial sweat and putting them under tanning lamps, he creates the feel of tropical heat in a Manhattan winter. Scene changes are covered by the transmitted blare of war news, taking the audience back to all the radio alarms of recent years.

Stage designer Jo Mielziner has constructed an ultrarealist setting of bulkheads and portholes, which permeate the comedy with rust and stagnation. But on the whole, the play is an affirmation—of war, death, decency—at a time when the country is already shaping its popular memory of WWII. *Roberts* expunges brutality and recalls death as a sweet regret. It not only locates Eisenstein's "womb of popular and national spirit"; it cuts into fresh veins of sentiment and nostalgia, releasing gushers of love and cash. This is the right play at the right moment.

It's a moment that lasts well into the 1950s, as *Roberts* turns into a barnstorming commodity fronted by blandly handsome actors—in the United States, John Forsythe; in London, Tyrone Power. From its beginning on the Alvin stage, in days not so far removed from the end of war, the play softens and expands, like a prosperous gut, to serve the new mood of the American audience. People forget how taut, ironic, and ambiguous the thing was meant to be. The film version—directed by a drunken, ailing John Ford—will arrive in 1955 as a Technicolor botch, the play's haunting edges only memories to those who'd seen it on the stage, and all but unimaginable to anyone who hadn't.

The *Roberts* play in its first form is recalled as strange and touching, and it wouldn't have become such a hit without Fonda. "He always wanted to face upstage," Logan says. "I had to use tricks to get him so the audience could see him work." Stage acting demands the actor project his voice and aura into the darkness, where the audience grasps it like a lifeline. Fonda's instinct is to look the other way. He underplays, stays quiet, all but hides; the audience is again left to feel what is hidden.

Some part of him is still the Omaha novice who dreads the nightmare of being watched. But now he has all the armature of experience, and can use reticence to his advantage: By stepping away from his watchers, he draws them closer. "He'll never be seduced by an audience," Logan continues. "He won't give them any more for their applause than he will without it."

People have come to *Roberts* only partly to laugh. Finally, they wish to experience some degree of loss. That may be the private logic to Fonda's underacting: His remoteness preserves the audience's unease. Unlike Marlon Brando, who in *Streetcar* puts everything on display, Fonda tells himself, no, leave people wondering if they knew you at all. Like a shadow that grows taller with distance, Roberts increases in stature as he approaches the death he believes he doesn't see coming.

∽

Like Fonda, Doug Roberts is a post–Pearl Harbor naval volunteer who has risen to the rank of lieutenant, junior grade. Like Fonda, Roberts's theater is the Pacific. Like Fonda, Roberts is a "typical eager beaver" who wants to see action, and does. Fonda wears his own navy cap and khakis onstage every night; the press make so much of the affinities between actor and character as to suggest that Fonda isn't acting the role at all, only remembering it.

Heggen has told Logan that, while writing his hero, he had Fonda in mind; and indeed the novel presents a man remarkably like the Fonda we've been following:

> There are people of wonderful conductivity who draw rather than repel the tenuous and tentative approaches that we call human relationships, and through whom, as through a nerve center, run the freely extended threads of many lives. . . . The quality they possess is not an aggressive one, nor a conscious one, and it can never be one acquired. It is native and inescapable and may even be unwel-

come to its inheritor. It admits of greater loneliness than is commonly thought possible.

Throughout *Roberts* rehearsals, as Fonda quietly commands the stage, Heggen lurks the theater in baggy, ash-stained suits, darkness circling his eyes, decaying teeth bared wolflike in occasional laughter. Thin and haunted to the point of neurasthenia, he is what Fonda might look like if drained of all but his doubts and demons. Both are deeply middle western; both studied journalism at the University of Minnesota and served in the Pacific. Like Fonda, Heggen joined the navy in part to escape domestic stress and professional discontent. Biographer John Leggett says Heggen had the "feeling, carried since his teens, of being doomed"; and the writer, like the actor, is fascinated by a man's need to take his doom straight.

Finally, recall how the hero dies—killed by Japanese suicide strike while sitting in a wardroom aboard his ship. It is exactly the death Henry Fonda did *not* die on June 21, 1945, when the USS *Curtiss* was rammed by a kamikaze. Though Fonda did not perish, for more than a thousand nights on the stage, he gets to imagine he did. As Roberts, he is portraying his own specter.

∽

At one stroke, he has traded Hollywood for Broadway, compost for caviar, family for free agency. He spends his days in rehearsal, his nights in French restaurants, town houses, and long black cars on the Avenue of the Americas. Henry likes his new life. On April 1, 1949, it's announced that he has contracted to star in *Mister Roberts* for its Broadway duration, as well as to headline the imminent film version—which will be shot, it's said, somewhere near Bermuda in the summer of 1950, with Josh Logan directing.

And the family? Henry stays in touch. In February, he admits to Earl Wilson that he's "feeling selfish about leaving his kids in Hollywood." For the first several weeks of the run, he flies back to Tigertail for weekend visits, but this proves burdensome, and Frances begins shipping the family's belongings east. By April, a house has been leased in Connecticut; in June, after school is out, the Fondas begin their residence on Pecksland Road in the upper-class suburb of Greenwich.

Tigertail—where Jane and Peter grew up, which Frances helped pay for, and whose planning and construction she oversaw—is left behind, all its rustic stone-built rooms emptied. Eventually, the house and grounds will be sold. Then, in November 1961, they will be destroyed in the worst brush fire in the history of Los Angeles, one that consumes hundreds of houses in Brentwood and Bel Air.

The Fonda children are told they must trade their Pacific playland for a murky eastern manse. The Count Palenclar House, as it is called, has a beautiful exterior, but its rooms are dim and unwelcoming; Jane evokes Charles Addams. Peter remembers its "musky, attic-like atmosphere," while the grounds and surrounding woods are distinguished by macabre vegetation: "Skunk cabbage, swamps, parasitic vines choking giant trees." Over time, it will be overtaken by what he can only call an "unknown darkness."

The kids detest Greenwich, find it snobbish, elitist, racist. The Hayward children are nearby—Margaret Sullavan, now divorced from Leland and remarried, has been in Greenwich for two years—and their presence helps offset the loss of Tigertail. But not enough.

Only Henry, it seems, is happy here, and he is happiest when going it alone. It's notable that while he seems robust during this period, his children—not to mention Frances—are persistently ill. Peter contracts pneumonia in the winter of 1948, and is hospitalized with fever while at camp the following summer. Jane begins her battle with bulimia, grows susceptible to viral complaints, bites her nails, and discovers a talent for injuring herself in falls. She hurts her arm in a roughhousing incident and is scared to tell her father. "Dad asked me if I'd washed my hands, and when I told him I hadn't, he exploded in anger, pulled me out of my seat and into the bathroom, turned on the faucet, took the broken arm . . . and thrust it under the water. I passed out."

Certainly Fonda has redemptive streaks of tenderness, and never abandons his children when they are in direst need. (When Peter is feverish at camp, for instance, Henry moves to the nearby town until he recovers.) A conscientious planner, he buys each of his kids 2 percent shares in the *Roberts* production. The broken arm incident may, like many childhood anecdotes, be an exaggeration, enlarged over time. Yet it stems from a child's real horror of a stern and retributive father.

It seems a trial for Henry to stay in the family home for long. Functions and responsibilities are always calling him away, and he takes an apartment in town. Jane persists all the harder in seeking her absent father's approval, while gradually letting go of the mother who increasingly, it seems, is letting go of everything.

Frances has begun sobbing spontaneously, and spending more time in her room. As an adult, Jane will be told by Frances's psychiatrist of her mother's increasing paranoia and feelings of hopelessness: "She began to feel she was ugly . . . that she was poor and fat."

Peter feels Frances isn't always "there."

∽

One night near the end of the first Greenwich summer, as Henry is leaving for a performance, Frances informs him that she is checking herself in to the Austen Riggs Center, a sanitarium in Stockbridge, Massachusetts. She encourages him not to worry—in fact, to spend more time in the city. Frances's mother, faithful Sophie Seymour, moves in to take care of the children.

Established by a tubercular Manhattan internist in 1919, and describing itself as "the center of American ego psychology," Austen Riggs has, by the late 1940s, become one of the most prestigious mental-health institutions in the country. Far from the state-funded snake pit of popular fiction, it is a model of the expensive, comfortable hospital-retreat, with its private rooms, neutral colors, and psychiatric idealism. Here, it's hoped, the nervous modern psyche will be soothed by peaceful scenery and fine-tuned by a staff of world-famous analysts.

The pioneers of psychotherapy, some of them employed at Riggs, are toiling mightily in these high Freudian days of postwar mind science. But there is only so much even the most dedicated staff can do to arrest human breakdown, particularly in settings that may encourage rather than combat a patient's sense of cloistered unreality. In *Women and Madness* (1972), Phyllis Chesler refers to the best U.S. mental hospitals as "special hotels or collegelike dormitories for white and wealthy Americans, where the temporary descent into 'unreality' (or sobriety) is accorded the dignity of optimism, short internments, and a relatively earnest bedside manner."

It is largely these qualities that make Riggs a favored refuge of the New England elite, as its members succumb in increasing numbers to psychic stresses both real and whimsical. Numerous celebrities and children of the rich and renowned log time there; Margaret Sullavan will experience a brief stay, as will her daughter Bridget.

Frances makes several trips to Riggs. Clearly she finds there some surcease of sorrow. It may satisfy coeval needs to take care of others, and be taken care of. "Perhaps one of the reasons women embark and re-embark on 'psychiatric careers' more than men do," Chesler suggests, "is because they feel, quite horribly, at 'home' within them. Also," she continues—a point relevant to Fonda's failure to answer Frances's emotional needs—"to the extent to which *all* women have been poorly nurtured as female children, and are refused 'mothering' by men as female adults, they might be eager for, or at least willing to settle for, periodic bouts of ersatz 'mothering,' which they receive as 'patients.'"

Frances's first commitment lasts eight weeks. Under the supervision of medical director Robert P. Knight, she undergoes intensive analysis, some of which is paraphrased in Jane's memoir—most tellingly, stories of abuse as a child and wife, the Seymour family history of mental illness, and Frances's overwhelming love and fear of her father. Surprisingly, given that electroconvulsive therapy is, in the late 1940s, the only treatment for severe depression, there is no suggestion that Frances receives shock treatments. It's probable, though, that she is injected with sodium amytal, also commonly used at this time, to facilitate truthfulness in therapy sessions.

Knight and his team work some kind of quick fix on Frances, yet she is home barely long enough to readjust to normal life. She returns to

Riggs a few days into 1949, claiming postholiday exhaustion. Has she finally found a hospital she likes better than home? What is it about the institution that draws her back—is it the vanilla-colored walls, the morning oatmeal, the wise, strong, fatherly men who listen?

∽

Frances has insisted Henry spend more time in New York, as if encouraging him to seek a liaison, a betrayal it will torture and please her to imagine in her Stockbridge cell. As *Roberts* rolls on through the spring and summer of 1949, Henry, following his wife's suggestion, becomes even more of a stranger, deserting the Gothic twilights of Greenwich for the well-lit stage of the Alvin, his demanding kids and depressed wife for the straightforward male romance he shares with Logan, Heggen, and the troupe.

Events make it inescapable that he will meet someone else while Frances is incapacitated. He is too much in demand; there are too many women casting their lashes and lusts his way—appraising his fine forty-four-year-old frame, his tanned jawline and nicely angled arm, perfect for clutching as flashbulbs pop.

The one whose gaze makes Henry look up, and look again, is Susan Blanchard. She is twenty-one years old and the stepdaughter of Oscar Hammerstein II, who, with partner Richard Rodgers, has most lately triumphed with *South Pacific* (coauthored and directed by Joshua Logan). Susan swims in the same splashy circles as Henry; the two wind up at the same parties, and discover rapport. She has done bits of stage acting, and even spent time under contract at Twentieth Century–Fox. She is familiar with the hype and whirl of the business, seems well adjusted to them.

Like Sullavan, she is small, even pixieish in appearance, with a face out of a locket. Her smile is a mischievous triangle and her eyes are hooded with intelligence, the suggestion of some ongoing inner dialogue. Amazingly for a woman of glamour in the 1950s, she wears black horn-rimmed glasses in public without self-consciousness. She has a sense of humor, and a lack of neurosis.

She has—no avoiding the word—youth. She is the opposite of what Frances has become: dreary, dolorous, old.

The two pursue an affair—at this point platonic, Henry swears. They stick to small, dark restaurants; only a few friends know. When Frances finds out, she will seem surprised. But some will claim she has known of the affair almost from the start, thanks to the grapevine of chatter and whispers running between New York and Greenwich.

Right now, though, she is still a patient at Austen Riggs, resting, recuperating, and receiving something she cannot get at home, from children, mother, girlfriends, or absent husband. But she must reemerge eventually: Unlike Henry, Frances cannot stand to be alone for long. To him, independence is life; to her, it is death.

∽

The spiral, from this point, is only down. Small gestures at regeneration barely interrupt the process by which a mind is buried in an accumulation of sadnesses.

Frances ends her second stay at Riggs, and again seems fine on her return—whatever that means to others' appraising eyes and smiling mouths. The Fondas move out of the Count Palenclar House into a sublet on Sherwood Lane, and Frances roughs out designs for the construction of a new home—Tigertail East, more or less. Around the same time, her daughter Pan—now seventeen and, thanks to Frances's efforts to secure for her the bequest of her late father's estate, one of the wealthiest heiresses in America—becomes engaged to Charles Abry of Philadelphia. He is also seventeen and, as heir to the S. H. Kress chain of five-and-dime stores, also splendidly wealthy.

Frances is excited by her daughter's engagement, though Henry's autobiography speculates she is equally disturbed by the approach of grandmotherhood.

But all plans are arrested when Frances is diagnosed with a kidney problem. It is sudden and serious. One biographer describes it as a "floating" kidney, or nephroptosis—quite simply, the unusual tendency of a person's kidney to descend into her pelvis when she stands. The treatment of the day is surgery to stabilize the organ. Today, some "float" is considered normal, and surgery might not be indicated; but in 1949, the condition was assumed to be life-threatening.

Frances goes under the knife in April. Her attraction to hospitals is outweighed only by her dread of her own body and its ravaging by age and illness. Imagine her horror, on waking, to discover that the surgery has left a foot-long scar across her midsection.

∽

Time will show that Henry is not as carefree as he seems. In these painful months, a few moments bear witnessing.

On May 19, 1949, the morning after *Mister Roberts*'s 522nd performance, Tom Heggen's body is found in the bathtub of an apartment on East Sixty-second Street. Empty pill bottles are nearby; an unused razor blade lies at the bottom of the tub. The coroner rules it a "probable suicide," but writer Alan Campbell, owner of the apartment, believes it was accidental. Josh Logan, too, will remain unconvinced: "I do know there was a time when Tom tried to die. But I'm sure that the time he didn't try was when he did."

Even if Heggen didn't mean to die that day, there is enough reason to suppose he meant to die. The themes of his writing up to and including *Mister Roberts* were death, isolation, and disappointment. "I don't much like myself," he'd written his wife during the war, before *Roberts* was even begun, "and I was no good to anybody." Logan's immersion in *South Pacific* had left Heggen feeling abandoned, and he'd been unable to develop a second novel. He was earning more than four thousand dollars a week from the play and other royalties; money was not his problem. His problem, if he was a suicide, was the depression that falls when the fear of failure sinks deep enough to edge out every option—most crucially, the option to fail, as Heggen probably would have, to duplicate the success of his first creation.

It may have amounted to a terror of boredom—one of the many names of death. Pointlessness yawns, swallowing the future, and the mind shrinks under the weight of so much empty time. Tom Heggen may have decided to meet that oblivion head-on, for staying alive without a reason is also death, as he knew. "The most terrible enemy," Doug Roberts writes in his last letter to the *Reluctant* crew, is "the boredom that eventually becomes a faith and, therefore, a sort of suicide."

A week and a half after Heggen's death, on May 29, Henry is the guest star on Dean Martin and Jerry Lewis's NBC Radio show. In the first skit, the pair are excited by having finally scored tickets to *Mister Roberts*. As they sit in the audience, Fonda is heard performing part of a speech. "Gee," Jerry gushes after the curtain, "Henry Fonda is really terrific, huh, Dean. That's what I wanna be—a great actor." He says *Roberts* has given him "the most vibrant, spine-tingling moments I've ever spent in the American theater."

"Really spine-tingling, huh?"

"Yeah. I felt just like somebody'd dropped a live frog down inside my shirt."

Convinced it is his destiny to quit comedy and become a serious actor, Jerry gets into Fonda's dressing room and presses the star for a job in the *Roberts* cast. After much cajoling, Henry offers him the part of the goat.

There is a fantasy segment in which a down-home girl, Daisy Belle, wonders with whom she should attend the big barn dance—Hank or Jerry. Fonda provides a drawling parody of himself, circa 1935. But he seems flat in the skit, distracted.

The show ends with Martin, Lewis, and Fonda joining voices for a sprightly hate song to a lover who has overstayed her welcome:

> *Drop dead, little darlin', drop dead*
> *I need you like a hole in the head*

Fonda moans the lyric far beneath Lewis's monkey mewling and Martin's lubricated lead, as if hoping to go unheard. He has been sluggish throughout the show; now he sings as if his stomach is full of rocks.

The day before the show airs, Frances writes to a friend about her kidney operation. "They just cut me in half," she says.

∞

In June, Frances, Henry, and Jane attend Pan's graduation from her Baltimore boarding school. Soon thereafter, Pan and Abry are married, Henry giving away the bride. Frances accompanies the young couple on their European honeymoon. Before returning to New York on the *Queen Elizabeth*, she writes to Watson Webb, her children's godfather, that "my better half will find me looking 100% better than when I left."

Frances speaks as if she still has hope that Henry is not lost to her. And in fact, it's around this time that the papers run photos of the two dancing and socializing at the Stork Club. They seem reasonably gay. Henry looks like what he is—esteemed, successful, the center of attention—while Frances is not worn or empty-looking at all, but beautiful, vital, proud. You would never know, from looking, that parts of both are already dead.

It is not long after this that Henry decides everyone—or at least he—has had enough. He inhales, sits Frances down in a quiet room, and asks her for a divorce. He says there is someone else.

"Well, all right, Hank," Frances says—or Henry will say she said.

He will recall how well she took the news, the sympathy and "understanding" in her response. He suspects more than he tells. But he seems not to realize how little he ever understood his wife's depression, or how cruel it is to interpret her final surrender as kindness and sympathy.

Frances has acquiesced to Henry's leadership at every point. She has left her eastern element for an uncertain life in Hollywood; allowed her husband free rein to come or go, live and work in other worlds. She has gone along with his need to enlist, knowing how much she would be left to handle on her own. She has agreed to be transplanted again, to a cold, lonesome spot in the suburbs, and to endure gossip as her husband escorts a young lady around New York. Her response to each request has been some version of the refrain "Well, all right, Hank."

If she can't be happy, she will at least direct her own misery. Frances takes it all inside, smiling the martyr's distant smile. And Henry believes, is willing to believe, that it is all right.

"The shock of Hank wanting to remarry," Frances writes to Watson Webb in the fall of 1949, after Fonda has removed himself from the Greenwich house to the top floor of a brownstone on East Sixty-seventh Street, "was almost too much for me—and too soon after my immense operation. . . . Since he has told me he hasn't been happy during our thirteen years of marriage all I can say is I wish him great happiness in this *new marriage*."

The emphasis is Frances's, and it undercuts the sympathy Henry has found so wonderful.

Frances has been nursing her pathos for a long time, and now it is handed to her on a plate. She is forty-one, and soon she will be alone. What does she imagine for herself? Her visions of the future may resemble those recorded by other depressives—Tom Heggen's fear of surrender to the suicide of boredom, or the featureless void described by Sylvia Plath in *The Bell Jar*: "I could see day after day after day glaring at me like a white, broad, infinitely desolate avenue."

Now Frances will move between planning a future and shrinking from it. First, on October 18, she has a new will written, apportioning her holdings between her children and mother, and excising Henry. It is a good move forward, a healthy act of spite. But around Thanksgiving, her lapses into psychosis become more extreme. Staying in Manhattan with her friend Eulalia Chapin, she speaks openly of suicide, and weighs insanity as a ploy to prevent Henry's remarriage. According to Jane, Frances hacks off her hair, and wanders her friend's Manhattan neighborhood in nightclothes. Chapin awakens in her apartment, to find Frances looming over her in the dark, examining her neck, curious to find the precise location of the jugular vein.

She is taken by her mother back to Austen Riggs.

More agony. On December 9, Pan gives birth to a premature infant at Hahneman Hospital in Scranton, Pennsylvania. According to reports, she and Abry have been vacationing in the Pocono Mountains, Frances accompanying them, presumably on furlough from Riggs. Frances writes to a friend, in fragments: "Pan lost her baby last Friday—premature—a girl who lived two hours—a difficult time."

Peter remembers that his mother spent Christmas week of 1949 at home, and "seemed all right."

It is just after Christmas that Dorothy Kilgallen, entertainment columnist for the *New York Journal American*, publicly breaks the story of the Fondas' divorce agreement, and Henry's desire to wed Susan Blanchard "as soon as it is legally possible." "Miss Blanchard is in her twenties, Fonda in his forties," Kilgallen tut-tuts. "It is understood Mrs. Fonda will take custody of the children without opposition from the actor, and also will be given an extremely large financial settlement." The tone of disapproval is not surprising: Some say Kilgallen has gotten the scoop directly from Frances.

In late January 1950, Frances is back at Riggs, and Henry meets with Dr. Knight to discuss her condition. Knight has little hope to offer. There has been further breakdown, more talk of suicide, decreasing contact with reality. Knight fears Frances will attempt the worst, and that Riggs is no longer equipped to secure her. He recommends she be moved to the Craig House sanitarium in the Hudson Valley town of Beacon, New York, forty miles from Manhattan. Craig is another exclusive, expensive refuge for the rich and self-destructive—Zelda Fitzgerald had been there in the 1930s—but it is designed for maximum watchfulness over those inmates who might be inclined to hurt themselves.

Frances is admitted to her last hospital on February 3.

∽

Having studied the void that is her future, the character in *The Bell Jar* speaks of being seized by a need for controlled action, directed toward finality: "I wanted to do everything once and for all and be through with it."

In March, Frances's caretaker at Craig House, Dr. Courtney Bennett, reports improvements in her condition. She seems less depressed, more aware of the people around her; she plays a skillful game of bridge. The fog may be lifting. Too early to tell, though, what it is revealing.

Accompanied by a nurse, Frances takes a day trip home to visit Sophie, Jane, and Peter. At one point, she excuses herself and goes upstairs to her bedroom. The nurse peeks in to check on her; Frances, startled, drops a box. The box is replaced and the nurse thinks nothing of it. But Frances has taken from it a small razor, which she hides somewhere in her clothing. That night, she smuggles it into Craig House. The date, Peter remembers, is April 7.

Exactly a week later, at 6:50 in the morning, night nurse Amy Gray brings juice to Frances's room and finds a note affixed to the bathroom door. It reads "Do not enter—call Dr. Bennett." The nurse alerts the doctor, who enters the bathroom, to find Frances on the floor, bleeding from a deep gash in her throat.

She is barely alive. Help is summoned, but Frances is beyond it. Within minutes, she has bled out. It is Friday, April 14, her forty-second birthday.

In the room are notes Frances has written to her children, to her mother, and to Dr. Bennett. The message of each is essentially the same: "I'm very sorry, but this is the best way out." There is no note for Henry.

Telephoned by Sophie, he rushes to Craig House. The two attend a hastily arranged funeral service at McGlassen & Son mortuary in Beacon, after which the suicide verdict is summarily entered by Dr. L. Edward Cotter, deputy medical examiner for Dutchess County. Frances's body is then removed to the town of Hartsdale, New York, where it will be cremated; the ashes will be interred with the remains of previous Seymours in the family cemetery in Ogdensburg, New York.

Sophie and Henry return to Greenwich and tell Jane that Frances has died in the hospital—of a heart attack. Peter, when he arrives home, is told the same.

"She was making a wonderful recovery and expected to be discharged soon," a bewildered Dr. Bennett tells reporters. The texts of the notes to Bennett and Nurse Gray are released to the press by Assistant District Attorney Edward Russell.

That night, Henry drives to New York, uncertain whether to go onstage—for *Roberts* must play again this evening to a capacity house. Backstage, he discusses his options with Leland Hayward and Joshua Logan, and, in what many have found to be the single most unfathomable fact about this very mysterious man, Henry Fonda—hours after discovering that his estranged wife has killed herself, attending her funeral, and consigning her remains to the flames—decides to climb into his costume and give his 883rd performance as Mister Roberts.

That can be taken as evidence of an actor's discipline, a husband's daze, an egotist's narcissism, or all of these. But the decision to "go on" is not uncharacteristic of actors. We think of Ross Alexander reporting to the set the day after his wife killed herself; and of Brooke Hayward's insistence, as a young actress, that she be allowed to give a scheduled performance in her Off-Broadway play, despite the discovery of her mother's body in New Haven earlier the same day.

Asked by Lawrence Grobel if the *Roberts* performance on the night of April 14, 1950, was the most difficult of his career, Fonda replies, "Probably." In the autobiography, he claims it is his own sober decision. But he tells Grobel that in fact Hayward and Logan convinced him to go on, and that he was "too numb" to resist—which makes Fonda seem less the controlled Christian Scientist and more the man struck helpless by a first premonitory wave of sorrow and guilt.

The next day, the papers report both Frances's suicide and Fonda's decision to perform—while noting pithily, if not wholly accurately, that Frances "apparently killed herself because of the actor's romance with a younger woman." The AP story states that Henry, "pale with fatigue," appeared at the Alvin an hour before showtime, as his understudy was preparing to go on. Assured by Hayward that few in the audience would have heard the news, and that press would be barred from the theater, Fonda agreed to perform. At night's end, a phalanx of friends rushed him to a cab.

Those who watch him onstage that night express admiration and mystification. A frequent spectator of the play says, "He was even sharper than usual." Stage manager William Hammerstein, Susan Blanchard's stepbrother, believes Fonda's performance is essentially identical to the 882 that have preceded it. "He went on and played and played very well," marvels Josh Logan; Susan says, "I think he didn't know what else to do."

But actor Eli Wallach—a young unknown hidden among the chorus of *Reluctant* crewmen—suggests the performance goes harder on the star than it appears from the orchestra seats. "When [Fonda] was out there," he remembers, "it was as if he'd been spun around three or four times until dizzy, then pushed out into the spotlight. He wasn't with it, but he made it through to the end."

∽

"Men commit actions," Phyllis Chesler writes; "women commit gestures." There is terrific aggression implicit in Frances's suicide, and in its theatrical manner. First, there is the exclusion of Henry from her will, then the smuggling of a razor from their home. Choosing a blade over pills means Henry can never tell himself her end was clean, painless, or accidental. And rather than open her wrists, she cuts her throat from ear to ear: a last broad red smile from the wife so fearful of losing her beauty.

None of the six messages she leaves is addressed to Henry. The act itself is the message.

Then there is the doctor's note. A few days after Frances's suicide, Henry receives a letter from Dr. Knight of the Riggs Center. The doctor assures him that the divorce request was not the cause but only the "immediate trigger" of the despair that led Frances to take her life, and that she committed the act "in a mood of exacerbated hopelessness." (Though this seems to contradict the premeditated nature of the act, not to mention the symbolism of Frances's having carried it out on her birthday.) Dr. Knight then suggests that Frances, aware of her slim chances for recovery, and sorrowful at her inability to make Henry happy, "arranged this solution" out of loving motives.

Let us not malign Dr. Knight, a cofounder of the Menninger Clinic, president of both the American Psychoanalytic Association and the American Psychiatric Association, and, by all testimonials, a caring man. But it's a fact that clever patients can manipulate those who would heal them. We wonder if Frances, upon deciding her ending, implanted these maudlin thoughts of martyrdom in the doctor's head—if, in effect, she authored that awful condolence herself. Certainly, Frances can hardly have left her survivor a more lasting legacy of guilt if the words had come from beyond the grave, written in her own hand.

As to the manner of death, there is clearly intent to its preparation and staging. In answer to Henry's acclaimed stage comeback, Frances's suicide is likewise a theater of dying; and no less is it an act of public assertion, a final naked display of what Frances had come to believe was her real identity—a human shell, cut in half and emptied.

On May 11, 1950, it is reported from Greenwich that Frances's will has been filed in probate and that it "disposes of an estate of more than $400,000 in real and personal property and $3,500 in Greenwich real estate." The principal beneficiary is Sophie, who receives the title to her Los Angeles home, one thousand dollars in cash, all of Frances's personal effects, and 60 percent of the residual estate. The remainder is to be divided between Jane and Peter, who will inherit Sophie's share upon her death. Pan, already wealthy, is left a house in Newark, New Jersey.

What is it that makes Frances's will particularly newsworthy, a month after her suicide? One thing: the beautiful, vengeful fact that Henry is not in it.

∽

Some years later, Hollywood columnist Sheilah Graham will describe a function at which "a tactless woman" asks Fonda this question: "What is it like to be married to all those women, and two of them committed suicide?" To which Henry replies, "Everyone has to save himself."

Though he has cared for his wife within the limits of his ability, though he has suffered stresses and regrets, Fonda has sacrificed few prerogatives through the fourteen years of this marriage. But we're not without understanding for him. He must feel despair creeping about his neck like the swampy vines of Greenwich. He knows he is unable to pull Frances from the hole begun for her in childhood, deepened in marriage to George Brokaw, and widened in every year of marriage to himself—a man uninclined to express feeling, lend emotional succor, or sympathize in depth with those closest to him.

As Fonda will say later, "It was just a bore to have a wife who wasn't always well." That cold candor harmonizes with words we've come across before. It may be that Henry feels as keenly as anyone around him—Sullavan or Frances, Heggen or Logan—that boredom is one of the many names of death. It may be that he himself tends to the very depression that has sunk, or threatens to sink, those remarkable individuals to whose mysteries he has always found himself attracted, whose frictions have fired his creativity.

The need to seek out such depths as Henry has gleaned in Frances, to venture so near to another's impulse toward death, and then to flee while pretending a lack of comprehension—this is selfishness. But it is also, to Fonda, as basic a necessity as work and freedom. If Frances has for many years been doomed to fall, he is equally doomed to go on, in both the performing and existential senses—doing creative penance for his emotional sins, tracking the elephant of doom as his black dog of fear takes the point.

His job, finally, is to act; his responsibility, to live.

Frances joins Aleta Freel, Ross Alexander, Tom Heggen, the others who have fallen before and will fall after. Given all she suffered, the wonderment may be that she held on to life as long as she did. Henry, though, must make it through to the end.

Part 2

7

The Right Man

With admirers, New York, mid-1950s

America couldn't be happier with him.

Come the 1950s—midlife and mid-century—as stars of similar vintage fall behind, Henry Fonda achieves cross-media ubiquity. He capitalizes on, contributes to, or somehow connects with virtually every entertainment trend and innovation of the time: television, wide-screen spectacular, Method acting, the inescapable Western. By dint of apprenticeship, luck, strategic compromise, and dedicated artistry, he has won the ability to do anything he likes. He has beaten the game.

It's only himself he can't figure out. He is forty-five. At the peak of his life and work, with youth behind him and age ahead, he is an ordinary man with ordinary questions. Where does he belong? What are the limits of his ability? Is he a good man or a villain?

Writer and critic A. Alvarez quotes Dante: "In the middle of the journey of our life, I came to myself within a dark wood where the straight way was lost. Ah, how hard a thing it is to tell of that wood, savage and harsh and dense, the thought of which renews my fear!" Alvarez then references the psychoanalyst Elliott Jaques, who reads those lines as a description of "'the mid-life crisis,' that long period of hopelessness and confusion, a kind of male menopause, which often occurs at some point in the thirties or early forties and marks the transition from youth to middle age."

Henry Fonda's middle age—the period following the ascension of *Mister Roberts,* and the low of Frances's death—is a dark wood full of thorns and dangers, with no clear path. It is his most volatile period— his most various in artistry, his most confounding in behavior—and it bespeaks a man whose straight way is lost.

It's to Henry's credit that he does not recede into his Dantean darkness. His middle age is ceaselessly productive and persistently interesting. As a public man, he is forever moving, relocating, remarrying, his eyes darting into new social sets, new creativities. As an actor, he goes places he hasn't yet ventured. But as a professional, he is newly demanding and combative. A new egotism drives him, a latent craziness that cracks his self-control.

Behind it is Frances. She hounds Fonda through these middle years, pushing him to work, fight, despair, live. Her own ordeal ceased with her death, but his has taken a new form. Through all the muddled episodes and mystifying works of these postsuicide years, the crux of his ordeal is to battle toward expression through a dark wood of guilt and pain, the thorns of an exquisite self-loathing.

And if he cannot find the straight path, he will hack one out—one that is crooked and difficult and even, in its purest moments, noble.

∞

Fonda prepares to make Susan Blanchard his third wife by shedding the coverings of his previous existence. He leaves the Greenwich house for another in the equally affluent suburb of Darien; abandons the Manhattan bachelor flat to lease a four-story brownstone in the East Sixties. The children are here and there, Jane immersing herself in friends and horses, Peter the ward of Grandma Sophie. Jane recalls that Frances's sister and brother-in-law threatened a custody bid around this time, and she suggests that Henry's inclination was to let his children go; it was Susan who convinced him to fight for them. A few months after Frances's death, Henry successfully petitions the Greenwich courts for guardianship of the assets she has left Peter, an estate totaling sixty thousand dollars.

The wedding occurs three days after Christmas, 1950. It is a small, chic affair held in the Upper East Side apartment of Susan's mother and stepfather, the Hammersteins. Neither of Henry's children is present. Despite its rebound aspects, not to mention the age difference, the marriage looks sunny: Henry and Susan are spotted around town, giggling. The children, far from thinking her an intruder, adore their young stepmother. She is the supportive older female Jane has never had, and an object of wonder to dreamy Peter.

The girl is a winner. Henry has good times with her. But he is the same parched and private man he was before.

They take their honeymoon on the Virgin Island of Saint John. And without any malign intent, ten-year-old Peter blows a hole in their getaway. While target-shooting with two friends on a skeet range near Ossining, New York, the boy mishandles a .22-caliber pistol and shoots himself in the abdomen.

The wound appears small, but as a handy chauffeur speeds him to town, Peter knows he is dying. Miraculously, a surgeon from nearby Sing Sing prison, with expertise in violent wounds, is on the scene. Dr. Charles C. Sweet finds damage to Peter's liver, stomach, and kidney; his heart has only just been spared. In the course of emergency surgery, near-fatal amounts of blood are lost. Three times, the boy's heartbeat ceases. Jane and Sophie are told he won't make it. Then adrenaline is shot straight into the struggling heart, and it returns to life.

All this time, Henry knows nothing. By the time a shortwave-radio alert penetrates his island seclusion, the mishap has hit the papers. Peter is listed in "very favorable condition"; Dr. Sweet says that despite needing three blood transfusions, the lad has made an "amazing comeback." Reaching the hospital, Henry finds his son still unconscious, and takes up vigil at his bedside.

Despite the rumors and surmises of ensuing years—even Jane has her doubts—Peter swears it is not a suicide attempt. Henry believes him, inasmuch as the circumstances do not seem to suggest he meant to hurt himself. But it's several hours before Henry knows what the circumstances are. How can he avoid the word *suicide* as his frail son lies strung with tubes, eyes closed in a face so resembling Frances's?

But Peter stabilizes and regains strength. Meanwhile, the third marriage becomes everyday life. Organs regenerate, blood regains its flow, and life rolls forward.

Parts of Fonda are invigorated as he enters his late forties—by marriage to Susan; by his new pastime of depicting superrealistic still lifes in pastel chalk; by the broad choice of theatrical works available to him; and overall by the possibilities that attach to being Henry Fonda at this point in time. Work and production, plans and projections put distance between him and the past. Frances fades from the visible plane; her ghost goes gray and indistinct in the memories of the living. "No one ever talked about Mom," Peter says of these days. "No one seemed to miss her. It was almost as if she had never lived."

By "no one," Peter means, more than anyone, his father. All is hidden in this man—until the instant when an opening appears. Dorothy Kilgallen has a spy in the room as Henry and Susan trade vows. "She remained cool and unflustered throughout the ceremony," the spy relates, "but he wept."

Henry has been through a lot, and middle age lends new poignancy to every emotion. We don't know if he cries because he is happy, or because he knows the vow he swears to Susan will not survive his need to keep her at a distance. We don't know if the tears are shed in anticipation or remembrance—thoughts of Frances, himself, his motherless children, the sad mess of life.

∽

On October 28, Henry gives his last Broadway performance as Mister Roberts. His leaving is due to a torn knee cartilage, which will require surgery and necessitate a twelve-week period of recuperation. Columnist

Whitney Bolton, present that last night, writes that in his final scene, Fonda "was almost unable to go on speaking. Emotion gripped him and tightened his throat." After the curtain, Josh Logan emerges to inform the audience of the special occasion and explain that the company has made a tradition of awarding a bottle of scotch to a departing cast member. Tonight, for the first time, the ritual will occur in public. "The handkerchiefs were out like moths in the moonlight," Bolton writes.

But Fonda is not finished with *Roberts,* or it with him. Star and specter will hit the road together in a nation-spanning marathon of performances between February and August of 1951. The itinerary has been announced far enough in advance for ticket orders to soar, and each midsize town to experience its own excitement. Launching in Pittsburgh, the road tour covers the belt line of Middle America, in cities where Broadway stars seldom appear—Charleston and Cleveland, St. Louis and St. Paul, Kansas City and Denver, Seattle and San Francisco—culminating in a farewell engagement at Hollywood's Biltmore Theatre.

"This is my first tour," Henry tells a Wisconsin reporter. "It's exciting: there's an added something about going out and playing before audiences all over the country." He has always loved the egalitarian grind of theater, whatever takes it away from cocktail entertainment and closer to soul-feeding labor. But the tour also has glamour and allure: To most Americans, Henry is still a movie star, something romantic and fantastic. Susan Blanchard accompanies him, and why not—she has youth and stamina and doesn't mind being photographed.

On March 19, the company, leaving Minneapolis by train, runs into a snowstorm and is stranded; that evening's scheduled performance in Omaha is canceled. Emerging the next morning, blinking in a world of white, Fonda promises a special extra show for disappointed ticket holders. But the secondary train cars, containing props and scenery, are stuck behind—which entails Fonda's addressing his hometown audience directly from the stage, explaining the layout of the *Reluctant* set, entreating each spectator to imagine the ship's towering hull and paltry palm tree, the cargo winches and goat on the gangway. Fonda and his costars then perform the show with nothing but their bodies and costumes, miming everything from the moving of crates to the climactic heaving of the palm tree.

In Iowa, fire breaks out on an upper floor of the Fort Des Moines Hotel, where the *Roberts* company is staying. A power cut strands seventeen-year-old elevator operator Joan Galusha in her elevator car, and Fonda, on his way to the lobby, is enlisted by firemen to help give the fainting girl artificial respiration. He is served up as a local hero: "If I get a chance, I'm going to see Mr. Fonda and thank him," Miss Galusha says. "He disappeared right after helping me." Mister Roberts and the Lone Ranger in one!

But the tour ends on a bum note. Josh Logan, concerned how *Roberts* will play before the Hollywood elite—he is keen to direct the movie—catches up in San Francisco. He finds the show's comic-dramatic friction has been lost. It seems the other cast members, in awe of Fonda, have begun to emulate his reserve; full of competitive underplaying, the action has gone solemn and slow, and lost its tragicomic tension. Asserting eminent domain, the coauthor-director steps in to recharge the comedy and restore the balance.

Fonda is deeply offended. He has effectively been directing the show throughout the tour and feels it is in fine shape. But he grits his teeth and shuts up—until the night before the Hollywood opening.

"I don't feel it's *my* play anymore," he explodes.

"No, you son of a bitch," Logan responds, "but it's mine!"

Despite his own annoyance, the director senses the subtleties of ego that are involved. Fonda "had become so identified with the part, and with the play," according to Logan, "that in his mind he was its guardian and I had become a guy who was contriving to spoil it by putting low laughs into it." Fonda goes so far as to tell Leland Hayward that he will not star in the much-anticipated screen version if Logan directs it.

Fonda and Logan are brothers; they fight that passionately, that whimsically. But this is a warning of other backstage scenarios to come in the next decade, dustups with a common denominator—Fonda's new intransigence against authority. His temper has usually been vented on those in his personal life, children or wives; now it is less discriminate.

His ego has usually manifested itself as aloofness; now it is an animal thing—prowling the dark wood, savage, protective of its territory.

∽

The new, makeshift Fonda family vacations in Malibu in the weeks following the *Roberts* road show. Henry must be happy, for all will remember it as a good summer.

Leland Hayward, now as mighty a theatrical producer as he had been an agent, sends along what he is certain will be the next hot play: *Point of No Return*, an adaptation, by Paul Osborn, of John P. Marquand's best-selling 1949 novel. It concerns New York bank executive Charles Gray and his personal and professional crisis at middle age. While sweating out a promotion, Gray revisits his Massachusetts hometown and has memories of youth, family, a girl loved and lost.

The story is founded on the same critique of petit-bourgeois and corporate values that later in the 1950s will become a successful model for "probing" fiction on the page, stage, and screen: *Executive Suite, The Man in the Gray Flannel Suit, Patterns, The Apartment*. The play is, in that sense, slightly ahead of the cultural curve, but that is probably of only marginal interest to Fonda. Something else about it gets into his brain. Though it's far from perfect, he signs up, then flies back to New York for consultations.

Fonda's first venture after *Mister Roberts* is guaranteed a sizable audience. On the instant of his agreement, capital and curiosity begin to flow. Rehearsals are announced for October 1, the Broadway opening for mid-December. Directing is H. C. Potter, spinner of dreary but popular screen whimsies (*The Farmer's Daughter, Mr. Blandings Builds His Dream House*), shepherd of high-minded stage hits (*A Bell for Adano, Anne of the Thousand Days*). Leonard Lyons reports that Hayward "will charge $8 top for Fridays and Saturdays, assuming a $37,000 weekly gross." By the time it opens, the play will have an advance ticket sale of half a million dollars—far more than even *Roberts* stimulated.

Previews commence October 29 at New Haven's Shubert Theater, where the show sells out and Walter Winchell's scouts herald it as "absorbing and generally entertaining." But Fonda again has trouble with his director; Potter, he feels, is unable to address key weaknesses in the play. Leland Hayward is forced to agree. Though the two are old friends, producer asks director to excuse himself, on the face-saving pretext of a prior film commitment.

On November 6, the play, minus a director and still only "generally" entertaining, begins a three-week stand at the Colonial Theatre in Boston. Hayward places a call to Greece, where Elia Kazan—the most influential director on Broadway, stager of modern milestones by Thornton Wilder, Arthur Miller, and Tennessee Williams—is vacationing. Kazan flies to Boston for a performance; his comments engender extensive rewrites and reconstructive rehearsal. Cast changes and final touches are added over two weeks at Philadelphia's Forrest Theatre.

Local reviews are again fine. But the new and improved production, Fonda feels, is little but an empty shell with a higher gloss. He plays the remainder of the previews "feeling that I was cheating on an audience in every possible way."

Less than a month has been devoted to pretryout rehearsals and getting the text in shape; even in published form, Osborn's adaptation reads like a work in progress. From day one, Henry knows there's something wrong, and he is ravaged by nerves and sleeplessness in the preview period. In Philadelphia, his throat bothers him, and a doctor finds bleeding fissures on his vocal cords: apparently, Fonda has been yelling too much in rehearsals.

What is he yelling for? "An honest second act," he says.

Everyone's instincts—Hayward's for the money, Fonda's for the art—are confirmed when *Point of No Return* opens at the Alvin Theatre on December 13. It's a hit, and a sizable one, but no magic attaches to it. The notices are glumly approving. "Sound, professional theatre work," Brooks Atkinson calls the play in the *New York Times,* while Richard Watts, Jr., of the *New York Post* respects its "expert showmanship." John Mason Brown of the *Saturday Review* says it is "distinguished throughout by the kind of professionalism which restores one's faith in the theatre." Other scribes plumb their souls for phrases like "impressive accomplishment," "expertly loaded," and "thoroughly efficient."

∽

Fonda is unhappy with *Point of No Return* and will remain so, though his involvement with it will be extensive—a Broadway run of 356 performances, another coast-to-coast tour, and even initial agreement to a Hayward-produced film version, which is never made.* Fonda is unhappy because he has taken on a play that is not there, a character not on the page, a core conflict not brought out but sketched in air.

What attracted him? Charles Gray is a protagonist Fonda feels he might understand, yet who exists at a safe remove—roughly his own age, likewise a veteran of World War II, with a wife, children, and an existence split between city job and suburban home. Gray is proud to suffer silently, though early hurts have left him stunted. A number of lines about ghosts and fate jibe with the inner logic of Fonda's career.

Such implications may have induced Fonda to hope the play would deepen with rewriting. But although Henry rages, and his throat bleeds, he will be unable to make *Point of No Return* work in a personal way, or as anything but a popular success.

What's missing, he's said, is "an honest second act." The climax of the second act is the suicide by pill overdose of Gray's father. In the novel, the son's discovery of the father's body is a memory swimming "deep beneath the waters of experience": "There was nothing to explain the spasm of fear which shook Charles except his father's utter stillness. He was out in the hall again, closing the bedroom door very softly, before he faced the full realization that his father was dead." The play presents the discovery as a brief spotlit flashback between overloaded dialogue scenes:

A single light goes up on the GRAYS' *living room.* JOHN GRAY *lies motionless, stretched out on the sofa, one leg and arm hanging*

---

* There is a 1958 teleplay version, starring Charlton Heston.

down. On the floor is a newspaper, an empty glass and a pill bottle.
CHARLES *is kneeling, dazed. He places the limp arm upon the*
body, kisses the forehead, reaches for the bottle and rises. Slowly he
places the bottle into his pocket.

"My life has been peppered with suicides," Fonda will say near the
end of his life, "and I don't like to think back on them." But in the post-
Frances years, suicide is what he cannot stop thinking about. *Point of*
No Return is his first dramatic gesture in its direction, but the crux is
hedged, the whole irremediably flawed. He wants to go further.

∽

Grimly focused, Fonda takes to the road with *Point of No Return,* em-
barking on a ballyhooed national tour days after the play closes at
the Alvin. For the next seven months—late November 1952 through
June 1953—he traverses the country, working hard every night. But is
he working to deepen the play, or to maintain a basic level of entertainment, an illusion of wholeness?

Either way, the tickets sell. Opening the tour in Baltimore on November 24, the company breaks the house record for nonmusical shows.
Similar returns will be counted elsewhere, along with glowing write-ups
from local critics. Not that anyone mistakes expertise for profundity. The
San Francisco critic admits *Point of No Return* "is not the greatest play
ever written, Heaven knows, but the combination of playwright, director
and actors has made it into a semblance of a great play." Henry, he finds,
makes "a thoughtful and forceful presentation, admirably calculated and
projected." That he has helped to calculate a semblance of greatness is far
from the lowest praise an actor might receive.

When Henry regroups after the tour to consider his options for the
autumn, he rejects or tables offers that appear frivolous (Edward
Chodorov's *Oh, Men! Oh, Women!,* a fashionable satire on the sacred
cows of marriage and psychoanalysis), are well outside his performing
repertoire (a musical based on the Steinbeck novel *Sweet Thursday,* for
which he takes extensive vocal training—a male Mary Martin he's

not), or are beyond his capacity to creditably purvey (the dying homosexual husband in an adaptation of André Gide's *The Immoralist*).

The choice Fonda makes is among the most fascinating and confounding of his career. The play itself, Herman Wouk's *The Caine Mutiny Court-Martial,* is well within his established range. But from the three options he is given by the producers—he may play either one of the two leads, or direct—the one he chooses is to play Lt. Barney Greenwald, a young Jewish lawyer. For Fonda to believe he can become Greenwald amounts to an act of hubris—one of the conspicuous few in this career of self-enforced limits.

The play is an extraction from Wouk's 1951 novel about a revolt aboard a World War II U.S. Navy ship performing routine duty in the Pacific. Lieutenant Maryk has, at the height of a typhoon, seized control from his skipper, Captain Queeg, who, he claims, froze. Greenwald, Maryk's defense attorney, believes Maryk is merely the tool of Lieutenant Keefer, a smug, navy-hating writer. Greenwald rescues Maryk by dismantling Queeg on the stand but then, in an epilogue, drunkenly confesses to remorse at his actions.

Wouk's novel, in addition to a Pulitzer, has a year on the best-seller lists. The play's popular profile as it approaches the stage far outdistances that of *Point of No Return,* or, for that matter, *Mister Roberts.* At the same time, Hollywood readies its film version, with Humphrey Bogart as Queeg and José Ferrer as Greenwald.

Fonda is sent the play by producer Paul Gregory and actor Charles Laughton, who have recently staged successful all-star table readings of verse plays by Shaw and Benet. Save for sex, Wouk's play has all the elements of a moneymaker: single set, showy star parts, precise construction combining courtroom drama with an underdog premise and two devastating dramatic twists. Henry would be a fool to pass.

∽

Counter to tradition, *The Caine Mutiny Court-Martial* will have its national tour before Broadway, not after, beginning on the West Coast and working east, logging seventy-odd performances before its New

York opening in January 1954. Susan will not be along this time: "One-nighters make it too tough," Henry tells a reporter. (For whom?)

With Fonda in place, the other roles are quickly filled. John Hodiak, dark-eyed incarnation of working-class brawn, plays Maryk, and the role of Queeg goes to Lloyd Nolan, a reliable second-level movie mug.

In early September, Henry flies to Hollywood, where rehearsals are to be held in the headquarters of the American Federation of Musicians. There, he finds actor Dick Powell has been hired to direct. The choice is an odd one: Powell's chief fame has been as a featured singer and dancer in gaudy Warner Bros. musicals (*42nd Street, Footlight Parade, Gold Diggers of 1933, 1935, 1937*). In the years since, he has worked with ambitious auteurs (Rossen, Mann, Minnelli), and even directed a low-budget crime drama (the 1952 *Split Second*). Still, his directorship of this prestigious stage piece is nearly as unlikely as is the conceit of middle-aged Henry Fonda playing a youthful Jew.

But the producers' choice of Powell may not have been a choice at all. Laughton biographer Simon Callow notes that Paul Gregory had "somehow" convinced RKO Pictures, already in production on the film version of *The Caine Mutiny,* to cede partial rights so that the play could premiere before the film. Most studios would have vetoed such a request. But in 1953, Dick Powell, in addition to being an actor and director, is a production executive at RKO—which may explain at one throw why those partial rights are granted, and a director without theatrical experience is hired to steer a major stage production.

Almost instantly, the enterprise turns sour. There are too many talents wound too tightly; rehearsals are a crash of egos, techniques, even sexualities. Alliances and enmities form: The cast members get along, but Laughton and Gregory are contentious; Laughton and Wouk grow close, but Fonda dislikes Laughton; Laughton belittles the cast, and everyone thinks Powell is in over his head.

There are ongoing troubles with the text. More importantly, the director, bred on movie sets, seems unable to shape performance and narrative away from the camera eye and toward the theater's living darkness. Fonda huddles with Nolan and Hodiak, and the consensus is that Powell must go. Laughton reluctantly agrees. In a messy negotiation, by which Gregory grants him director's billing and 2 percent of the gross profits, Powell is dismissed. But the producers have not heard the last of him.

∽

Laughton takes over as director. If Powell's shortfall is inexperience, Laughton's is a command of theater so lordly, it is close to contempt. Cast member Charles Nolte remembers being ridiculed at length for his vocal mannerisms, and no fewer than three cast members are driven to walk out.

Laughton's training is steeped in artifice and attitude. A closeted gay man with masochistic leanings, he suffuses his performances with the odors of sensualism and self-loathing. Fonda's style is as no-nonsense as Laughton's is rococo, and he normally smells of nothing more louche than Old Spice. So perhaps it is both chemical disgust and a Mister Roberts–like defense of "the crew" when, at mid-rehearsal one day, Fonda impales Laughton on the spear of a direct and mortifying insult, delivered before the entire company: "What do you know about men, you fat, ugly faggot?"

The remark is both an offense and an impertinence—like asking a bee what it knows about flowers—but it characterizes Fonda's explosiveness in this period. It speaks as well to control: Fonda is more intent than ever on being the shaping intelligence, the decisive energy behind anything he is in. He knows his attack on Laughton will damage the older man's authority, while defending the cast will empower his own position.

But the other actors may also secretly fear the spear of his anger. "I consider Fonda the most interesting actor with whom I worked for many reasons," Nolte—who also happens to be gay—will tell an interviewer some fifty years later. "I did study his acting technique because I was witness to it at first hand, and close up. It struck me as highly professional when it wasn't frighteningly demonic."

∽

Yet somehow *The Caine Mutiny Court-Martial* makes it to port. Previews in Santa Barbara are followed by the San Diego premiere on October 13, and rapt audiences and rave reviews in city after city. Fonda has "the gift," a critic writes after the November 4 show at El Paso's Liberty Hall, "of commanding more attention even when his back is to the audience than most actors can scrape together with a spotlight and ten-piece orchestra."

By early December, the advance Broadway ticket sale is approaching $800,000. But chatter about dissension in the company persists. Columnist Wood Soanes has written that Henry is cold-shouldering both Hodiak and Nolan, "and is eager to get out of the proceedings," suggesting it is because Nolan's reviews have outshone his own. Louella Parsons likewise claims Fonda has stayed "aloof" from his costars during the Chicago layover, and that his "unwillingness to take any direction is said to be one reason that Dick Powell withdrew from the play."

"What direction?" Lloyd Nolan snaps the next day. "Powell doesn't know anything about directing a play. . . . Charles Laughton took over a week before we were to start out and saved the show." And what of Henry's aloofness? "It's a lie," Nolan says. John Hodiak is moved to phone Parsons and quash the rumors. "[We're] just one happy family, and except for a few minor misunderstandings we are all very congenial." Parsons reserves her doubts: "[A]t least five people" tell her Fonda has been difficult.

Then Powell reappears. He has, by legal fiat, been billed as director throughout the tour; when it arises that Laughton will be so credited in New York, Powell moves for an injunction to block the opening. He tells a reporter he wasn't fired; he quit. Why? "I got into a slight squabble with Henry"—though one report has had an enraged Fonda putting his fist through a door. "He threatened to quit unless it was done the way he wanted. He's like that, moody."

In the end, Powell cannot raise the $1.5 million bond needed to block *The Caine Mutiny Court-Martial* from making its scheduled debut at the Plymouth Theatre on January 20—which it does, to acclaim across the board. Kerr of the *New York Herald-Tribune* calls it "thrilling"; Atkinson of the *New York Times* says "shattering." "Powerful, impressive," writes Watts of the *New York Post;* "magnificent," offers both Coleman of the *Mirror* and McClain of the *Journal American;* "brilliantly exciting," contributes Hawkins of the *World-Telegram and Sun.*

Earl Wilson believes it is "one of the great shows of our time." Legendary theatrical producer Billy Rose compares the play favorably with the bloated film version (another thorn in Dick Powell's side), calling it "a throat-grabbing chunk of life." Columnist Mel Heimer writes, "I am in that near-comatose state where I feel it may be the finest thing I ever have seen in the theater."

∽

Maryk, just acquitted, is celebrating with his shipmates. Greenwald staggers in drunk. He baits Keefer, whose war novel lampooning the regular navy is approaching publication. Then the lawyer describes the shame he feels. Queeg, though petty and paranoid, represents the unsung military that protected democracy between the wars, while cynics like Keefer pursued private ambition and Hitler incinerated European Jews for soap.

The *Caine* mutiny violated the sanctity of rank in wartime; the acquittal ratified disloyalty. "Queeg deserved better at my hands," Greenwald says. "He stopped Herman Goering from washing his fat behind with my mother."

Greenwald's indictment lifts *The Caine Mutiny Court-Martial* to within reach of the great American plays—not because it makes sense, but because it makes drama. It is up to Fonda to render Greenwald's ethnic terror convincing and real; if he fails, the play is sabotaged by a wet lump of desperate jabber. But on those nights when he breaks his own emotional limits, the epilogue carries the play past any spot where an audience might safely have left it behind.

Greenwald enables Fonda to portray a man done in by his own controlling nature, whose triumph brings desolation. Henry calls the epilogue "the toughest scene [I've] ever played." He is uncertain how to deliver it, before realizing the only approach is to create the emotion anew in every performance, from first mutterings to final condemnation, inebriation to rage. He must reexperience that mounting ferocity each night as if for the first time.

He cannot always manage it. But on those nights he does, Fonda breaks down and cries.

∽

Fonda at middle age has his fists in a perpetual clench. But when violence comes, it is not he who delivers it, but his director. The punch is a drunken flail, packing more pathos than power. It is especially sad because the director is John Ford, who more than any filmmaker has had the sensitivity to see what lies beneath Fonda's skin, and the love to bring it out.

Ford is directing the film version of *Mister Roberts,* for which Henry has been drawn back to Hollywood after a seven-year absence. Smash play, legendary director, beloved star, big budget—the dominoes are lined up for a box-office hit and a great film.

The picture has been under discussion since 1948, when it's assumed that Joshua Logan will direct Fonda in Caribbean locations. But plans are postponed, partly by the continuing success of *Roberts* as a touring commodity. By late 1953, that success has crested, and the gears crank again to hoist a *Roberts* for the screen. Leland Hayward produces, and Logan, per the assumption, is tapped to direct; but he and Fonda are still on the outs, and Logan is besotted with Marlon Brando, the new Method sensation. William Holden is mentioned as a fallback, while Fonda—felt to be past his peak for playing young naval officers—is barely in the running.

But Hayward begins to question the wisdom of handing the film's costly reins to Logan, whose only movie experience has come fifteen years before, in the form of codirecting one film and dialogue-coaching two others. Hayward asks him to step aside in favor of John Ford, surefire when it comes to sea stories and masculine comedy. (Ford's involvement also promises the cooperation of the U.S. Navy.) Logan, understandably peeved, claims Ford has never even seen the play and, further, that he has disparaged it as "homosexual" in nature.*

Soon after Logan's axing, Louella Parsons makes it known that Hayward and Warner Bros. want Brando. But Brando's involvement is complicated by the lawsuit threatened by Twentieth Century–Fox for his refusal to appear for work on a Michael Curtiz picture, *The Egyptian*. Meanwhile Fonda, "who has aged considerably since he starred in *Mister Roberts* on Broadway," will shoot a screen test for the lead, Parsons reports. "However, there's a possibility he will play the role of the doctor instead of the younger man." What ignominy for Henry, to move up an age bracket and down a billing level in a property for whose popularity he is chiefly responsible.

But John Ford speaks: "Bullshit! That's Fonda's part." He even makes his own participation contingent on Fonda's hiring. Within days, Parsons will announce that Hayward and Jack Warner have decided, in closed conference, to give Fonda the role. Two eminences of an earlier Hollywood, James Cagney and William Powell, are cast as the Captain and Doc; hot young Jack Lemmon will play Pulver.

When his *Court-Martial* contract expires at the end of May and Hayward sends notice that *Roberts* location shooting is set for September 1, Fonda chooses to depart the play and grab the movie. His return to the screen after seven years is an important story, both publicly—it gets the cover of *Life*—and personally. To fuse his two acting selves in the consummate realization of the role that has arguably meant the most to him is a rare chance. To avoid jinxing it, he denies having meant to abandon the movies, or disliking Hollywood: "I had no intention of quitting Hollywood when I left. Three great plays . . . just kept me away. I never intended to pull up stakes."

Much publicity attends initial filming on Midway Island, where Ford shot his great battle documentary more than a decade before, and not far

---

* The first claim is certainly false (many, including Fonda, said Ford saw the play multiple times), and the second probably so, with the "homosexual" bit making us wonder again how repressed were Logan's true desires: accuse your enemy, etc.

from the vortex of Fonda's own navy service. Sailing out, Henry poses with Susan and the kids against the blue waters off Hawaii. He retains all the charisma of the Hollywood star: Pearl Harbor looks like his private swimming pool.

∽

Fonda's command, so inseparable from his coldness, is impressive. He travels between the divergent worlds of theater and film stardom without any evident bump to the psyche; he resumes the movie star's mask, and the stress it conceals, that easily. The gap between 1948 and 1955 might never have occurred, except that Fonda looks what he is—namely, seven years older. Taut, wiry, a most attractive middle-aged man, but one who is too old to be playing Mister Roberts.

On the set, though, he's more the coiled snake than ever, where John Ford is, from the start of shooting, an angry boar flashing its teeth. The old man's alcoholism is peaking, and his health is poor; even at his best he is, in Fonda's phrase, "an Irish egomaniac." Worst, Ford seems bent on making *Roberts* into, imagine this, a John Ford picture—broad comedy and ample slapstick, lusty men and busty women, a *Quiet Man* on the waves. With his screenwriters, Ford has reworked the elusive thing that haunted the Alvin stage into a thick-skulled service comedy about lugs on a tub. The tumultuous shore leave, for instance, is no longer suggested by the crew members' shredded clothing and black eyes; now it is a full-scale disaster romp with rioting sailors, club-swinging MPs, and a motorcycle flying into the drink.

Immediately, Fonda sees the movie shaping up as dumb and unfunny. He has been investing ever more of his ego in controlling the shape and direction of his projects; here he finds the story and character he most prizes being wrested away. But because it is Ford, Henry doesn't shout—as he has lately shouted at Logan, Potter, Powell, and Laughton. Instead he goes sullen. His scenes lack snap; his body is drawn and hostile; there is no bloom of youth on his Roberts. And his off-camera mode is passive-aggressive, even mutinous: According to Jack Lemmon, Fonda encourages the younger actor to "screw up" his scenes, which involve much of the farcical business Ford enjoys and Henry detests.

Finally it comes to a head. Stories vary, but most place the confrontation in the privacy of Ford's room after hours. The director has requested a private conference. What's eating you? he asks Fonda. Henry starts to explain—and Ford, unaccustomed to being answered by his actors, cuts him off with accusations of treachery. More words, getting hotter. And suddenly, Fonda feels a blow to his chin, coming from Ford's aged but wrathful fist. Fonda is propelled backward over a table.

This is followed by tears and remorse. Ford appears at Henry's door to apologize. But the subtle bond that distinguished the partnership has snapped.

It's the most dismal episode in either man's professional life. The two will have clipped and sarcastic exchanges on the *Roberts* set, and speak only occasionally in the years following. But in 1971, Fonda will contribute an affectionate anecdote to Peter Bogdanovich's valedictory chronicle, *Directed by John Ford;* and to the end, he will speak of "Pappy" as one of the greats.

In an interview conducted in 1973, Ford's grandson Dan asks him his feelings about Fonda. "Just a great actor, a real professional," the director says, gruff and phlegmy, his voice full of tobacco, whiskey, history. "All in all, just a fine man."

He offers a tall tale or two about their virgin encounters on *Young Mr. Lincoln.* There is a pause. Though he has been reminiscing about the first time he and Fonda worked together, Ford may be more keenly recalling the last time. It's as if a chasm of nearly twenty years is being mulled in the gap between sentences. For when he speaks again, Ford notes that Fonda had "a fine war record. He never advertised the fact, but . . . I'm very proud of him. He was in the Navy."

Those are Ford's last recorded words on Fonda; he will die a few months later.

∽

After the apology, Ford begins boozing in earnest. Somehow, he survives the remainder of the Midway shoot, further locations in Hawaii, and a few working days in Hollywood, as the production nears a state of chaos. (Leland Hayward remembers Ward Bond, a supporting player— and no moderate drinker himself—serving as uncredited director during Ford's spells of alcoholic unconsciousness.) Finally, Ford is overtaken by gall bladder distress and removed from the filming: an honorable, if painful, out for everyone.

The rest of the scenes are shot by Mervyn LeRoy, a decent-minded hack with the pictorial gifts of a warehouse foreman. And in a final irony, the film's presumptive first director, Josh Logan, is called upon to contribute several bridging scenes and dialogue inserts, and even to re-shoot some slapstick—most of it so corny and clanking it matches seamlessly with Ford at his crocked Irish worst.

Released in the summer of 1955, *Mister Roberts* gets celebratory reviews and becomes one of the top moneymakers of its year. It is still considered a beloved film today; although, as with many works so des-ignated, it is rarely mentioned, for the simple reason that it is an embar-rassment. A story that calls for a poet's sad touch is covered with Ford's fumbling thumbprints; the skeletal play becomes a wide-screen whale spouting gouts of buffoonery and sentimentality.

Mister Roberts had, in no small sense, saved Fonda. He has done the role on stage, radio, television, now film; and after seven years, a thousand-plus performances, and miles beyond number, he consecrates to history a hollow Leviathan. The picture will be a hit—but then, so will the likes of *Operation Petticoat* (1959) and *The Wackiest Ship in the Army* (1960), lubricious and witless co-optations of the *Roberts* model. It will even be taken for a classic. But Fonda knows it is crap.

"I despised that film," he says of *Mister Roberts*. At least he has the memory of what was.

∽

Come the 1950s, television presents itself as the ideal screen for Fonda's blander aspect. The new entertainment appliance, which by 1953 sits in half of all American homes, will be blamed for much ill-defined social evil; it will plug straight into every American tendency to complacency, conformity, and imaginative sloth. So it's not in the happiest sense that Fonda seems made for it—as do numerous other, less talented members of his acting generation, from Robert Cummings to Robert Young. Henry's thinness and pallor blend with the transmission fuzz of early broadcasts; his darkness is diminished and his dullness magnified by the unsubtle camera, the gray-and-white image.

Fonda will have been on television for years by the time it ceases to be called a fad. His first appearance is in April 1948, on a show called *Tonight on Broadway*—two weeks into the run of *Roberts,* he is interviewed live from the Alvin Theatre. In October 1950, he performs a *Roberts* scene on ABC's *Showtime USA*, and in July 1953, he plays his first original TV part—the title character in *The Decision at Arrowsmith*, an adaptation from Sinclair Lewis.

In 1954, Henry is offered a substantial sum to front his own show. *The Star and the Story* is a half-hour anthology series guest-starring the requisite supply of second- and third-echelon movie veterans. The show's subject matter, judging by the episode listing, displays a curious dependence on the short stories of Somerset Maugham.* Fonda's contribution is his name, a brief introduction to each story, and two product endorsements per episode, delivered straight to the camera. The show is not unsuccessful (thirty-nine episodes are broadcast between January 1955 and April 1956), but it's the commercials—Fonda hoisting a glass of Rheingold to extol it as "the largest-selling lager beer in the East"—that get the most attention.

Endorsements are not new for Henry—since 1936, he's been hired to sell shirts and shoes, razor blades and self-sealing envelopes, Schaefer beer and Camel cigarettes—but they've always been in print; some onlookers question the propriety of a great actor pitching products via the tube, as opposed to in the pages of *Collier's.* TV critic Hal Humphrey,

---

* The show's full title was *Henry Fonda Presents The Star and the Story*. Amazingly, given still-recent events, Dick Powell was among its coproducers. See *Fresno Bee*, 7/20/1954.

while admitting the power of $150,000 as an inducement, finds it "appalling to see an actor of this stature going so commercial and mediocre." The star is more of a realist. "I am an actor and this is part of acting," Henry says. "Yes, I am being very commercial, and for commercial reasons. I am getting more money for this than I would for a movie."

Clearly Fonda has a pragmatic relationship to the medium that will keep his name current and his face familiar to the end of his life. He doesn't condescend to TV, but he exploits it, with exceeding deftness, as a ready source of cash, publicity, exposure; as a place to assert his independence as an artist-entrepreneur; and as a medium with the power to transmit fine touches and delicate strokes to millions, amid what FCC chairman Newton Minow will call a "vast wasteland" of pap programming.

Also in 1954, Fonda becomes infatuated with *Clown,* the autobiography of circus performer Emmett Kelly, whose silent hobo Weary Willie has recently been featured in Cecil B. DeMille's *The Greatest Show on Earth.* Circus movies are in vogue just now—following DeMille's will be *Carnival Story, Trapeze,* and *La Strada*—and Henry believes there is a feature film in Kelly's book. Hollywood doubts it. *Clown* is no account of a tortured artist, but the story of a well-adjusted entertainer who finds a successful niche. Where's the drama?

Henry has had a "secret ambition," he says, to play Kelly ever since seeing him perform in the mid-1930s. He buys the book, commissions a teleplay, assembles a deal; after wrapping *Roberts,* he learns basic trapeze moves and studies Willie's style in counsel with Kelly himself. His idea is that the presentation—filmed, not live—will serve as a dry run for the movie version. "I want to do the picture," he says, "and that's the only reason why I'm doing the TV show." The half-hour production accrues a budget of nearly eighty thousand dollars, making it the most expensive film yet made for television.

Despite good ratings and reviews, *Clown,* which premieres on the *General Electric Theater* of March 27, 1955—introduced by host Ronald Reagan, sponsored by the company that promises "a better America through chemistry"—vindicates Hollywood's judgment, not Henry's.

More concerned with manufacturing drama than with being dramatic, the show is stilted and grudging.

That is, until the climax, when the clown's lachrymose ballet wows the crowd, and we finally understand what Fonda sees in the material. He is engaged both by Willie's isolation—so poetically mute that it risks ickiness—and by Emmett's desire to disappear behind the mask and mummery of this sweet, alien creature. As Emmett, Fonda is tight-faced, unappealing; reborn as the clown, he is miraculous. For five or six organic minutes, this stiff and serious man stages a dance in slow motion.* Whether cracking a peanut with a sledgehammer or sweeping his spotlight under a canvas flap, Fonda moves dolefully, sensually, in a perfect stylization of melancholy and vanishing.

Just two months later, he is pursuing similar quarry—but this time with words, words, words. On May 30, NBC's blue-ribbon drama slot, *Producers' Showcase,* airs *The Petrified Forest,* Robert E. Sherwood's theatrical chestnut about a motley assortment of people held hostage in an Arizona diner by a gangster, and about a writer who sacrifices his life to free a forlorn waitress. Humphrey Bogart stars as the gangster, Duke Mantee, the part that made him famous on Broadway in 1935 and in the following year's film version; Lauren Bacall is Gabby, the waitress; and Fonda plays Alan Squier, the writer who walks out of the desert sweating pathos and poetry.

Squier is a bitter romantic and gaseous failure who references the modernist shibboleths of Eliot and Jung, and bemoans belonging to "a vanishing race—the intellectuals." Fonda isn't a disgrace in the role, but intellectualism sits on him like an expensive hat on a pretentious woman, and he overappreciates Sherwood's fancy-pants dialogue.

The role is humbug, yet it takes Fonda two steps closer to his secret post-Frances theme of suicide. Squier arranges to be murdered by the gangster so the waitress may claim his life insurance and bankroll her

---

* Henry was among the celebrity clients of pioneering New York yoga instructor Blanche DeVries. See Robert Love, *The Great Oom: The Improbable Birth of Yoga in America* (New York: Viking, 2010), 339. See also *Lowell Sun,* 11/30/1950, and *NBN,* 51.

escape. And so it happens: The writer is put down by a well-placed bullet and dies, sainted, in the waitress's arms. Like Frances, Squier believes his sacrifice will set a loved one free. But her act was a curse disguised as a gift; Squier's is an ancient literary device—a redemption. As Abe Lincoln redeemed American myth, Alan Squier redeems the myth of the noble suicide.

∽

Fonda the celebrity works hard for his audience's attention and then tests his ability to dodge the light he has drawn. Fonda the husband is wired the same way: Having acceded to wedlock, he does his best to exist as if he is alone in the world. Henry's third marriage is barely two years old before rumors of disunity begin; they are denied, but in fact the couple are spending less time together (Susan has not joined Henry's last two theatrical tours), and their mutual infatuations—his with youth, hers with sincerity—break down under the dull test of daily living.

As couples do, they figure to fill the space that separates them with a child. Though she cannot become pregnant, Susan's relations with Jane and Peter in the months after Frances's death—encouraging them to explore feelings Henry will not admit exist—prove she has a way with kids. As for Henry, he may be lukewarm on children, but he loves babies. So in November 1953, they adopt an eight-week-old girl, whom they name Amy. Buoyant and engaging, untouched by dark Fonda memory, she is doted upon by all.

But the marriage will not be saved. Susan is well aware of Henry's discomfort over the difference in their ages. Perhaps guilt over the suicide, and a sense of being publicly judged, makes every social convention keener in him. As if rebuked by the youthfulness he once sought, Henry becomes less Susan's husband and more her headmaster; Peter describes his father as being "astoundingly restrictive" with regard to Susan's desires to dance, romance, and socialize.

Susan admits to being fearful of him. Fonda's response to emotional distress is punitive, bordering on sadistic. On their honeymoon, the couple swim on the beach; Susan places Henry's wristwatch in the sand, to find later the tide has taken it away. Ashamed, she begins to sob. Henry fixes her with a cold stare. "Don't cry," he says. "Crying is disgusting." She must excuse herself and expend her tears behind a rock.

That is the marriage's ominous beginning. Its end arrives near a movie location in Rome. In the summer of 1955, Fonda flies to Italy with Jane and Peter, Susan to arrive later with Amy. He has come to star in an epic realization of *War and Peace*, costarring Audrey Hepburn, and shot at Cinecittà film studios by the colorful Italian producer Dino De Laurentiis. It's to be one of the heaviest spectaculars yet mounted—"probably the biggest movie ever made," a grinning Dino claims. The Tolstoy epic, as yet unmolested by movies, is lately the focus of competing desires: David O. Selznick and Mike Todd are among the would-be adaptors whom De Laurentiis has beaten to the post. The movie will have sixty speaking parts; eight thousand soldiers and three thousand horses will be supplied by the Italian army. The budget is six million dollars, with a projected running time of four hours.

Fonda is lured by the money, and by the challenge of portraying Pierre, Tolstoy's idealist-intellectual, who bounces corklike on the tide of the Napoleonic wars—a forerunner of every idealist-intellectual Fonda has ever played. Except that Pierre is fat, unglamorous, a cuckold—not a hero, but a slogger, a seeker. Perhaps the mask will fit, as had the clown's, and the real Fonda will disappear for a while.

∽

But this mask only magnifies him. Every actor has his limits, and no wish to transcend them will provide what technique and physique do not. Fonda's best work always emanates from his face and body; it seeps out, coalesces, *happens*. Everything about his Pierre, from shaggy black hairpiece to philosophical maunderings, is pasted on the surface. He will get better as the film progresses—will grow weary from the warlike grind of the four-month shoot, to arrive at a last defeat that looks real and has weight. But it is hardly a whole performance. In fact it's one of Henry's worst, in a film as large, extravagant, and trivial as international committee can contrive.

His mood is bad throughout the filming. "You understand, don't you," he asks the director, King Vidor, early on, as if in warning or challenge, "that I can be a real son of a bitch?" Having approved a first script by novelist Irwin Shaw, Henry finds his daily pages are a farrago of fiddlings imposed the night before by Vidor and his wife. De Laurentiis provides his star with a lavish hotel suite, personal driver, and Roman ransom of daily luxuries, but he refuses to let Fonda deglamorize Pierre: No fat suit on my Fonda, the Italian commands, and no glasses! Henry says he must wait for Dino to leave the set before slipping his specs back on; though assuming the producer ever looks at rushes, Pierre's glasses must be an agreed-upon thing, as Fonda peers through them owl-like for two-thirds of the picture.

Fonda, always ready to admit he has avoided seeing many of his own movies, will not bother himself to view this one. "If I'd seen it," Henry will say of *War and Peace* a year after its release, "I'm sure I would have to tell you that I was lousy."

The family, as usual, is left to its own devices. Jane and Peter find sundry adventures up and down the Appian Way, among romantic ruins and at embassy dinners; both claim to lose their virginity this Roman summer. But Susan is the wife, she has the baby, and she is stuck. Weeks go by; she and Henry see little of each other. Parts of the heart die every day.

"It was as if we were sort of passing each other on different levels, not really connecting," Susan will tell journalist Barry Norman two decades later. "He was a very self-sufficient person in terms of his work." Susan wants what most wives want—sustained intimacy—and Fonda has failed her, as many husbands fail their wives. He is an extraordinary success, and an ordinary failure.

She leaves. Like Frances, she must have that moment of realizing what her future with Fonda will be; but she is not so susceptible to despair. Susan is in some ways her predecessor's happier twin—a daughter of privilege, familiar with society and eager for experience, but lovingly raised and unburdened by self-hatred. Though hurt by Fonda's harshness, she is simply too healthy, and youthful, to be brought low by his neglect or his judgments.

She means to live a life, as long and happy a life as she deserves.

∽

She bids Henry good-bye and informs him she's returning to New York with the children. Whether or not he has the right to be, he is stricken. For the second time in their life together, Fonda weeps. He makes repeated transatlantic phone calls, pleading for reconsideration, but Susan, wiser and tougher than her age, holds firm and doesn't look back.

The separation will be officially announced in December; the following May, Susan, petitioning the court in Reno, Nevada, will be granted a divorce decree by District Judge A. J. Maestretti on a charge of "extreme mental cruelty"—a formulaic indictment, but probably not so far off the truth, although Fonda, through his attorney, will make a formulaic denial. Susan will be granted sole custody of Amy, but she will allow Henry generous visitation throughout the girl's childhood.

By the time the divorce is finalized, he will be in another place entirely. For now, he is stuck in Rome, shooting his scenes of slog and hunger, in his off-hours haunting art galleries and corner cafés, perfectly alone and miserable with it.

We might call that irony, or an apt turning of tables. But failure is not villainy: Without evil intent, Fonda has again gotten himself in a foolish position, an impossible relationship. Susan has problems with Henry's stinginess and denial of intimacy, but for him, the marriage is cracked in another way. Whatever happens between them, he will feel shame: if the marriage continues, the shame of the age difference; if it ends, the shame of being a three-time loser.

But for every door that closes, a window opens; and who knows how many brightly feathered birds fly through Fonda's open window in these weeks? Rome, like all large cities, is also a small town—as well as cradle of the paparazzi. So Henry's sudden singleness is well known, and he becomes the subject of more gawking and gossiping than he's known since before he married Frances. He commiserates nonphysically with Audrey Hepburn (who is having her own troubles with husband Mel Ferrer), and is said to have a brief affair with his other female costar, Anita Ekberg, at this moment one of the world's most desirable women. He is spotted solo at the Venice Film Festival. Though Walter Winchell transmits Fonda's denial of a split with Susan, the Broadway blabbermouth also reports Henry "laughing" with Italian starlet Loren Pastini.

Our man is in a highly public sulk—yet so poised in his woundedness, so long and fine in a tuxedo, that he can't help but make sulkiness alluring. Among the rare birds who flock about him, pecking crumbs of intrigue, is a twenty-four-year-old baroness named Afdera Franchetti.

Her looks suggest a hot-blooded European version of Susan Blanchard, with a similar knowing cast to the eyes, a tease on the lips. According to her, she and Henry meet at a dinner party, where she tempts him with persistent requests for condiments and side dishes. The symbolism is fit for a novel: She salts his open wound, peppers his curiosity, promises a generous appetite and challenges his ability to meet it. She fancies his elegance and separateness. "There was something pure and sensitive about him," Afdera offers in her ghostwritten memoir. "His eyes were very blue, cool and detached. He looked untouched and untouchable."

Fonda is taken by her gaze, her insouciance, and perhaps the transparency of her flirtations. Maybe his real connection with Afdera is beneath his consciousness, somewhere in the viscera. She writes of a feeling that is "barbaric and primeval—the hot blood of my ancestors": perhaps she awakens some of Fonda's ethnic corpuscles? He is of Italian descent, too, after all. Rome is called the Eternal City; and some would say the Latin trace, once in the bloodstream, never leaves it.

∽

Afdera and Henry edge into a platonic affair, appearing as companions at parties and galleries, enjoying the conspiratorial humor of "friends" who know they are tempting themselves and each other. But even to pursue friendship is risky for these two in a land where manly saber rattling is still a way of life. Fonda is not officially separated, let alone divorced, and Afdera is publicly affianced to Augusto Torlonia—Italy's so-called "Lord of Earth," a pistol-toting duke who in 1949 has survived an assassination attempt by a shepherd employed on one of his many estates.

Afdera combines the flexible morality of the international set with the resilience of the peasant, and she has the face of a sophisticated cherub whose smile is animated by centuries of violence and decadence. The Franchettis exist in the middle echelons of old-world nobility, a lineage of minor counts and consorts, existing on money from ancient bequests. Their bloodlines connect them to a legendary Europe of curses, palaces, plots; their kind—some call it aristocracy; others, like Peter Fonda, call it "Eurotrash"—are accustomed to privilege, to scandal, to upheaval. They take nothing overly seriously, least of all pain. Afdera in particular rejects gloom absolutely.

But Franchetti history may leave her no other choice. Her father, a friend of Mussolini and famed explorer of North Africa (Afdera is the name of a live Ethiopian volcano), was killed in a plane crash when his daughter was three—the result, according to rumors, of a bomb planted by a prewar provocateur. The war years were desolating for the family. After the Fascist takeover, the Franchetti palazzo on Venice's Grand Canal was occupied by the Nazis; later, it was liberated—that is, reoccupied—by the Americans. Afdera's beloved older sister, a nurse afflicted with tuberculosis, survived a hospital bombing but was left with shattered nerves and anorexia, and died an early death. Her mother, a delicate case, succumbed to depression and hysteria. A wasting illness will bring her demise not long after Fonda has entered the picture.

The Franchettis have internalized the emotional extremes of an extravagant history. Rape and domination are the way of the world, love and brutality complementary flavors in the sauce of life. Afdera's father proposed to her mother by submerging her head in a canal until she said yes. A generation later, Afdera will be beaten by her brutish brother after he learns she has chosen Fonda over the titled Torlonia. She doesn't bother forgiving such acts, because they are not considered real offenses: The baroness respects physical violence as the sign of a masterful male.

She is impossible. There's clearly more to her than that, yet she lives and thrives by such games. You want to shake her. Then you see that cherubic smile spreading, asking for the back of your hand, and you realize how complex is the psychology of a woman taught to hold what she has, and gather more, by getting men to hit her.

On the surface, there's little to the baroness but looks, high blood, and joi de vivre; but, using them to the full, she makes her impression. Afdera's may be one of the many gamine faces and footloose spirits that go into creating the character of Holly Golightly in *Breakfast at Tiffany*'s, which her friend Truman Capote is writing during the Fonda years. She was a teenage idolator of Ernest Hemingway, of whom her brother is a close friend; when *Across the River and into the Trees* was published in 1950, it was speculated (mainly by Afdera) that she had inspired the novel's young Italian heroine. Even before Fonda appeared, Afdera had splashed in many fountains, pursued many adventures, known many nights when it must have seemed the stars shone for her alone.

To Henry she is something new, and most unlike any of his previous wives: She lacks Sullavan's histrionics, Frances's depression, and Susan's emotional expectations. Asked in later years to sum up the woman who will be his fourth wife, phrasemaker Fonda will simply say, "She's a character." Which is middle western code for *She's crazy.*

After the filming of *War and Peace* ends, the two share a tour of Venice. Henry invites Afdera back to New York; Afdera's fiancé, inexplicably unaware of her interest in Fonda, consents to this final spurt of premarital freedom. In New York, she stays at a hotel, rather than at Fonda's new, recently purchased residence—an elegant four-story town house on East Seventy-fourth Street, off Lexington Avenue. But word of the relationship travels fast, as she knows it will. With maximum dexterity and minimum personal unpleasantness, Afdera has forced the duke's hand: In a rage heard across Rome, he severs the engagement.

Plainly, she knows the fine Italian art of subterfuge. Henry's complicity in all of this is unknown.

∞

It is near Christmastime, 1955. Fonda is already shooting his next film, *The Wrong Man,* a crime drama directed by Alfred Hitchcock, on locations in Manhattan and Queens. Afdera returns to Rome—says she finds the film "sad and boring."

She would. Her aversion to *The Wrong Man* is as comprehensible as Henry's interest in it. The picture has nothing to do with the Fonda of the breezy, charming Roman affair, and everything to do with the man obsessed by the memory of his dead wife.

8

The Wrong Man

12 Angry Men

In late 1947, Fonda traveled to New York to interest Josh Logan in a film project. Instead, Logan introduced him to Tom Heggen and *Mister Roberts,* and the project was sidelined.

It was to have been a film of John O'Hara's *Appointment in Samarra*. Published in 1934, the novel is set in the fictional Gibbsville, Pennsylvania, among the upper middle classes. It follows Julian English, a self-loathing drunk and eventual suicide, and his downfall over a four-day period. The tragedy is Julian's inability to evade his doom, or himself—hence the title, with its metaphor of fate derived from an Arabic folktale.

Henry Fonda had met and become friendly with O'Hara just before World War II. He'd induced O'Hara to write a screenplay adaptation of *Appointment,* and around the same time, the novelist was credited as a contributor of "original material" to the Fonda-Stewart segment of *On Our Merry Way.* In a September 1948 *Saturday Review of Literature* article, Fonda cited *Appointment* as being among his current reading.

The film was never made—partly because *Roberts* intervened, partly because no studio at that time would have financed the straight filming of such a downbeat narrative. The novel is candid about sex, adultery, the ethnic hatreds of suburban enclaves, and all manner of dirty games. How could postwar Hollywood have made a decent movie of it? But O'Hara continued to hope. In 1963, he bemoaned the difficulty of casting an ideal Julian, saying he would have preferred Fonda "in the old days"; two years later, he is staunchly insisting, against studio pressure, on retaining the suicide ending. The project was an object of interest as late as 1969, with Paul Newman the likeliest star.

Fonda had to know that the novel would never reach the screen uncompromised. Yet something in his more than forty-year-old body would not surrender the prospect of playing a not yet thirty-year-old wastrel, the crumbling center of a story whose dramatic arrangement is to foreclose hope on a suicide. Would not surrender it, anyway, until *Mister Roberts* came along—the story of another death wish, with the advantages of being both commercial and a stage play, and therefore a way of escaping home and Hollywood.

Fonda had already demonstrated his interest in the theme of self-destruction. Surely he felt he knew something about Julian English, and that Julian knew something about him. The character's complex combines guilt, a loathing of domesticity, and an overwhelming awareness of his own weakness. Fonda's interest came at the time when life with Frances had passed its point of no return; perhaps he hoped, by making the movie, to divert some disaster of his own. Or maybe he wanted the opposite—to risk a crack-up of art and life.

Fonda's interest in the O'Hara novel suggests many possibilities. What is not possible is that the role of Julian English meant nothing special to him—that in pursuing the character he was not pursuing another specter, another version of himself.

∽

The more phantasmal Frances becomes, the more she emerges as the most urgent and interesting presence in Henry's work. She haunts *The*

Wrong Man—though Hitchcock would bristle at any suggestion that the film might be as personal for Fonda as it is for himself.

Hitchcock first sought Henry to star in the 1940 *Foreign Correspondent,* and again two years later in *Saboteur,* but the teaming has had to wait for its perfect moment. Based on fact, *The Wrong Man* revisits Hitchcock's favored scenario of the innocent man implicated by circumstance, while the hero is another of Fonda's dogged sufferers. The source is Herbert Brean's 1953 report, published in *Life* magazine, of a real case. Christopher Emanuel "Manny" Balestrero, bass player in the house band at the Stork Club, is charged with the armed robbery of an insurance office, jailed, and tried. As he is fed through the system, his wife, Rose, shrinks to a state of near catatonia. Exoneration comes only by a fluke: The robber is caught committing another crime. But the wife, so far as we see, gets no better.

As a Hitchcock film, *The Wrong Man* has clear themes—the randomness of fate, the fragility of identity—and a clear failure. The first half, recounting Manny's arrest and imprisonment, is quiet, objective, and paced with "the somnambulistic quality of a bad dream," as Brean described the real Balestrero's experience. A break occurs when Manny is released on bail and focus shifts to his wife, from Manny's martyrdom to Rose's depression. Hitchcock reckoned this a misjudgment, and undeniably, a certain tension is lost in the break.

But as a Fonda film, *The Wrong Man* has a different unity. The shift becomes Manny's—the transfer of his anxiety from himself to his wife. The film's "personal" element passes from Hitchcock to Fonda, our focus from the director's passive observation to the character's encounter with his wife's depression.

What actor and director share is a fascination with watching: the robbery victims who identify Manny from sheltering darkness; the gawks of his children, prosecutors, jurors; and finally, Manny's own helpless regard of Rose's decline. But where Hitchcock is fascinated by the power of the gaze to instill fear, Fonda demonstrates the limits of witnessing as an instrument of empathy. His great screen characters have been men who act because they see. But although the Catholic Manny trusts in redemption, he can do nothing to help his wife. Witnesses in this story have the power to judge, but not to understand; to condemn, but not to save.

Probed for Fonda's fixations rather than Hitchcock's, *The Wrong Man* reveals a new logic. Its first half is unified because it posits a problem with a solution. The second half, dominated by the wife's melancholia, offers no solution. Without it, there is neither hope nor drama, only decay. In Hitchcock's terms, the film fails because it has strayed from a resolvable crisis to an irresolvable one; but in Fonda's terms, this parallels the hero's inability to save his wife.

A key scene is Manny's meeting with Rose's psychiatrist. The doctor suggests she belongs in a place that will give her the treatment she needs. "You mean an institution?" Manny asks. The shot is medium close on Fonda as he stares away from the doctor, who speaks of the "maze of terror" in which Rose is caught. All that he says applies to Frances:

"She's living in another world from ours . . . a frightening landscape that could be on the dark side of the moon."

"And I'm not there?"

"You're there. And the children are there. But not the way you *are*. Monstrous shadows that say hateful things. Now she knows that she's in a nightmare, but it doesn't help her to know. She can't get out."

"Is it incurable?"

"No case is incurable."

Art is not imitating life here; it is cutting life open. Can Henry be thinking of anything but the day, some seven years earlier, when he and Dr. Knight agreed to commit Frances to the sanitarium where she ended her life?

Fonda's gift for vibrant understatement allows him to center Hitchcock's bold visual ideas while being as self-effacing as a screen star can be. Manny is repeatedly defined as the passive center of an oppressing frame; to anchor the film, Fonda must show subtleties of fear in the face of a man almost too scared to breathe.

So the most memorable images are silent: an extreme close-up through the slot in a cell door, Fonda's face hidden but for his desperate eyes; Manny's lips moving in prayer as a dissolve melds his face with that of the criminal. In an amazing scene, Manny falls back against the cell wall, and the camera swirls as the shadows of the bars thicken and darken. This predicts both the horrified dream states of *Vertigo* and the shower drain of *Psycho*. It is an overflow of panic, with Fonda's face perfectly, passively expressive of a man surrendering himself to fate, as a martyr to flames.

The film ends on a pathetic encounter in the sanitarium, Manny walking out of Rose's room and down a dark corridor—a shot to be repeated in *Vertigo*. Music rises to drown the desolation and carry us to the closing image of a faceless family strolling beneath palm trees: The Balestreros, end titles tell us, made it through, and now live happily in Florida. It's a Hitchcock trademark to linger on human wreckage before insisting at the close that everything has come right. But Fonda and Hitchcock have gone too far into their fears, separate and shared, to make credible such a simple happiness.

∽

The Fondas vacation in Kennedy country—Hyannisport, Massachusetts—over the summer of 1956. Afdera visits Henry there; she also meets Jane and Peter for the first time, and their mutual disdain is immediate.

But Henry and his new lover have found a level of amusement. Each distracts the other from the deeper, uglier stuff of life. If their decision to marry has the almost ironic quality of an accession to entertainments that will not last, that doesn't belittle it: Nothing could be more human than the shared desire of two scarred people to be entertained for a while.

On March 10, 1957, they are married in the library of the Fonda town house. Seventeen-year-old Peter is best man, and Afdera's eyes are still puffy from the beating administered by her brother. (Later, she will go to the macabre length of scissoring her eyes—only her eyes—from every wedding photograph.) The newlyweds spend a brief, flu-ridden honeymoon in a Canadian chalet, followed by a few weeks in Hollywood. The summer is spent in a villa on the Mediterranean: The avowed purpose is a second honeymoon, but Jane, Peter, and assorted friends accrue over the weeks. Henry and the baroness attend the Cannes Film Festival, socialize with Garbo, Hemingway, Picasso, and Cocteau, and witness the running of the bulls in Pamplona.

As Henry's soul seeks resolution and his face perfects the arts of despair in *The Wrong Man,* he publicly acts out a version of *la dolce vita*—tags along as Afdera gathers glamour, plans parties, and redecorates the town house (she likens it to "a dentist's waiting room, or the Hilton, Nebraska, circa 1950"). Henry spends many hours alone, reading novels and scripts, doing yoga, painting. (It's in these years that his realistic oil studies of objects and textures begin to attract serious demand among friends and collectors.) But mostly their married life is a welter of soirees and events, villas and yachts, comings and goings; the town house is home base, but effectively there is no home. (Peter calls this the Fondas' "renting period.") It is all financed by a diverse and almost unbelievably constant stream of product from Henry.

We wonder how he tolerates the pace, but the truth is that he demands it: Too much leisure means indolence, and indolence is sin. Look at the amount of business logged merely in the months between Hyannisport and the wedding:

In early summer 1956, Fonda acquires film rights to Reginald Rose's teleplay *Twelve Angry Men,* and forms a company, Orion Productions, to make it; he and Sidney Lumet—a young television director making his first film—shoot it in a West Fifty-fourth Street studio over three weeks, while Henry commutes to and from Hyannisport. In the autumn, he is in Hollywood filming a Western, *The Tin Star,* and stumping for presidential candidate Adlai Stevenson. After, he flies to Florida with Alfred Hitchcock, meets the Balestreros, and films the closing of *The Wrong Man.* He then signs for a part in *Stage Struck,* a drama directed by Lumet, and continues planning for the film version of *Clown.* After the turn of 1957, he does publicity for *12 Angry Men* and shoots his *Stage Struck* scenes. Throughout, he is a harried father taking calls from Peter's headmaster, and a frequent flier to assignations with the baroness.

"Medics are warning Henry Fonda to take it easy," writes columnist and old friend Erskine Johnson in the midst of it all.

But it's the schedule Henry will maintain for the next several years: months in New York, doing plays; months in Hollywood, making movies; days and weeks between taping TV shows, voice-overs, promo inserts, and sundry one-offs. He is as industrious as a honeybee, constructing a hivelike world out of work. Afdera admits to a lack of ambition ("Each achievement is just another enslavement that drives you on to achieve the next thing"), but as a voyager in her own life, she doesn't lack guts. For Henry, work remains less an adventure than a way of staying involved with his past, his memories, himself—of staying troubled by what troubles him.

Life, meanwhile, is the diversionary *now* of travel and temporary homes, contracts and children's crises, ordering and managing the far-flung components of a wealthy and celebrated life.

∽

He stays solvent by pinching pennies, taking good advice, being realistic. He has lucrative investment stakes all over the place—in Broadway shows (not only his own but others', like *South Pacific*); in Southwest Airways (cofounded by Leland Hayward in 1941, it will become Pacific Air before merging with larger carriers); in Oklahoma oil. His entry into television, as both actor and product pitchman, has been immediately and conspicuously remunerative.

And it had been announced in early 1955 that he had—like other top stars in this new era, pressured by TV and freed by the breakdown of studio oligarchy—signed an independent production deal. Rather than limit himself to what is offered, he will pursue and develop projects on his own behalf, and distribute them through United Artists. The agreement pays him handsomely to make six pictures over three years, starring in at least three of them.

It's also with commerce in mind that Henry makes his "comeback" as a cowboy. On television, the late 1950s are ruled by the likes of *Gunsmoke, Wagon Train, Maverick;* at the cinema, by the horse operas of Ford, Hawks, Mann, Boetticher, and Sturges. It is the Western's commercial if not artistic, peak and Henry sees where he fits: too old to play a classic cowboy, just right to play the cowboy's mentor, or a good-bad man on the far side of his prime.

In Anthony Mann's *The Tin Star* (1957), he is a bounty hunter teaching the rudiments of six-gun morality to greenhorn sheriff Tony Perkins. Mann directs to listless formula, and Fonda matches him in projecting an authority as boring as it is convincing. Nearly as inert is *Warlock* (1959), with Henry as a marshal for hire shielding a fledgling township from marauders. The most compelling element is Fonda's Clay Blaisdell, a man with substance, soul, and a capacity for betrayal. Henry, vests and guns glittering, looks great and gives the character coherence; the whole might have worked, had it a director who knew actors, who knew how to cut and frame on the human pulse—like John Ford. Instead it has Edward Dmytryk.

In early 1957, Fonda is quoted to the effect that he will never star in a TV series. Two years later, he agrees to star in one, and it's a Western. *The Deputy* is one of the most frankly mercenary moves of our man's career. Propositioned by cocreators Roland Kibbee and Norman Lear, Fonda doubts that the bullet-riddled TV schedule can stand another Western. But he is persuaded, he says, that such a commodity will enable him to "save a dollar . . . And I could use a saved dollar." His representatives devise the most lucrative, least strenuous arrangement: He will star in only six of the initial thirty-nine episodes, while contributing walk-ons to the remainder. A makeshift production entity, Top Gun, is established to collect his end of the profits.

Henry's Simon Fry is "Chief Marshal of the Arizona Territory" and mentor to the deputy of the title, played by Allen Case—a young actor of blinding ordinariness, supposedly handpicked by the star himself. Henry is so forthright about being in it for the money that by the time *The Deputy* premieres on NBC on September 12, 1959, the press is virtually scornful of the enterprise. TV critic John Crosby declares that the opening shots of bandits heisting a train "looked so startlingly like *The Great Train Robbery,* the very first movie ever made, that I thought the industry had been set back about eighty years."

While not the worst TV series to carry Fonda's name—that is still years off—*The Deputy* is barely passable as overnight fodder for rerun insomniacs. The plots are inane, the acting adequate to rotten, the sets slapped up. Henry walks through without sweat or other human juice. "I guess he doesn't plan to kill himself with overwork," Crosby mutters.

The show exists for two seasons, has a brief life in syndication, and disappears up its own vacuum. But in the diversionary now, it is making money and doing its job. Surely Fonda, having just produced and starred in a film that received great reviews, international awards, and an Oscar nod, can taste the irony. That film, *12 Angry Men,* has been acclaimed, yet it sold scarcely enough tickets to fill a bread box; *The Deputy* is recognized as an emptiness, yet it wins ratings and renewal. Fonda labors on the former, and makes a dime; moseys through the latter, and makes a mint.

MCA Television and Top Gun squeeze a small fortune from *The Deputy.* The Western genre is left a bit more depleted, the irony is swallowed, and the dollar is saved.

∽

Of the four plays Fonda stars in between 1958 and 1962, only one—Ira Levin's *Critic's Choice*—is an obvious concession to the diversionary now of money and profile: light comedy, with Henry playing the unlikely combination of powerful theater reviewer and desirable husband-stud, all-around right man. The others place him as the wrong man in a sad situation—confused, angry, depressed, dying—and pull him toward the ending and exorcism of these years.

In spring 1957, Fonda is sent *Two for the Seesaw,* the first play by William Gibson, a novelist (*The Cobweb*) and TV playwright (*The Miracle Worker*) of growing reputation. It observes the brief love affair between two lonesome New Yorkers: Jerry Ryan, an uprooted Omaha lawyer, and Gittel Mosca, a dancer from the Bronx. Taciturn Jerry has fled smothering marriage to a wife who is undergoing a breakdown; tempestuous Gittel has an ulcer and abandonment issues. They are the sole characters.

None of the other principals has any Broadway experience. Producer Fred Coe is a past colleague of Henry's, having put *The Petrified Forest* on TV two years earlier. Director Arthur Penn is a graduate of the Actors Studio and veteran of television, whose first film, *The Left-Handed Gun,* is in the can but as yet unreleased. Anne Bancroft, playing Gittel, is a Method adherent and unknown of twenty-six who has spent a few years on the Hollywood margins; *Seesaw* will be the Broadway debut of the woman soon to become, and remain for several years—until she is supplanted by Jane Fonda—the best actress in American movies.

Fonda stalls on a commitment: Jerry, he feels, is "underwritten." In mid-June, a reading is held at East Seventy-fourth Street. Henry is charmed by Bancroft, wooed by Coe and Penn, troubled and tantalized by Jerry's unyielding character. After he leaves with Afdera for their Mediterranean summer, Gibson dispatches rewrites from the States.

Henry is drawn in. He needs a play for the winter, and perhaps he feels challenged by these Actors Studio upstarts, with their emphasis on self-analysis as the key to truth. And the play itself—there's something irresistibly right and inexpressibly wrong with it. It has a flaw and a flavor, a quality and a lack, *something* Fonda must try to master. Despite his doubts, he sends a cable from Europe: "Start it rolling. I am yours." There's grim resignation in the tone, yet upon his acceptance, the eighty-thousand-dollar budget magically appears—a quarter of it Fonda's own money.

Though Gibson comes to believe Henry is miscast as Jerry, in reality the match is too perfect. Actor and character share Omaha origins, emotional limitations, unstable wives, and rageful habits. The problem with the text, everyone agrees, is an imbalance in intensity and sympathy between the characters: Gittel has humor and passion, while Jerry comes across as vague and truculent. She has desires; he has moods.

Playing such an unattractive version of himself ties Henry in knots. He will engage in verbal and even physical confrontation with Coe and Penn, but mostly, his anger will focus on the playwright. William Gibson has read his star too well. Despite the fact that he, like Tom Heggen, has not met Henry before, his intuitions have discerned Fonda's type in other men; but where Heggen sculpted the hero, Gibson has drawn the bastard.

Has Henry taken the role to get closer to parts of himself, only to reconsider because they are the most unsavory parts? Does he condemn the playwright for failing to redeem his weaknesses, to deliver the actor from himself? Gibson, it seems to Henry, has left him dangling from a public scaffold constructed of his own worst traits.

His discomfort may run even deeper. The playwright's wife happens to be Dr. Margaret Brenman-Gibson, a psychoanalyst at Austen Riggs during Frances Fonda's stay there, and a close colleague of her doctor, Robert P. Knight.* In *The Seesaw Log* (1959), his diary of the play's production, Gibson mentions neither his wife's professional identity nor Fonda's past connection with Riggs; it seems doubtful they ever discussed the one thing besides the play they had in common. But when Henry meets Dr. Brenman-Gibson, he is conspicuously ungracious.

Throughout November rehearsals, Gibson rewrites, and rewrites. Up to the opening, the play is in flux. Henry likes Bancroft, but their aesthetics are at odds: As actress and director discuss motivation, Fonda sits watching, Gibson writes, "with a fixed tolerant smile . . . a stony witness." Asked to improvise with Bancroft, a bemused Henry simply declines.

Gradually, he isolates himself from the cast and crew; he and Gibson cease to speak; his performances grow erratic. The play has its first preview on December 5 in Washington, D.C. The AP correspondent gives Bancroft high marks for "zest and fine realism," but Fonda "doesn't reach any great dramatic peaks." Subsequently, at a rehearsal in Philadelphia, Fonda and Coe come close to blows. The mood is so dark that a nauseous Bancroft must be tended by a doctor.

Finally, they open on Broadway, at the Booth Theatre on January 16, 1958. Before the curtain, Gibson appears at Fonda's door to wish

---

* Gibson's novel *The Cobweb* is set in a thinly veiled version of the Menninger Clinic in Kansas, where both his wife and Knight had worked.

him luck—and the star nearly loses control, shouting at the playwright to get out. He tells Gibson he feels let down, set adrift, abandoned. Their relationship is finished. For Gibson, the tirade caps what he calls "the most odious experience of my life."

In spite of all this, the show works. The audience is piqued by the cold-water realism of George Jenkins's tenement-flat set, and the ambient street sounds heard over the scene changes. The play has a feel of the city and eight million hidden lives; the mood is one of hard-earned intimacy between man and woman, actor and actress. Bancroft receives superlatives (Walter Winchell announces "the birth of a star . . . Broadway's newest Miss Radiance"), while Fonda throws off such magnetism that he cannot help but win his audience even while playing a son of a bitch.

Yet the play's success leaves Henry feeling a fraud. Convinced Gibson has failed him, he may secretly know he has failed himself. It has been his job to humanize Jerry Ryan, but he has not been able to believe in the man's decency—that is, his own—enough to do so. Feeling broken on the rocks of his own limitations, he has raged at others for not setting him free.

Still the audience cheers. *Seesaw* will spend almost two years on Broadway, tour America's regional theaters, become a popular summer-stock property, be made into a drab film version, and finally return to Broadway as a musical. Fonda the investor will reap many returns from the play before selling his quarter share at what is reported to be a 300 percent profit. But Fonda the actor will leave exactly six months after opening night—the swiftest escape his contract allows.

∽

The antidote to bitter success in cold Manhattan is California breeze. The summer of 1958 is spent on the Malibu beach with Afdera and the kids. Fonda then lingers in Hollywood for the remainder of the year, making movie deals, cropping his charisma to fit fluff. Though he told Paris reporters a year earlier that he "can't stomach Hollywood," he knows his commercial viability, and hence his lifestyle, will not be sustained by two-character dramas at the Booth Theatre.

He signs for *The Deputy,* shoots *Warlock* in Hollywood and Utah, and, after a Christmas in New York with Jane and Peter, returns for a romantic comedy called *The Man Who Understood Women.* This negligible item places Fonda next to hot international star Leslie Caron in the story of a starlet and a "genius" movie producer. Henry's performance is impressively committed, if only to the consequence of nothing, while the film itself is stupefying—as scattershot as a riot, as indiscriminately colorful as a vomiting of jelly beans, yet supremely dull.

Coming through Roberts, Greenwald, Pierre, Manny, and Jerry, Fonda has become rather a connoisseur of misery. To engage him these days, a part must tap into his sense of pain, not pleasure, and it will be a while before he can begin to be convincingly loose and funny again. For now, all of his caring, and all of his neuroses, are poured into the deep black funnel of the theater. His collaborative tempers have been getting shorter, his creative nerves rawer; being "uncompromising" has meant imposing his will and enforcing his interpretations.

This obsession with control has acted as cover and compensation for a deeper one. Henry's goal onstage in this decade has been to examine states of helplessness and melancholy, to delve into depression and death. His concurrent screen work has mostly incarnated solidity, self-determination; but his stage tendency is toward a portrayal of total vulnerability, a final baring of psyche and skin.

∽

In the fall of 1959, back in New York, rehearsals begin for another play: a minor work, but a major move toward the secret themes. Robert Anderson's *Silent Night, Lonely Night* is a talk-driven piece about two married people sharing Christmas night at a New England inn. The woman is mulling a separation from her absent husband; Henry's character, John Sparrow, is visiting his wife at a nearby asylum, where she has been driven by his philandering. The two converse through a long night and into the day; dust settles as the actors drift across a cozy, antiquey set.

Despite its humanistic decency, the play is as meager as an episode of *The Deputy.* Costarring Barbara Bel Geddes and directed by Peter

Glenville, *Silent Night* proves uncommercial because of its air of defeat, but that doesn't mean it isn't trying to be liked. "I'm so sorry" is a dialogue motif; another is "That's so sad." And it has a fashionable fix on alienation, which forces Fonda to twist himself under lines like this: "I imagine if we could hear all the stifled cries for help in the world, it would be deafening."

Opening at the Morosco Theatre on December 3, *Silent Night* is welcomed as enthusiastically as a sick aunt. Brooks Atkinson calls it "excessively verbose" and "uneventful," and regrets the "slow, ruminative pace" of Glenville's staging. Even the odd defender, like Jack Gaver of UPI, offers only oblique praise: Fonda and Bel Geddes, he feels, are so good "that I find this talky, almost motionless drama of loneliness an appealing entertainment. Certainly it is a play that could be deadly in the wrong hands."

The broader feeling is that any hands would have been the wrong ones. The show closes after three months and a solid 124 performances, but it goes in the books as a failure.

Fonda cannot have mistaken Anderson's play for dynamic theater. What interests him is the chance for performing therapy—getting closer to personal mysteries in the costume of a character hauntingly similar to himself. Like *Seesaw*, *Silent Night* is about a married man alone with a woman, a man whose depressive wife suffers offstage. But where Jerry Ryan is controlling and selfish, John Sparrow is kindly and sympathetic, attributing his own sexual and emotional betrayals not to hedonism or narcissism, but to the higher syndrome of alienation.

Adultery, asylums, depression, suicide—not one of Henry's Frances-related preoccupations goes unreferenced. The unseen spouse is a kind of specter: Unwilling at first to admit her condition, Sparrow pretends she is dead. She is to the play what Frances has been to Henry's art in these years—the absent body, the open wound—and the play allows Fonda to fulfill a fantasy of happier endings: The despondent wife clings to life, and the husband's final resolve is to stay by her side, come what may.

Though *Silent Night, Lonely Night* will not make great profit, loft the art of the stage, or be remembered far beyond its season, from Fonda it is an offering, a Christmas gift to the ghost. Yet the gift is wrapped in sadness: There are limits on the ability of actors and other mortals to rewrite the past.

∽

These few months—late 1959 through early 1960—are a convergence point, at which the feminine planets in Fonda's orbit come into alignment. As rumors of discord with Afdera creep out, Henry goes onstage as John Sparrow to relive memories of the wife who died. On New Year's Day, a month into the run of *Silent Night,* Margaret Sullavan is found dead in New Haven. In February, Jane has her Broadway debut, and appears with beaming Dad on the cover of *Life.* And in these very weeks, Henry's newest movie will open in cinemas across America—*The Man Who Understood Women.*

The fourth marriage has begun to devolve from novelty to routine for two companions who feel lonesome in each other's company. The summer of 1960 is again spent in Hollywood, but Henry and Afdera are often at different parties. Both attend the Democratic National Convention, held in Los Angeles in July—nominee John F. Kennedy and his wife, Jackie, have been dinner guests at the Fonda town house—but their escapades are separate. The gaps between them widen. She enjoys entertaining; he does not. She is amused by her own immaturity; he is bored by it. Both play manipulative games, but the games have different rules.

The marriage is attenuated through the summer. When rehearsals begin in the fall for Fonda's compulsory wintertime play, the choice of material suggests compromise—with commerce, with comedy, with the careless and carefree view of life promoted by frivolous farce and aristocratic wives. *Critic's Choice* is the opposite of the "sad and boring" work that has lately taken Henry's attention; it is Henry trying to fit another man's dinner jacket.

If *Seesaw* evokes the volatility of the Sullavan marriage, and *Silent Night* the depression of the Frances years, *Critic's Choice*—which opens at the Ethel Barrymore Theatre on December 14—offers a likeness of

Afdera's Fonda: Hank the glamour boy, suave and socially adept. As a drama critic faced with reviewing his wife's saccharine play (a situation based on the marriage of *New York Herald Tribune* critic Walter Kerr and playwright Jean Kerr), Fonda indulges his middle-aged penchant for tiresomely sardonic types who speak in pronouncements. The play is staged by Otto Preminger, reuniting with Fonda thirteen years after *Daisy Kenyon,* and aspires vaguely to an air of old Hollywood screwball comedy—minus any wild strokes of genius.

Like everything Ira Levin writes, *Critic's Choice* is constructed with exceeding finesse: The thing makes sense. But it is fatally cute, with the stench of something too eager to be a hit. (Some of the stench may come from Preminger's gaseous backstage outbursts, which cause Gena Rowlands, the actress first cast as Fonda's romantic foil, to be replaced in previews.) Notices are tepid, and the show ends after five months and 189 performances: a hit, but far from a knockout.

On January 20, 1961, JFK is inaugurated in Washington, D.C. Henry cannot attend: *Critic's Choice* is sold out for a benefit that night. But Afdera is in Washington, and, making the rounds of parties, she experiences private moments with Prince Jack. These do not lead to intercourse, astonishingly, but to insight: The baroness, like many others her age and younger, gets the sense—as if passed telepathically through JFK's crinkly eyes and white teeth—that enormous changes are in the wind.

"I was discovering myself," she will recall in her memoir, sounding like a budding flower child. "I was too deeply affected by all the many changes that were taking place. I was in tune with the present." Whereas Henry, she comes to feel, is stodgy, close-minded, redolent of things past. "The 1960s were with us like a hungry lion, and everything I was feeling instinctively my husband was too old and too well-established to appreciate fully."

Who can be certain what she wants, other than to be a single girl again? Come to that, what has Afdera *ever* wanted with Fonda? She knows the true answer, and offers it frankly: He is "the father I never had." Her own father died before she knew him; growing up in a world of male privilege has taught the baroness that her power lies in cunning and manipulation. When Fonda appeared, she was twenty-four, yet essentially a child; a few years on, she has achieved a teenager's maturity, and found a teenager's sense of revolt. In time, like many aging postadolescents, she will look back with regret on the home she left, and wonder what leaving cost her.

"If it had been maybe ten years later," she muses, "I might have understood more and tried to work things out better and do what he wanted me to do." With such violence in her father's legacy, she may have been attracted to the aspect of Fonda that is parental and punitive. Afdera even claims Henry hit her—once, and only once. "Just the slightest of slaps," she swears, though he is overcome by remorse afterward. She admits she has goaded him to it, and that "if he had done it more often, I would have respected him more."

This is the same woman who decides that Fonda is too backward to meet the coming age. Yes, Afdera is impossible. What does she want—to be punished or pampered, caged or liberated?

When she requests a divorce, Fonda implores her, as he had implored Susan, to reconsider—again, less out of love than shame. The separation is announced on March 16, and hopeful Henry paints it as "completely friendly, a chance for us to work out certain problems in our marriage." But Afdera sounds wised-up, rueful, and ready to take the blame. "I can only reproach myself," she tells the press. "Hank is an admirable man. I guess I was too immature." Meaning, she has already moved on. Only a lover with the next adventure in sight can part so generously.

After obtaining a quickie divorce in Juárez, she flies back to Rome. Stoic Henry finishes out the contracted run of the Levin comedy.

Afdera will always have money, or find money; and since for her everything stems from lire and the accoutrements of the good life, she will always find a way to be happy. But she will remain torn between freedom and the cage. On July 31, 1966, she and a traveling companion, pop artist Mario Schifano, will be arrested at Rome's Fiumicino Airport for smuggling marijuana, a charge carrying a maximum penalty of eight years. Afdera, who will freely admit to carrying Schifano's stash, is not innocent of the illegality of the act, only of why it would matter to anyone. After three months, the sentence is suspended and a fine imposed, but Afdera spends the intervening time in jail.

But she will absorb the bad publicity, the distaste attaching to a glamour girl whose days in the spotlight, along with her youth, are fleeting. She'll move forward with the resilience of one born certain that life is a banquet, and that some courses will be finer and rarer than others.

∽

In September 1961, our man is back in Hollywood. *Critic's Choice* had its last curtain on May 27, and Fonda, accepting Preminger's offer of a plum part in his next big-budget screen controversy, *Advise and Consent,* has rented a Bel Air house for the months preceding initial shooting.

Save for the odd comely companion, Henry is alone in these weeks. But he cannot abide idleness, and so has chosen to squeeze himself into the crowded mural of *How the West Was Won,* an all-star Cinerama spectacular directed in relays by John Ford, Henry Hathaway, and George Marshall. Obscured by cocked hat and ropy mustache, Fonda plays a buffalo hunter and Indian scout in the segment done by Marshall—the only one of the three directors with whom he has no contentious history. It's a rich, leathery piece of acting in a film that, for all its bulging sense of land and space, is in no small measure a racist whitewash.

So it is September, and the old lots at Twentieth Century–Fox are being torn down for real estate development. How the West was won, phase two. Fonda strolls through the ghost towns with a journalist, taking in the half-demolished buildings and displaced facades. "I made my first picture, *Farmer Takes a Wife,* on one of those sets," he says—you can see him pointing. Here, he shot *Way Down East;* over there, *Young Mr. Lincoln* and the James brothers movies. The *Ox-Bow* and *Clementine* streets too are nearby.

"Now they're going," he says. "It's kinda sad."

Just a few weeks later, the hills between Brentwood and Bel Air will catch fire, and Tigertail will burn down to black ash and disperse in the Santa Ana winds.

Henry is nearing sixty. Time steals up on a man, and suddenly it is on his back. Though still straight and strong, each year he hunches a bit more with the weight of time. Another wife has come and gone, another half decade. Now whole continents of his past are vanishing; and part of that past—Frances—remains as a persistent sorrow. We imagine this as a point of reckoning; of putting memory to rest, and the mind at ease.

It will be done only through a part; only through work. Henry knows no other way. The parts have always found him, the great parts—Lincoln, Joad, Earp, Roberts, Balestrero—which he has needed as they have needed him. He has given the parts life, and they have allowed him to symbolize himself. And within each part, *the scene*: Abe at the graveside, Tom leaving the camp, Wyatt watching Doc, Roberts saying good-bye, Manny walking down the asylum hall. Each has been a statement of self as well as communion with another—a settling with obligation, a facing of ghosts, a farewell.

He needs another chance like that: a chance at an ending.

Hints of it turn up in Fonda's remarks, these latter months of 1961. Walking through the Fox lot, he allows he'd like to make more movies, perhaps get off the stage for a while. But something is stopping him. A new play has been offered, and its producer is telling Fonda it could be the greatest role he has ever played.

It will not prove to be quite that. But it will conceivably constitute "the greatest acting challenge of his career," as he will later call it. It will become a major project, a personal need. Henry will care about it as he has cared about little else lately.

And he would like to give us a sense of what is coming. Just before the end of the year, he announces he has agreed to do the play he'd been considering in September, and that it is "about a writer who kills himself."

∽

In late 1954, Charles Christian Wertenbaker—a novelist and journalist living with his wife and children in France—is given a few months to live: He has intestinal cancer. Rejecting hospitalization and life support, he chooses to spend his last days at home, suffering a hellish decline with the aid of black-market painkillers. Finally, at his limit of endurance, he opens his wrists with a shaving razor.

Lael Tucker Wertenbaker not only approves her husband's suicide but aids it. And then writes about it: Her nonfiction chronicle *Death of a Man* (1957) spares no detail of Wertenbaker's rapid and degrading demise. At the time, *euthanasia* is an unknown word, cancer goes unmentioned in obituaries, and Lael's book is not read easily. It is then forgotten by all but playwright Garson Kanin. Known for his comedies, particularly the stage and movie hit *Born Yesterday*, he has aspirations to drama; he reads Lael's book and is gripped by the need to put it on the stage.

His adaptation is titled *A Gift of Time*. William Hammerstein—Susan Blanchard's stepbrother—signs on as producer; it may be at his suggestion that Henry Fonda is asked to star. Good sense would tell our man to decline: He has numerous commitments pending, and the play is looking at a late start in the theatrical season. The sterner reality is its subject matter. Who will pay to witness a man's slow death from cancer?

It sounds unmanageable, or unwatchable. Kanin may be moved by the challenge of it, but Fonda has his own reasons to make the attempt. Together, they have the power to conceive and construct a show that wisdom says should not be done. Will they do it? Will they do it without flinching?

∽

Fonda's schedule is already backbreaking: ten days of location shooting in Washington, D.C., for *Advise and Consent;* the New York taping of *The Good Years,* a Lucille Ball TV special; the Hollywood taping of *Henry Fonda and the Family,* a Henry Fonda TV special; and a brief trip to Paris for a one-day cameo as Brig. Gen. Theodore Roosevelt, Jr., in *The Longest Day,* Darryl F. Zanuck's mammoth chronicle of the D-Day invasion. (A fat check and high-line exposure in the most heavily hyped war movie yet made can be Fonda's only motives for reuniting with Zanuck.)

Beyond these obligations, Fonda must not only schedule rehearsals and preview periods for *A Gift of Time*'s late-February opening but also make a research trip to Ciboure, the village on the Basque coast of France where the Wertenbakers lived. In November, Henry meets Lael in the company of his costar, Olivia de Havilland, who is making her comeback after long absences from screen and stage. They journey, she tells an interviewer, "to the radiologist's, into the waiting room and into the room where the X-rays were first shown . . . We went into all the rooms of the house where the Wertenbakers lived."

"We talked to Wertenbaker's doctor and some of his Basque friends," Fonda adds. "What strong faces they had."

It is unusually immersive, almost Method, the way Fonda stretches his body and abilities to play the dying man. He spends an hour a day studying the rudiments of classical guitar, which he'll play onstage. Already rail-thin, he fasts to drop more pounds.

Almost the entire burden of this risky, costly show rests on his shoulders. Aside from de Havilland, there are no stars. The production requires a large cast and technical management on a level usually reserved for musicals. Kanin envisions a montage approach, with scenes ranging from several spaces in the Wertenbaker home to cafés, doctors' offices, a hospital room, even the deck of a transatlantic liner. Boris Aronson's tripartite set offers multiple centers of action, each with its own props, furniture, and lighting cues; often all three are active at once, with scenes overlapping.

The rush to opening is intense, the physical stress on Fonda terrific. It's unlikely that he has ever given himself so completely and recklessly to a role.

It culminates January 27, 1962, when *A Gift of Time* begins previews at the Shubert in New Haven. The stars are rewarded with curtain calls and roses, but in truth, people have been turned off. A playgoer sends an angry note to the *New York Times,* expressing outrage "that the theatre should concern itself with so unpleasant and painful a subject." The review in the *Bridgeport Post* augurs the notices to come: The actors are fine, the play simply too much—ten scenes over two acts "is a long time to watch a man creep constantly nearer the grave."

The Broadway opening comes February 22, at the Ethel Barrymore. Word has traveled from New Haven that the show is a downer. Ticket demand is so low that the producers have been unable to sell a single "party" block of seats in advance—unheard of for a Fonda play.

∽

On March 11, Fonda and de Havilland appear on *The Ed Sullivan Show*, performing a scene in which the Wertenbakers return to Europe by ship. Cancer being unmentionable on TV, Sullivan's setup says only that the hero "faces death from an incurable malady." Based on this clip, the play looks maudlin—dialogue precious, acting stagy in the worst way. Olivia de Havilland basks in her own nobility, and Fonda affects a gruff, scratchy voice, a force that comes across as boorishness.

The televised scene ends on a kiss. On the Barrymore stage, though, it continues—and turns abuptly into something quite different.

"Lael!" Charles shouts from his deck chair. "Oh, Jesus."

Terrified, he asks his wife to cover him with a blanket. They leave the deck (*lights down, stage right*) and arrive in their cabin (*lights up, stage left*). Charles stumbles into the bathroom, ordering Lael not to follow. An abscess has burst in his colon, and he is leaking blood and feces from an unhealed surgical incision. In a scene that suggests bedroom farce re-cast as biological nightmare, Lael races about in search of sanitary nap-kins. As she bandages her husband's reeking wound with a belt of Kotex, the couple's mad laughter is heard from offstage.

Interludes of humor and sentiment become fewer as the disease spreads and the end approaches. Charles says good-bye to a friend, then fumbles down some pills and passes out; demented with pain and medi-cation, he abuses his wife. Fonda's form grows wispier, the stage darker.

Lael had described her husband's suicide in excruciating detail—a hurried swallowing of pills; injections of morphine into the leg; finally, the drawing of a razor across each wrist, the ebbing of blood, the dying embrace suggestive of a pietá. The stage rendition is faithful to the extremity of the scene. "I love you, I love you," Lael whispers, holding Charles, "please die."

A cut and bleeding corpse, a survivor asking release; after that, silence, and a black stage. The thing is finally done: Henry Fonda has committed suicide before his audience.

Henry's press agent, John Springer, says the Barrymore first-nighters are "stunned," and he remembers Paul Newman backstage, extolling "the God damnedest, greatest performance I've ever seen." Certainly, many are stunned because they are moved. But they are also stunned that such an ordeal should ever have been staged.

Critics too are uncertain. Richard Watts, Jr., of the *New York Post* finds it "one of the most depressing plays ever written." Howard Taubman of the *Times* writes that the play "does not achieve tragic dimension." "Strangely unmoving and dramatically slack," says *Time*. Famed stage director Harold Clurman, reviewing for *The Nation*, calls Fonda "the best thing in the play as it now stands" but says the characters are "ciphers . . . pegs for pathos." In the *Herald Tribune*, Walter Kerr likewise appreciates the star's "plain, unblinking, straightforward and unbelievably controlled" performance. But the play fails by outweighing fiction with realism: "The real thing has usurped the place of the ritualized thing, the drama of death has given way to the presence of death."

The show is officially not a hit. Lights go out for good on May 12, after ninety-two performances. Anything longer might have proved unendurable for the stars: Fonda has continued to lose weight after the opening, and de Havilland is rumored to be covered with bruises. Briefly, and improbably, a film version is rumored—to be co-produced by Kanin and Fonda and shot over the summer of 1962, on French locations, with both stars repeating their roles. But the rumor stays a rumor.

The Ethel Barrymore Theatre seats barely a thousand people—which means that far more viewers have watched *The Deputy* on any given Saturday night than have seen *A Gift of Time* during its entire run. To

Fonda, that is probably just as well; his labor in this play has been a private act of empathy and remembering. He has done it for Frances, and for himself—not for the public, and not for history.

He has staged a proper ending. It is important that the ending be witnessed, and just as important that it be hidden: presence as absence. In *You Only Live Once,* he hides his hands; in *The Grapes of Wrath,* he turns his back; in *The Ox-Bow Incident,* we do not see his eyes; in *Mister Roberts,* he faces upstage. In *A Gift of Time,* hiddenness is again called on, as both theatrical "cheat"—how to realistically depict the cutting of wrists, the release of blood?—and personal catharsis. The stage direction reads "*His back is seen, and her face, watching.*" There is a witness to the act, but it is not us.

His post-Frances career is brought to a climax. If on the stage Henry has become Frances, dead by a razor, in life he has been more like Lael, the witness to a loved one's decline, the pleading survivor. "I love you, I love you, please die."

Remember the graveyard: The stick points at the grave, and back at the man. Fonda's fate all along, his curse and his cure, has been to become the thing that haunts him. In performing suicide, he has dramatized an obligation to Frances. Whatever understanding he achieves is tardy, and only symbolic, but Fonda can hardly take symbol, or the autobiographical implications of his recent roles, further than this—to introject the loss that has, for more than a decade, shadowed him; and to bleed Frances from his veins while joining her in the loneliness of the last act.

∽

For Henry Fonda, right man—husband, father, master of control—the psychology of self-annihilation is a thing not to be discussed. But for Henry Fonda, wrong man—artist of sorrows, bearer of obligations—it may be the truest, deepest language he knows.

Go back to late 1935. Fonda is still a fresh face in Hollywood, with two starring roles to his credit, and buzz already that he'll be the screen's next Lincoln. He has much to be proud of. Yet these may be his worst of times, with such exhilaration and loss in so brief a period.

December 25, 1931: He marries Margaret Sullavan.

March 1932: Hank and Peggy separate; she humiliates him with Jed Harris.

October 5, 1934: Herberta Fonda dies.

October 7, 1935: William Fonda dies, one year almost to the day after his wife. Henry leaves the set of *Way Down East* to fly hurriedly to Omaha.

October 31, 1935: A small item appears in newspapers across the country, informing fans that Henry Fonda, presently shooting *The Trail of the Lonesome Pine* at Big Bear Lake in California's San Bernardino National Park, has nearly died from carbon monoxide poisoning. He had been listening to his car radio while running the motor—presumably in an enclosed garage—and was rescued by an assistant director who found him slumped in the seat.

November 16, 1935: Another version of the same incident is printed. It was late at night, and Henry was testing his car battery. He let the motor run. For entertainment, he turned on the radio; for warmth, he shut the garage doors. "They got him out just in time," the story says.

Fonda, in his enigma, leads us to ask the plausible worst—whether the incident was misadventure, as the reports imply, or his attempt, perfunctory or in earnest, to end his own life. We wonder if we have been placing Fonda at too objective a distance from suicide. Maybe his life is, as he has said, "peppered with suicides" for the simple reason that like finds like. Maybe for him the wish for oblivion is no mere witnessing of another's pain, but a thing inside, which he feels or remembers every day. Maybe the stick points at the grave, and back at the man.

There is much to recall in light of this. The dark around the eyes of William Fonda; Jane's remarks on the strain of family melancholy, and what she speculates was her father's genetic vulnerability to depression; Henry's history of befriending, and sometimes marrying, suicidal people; all the roles he has played in which despair is the stain, and suicide the cleansing.

We recall as well Henry's long-nurtured desire to play Julian English, the doomed hero of *Appointment in Samarra*. We note that the novel appeared in 1934, a year before the incident at Big Bear Lake, and that Julian ends his life in a car seat on a cold morning, his lungs full of carbon monoxide.

9

New Frontier and Hidden Agenda

Fail-Safe

Election Day is a farce to many Americans, but beneath that disgust runs an ever-receding memory, or myth, of our shared political life's having once been a richer thing. We believe it was different long ago—that other choices existed, that our politics had soul, sadness, honor, caring. That is why Lincoln remains our most revered president: We mourn the example we've lost, the absent father of our politics.

There is an ache in us. Mostly the ache stays hidden, for exposing it would mean admitting fear, doubt, ambiguity—everything Americans loathe. Yet because the pain is no less real for our denial of it, we have always needed a myth, a film, a fable to salve it. That hunger for fiction admits gaps in our reality.

As a young actor playing a martyred president at a crucial time, Henry Fonda slips through the gaps. He gets inside our dark mind, our ongoing political fable. Across four decades, nine chief executives, and innumerable changes, he stays there. He persists as a memory that, having first evoked Lincoln at the apex of the New Deal, returns more than twenty years later on the New Frontier. He embodies a sense of what we were, still ache to be, and fear we can never be again.

∽

Everyone knows the history that is made on November 22, 1963. But the year that follows, through which we trace the issue of that day, is just as crucial to the subsequent course of American affairs. The period of collective recovery from the assassination of a loved and hated president, 1964 is also an election year. John Kennedy's successor, Lyndon Johnson, thrashes deeper into the Asian jungle and pushes the Civil Rights Act into law. In response to the hawk rhetoric of his opponent, Arizona senator Barry Goldwater, Johnson's handlers devise a historic campaign commercial—a girl plucking a daisy, her voice melting into a countdown, the daisy into a death cloud—which is broadcast once on September 29, and never again.

In 1964, Martin Luther King, Jr., wins the Nobel Peace Prize. Former B-list leading man Ronald Reagan plays his last film role—a sleazy crime boss in Don Siegel's remake of *The Killers*—and gives a nationally televised speech in support of Goldwater, which is the beginning of his own, infinitely more successful career in politics. The Free Speech Movement is born in Berkeley, setting off passions and plots that Reagan will combat as governor of California.

Conflicting ideologies are more clearly defined in 1964 than they have been since New Deal days. It is exactly what Reagan's speech calls it: "A Time for Choosing." It is also the year that climaxes Henry Fonda's ascension to the presidency of the screen.

In 1960, many see the contest between JFK and Richard Nixon as a choice between new and old, life and death. Kennedy's Cold War stance is not far left of Nixon's, yet his candidacy promises a return of liberal principle and creative atmosphere after a decade of conservative stagnation. And when JFK arrives, Fonda is already there, equipped with leftist bona fides and populist associations. Appearing in a succession of political roles, he emerges as the soul of what Arthur Schlesinger, Jr., court historian of the Kennedy White House, would term "the vital center," dramatizing the mainstream American identity in days of excitement and crisis.

Behold the New Frontier. The phrase doesn't originate with Kennedy. As William Safire notes, it is "in the air" for months before JFK patents it in his acceptance speech at the 1960 Democratic National Convention. But at that moment, with so much else in the air, the words are a chime—the song of American ambition reaching forward and back at once, prairie cool and cowboy flash in the new world of IBM and superhighway. The great traumas of the century are past, while powers of justice and technology are on the march. "New Frontier": why not!

Of course it is only a golden moment, and its memory will be muddied over the next three years in a series of setbacks and advances, gross losses and irreducible wins. These are humid, bubbling times, but the lid is still firmly on the pot. Then everything changes: Kennedy is dead. A piece of his head flies off, and with it the lid. America is revealed as a cauldron—conspiracy, clamor, riot, war—that has been slow in the boiling.

Politics and image will mix in new ways. More than any star of his generation—save John Wayne, who from *The Alamo* (1960) to *The Green Berets* (1968) defends Hollywood's hawk agenda throughout the raucous decade—Henry Fonda is in that mix. Like "New Frontier," he is a stabilizer in the midst of change. Histories speak through and circulate around him, as they do through and around Wayne; simply by moving, speaking, advocating, these men connect eras and create meanings.

As J. Hoberman writes, Fonda in his changes has "tracked the trajectory of tormented liberalism—forged in the crucible of the 1930s, tested under fire during World War II, purged of its Communistic tendencies in the late 1940s." His political metamorphosis achieves absolute form just as the country is emerging from Eisenhower's "politics of fatigue" into Kennedy's radiant newness; at the moment he is needed, Fonda lives again in the cool mien of Camelot elder statesmanhood.

Our man is middle-aged by Kennedy time, and hardly a political innocent. Many years lie behind his emergence; numerous battles inform his choices.

∽

Starting in the late 1930s, Fonda is firmly identified with his industry's burgeoning liberal element, an identification encouraged by his involvement with both political causes and cause-driven films. *Blockade* is an unmistakable gesture in favor of the Spanish Loyalists; *The Grapes of Wrath* distills New Deal spirit; *The Ox-Bow Incident* jibes with controversy over lynching in the South; *The Long Night* puts a socialist spin on the plight of war veterans; even Fonda's blink-and-you-miss-it cameo in the all-star antifascist thriller *Jigsaw* (1949) states his ongoing leftist allegiance as the Cold War begins.

Under "political party," the California Voter Registries for 1936, 1940, and 1942 list Henry and Frances Fonda as "DTS" ("declined to state"); not until 1946 do they declare themselves as Democrats. Before Pearl Harbor, Fonda identifies less with a party than with the Popular Front, an unofficial, unincorporated confederation of antifascist groups in America and Europe. Positing fascism as the chief threat to individual liberty and collective security, the Popular Front unites mainstream liberals and more radical groups; for a few years, lefties of all stripes—and even a few freethinking conservatives—find, if not synthesis, common cause.

Fonda's earliest affiliation is with the Anti-Nazi League, whose Hollywood chapter is founded in July 1936. The ANL's mission is to promote—through rallies, ads, and other political appeals—a categorical denunciation of the Third Reich. Among its founders are screenwriter Dorothy Parker, director Fritz Lang, and actor Fredric March; members include James Cagney, Edward G. Robinson, Gale Sondergaard, Paul Muni, Bette Davis, Melvyn Douglas, and Douglas's wife, Helen Gahagan. Film historian Charles J. Maland calls the ANL "the most prominent manifestation of Popular Front anti-fascism in Hollywood," and Fonda's involvement signals his perennial location on the activist spectrum—left of center, within firm boundaries of democratic dissent.

The Anti-Nazi League quickly makes a name for itself. In 1937, Benito Mussolini's son Vittorio visits Hollywood to study film production; but his reception—clouded with espionage rumors, supposedly spread by the ANL—is so unpleasant that he leaves almost instantly. The next year, Hitler's documentarian, Leni Riefenstahl, comes to town, and the ANL places an ad in *Daily Variety,* calling for an orchestrated shunning. The climate convinces Riefenstahl to postpone American exhibition of *Olympia*, her documentary about the Olympic Games in Berlin, for several years.

As its profile and influence crest, the ANL comes under official scrutiny. In 1938 Martin Dies, Democratic representative from Texas, convenes a panel to investigate Communist influence in domestic affairs. The Anti-Nazi League is rumored to have made financial contributions to Communist groups; as far as Dies is concerned, write Larry Ceplair and Steven Englund, the ANL is "a front for the Communist Party, pure and simple." League representatives hasten a telegram to his committee, "challenging it to substantiate [its] charges." Dies promises to do so with a series of hearings—whereupon the White House and Congress are deluged with telegrams from Hollywood and elsewhere, demanding the investigation be nullified and the committee disbanded. Amazingly, the assault on opinion works: Dies, citing a "lack of funds and time," cancels the hearings.

The victory is only contextual: Right now, most Americans fear Nazism more urgently than communism. Hitler and Stalin have yet to sign their nonaggression pact, and the Soviet Union is America's ally in a world about to be at war. The Anti-Nazi League has the future on its side.

But the future has a way of becoming the past. In seven years, the war will be over; with Hitler and Mussolini gone, Stalin will be redrawn as America's ultimate foe, and the Dies committee will return to make good on its first threat. By then, it will have mutated into a far more sophisticated form under its official designation, the House Committee on Un-American Activities.

∽

The Popular Front agenda had demanded visibility, active dissent. In contrast, the Cold War is about hiddenness—official secrets, security councils, exposure as damnation. The politicians to whom, in Leslie Fiedler's words, "'Red' really means loud-mouth or foreigner or Jew" have intuited that communism is the next enemy, secrecy the new source of power. Opportunism, fervor, a populace in equal parts panicked and passive create what becomes known, even before it is over, as the Mc-Carthy era, after its chief visionary and loudest crusader, Senator Joseph McCarthy of Wisconsin.

McCarthy is right: There are spies inside the U.S. government. Definitive or at least credible cases have been made against Harry Dexter White, senior Treasury official and architect of the World Bank; Julian Wadleigh of the Department of Agriculture; Duncan Chaplin Lee, assistant to OSS director William J. Donovan; Alger Hiss of the State Department; and others. But the powerful spy rings of the 1930s and 1940s are defunct well before the height of the Red scare, and many quondam communists, fellow travelers, weekend pinkos, and all-American rabble-rousers are snagged in the net of the great McCarthy and HUAC fishing expeditions. Even Ronald Reagan will admit, long after his conservative conversion, that in these years "many fine people were accused wrongly of being Communists simply because they were liberals."

Fonda is off to the side, observing. This is some of what he sees:

In October 1947, HUAC, chaired by New Jersey congressman J. Parnell Thomas, schedules hearings on communism in Hollywood. In support is the Motion Picture Alliance for the Preservation of American Ideals, led by John Wayne. Among the committee's "friendly witnesses" is Reagan, head of the Screen Actors Guild and—along with his then-wife, actress Jane Wyman—an FBI informant on Commie scuttlebutt. Meanwhile, industry Left-leaners, branding themselves the Committee for the First Amendment, establish a presence at the Washington hearings in the form of a delegation led by Humphrey Bogart, Lauren Bacall, and John Huston.

The hearings are dominated by the testimony of the Hollywood Ten—a group of screenwriters hostile to HUAC. Among them is John Howard Lawson, one of the few openly Communist writers in Hollywood, and author of the Fonda-Wanger *Blockade*. Lawson's appearance, while courageous, is also arch and self-righteous; refusing to answer direct questions, he lectures. Ultimately, he is escorted from the dock by police. The next day's witness is Dalton Trumbo, who is likewise charged with contempt and jailed.

Trumbo explains the refusal of the screenwriters to answer questions: "The accused men made their stand before the Committee to reestablish their right of privacy, not only in law but in fact." But many feel that such intransigence has only made HUAC's job easier. "It was a sorry performance," says John Huston of the Hollywood Ten testimony. "They had lost a chance to defend a most important principle."

Like the Anti-Nazi League, the Committee for the First Amendment has started out full of vigor, charged with mission. But now history is on the other side. Out of fear, exhaustion, and a desire to get back to business, the movie industry, like most of America, makes a willing exchange of democratic danger for bureaucratic surety. It's the first phase in a transformation that will climax in the late 1960s, after assassination and cover-up have woven themselves into the patterns of American thought—the transformation, in Greil Marcus's words, "of what in the United States had been taken as open, public life into private crime or hidden conspiracy."

∽

Most of Fonda's work with those blacklisted occurs after the blacklist era has ended. In 1959, *Warlock* is directed by Edward Dymtryk, Hollywood Ten member, who, after going to jail for refusing to testify before HUAC, reconsiders, then testifies twice, naming several of his former associates in the Communist party. *Fail-Safe* (1964) is scripted by the blacklisted, nontestifying Walter Bernstein, and *Madigan* (1968) is cowritten by Abraham Polonsky, Hollywood Ten member and subsequent exile.

Apart from *Blockade,* Fonda's preblacklist filmography contains only one instance of "social propaganda" from a known Communist source. *You Belong to Me* (1941) is written by Claude Binyon, from a story by Dalton Trumbo—in later days the grand old man of the blacklist, a hero retrieved from 1950s pseudonymy to write *Exodus, Spartacus,* and others. This minor comedy has Fonda as a pampered, sickly millionaire married to a domineering doctor (Barbara Stanwyck). Feeling emasculated, the millionaire takes a pseudonym—aptly—and a low-level sales job in a department store; when the ruse is discovered, he is brought into the manager's office to face representatives of the employees' union.

Actor Larry Parks—in 1941 a nobody, five years later a star for his turn in *The Al Jolson Story*—plays the man who speaks for the union. Two other workers, one of them played by the familiar character actor Jeff Corey, look on silently. The employees demand the millionaire's firing, on the grounds that he is depriving a needy man of a job. Parks pronounces the underdog's right to a fair shake, and a fast-moving film stops dead for an insertion of ideology in the form of undramatized speech. It is, undeniably, propaganda, albeit in the service of compassion and economic good sense.

But there's a twist. The playboy protests that *he* needs the job, too— not for money, but for personal reasons. Not buying it, Parks tells the manager, "He refuses to argue his case openly and above-board. He classifies his defense as"—uttering the next words as if they are dirty— "something *personal* and *private*. He hasn't given a single reason why he shouldn't be dismissed immediately." This is starting to sound familiar.

Fonda asks the manager to recommend him for another job. "You mean take it away from some other poor fellow?" Parks interrupts. "I promise you that when we get through publicizing your case, there won't be a company in the United States willing to hire you."

None of these people knows what is to come in the next ten years. But we do.

Fonda's millionaire backs off. Before leaving, he turns his severance pay over to the employees' fund.

Nine years later, Larry Parks will be subpoenaed by HUAC. In an emotional testimony, he'll admit to having briefly been a member of the Communist party. He'll name names, and, despite repenting, will find himself unemployable in Hollywood. As will Jeff Corey, who doesn't cooperate with the committee, and who until his mid-1960s reemergence in supporting parts sustains himself as an acting teacher. As will Dalton Trumbo, who justified his refusal by exalting "the right of privacy, not only in law but in fact." These men will be damned with the same phrases heard in *You Belong to Me,* their careers crippled by the same threats; but here and now, they endorse the language and logic of the blacklist.

It is a hard irony, at the least; at the most, a warning against dogma, and a suggestion of why a man like Henry spends most of his life closer to the political middle than to any extreme.

Jane Fonda will later criticize her father for not taking a public stand against the blacklist, without taking into account that many good men and women were in the same position. It's true that in his postwar politics, he is usually supporter rather than activist. By the end of 1947, he is out of movies and in the theater, a zone of limited influence that doesn't really interest the investigating committees.* Unlike other Hollywood liberals, such as Edward G. Robinson and Melvyn Douglas, Fonda will not suffer the fate of being graylisted in the 1950s, when stars must make the crucial transition from movies to television. He grows distant from old friends Ward Bond and John Wayne because of the Red scare but does not rescind the relationships entirely; he continues to socialize and work with those men and others who have complied with HUAC.

Maybe that is Henry's compromise, and maybe he makes it because he knows how compromise works. He is no more a radical in his politics than in his art, but his politics, like his art, are honest and devout, and have much to do with remembering. He has a broad and a large view; he knows the landscape. So he pitches his tent in the middle ground. It's only a fact: People usually last longer, living in the center.

---

* However, in these years Fonda was a prominent left-wing voice in radio. He played a scientist in "Rehearsal" (broadcast on Independence Day, 1946), an installment of *The Fifth Horseman,* a miniseries arguing for United Nations control of nuclear weapons. *A Man with a Cause* (aired May 17, 1948), with Fonda as a government official, concerns the plight of Holocaust victims and other European refugees seeking passage to the United States. Sponsored by the Citizens' Committee on Displaced Persons, it addressed the postwar rise in American xenophobia, particularly the prejudice against European Jewry so often implicit in anti-Communist rhetoric.

Though he will become a bitter detractor of Dwight D. Eisenhower, Henry initially supports his 1952 presidential bid. In the late 1940s, the former Supreme Allied Commander is courted as a candidate by both parties; and his declaration as a Republican does not alter the general perception of him as a political moderate, and an alternative to the current chief executive. Isolationists are angered by Harry Truman's infusions of American force and money into Europe through NATO; interventionists by his fumbling administration of the Korean War; liberals by his investment in hydrogen bomb testing and the mandating of federal loyalty oaths. The moment is felt to call for a cleansing.

It's hard to say what liberals believe Eisenhower will offer them beyond the reflected glow of guts and glory, a mystique to which not only right-wingers are vulnerable. Opponents of blacklisting may hope Eisenhower's military credibility will retard the trend toward the patriotism of fear. Fonda is sufficiently soured on Truman not just to endorse his opponent but also to narrate a long-playing record, *Ike from Abilene,* distributed by the GOP as a bonus for campaign donors.

But hopeful liberals don't like Ike for long. Weeks before the election, a cluster of notables stages a public defection from Eisenhower to his Democratic rival, Illinois governor Adlai Stevenson—a candidate they have seen up to now as unelectable. Fonda joins this mass defection, which includes John Steinbeck, Cornelius Vanderbilt, Jr., Edna Ferber, John Jacob Astor, and Oscar Hammerstein II. Stevenson's campaign manager reckons the disillusionment is "based on the compromise, the shifts of position, [and] the abandonment of principles" exhibited by Eisenhower, such as his failure to condemn Senators McCarthy of Wisconsin and Jenner of Indiana—the two biggest Red-baiters in Congress—and his devil's pact with the ultraconservative Senator Taft of Ohio. "Eisenhower seems to have lost the ability to take any kind of stand on any subject," Steinbeck writes.

Then, at the Republican National Convention in July, the candidate grips the hand of another man whom, like Taft and McCarthy, he needs but secretly despises. Richard Nixon is the Republican senator from California, a key member of the House Committee on Un-American

Activities, and star prosecutor in the Alger Hiss espionage trial of 1948. Nixon is a rising star, a force; like a true believer with a talisman, he has gripped, stroked, and squeezed the postwar panic around communism. That prescience will make his career, and shape the next three decades of life in the United States.

Witnessing the clammy grip of compromise at the convention, Fonda must utter curses. He remembers Nixon. Not just from the Hollywood-HUAC hearings, from which the California senator, after questioning Jack L. Warner and delivering the committee's mission statement on opening day, largely absented himself, and not just from the Hiss trial. No, Fonda remembers him most keenly from the 1950 California Senate race, which pitted Nixon against Democrat Helen Gahagan Douglas, representative since 1944 of Los Angeles's highly liberal Fourteenth District.

A former opera star and actress, Gahagan had her spotlight moment as Queen Hash-a-Motep in the 1935 camp epic *She*. Married to actor Melvyn Douglas, Gahagan went into politics. Fonda was a friend, but he'd have found common ground with Gahagan if they'd been strangers: In terms of her beliefs, she was Henry Fonda in a dress. During the 1930s, she was a Popular Fronter and proponent of the New Deal; as a Democratic party novice, she made her name advocating for labor and small farmers.

In the House, Gahagan was a staunch liberal, but no pinko. As Stephen E. Ambrose would later note, "she had spurned Henry Wallace's Progressive Party in the 1948 election, which was a litmus test for fellow travelers." She was less than completely predictable on foreign policy, challenging both Communist dictatorships and the Truman Doctrine of unilateral aid to Communist-besieged Greece and Turkey. Significantly for Fonda, she sponsored an antilynching bill in 1947, just as hangings of black men in the Carolinas were making headlines.*

Henry always had a thing for nervy, chance-taking women. He must have appreciated the fact that, to run against Nixon, Gahagan had to

---

* The bill was defeated by the southern congressional contingent, as it would be when Gahagan reintroduced it two years later.

buck her own Democratic leadership. Assured of party support if she would wait until 1952, when incumbent Sheridan H. Downey had pledged to retire, Gahagan refused. Withdrawing, Downey threw the party's weight behind Manchester Boddy, the only other Democrat; and when Gahagan edged out Boddy, Downey became a prominent supporter of Nixon. By splitting their own vote, the Democrats—not least Gahagan—had already cleared much of Nixon's path for him.

A tight team of Republican schemers did the rest. In a symphony of smear orchestrated by campaign manager Murray Chotiner but played to the hilt by a possessed Nixon, Gahagan was dubbed the "Pink Lady." Anti-Gahagan flyers were printed on pink paper; voters received anonymous phone calls whispering of un-American associations. The campaign was an innovation in character assassination, the linking of vagaries in a chain of fear connecting the voting booth to the chambers of foreign power.

Nixon defeated Gahagan, and the 1950 race made history. It was not the first political contest to pivot on the threat of cultural war between the liberal powers of Hollywood and the interests of the American majority; nor was it the first race to be won on charges of disloyalty. But it took these stances, and the tactics they entailed, to new levels of audacity—Nixon's passion as he shouted the slanders, his leveraging of lofty progressive ideals as weapons against themselves, his persona combining the attack dog and the aggrieved mutt.

The maw of conservative backlash opened to vomit up a new age of malice. Nixon's aura would overhang, underlie, and finally enshroud every other movement of the postwar period: Every important American development seemed to react against or quail beneath the darkness released in these early years of HUAC and Helen Gahagan. It is the defeated Pink Lady who tagged Nixon with his most enduring nickname: "Tricky Dick."

Come 1952 and Nixon's placement on the Eisenhower ticket, many have forgotten the California smears—if they ever heard about them to begin with. But others remember. As Herbert S. Parmet observes, "Long after Watergate and the evidence of abuse of power, long after

the passions over Vietnam subsided, middle-aged liberals invariably ex-
plained their hatred toward Nixon by citing 'what he did to Helen Gahagan Douglas.' "

This was true for elderly liberals, too. In his last interview, Henry
Fonda will say he has hated Nixon ever since his annihilation of Helen
Gahagan Douglas. "Such fuckin' lies," Fonda mutters, as if disbelieving
still the phenomenon of a man like Nixon.

∽

The two of them make an unlikely pairing. Differences are obvious:
Where one is melancholy, the other is brooding. Where one is stoic, the
other is self-pitying. One is a liberal Democrat, the other a conservative
Republican. One is a friend of Gahagan, the other her destroyer.

In *Nixon at the Movies,* Mark Feeney writes that Fonda "can be seen
as an almost metaphysical epitome of the anti-Nixon: light against dark,
scruple against grasp, secular grace against secular sin." Yet at the same
time, he incarnates a Nixon essence in spite of himself. "What makes
Fonda the supreme liberal icon of the screen isn't the fineness of his intelligence, the finickiness of his bearing, or even the unique ineffability of
that faraway gaze . . . No, it's that he's happiest, or at least more grati-
fied, when his cause is lost. Nothing could be more Nixonian."

Both Fonda and Nixon were raised in sectarian churches—Christian
Science and Quakerism—that emphasized austerity, servitude, repression. Both served in the navy in World War II, stationed on Pacific vessels, working in tandem with the air force. (Feeney quotes a navy friend
of Nixon's: "If you ever saw Henry Fonda in *Mister Roberts,* you have a
pretty good idea what Dick was like.") Both are gifted with superhuman
control yet are capable of flagrant and dramatic outbursts. Emotional
chaos is suppressed, released indirectly and often destructively, as inner
mechanisms work overtime to channel the psychic overload.

From there, though, the two fork as radically as lightning bolts. Out
of Fonda's darkness comes empathy. Even his loners and killers are men
with the capacity and compulsion to feel others' suffering; the drama
lies in their transformation by this awareness. Out of Nixon's darkness

comes a vision of vengefulness, of others being made to suffer. Payback is the true drama of the great noir candidate; as John Erlichman (J. T. Walsh) says in Oliver Stone's *Nixon,* at the apex of the Vietnam War: "We've got people dying because he didn't make the varsity football team."

Fonda's insides are in disarray, however ordered his exterior. Nixon's innards, though, bespeak another level of madness—a muck of resentment, self-pity, and incomprehension that pours forth in the breakdowns and alcoholic fugues of his administration's final days. But because the consummation of Nixon's personal grudge happens to coincide with the post-1968 shift from liberation to repression, he is appreciated as a "great American" precisely for his pathologies. It is a disastrous alignment of social and personal forces—that old black magic some call historical inevitability.

Nixon's visionary move will be to turn the discontents of the white working and middle classes into a political weapon, the disregarded "silent majority" into the obstreperous power that will one day beat America's radicals back to the margins. His boldness will be to embody his own paranoia so fully that America will spend several tragic years taking his image as its own, and years more paying the price.

With the Gahagan campaign, Nixon was teaching the underdogs that they had teeth, and that teeth were for biting. The New Deal was over.

∽

Adlai Stevenson is a New Dealer, United Nations delegate, peacemonger, and (the word is invented for him) egghead. He is known to read books and worry over nuances. Nothing could be easier for the Republicans than to neutralize Stevenson by branding him "intellectual," as Gahagan was branded "pink." Ike, the war hero, wins soundly in 1952.

But four years later, Stevenson is again the Democratic nominee, and Fonda campaigns on his behalf, headlining rallies and delivering speeches. At a Students for Stevenson gathering at New York's Barnard College, he says, "It is the sum of the little tiny selves which make a nation, and we must be mighty good to have made ours so good." Often the words Fonda delivers are just that redolent of 1930s folk speech, that evocative of Tom Joad and the big soul—unsurprising, since John Steinbeck writes them.

When the Democrats stage a cross-country fund-raiser on October 20, 1956—twenty-nine banquet halls linked by closed-circuit television in a spectacular called "Seventeen Days to Victory"—Fonda is at the Hollywood gathering, along with Eleanor Roosevelt, John F. Kennedy, Frank Sinatra, Marlon Brando, Harry Belafonte, and many others. Recapping the affair, D.C. columnist George Dixon notes that the famed faces were not well-treated by the broadcast technology. "Henry Fonda looked more scary than the Phantom of the Opera. . . . I was informed on the way out that the screen was a personal contribution of Republican National Chairman Leonard Hall, and that Richard Nixon was operating the projection machine."

It's a microcosm of the Stevenson candidacy. Money, intellect, and liberal star power cannot prevent even a fund-raising gala from seeming a hapless colloquy of well-meaning losers. Elections are secured or surrendered on an accumulation of such perceptions. Eisenhower takes his second term more easily than the first.

∽

Shot in the midst of the 1956 campaign, *12 Angry Men* is a statement of ethical humanism, a blacklist-relevant warning against scapegoating and prejudice. Fonda makes it for the message as much as for the drama— and this fact has its bad effect on his performance. Less than a fleshly composite of living behaviors, his character is a moral beacon, dispassionate and unsensual, a man you ought to vote for but might not. He is Adlai Stevenson.

Simple situation: A roomful of jurors debates a murder case, and one of them, a solitary holdout for reasonable doubt, fights to sway his fellows from a hasty and unjust verdict. Such is Fonda's personal interest in the project, and in playing the holdout, that he makes *12 Angry*

Men his sole excursion as a film producer, and locates a TV director, Sidney Lumet, to shoot a cast of tough actors in a filthy room.

Though it fails commercially, the picture is soon recognized as both a drama of terrific impact and a superior civics lesson. Its success is mostly attributable to formal competence, clockwork exposition, and the dramatic advantages of a small, hot space full of street-level accents and sweating faces. The weak link is Fonda, who *doesn't* sweat: Juror number eight is so virtuous, he lacks even glands.

He is strange, this juror—aloof. When another man attempts conversation, number eight only grins and stares straight ahead. A rest room scene gives Fonda some naturalistic hand-washing business to engage in while a burly New York actor (Jack Warden) sounds off nearby, but it also tips us to the fussiness of this hero: He dries each fingernail in succession, grooms each cuticle. Number eight is a control freak, this man who doesn't sweat or socialize, who only smiles the oddest, most alienating smile.

The film *12 Angry Men* stands among the best-crafted fantasies of liberal heroism ever to come from Hollywood, as well as being one of the films that give Henry Fonda his stature before the popular audience. But atmosphere and acting, more than ethics, carry the force of the drama, while the producer-star is less a bleeding heart than a glass of milk: tall and white, contained and cool. Did we mention he resembles Stevenson? We see why so many voters—not only conservatives but also liberals craving boldness, rhetoric, glamour—could not get behind a man so impeccable and unexcitable. There's a dearth of passion in this character, dryness in place of the spurt of life.

To this day, *12 Angry Men* is screened in high school classrooms. It should be. It lets each of us believe we can be the hero, the holdout; shows us how, as citizens, we ought to behave. But no one should place it on a level with *Young Mr. Lincoln*. Its limitation as art and politics is to shortchange the democracy it extols. It lacks the mystery, danger, and confusions, the dark potential and black magic that live in democracy, and in its great fables. *Young Mr. Lincoln*'s humanism shines the brighter for its pervading dark and persistent fear. *12 Angry Men* has more in common with campaign commercials, which reduce the redemptive lies of myth to planks in a party platform.

∽

In 1960, Stevenson's place is taken by the young senator who had just missed becoming his running mate in 1952. John F. Kennedy has been a figure of swelling glamour since emerging as a Massachusetts congressman in the same freshman class with Nixon. Since then, he has risen to the Senate and paid his dues as a team player—sponsoring no innovative bills, leading no brave charges, but proving himself a reliably telegenic face and pleasing voice in party politics.

Like most erstwhile Stevensonians, Fonda shifts allegiance to JFK. The choice seems clear: Kennedy is younger and handsomer; he radiates athleticism and cool millions; he has hair. But it is a compromise, as well. The fact that both the senator and his younger brother and chief adviser, Robert, are, like Nixon, past allies of Joe McCarthy must give Henry some troubled hours.* Fonda might prefer a candidate as intellectual, irreproachable, and experienced as Stevenson. But he has had enough of losing.

And he finds rapport with JFK—knows him "intimately," he'll say years later. The two share numerous traits. Kennedy, as Gore Vidal writes at the time, "is withdrawn, observant, icily objective in crisis, aware of the precise value of every card dealt him." We picture Hank and Jack relaxing, chatting in low masculine tones in the library at East Seventy-fourth Street, enjoying scotches and cigars brought by Fonda's Puerto Rican houseboy. They are men of the world, conversant in history, literature, art, travel, women—what are known as the finer things. They talk about the movies, no doubt: Joseph Kennedy, Sr., philanthro-

---

* "Perhaps I was wrong in McCarthy's case," Kennedy would admit later—in words narrated by Fonda in the 1966 NBC special *The Age of Kennedy*. "Perhaps we were not as sensitive as some and should have acted sooner. That is a reasonable indictment that falls on me as well."

pist and ambassador to the Court of St. James's, Prohibition bootlegger and paramour of silent-screen goddesses, has deep, dirty roots in the film business, and his eldest living son, bedding starlets and cultivating celebrity, will decorate his own presidential campaign with Hollywood dazzle.

But Fonda's approbation may go beyond the sharing of such moments. Kennedy embodies complementary disciplines of professionalism and suffering: his father a man of devouring ambition, who sees his sons as arms of his ambition; his older brother, blown up in a World War II fighter plane; his own mettle tested in the Pacific, where he rescued himself and his shipmates on PT-109; his body racked by back and leg pain, cortisone injections to delay the creep of Addison's disease. Stricken with an infection after undergoing back surgery in 1953, he comes so close to death that last rites are read over him. No one who knows Kennedy "intimately" doubts his toughness.

His compulsions—political, intellectual, sexual—are right for this moment. They go outward, not inward, and seem to increase the common energy. Compulsion in JFK is sexy, a positive charge; where it darkens Nixon, it gives Kennedy his glow. Whatever his secrets—and there are plenty—he comes across as an ad for openness, frank seduction, glamorous visibility, where Nixon is the picture of a man accustomed to living in his own shadows.

JFK is nominated at the convention, and Henry is there, participating in a staged spectacular at the L.A. Coliseum as Kennedy christens the New Frontier. Feeling the magic, Fonda shifts in the following months into high campaign gear. Emcees a Democratic rally in Long Beach; chairs the Hollywood Program Committee for Kennedy; sits on the dais as the candidate regales an audience of 200,000 in Manhattan's Garment District; stars in a four-minute campaign ad that details the PT-109 story (and draws a direct link between JFK and FDR); and even joins Jackie Kennedy in a TV special exhibiting the Camelot couple's family photos and home movies.

Fonda goes all out. And this time his man is elected, JFK defeating

Nixon in the closest presidential contest of the century—a retrospective hint of the silent majority's readiness to snatch history back from the youngsters and dissenters who have, in this open moment, claimed it.

Three weeks after Kennedy is sworn in, Henry appears on *The Ed Sullivan Show* to recite Lincoln's second inaugural address and bestow, by proxy, the Emancipator's blessing on the new administration. Later, JFK will appoint Fonda to the advisory board of his National Cultural Center, to serve in an honorary capacity with the likes of George Balanchine, Agnes de Mille, Robert Penn Warren, and Thornton Wilder. When on May 19, 1962, Kennedy holds his famous birthday party at Madison Square Garden, Fonda will be an honored guest. The president will thank him in his address, and Jack Benny will tease our man's well-known sympathies by pointing him out as "a registered Republican and vice-president of the John Birch Society."

Henry will laugh along with everyone. Maybe America is coming back around to something he can recognize—less fearful and closed, less about the angry will of the majority and the politics of attack. He believes in Kennedy, but more than that, he has refused to harden into suspicion or shrink to exclusionism. Unlike others—John Ford, Duke Wayne, Ronald Reagan—he has preserved his liberal faiths through these dank years of blacklisting and panic, compromise and lies. And here he sits in the Garden, in the glow of a president he admires, whose own compromises and lies he does not know, or can live with.

In America, you hope for something better. Henry has the right to laugh.

∽

Energized to find himself back on the winning team, he signs on for a series of roles—*Advise and Consent* (1962), *The Best Man,* and *Fail-Safe* (both 1964)—that constitute his first engagement since the 1940s with political content. Each comes out of Cold War anxiety over bombs, Communists, queers, enemies within; taken in sequence, the films advance in their evocations from the recent past to the hot present to the bleak beyond, writing a mordant postwar prognosis in paranoid style.

Adapted from Allen Drury's 1959 best-seller, *Advise and Consent* is a potboiler whose subject is the hidden agenda: Everyone in this perfervid Washington is hoarding secrets, telling lies, or threatening blackmail. Though filmed in the first year of Kennedy's presidency (and ornamented with the stunt casting of his brother-in-law Peter Lawford as a randy northeastern senator), *Advise and Consent* is not really a Kennedy movie. Full of sinisters and subversives, the Otto Preminger drama is imbued less with optimistic auguries of the New Frontier than with the combined piety and paranoia of the Nixon-McCarthy years.

For the novel, Drury had reconstituted a number of recent personalities and scandals from Capitol Hill, centering them on what was roughly a replay of the Alger Hiss trial. In 1948, journalist Whittaker Chambers claimed to have been, some ten years before, a link between New Deal bureaucrat Hiss and Soviet contacts. Questioned by HUAC, the patrician Hiss denied being a spy, while Chambers—a repentant former Bolshevik—looked the classic self-loathing snitch. But Chambers held to his story, and evidence was produced to support it. Tried twice for perjury, Hiss spent forty-four months in prison.

The effects were far-reaching. The witch-hunt gained credibility, while the residuum of the New Deal was cast in the worst possible light. Chambers's tormented conversion from communism to God, capital, and *Time* magazine was deeply influential on, among others, Ronald Reagan. Richard Nixon had been HUAC's main interrogator on the case, and he brandished it for years thereafter as his sole unimpeachable win.

In *Advise and Consent,* Robert Leffingwell, a liberal diplomat, is nominated for secretary of state by an ailing Rooseveltian president; the appointment is imperiled by the surprise testimony of a man claiming he and the nominee once belonged to the same Communist cell. Leffingwell reduces the witness to incoherence and his charges to slander. As it turns out, though, the charges are true, Leffingwell's defense a lie foisted on a credulous committee, several members of which have their own soap operas bubbling on the side.

The film's accuser, approximating Chambers, is portrayed by Burgess Meredith as a trembling Judas, while Fonda's Leffingwell combines the righteous bearing of Hiss with the intellectual-political profile of Steven-son. Watch how Fonda's body glides and his focus narrows as Leffing-well demolishes the dubious witness: Like a bird of prey, he circles and swoops as the mouselike Meredith dissolves in confusion and pathos.

"There is something a bit wicked, perhaps too wicked," Andrew Sarris writes when *Advise and Consent* is released, "in casting our most truthful actor as a liar." But Leffingwell is less a villain than a kind of pod person, a bureaucratic simulation of liberalism. It may be more un-nerving to see Fonda as a pragmatic opportunist than as an outright scoundrel, but he plays the role with bracing clarity: His Leffingwell is a man with little if any soul left.

∽

That same suggestion of a cagey, self-preserving amorality just barely carries over into *The Best Man*. Into its first shot, in fact—a shot that is also the high point of Henry's performance. As a presidential candi-date, he watches his own image on television, head bowed slightly, eyes level. A hand contemplatively pinches the mouth, covering the lower half of the face. The character is thus defined as observer, ironist, man above; a shrewd analyst who knows his modesty is his meal ticket; and a candidate half-hidden from the public to which he shows an open face.

This is brilliance—Fonda's dimensional arrangement of a few physi-cal elements in a shot that lasts mere seconds yet tells so much. Already, the movie is exciting. And it will stay exciting, though Fonda's part requires him to cede the fun of irony and vanity to those around him. As in *12 Angry Men*, it is his job to be the irritating voice of conscience, and to anchor a cast of characters more colorful, extreme, and other-wise entertaining than he.

Directed by Franklin Schaffner and adapted by Gore Vidal from his hit play, *The Best Man* shares with *Advise and Consent* an insider's perspective, a yoking of communism and homosexuality as political panic points, and a commingling of stars with well-known nonactors. But where Drury and Preminger imagine workaday Washington as a paranoid's panorama, Vidal and Schaffner breathe deeply and happily the air of political carnival.

The carnival is a Democratic convention, implicitly set in the very near future of 1964. Despite Vidal's contestants—Secretary of State William Russell (Fonda) and Senator Joe Cantwell (Cliff Robertson)—being based on Stevenson and Nixon, this movie is Camelot through and through: an athletic stride out of the dark 1950s, with hearty treacheries bathed in sunshine and "vigah." It moves the story's setting from Chicago to Los Angeles, site of Kennedy's benediction; a year earlier, Cliff Robertson played the young JFK in *PT 109*; Cantwell is a perverse composite of Nixon, McCarthy, and Bobby Kennedy; and the president, according to Vidal, contributes critique and even "a couple of lines" to the screenplay. Funny, fast, oddly sexy (there's a good deal of exposed flesh, even Fonda's), the movie unreels as if under the approving gaze of Prince Jack himself—alive when it is filmed, dead by the time it opens.

Kennedy has at least as many secrets as the average president, and Vidal's narrative mechanism, like Drury's, shifts on blackmail: Cantwell threatens to expose Russell's nervous breakdown, and in response, Russell's camp retrieves a gay innuendo from Cantwell's navy days. Whereas his rival is challenged by nothing but the expedient of the win, Russell must weigh the value of victory against the compromise of principle.

It would be easy to undervalue the subtlety of Fonda's acting, which is all feelers and focus, all quiet attention. A continuity of spirit runs between Russell's affectionate regard of the barnyard-blustering, terminally ill president (Lee Tracy) and the fascinated, revolted gaze he levels at Cantwell upon seeing through his rival's humanoid crust to the pod within. Russell is both admirable and maddening, a man of wit and implacable standards, gentleness working against innate emotional limits. A man of nuances.

Which makes him—yes—Stevensonian. Unelectable. Russell, declining to answer blackmail with blackmail, bows out of the race. But he ensures Cantwell's defeat by pledging his delegates to a third candidate, a dark horse of presumably centrist stances. (As if that weren't another kind of compromise.) It is hardly obvious, in the end, whether Russell is "the best man" or merely a loser who, in the words of the barnyard president, is "having a high old time with [his] divided conscience."

Fonda lets us make of him what we will. As a man of sense, a Hollywood long-timer implicated in some of the best and worst screen product of the last thirty years, and a history-minded American, Fonda plays the character subtly enough to leave the conclusions to his audience of invisible judges. As Russell rides off in the last shot, he is neither best man nor worst man, nor even the troubled soul of American liberalism. He is, in every sense, just a man.

∽

At the moment JFK is killed, Hollywood is in the midst of an unprecedented cycle of political thrillers and dramas: black-and-white movies full of stark figures and omens, paranoid visions taken to their all too conceivable ends. Unlike the anti-Axis thrillers of the 1940s, these pictures posit fascist threat from inside American institutions, thus turning J. Edgar Hoover's warning of an "enemy within" against itself.

Advise and Consent and *The Manchurian Candidate* appeared prior to Kennedy's death, while others—*The Best Man, Seven Days in May, Fail-Safe, Dr. Strangelove*—are completed or in production when the news comes from Dallas. The assassination, among its other reverberations, sends studios scurrying to reconfigure release schedules, manage the sudden blurring of satire and bad taste, and loop new dialogue for a changed world.

The release of *Seven Days in May,* about a militarist coup against a liberal White House, is postponed. *The Best Man,* announced for the summer of 1964, is expunged of Kennedy references. *PT 109* is withdrawn altogether. *The Manchurian Candidate,* augury of Oswald, conspiracy, cover-up, and despair—basically, the rest of the 1960s—will likewise vanish for many years. *Strangelove,* slated for a mid-December premiere, is pushed off to late January; a mention of Dallas is redubbed. The climax of the Kubrick film—a Mack Sennett pie fight between diplomats and generals—has already been excised for reasons of length and style; so audiences will never hear George C. Scott intone over the inert body of Peter Sellers, "Gentlemen, the president has been struck down in the prime of his life."

Such atmospheric coincidences and piquant parallels occur all the time. But in the 1960s, they are occurring *all the time.*

And Henry is in demand. In the months leading up to the assassination, there are more presidential roles than there are Henry Fondas to fill them. He must decline to play the chief executive in *Seven Days in May,* John Frankenheimer's follow-up to *The Manchurian Candidate,* because he has already agreed to play the same part for his protégé Sidney Lumet in the film of another recent doomsday novel, *Fail-Safe.* After that, he will go straight into *The Best Man.*

"I'm beginning to *feel* like a Kennedy," he says, laughing, in March 1963.

He is sitting in a dentist's chair in Beverly Hills when the president is assassinated. He returns home, to find the television consumed by violent non sequitur: shaky video from Parkland Hospital, raw footage from Dealey Plaza, face after face stunned blank or twisted with grief. Reporters race around Dallas, chasing scraps of rumor, and Henry falls into a chair to stare with the rest of the country. For the next few days, American life is telescoped through the TV tube in a dense frenzy of cameras, cops, microphone sticks, a nation of hallways and briefing rooms and emergency ramps.

Three years later, the world scarcely more settled than it was on that day, Fonda will participate in an NBC special, *The Age of Kennedy.* Chet Huntley's narration of the late president's political career will be interspersed with stiff but stately excerpts of Kennedy prose, read by Henry. Among the passages rendered in his inimitable tones—so flat, so plain and gentle—is this one, from the last chapter of *Profiles in Courage:*

> The courage of life is often a less dramatic spectacle than the courage of a final moment; but it is no less a magnificent mixture of triumph and tragedy. A man does what he must in spite of personal consequences, in spite of obstacles and dangers and pressures—and that is the basis of all human morality.

If the passage speaks to the heroic image Kennedy saw in his head, it says more than a little about the Fonda hero—that image long predating Kennedy's, upon which the younger man may have modeled some of his own moves, set some of his own standards; that image whose constancy preserved the idea of an America in which Kennedy and the generation he helped awaken could one day grasp their chance to make history.

Devastation is hard to register in a man like Henry, who holds so much back. This was the first president since FDR to excite his admiration. He watched as Kennedy silenced Nixon; ate meals and downed liquor with the now murdered man; enjoyed the individual and applauded the figure. Now the man has become a ghost, joining the others Fonda has collected in his lengthening life.

∽

Artistically, Henry will wander in the wilderness of the late 1960s and early 1970s. Kennedy's murder, besides blowing the lid off, upends the fragile balance of ideals and energies upon which both the New Frontier and Fonda's resurgence as cinematic statesman have been based. As if shocked into retrenchment—or merely sensing that the hour has passed—he will not play a president again for fifteen years.

Three decades have passed since he came on the screen: time enough to have established the contours of an image, for those contours to have sunk in as assumptions, and for those assumptions to come up for questioning. To large segments of the audience, old notions of screen heroism do not survive in the post-Kennedy years as anything but ironies. This is partly the fault of the stars, directors, and studios who flog a dying beast long after foreign film has raised the call for innovative technique and new approaches. In 1967, Pauline Kael delivers a sour elegy for the classic horse opera:

> What makes it a "Western" is no longer the wide open spaces but the presence of men like John Wayne, James Stewart, Henry Fonda, Robert Mitchum, Kirk Douglas, and Burt Lancaster, grinning with

their big new choppers, sucking their guts up into their chests, and hauling themselves onto horses . . . stars who have aged in the business, who have survived and who go on dragging their world-famous, expensive carcasses through the same old motions.

Every era must transmogrify a received image of heroism into something that is new, if only to itself, while dismantling the older model. But those brought up under the sway of that earlier heroism will feel its loss even as they refit it to new attitudes. And so a number of American writers of the 1960s see, or believe they see, Henry Fonda's face in unexpected places.

As Tom Joad, Henry burrowed into James Baldwin's imagination back in the 1940s, and left there an image of refusal to be recalled and reclaimed during the civil rights struggle. In 1961, Joseph Heller publishes *Catch-22,* a novel that becomes a sacred text of the antiwar movement. One of its characters is Major Major, a laundry officer whose wish is never to be noticed—a wish made impossible by his "sickly resemblance" to a certain movie star: "Long before he even suspected who Henry Fonda was, he found himself the subject of unflattering comparisons everywhere he went. Total strangers saw fit to deprecate him, with the result that he was stricken early with a guilty fear of people and an obsequious impulse to apologize to society for the fact that he was *not* Henry Fonda." *

Again in 1968, Fonda—both the man and the image—is on the political scene. The man is heard voicing ads for the Democratic Study Group, and narrating *Pat Paulsen for President,* a pseudodocumentary about the *Laugh-In* comedian's bogus run at the White House. The image appears at that year's Democratic National Convention, where Norman Mailer describes contestant George McGovern as "a reasonably tall, neatly built man, with an honest Midwestern face, a sobriety of manner, a sincerity

---

* Stunned to find his name in Heller's novel, Fonda talks to Richard Brooks, flagged in 1963 as most likely writer-director of the film version. "I'd like to be in your movie," he tells Brooks, "but I guess the Henry Fonda part is the only one I could play." What a pioneering meta-moment that would have made. See *Lowell Sunday Sun,* 10/20/1963.

of presentation, a youthfulness of intent, no matter his age, which was reminiscent of Henry Fonda."

Four years later, McGovern is his party's frontrunner, educating America daily in the limits of his charisma. Now Mailer turns the South Dakota senator's presentation as the "prairie populist" inside out, revealing dullness and piety as the obverses of sincerity and virtue. "There is a poverty of spirit in the air," he writes; "a paucity of pomp and pleasure which [his] very moral principles forbid." When he speaks of McGovern carrying "an absence of rich greeting, a delicate air of the cool," Mailer is describing with precision the Fonda of *12 Angry Men* and the campaign stump.

Like Michael Herr in *Dispatches*, invoking Lt. Col. Thursday as precedent in America's psychic mythology for the Vietnam aggression, Mailer puts Fonda's image to the acid test of modernity. Attractive as our man might be, on the screen and in the flesh, new times force new recognitions: Yes, people begin to realize, there has always been a profound piety to Fonda—an archness, a fear of passion. He appears unyielding in a time when previously iron structures—government fortress, war machine, racist institution—are being pressured to yield; he opposes nakedness in a day that calls for the clothes to come off.

American piety itself is under siege, and Fonda is guilty by association. His best films have opposed pieties of authority and patriotism, even when they were pietistic in style; but his dignity and familiarity—exactly what had positioned him well as New Frontiersman—set him back in the post-Kennedy years. Thanks in great part to the public criticisms directed at him by his daughter and son, Fonda is felt to carry the musty odor of outdated liberal traditions. Where he had for so long been an answer to American wants and needs, he is now—for the first time, really—out of date. He simply does not speak to what America is in 1966, or 1968, or 1970.

For these writers, Henry Fonda lives, but he lives in memories of another America. He is a symbol now of old weight; a symbol, too, of the better aspects of vanishing days. As these writers' memories are challenged by modern brutality and the call of relevance, Fonda's face is reexamined with fresh eyes—or transposed onto strangers like Major Major, so that something like that remembered heroism might be spotted again, even if fleetingly, in the confounding features of a lost American whose sole wish is to stay lost.

∽

In June 1972, marauders break into the Democratic National Committee headquarters in the Watergate Hotel in Washington, D.C., for the purpose of bugging telephones. They are nabbed, and their plot traced to a cadre of Nixon aides: Tactics once tested on Helen Gahagan are now the circuitry powering the White House as a dominion of the hidden. Slowly, a presidency is dismantled by revelations of dirty trickery, of democracy diverted by men crouching in corners. Oval Office tapes reveal Nixon's complicity, and he resigns to avoid impeachment.

For a solid year, through the drama of investigation and resignation, the country tastes bile. *How could we have been so duped? How were we so used?* Disgust breeds desires for revenge and purgation, but also renewal. America wants to invest trust in a man it respects. Don't look at me, says Vice President Gerald Ford, who, in pardoning Nixon, frustrates the revenge instinct and outrages his pact with the people. Americans will enjoy only secondary revenge for Watergate—through a refusal to elect Ford in 1976.

Again the times respond to Henry Fonda's enduring presence. After a decade of portraying mostly nonheroes and nonentities, he will star in a one-man stage show and send the country into raptures of admiration for a long-dead lawyer, a man it would find hard to tolerate were he still alive—a deep-grain radical contrarian who defended socialists and murderers, claimed crime was caused by mental illness and poverty, and had the gall to say the Bible couldn't be taken literally. After that, Fonda will make a private industry of playing upper-level bureaucrats, the highest officers of civic, military, and even cleric administration.

Soon he is nearly as much the president as Ford, and far more respected. His authority is so entrenched, it is scarcely noticed—which is to say it lacks surprise. His political performances of the Kennedy years had that surprise, the vibrancy of an ideal newly realized. And they came at a point when history, it seemed to many, had turned a new page, upon which any man or woman with a claim—including Henry Fonda, carrying baggage stamped "New Deal," "Popular Front," "Old Left"—could mark his or her name.

But now Fonda is in a rut with these roles, as the country is in a rut with itself: ruts of fatigue and old habit, of "malaise." So it may be Henry's way of jumping the rut when, in 1976, year of election and bicentennial, he makes a television appearance that pivots on his *refusal* to lead. On January 26 and February 2, CBS airs a two-part episode of *Maude,* a sitcom produced by Fonda's old associate Norman Lear.

It begins in Maude's living room, where the indomitable heroine (Bea Arthur) has established a campaign headquarters. The campaign: Henry Fonda for president. Maude has conceived it in the midst of a manic depression, but she is also motivated by a genuine disgust with American politics.

Only, Fonda has not been informed of his candidacy; and Maude's husband, Arthur, tells her it's stupid to nominate an actor for president. When Maude asks whom *he* wants for president, and Arthur says Ronald Reagan, the studio audience explodes with laughter.

The campaign hurtles forward. Maude's grandson says Henry has won a mock election at school ("He clobbered Tony Orlando and Dawn"). Maude advances Henry's daughter Jane as his perfect running mate. Then, shockingly, the fantasy takes form: Drawn in by a false invitation, Henry Fonda is at the doorstep. All stare in astonishment as he towers over them, a wintry monument in a Burberry coat.

The truth comes out. Somewhat aghast, Fonda protests that he knows nothing about being president; that he is unqualified and inexperienced.

"Mr. Fonda," Maude says, "you have something that no other candidate has . . . spiritual honesty. Mr. Fonda, you are the quintessential American, and the only one who can bring to this country the leadership it so desperately needs."

Henry informs Maude that she has, essentially, mistaken a man for a phantom. The words are sensible, but they ignore the degree to which, even if he cannot be the president of our waking lives, he has become the president of our movie fantasy. Maude may be nominating a phantom, but she is also nominating the actor through whom phantoms of idealism continue to exist as potentials.

Before leaving, Fonda repeats the words first uttered by General Sherman after the Civil War, when someone suggested he try for the presidency, and more recently paraphrased by Lyndon Johnson as he declined a second term in the White House.

"If nominated," Henry Fonda says, "I will not run."

Four years later, Ronald Reagan is president. It's Morning in America, and the end of an era.

∽

Perhaps Fonda's tenure as dream president ended at the moment it peaked—back in 1964, when *Fail-Safe* opened. Based on a Eugene Burdick–Harvey Wheeler novel serialized in *The Saturday Evening Post* (supposedly it was read by JFK himself), it begins with World War III triggered by a computer malfunction. Filmed in the spring of 1963 and released late the following summer, into a presidential race with world annihilation a central issue, it has the effect both of prophecy and of remembrance. And every representative terror of this last moment before anticipation turns to dread plays out in the face of Henry Fonda's president.

The movie is a true left-wing conspiracy—directed by old-line New York liberal Sidney Lumet; scripted by blacklistee Walter Bernstein; produced by United Artists vice president and founding member of Hollywood SANE (Committee for a Sane Nuclear Policy) Max Youngstein; and headlined by Fonda, who as the film appears is campaigning for LBJ against the putatively bomb-crazy Barry Goldwater.* Henry is

---

* In the fall of 1964, Fonda joined an "airborne political road show" for the Democrats, appearing at airport rallies throughout the western United States, and he narrates a syndicated TV special called "Sorry, Senator Goldwater . . . The Country Just Can't Risk It," which ran days before the election. See *Long Beach Independent,* 10/21/1964; *The* (Madison) *Capital Times,* 10/30/1964.

a longtime proponent of disarmament, having starred in the post-Hiroshima radio drama "Rehearsal," about the detonation of a super-bomb, and narrated an episode of *Eight Steps to Peace* (1957), a series of shorts about the United Nations' nurturing of détente via weapons treaties.

Despite the weight of its collective convictions, *Fail-Safe* comes across as a pure thriller, dynamic and unrelenting. A U.S. bomber group is reaching its assigned fail-safe points at the borders of Soviet airspace, when a computer blows a chip and transmits an attack code. As American and Soviet officers collaborate in pursuing the bombers, the American president—installed in a White House bunker, connected to the Soviet premier by telephone—tries with increasing desperation to avert the inevitable.

Wait, moviegoers ask, haven't we seen this? *Fail-Safe* reaches theaters several months behind *Dr. Strangelove,* with virtually the identical plot, and has the sorry fate to be a brilliant movie overshadowed by an exhilarating movie—a movie so fearsomely funny that its nihilisms have the ring of laughter in the cosmic madhouse inhabited by Swift and other comedians of the unthinkable. But *Fail-Safe* is both more dramatic and more earthbound than Kubrick's spiraling absurdity. Instead of up, *Fail-Safe* goes down—into the bunker, the Pentagon, the gut.

The unnamed president of the novel is a dead ringer for JFK. But as a Kennedy impersonator, Henry Fonda is no Vaughn Meader; to the role of president, he brings only himself. That is plenty. The bomb gives the film its relevance to the Cold War, to the latest election, to the world of 1964, but Fonda is present to give this moment its past—the long ago of Lincoln, and the closer context of twentieth-century American liberalism.

Greil Marcus notes the recurrence of Lincoln imagery in *The Manchurian Candidate,* busts and portraits that appear "more muted and saddened in each successive scene, forced to bear witness to plots to destroy the republic Lincoln preserved." In *Fail-Safe,* that role of helpless witness is taken by Fonda. Lumet shows him with head bowed and eyes closed, sitting beneath a large clock, bearing the weight of time. If we know Fonda, we know this president is not only listening, he is remembering—thus the sense of pastness. Presentness is in the immediacy of his readings, his shifts between control and panic. You *believe* Fonda in this nightmare setting, as he feels his way through a scenario of destruction no American actor before him has modeled.

First emerging as a tall black shadow advancing down a hallway, the president is seen from behind as his young interpreter stares at the back of his neck, the private face a silver smear in the elevator door. From there, the Fonda body is divested of dominance, the face stripped of privacy. With Fonda confined to the bunker, Lumet uses his star's height and slimness geometrically, and then bores in with close-ups, huge views from the vantage of a mesmerized fly, as Fonda attempts to negotiate apocalypse by phone.

His eyes become a register of the film's action, "a reproach to worldly vanities." Shouting into the hot line, the president asks if it's possible that one of the fighters might reach its target; when it's announced that it is, Lumet cuts to a single Fonda eye filling half the frame. In the Pentagon, a pitiless strategist (Walter Matthau) argues for an all-out nuclear strike. "History demands it," he intones; at the mention of "history," Fonda's eyes open and his head snaps up. Contemplating the casualties, Fonda asks, "What do we say to the dead?" There is history behind this moment—both the country's and the actor's: When Fonda invokes a responsibility to the departed, it is something very close to a statement of soul.

The moment that fulfills the story and creates continuity with the past comes when the president commits himself to the only act of good faith he can offer. If Moscow is destroyed, he swears, he will order the bombing of New York City—where, in addition to eight million people, his own wife happens to be. Fonda says the words haltingly, as if not trusting the sound of his own voice; and as he does, he covers his face with his hand, shadowing his features from the audience's view.

It's one of his great scenes. With nothing but a hand, a voice, and a shadow, past and present are joined, and epiphany crafted. All the submerged intensities of Fonda's performing history return to fill the scene, to expand its dramatic and political contexts. At the same time, acting out a world-changing ending—imagining the moment when the lid flies off—Fonda holds his hand exactly where the third bullet will, a few months later, enter John Kennedy's brain as he rides in an open car.

∽

We'd like to plumb the moment, take it apart, find its cogs and springs. But it's impossible: We cannot quite "see" what we are seeing. Rather, we feel what we are not seeing—that hum of history, that Lincoln tone still thrumming beneath the machine noise of *Fail-Safe,* of American life as it now is, as it is about to become; a heroism that hates to kill, that instead of boasting "Bring it on" asks, "What do we say to the dead?"

That is the agenda, open and urgent in Lincoln's America, that has become all but invisible in ours, and which Fonda, in his hiddenness, revives for us. At the eve of world war, *Young Mr. Lincoln* sounded the pure and decisive tone of myth, originating within Eisenstein's "womb of national spirit." The tone sang of integrity, equality, beneficent destiny; of affirmation against darkening skies. And it would sound but once.

Yet it persists as memory. Henry Fonda helps to sustain it in the dark of the movie mind, while the presidents of his time transform and deform it in the bright light of the arena. After *Young Mr. Lincoln,* no actor is more identified with the presidential role than Fonda, and Fonda is inconceivable as any other kind of president than Lincoln— that bearer of burdens who, when he looks past the faces of ordinary folk, sees eternity looking back. Lincoln was one of the very few men to ever suggest this depth in our White House, and Fonda is fit to represent him, because damned if he doesn't act like he knows some of that burden.

The older he has grown, the more Fonda's face has become the picture of memory, the more those Lincoln tones are the plaintive music of his voice. He need only present himself for us to know the ache, sense the hidden, feel that other, heroic past—just as if it truly happened, as if we were there when it happened.

As if it might happen again: even now, today.

10

He Not Busy
Being Born

*Once Upon a Time
in the West*

On a ranch in California's Conejo Valley, some fifty miles northwest of Hollywood, Henry is trying to shoot a movie—a Western
called *Welcome to Hard Times.*

"I've made lots of westerns here," he tells a reporter, "but it won't be
long before even this place is gone."

Just over the rise, bulldozers roar, clearing acres earmarked for the
planned suburban community of Thousand Oaks. How the West was
won, phase three.

∽

The 1960s are about novelty, evolution, reinvention—in one word,
transformation. The works and acts of visionaries as different as Martin
Luther King, Jr., and the Beatles, Muhammad Ali and Norman Mailer,

James Brown and Jane Fonda have in common a desire to destroy the accepted limits on social behavior and human capability. The decade's defining figures are determined to live up to the transformative demands they have set themselves; that, and the enormity of popular response to this wholesale questioning of the traditional, is what makes the 1960s a glorious rupture in our recent time.

But for others, tradition is life. A man inclined to prize old values and protect old wounds is bound to feel he was not made for these days. Venerated by one segment of society, he may find himself the target of another, one whose faith is defined in a line of Bob Dylan's: "He not busy being born is busy dying."

This man may feel that even his children are hastening that end. By decade's end, "Kill your parents" has become the Dylan line's sinister complement. Parricide, the unvoiced desire, finds voice in some widely noted words and images—Jim Morrison climaxing a Doors song by raping his mother and murdering his father; 1968's *Wild in the Streets,* in which a nineteen-year-old becomes president and parents are force-fed LSD in pogroms; Weatherman Bill Ayers's declaration, "Bring the revolution home. Kill your parents. That's where it's really at"; or Charles Manson warning straight America that its children are *"running in the streets—and they are coming right at you!"*

∽

In 1966, Henry Fonda becomes an institution. His sixtieth film, *A Big Hand for the Little Lady,* is released in June; later that month, a party is held at New York's swanky L'Etoile restaurant to mark his third decade of Hollywood stardom. The celebration serves as overture to a Fonda film retrospective at the New Yorker Theater, and as coda to his stage comeback in a hit comedy, *Generation,* now closing after three hundred performances.

The play has more than done its business, and Henry's reviews have been impeccable. But it may chafe him to find anniversaries and retrospectives suddenly abounding. In a piece accompanying the retrospective, Peter Bogdanovich writes: "Were he never to play another role, his

Lincoln, his Mister Roberts, his Earp, his Tom Joad would have immortalized him . . . as a special, most individual aspect of The American." The words are truthful and sincere, and sound like an elegy.

Right now, the Fonda kids are more to the point. As Henry celebrates his thirty years in movies, Peter—currently on drive-in screens as a drug-taking, church-wrecking Hell's Angel—is arrested in Los Angeles in connection with a quantity of marijuana. Across the ocean, Jane—now an expatriate actress married to a director of glossy erotica—sues *Playboy* magazine for publishing nude photos of her.

Henry's son and daughter are driven in the sixties toward the eternal goal of youth: the first expression of self. They take every chance that comes their way, and glory in the risk of going too far. By pushing limits, they tempt the disaster that lies behind the decade's promises, and place themselves among those who will define its ending.

∽

At Boston's Colonial Theatre at the dawn of the decade—January 29, 1960—*There Was a Little Girl,* written by Daniel Taradash and directed by Joshua Logan, opens in previews. The girl is played by Jane Fonda, her father by the veteran actor Louis Jean Heydt. The curtain rises; first scene goes smoothly. Then Heydt exits—and drops dead. Heart attack. With an announcement to the audience, the show goes on, Heydt's understudy filling in.

Consider the moment. Jane, only twenty-two and playing a daughter, loses her "father." Josh Logan is a beloved uncle who has exploited familial anxiety to goad his protégée: "You're going to fall behind your old man," he tells Jane in rehearsals. "When the curtain goes up, there'll be a ghost of your father sitting in the chair." And Heydt, we note, is fifty-four when death finds him in the wings—exactly Henry's age.

Jane spends the best part of her career working off of her father's silent example, his ghost in the chair. He is present from the start, when Jane is seventeen and a graduate of the Emma Willard School in Troy, New York. In June 1955, the Omaha Community Playhouse stages a week of benefit performances of Odets's *The Country Girl,* starring

Henry. Jane is suggested for the ingenue, a part requiring tears. Dad leaves daughter to find her own emotional motivation, and to do so, she pretends that her father is dead.

Her next guru is Lee Strasberg, whom she meets in the summer of 1958, when the Strasbergs and Fondas are neighbors on the Malibu shore. Guiding force of the Actors Studio, he espouses a variety of the Stanislavskian Method, which emphasizes the player's personal experience. Actors fear his critique but adore him for elevating them to equality with directors and writers. Jane requests private lessons from the master and gets them, for one reason: "There was such a panic in the eyes," Strasberg will later recall.

Jane is a docile girl who imagines herself a rebel, a beautiful girl who hates her looks, a daughter who worships her father but must erase him to create herself. She has spent a listless year at Vassar, forlorn months as an art student in Paris. Acting has been "a bit of a romp," no more. But Strasberg gives her permission to take the romp seriously, and a vocabulary to define what her father refuses even to discuss.

He introduces her, for instance, to the idea of the "counter-need," a secret desire contradicting each conscious motivation. He also informs her that the ability to understand any dramatic act is already contained in her personal store of buried dreams and dread wishes. As Jane explains it to Lillian Ross in 1962, you needn't commit murder to understand how murder occurs, for "somewhere inside yourself, you will find some relevant experience."

Like wishing your father was dead?

∽

Peter is more closely shadowed, it seems, by his mother. He and Frances share queer bonds—beginning with the Johns Hopkins trip, mother undergoing hysterectomy as son is probed in another room. In the cold chambers of her last years, Peter is often the only witness, apart from medical professionals, to Frances's decline. Her long fade and abrupt disappearance implant his lifelong sense that grown-ups can't be trusted—that authority itself is a lie.

"Difficult and very sensitive," Susan Blanchard describes him as a boy. He grows up with a tendency to illness, and an itch for dangerous games. That he doesn't directly intend to burn his father's acreage or shoot himself in the stomach does not mean the acts are unmotivated: No small boy plays with fire and guns because he is free of anger.

In his junior year at boarding school, Peter is involved in an incident: an instructor, referring to Henry, asserts that any man married so often must be "a no-good son of a bitch." Peter attacks the man physically, not ceasing until pulled away by others, and the aftermath intensifies his certainty of adult conspiracy.

Withdrawn from school, sent back to Omaha and placed in the charge of his aunt Harriet, Peter declares himself "not part of this system." He studies at the University of Omaha, connects with other misfits, and rehearses for life as a square peg. During family summers, Peter and Henry share private moments, but never enough of them.

The boy cannot but imagine himself a disappointing son. To prove himself in Dad's arena, Peter ventures into acting. In 1961, he stars at the Omaha Community Playhouse, and does a summer apprenticeship at the Cecilwood Theatre in Fishkill, New York. By the end of the year he has secured his Broadway debut: *Blood, Sweat and Stanley Poole,* a military comedy, earns Peter fair notices ("a rare combination of total self-assurance and appealing modesty," says *Life*). Soon into the run, he marries twenty-year-old Susan Brewer, stepdaughter of Noah Dietrich, who has recently ended his tenure as Howard Hughes's chief adviser.

Our rebel is on the rise, with solid neophyte credentials and high-ranking in-laws. If Peter never becomes his father's equal, at least he may cease to be a disappointment.

∽

Jane moves to New York in the fall of 1958 to continue with Strasberg. She models in town and works winter stock in Fort Lee, New Jersey, where an unknown Warren Beatty, at a rival theater, is prepping for Broadway. At the guru's encouragement, she enters psychoanalysis.

Henry doesn't get any of it. "I don't know what the Method is," he says in 1962, "and I don't care what the Method is. Everybody's got a method." Some methods are less agreeable than others to a man of Henry's limitations and background. Method actors, in Norman Mailer's summary, "will *act out*; their technique is designed, like psychoanalysis itself, to release emotional lava." But Fonda no more welcomes an actor's lava than he does a wife's tears or a child's diarrhea. The neediness and gabbiness of the Method revolt him: "Analysis," he says, "is a way of life for them."

But Jane continues with her facial calisthenics and miming exercises, her analysis of ego and art—until sidetracked by Josh Logan, who offers her an exclusive contract for stage and movies. He wants to test her beside his other discovery, Warren Beatty, her fellow veteran of Fort Lee, in a soap opera. That script proves unconquerable, but Logan, still keen to mate his virginal beauties, adapts the play *Tall Story,* a college-basketball farce. Beatty drifts from the picture, and Anthony Perkins is substituted.

Making her first movie, Jane feels trapped inside what she will later call "a Kafkaesque nightmare." She is horrified by her screen test: "I left the projection room in a state of shock, with a resolution to lose weight." Logan suggests she have her jaw surgically fractured and chiseled, and her back teeth pulled to achieve the gaunt glamour cheeks of the moment. (More than likely, he is projecting his own body issues onto her.*) But Jane resists his advice and makes a fetching screen debut when *Tall Story* appears in early 1960. Strikingly physical, she is unvanquished by the stagnant air and ugly look of the film; her focus is total, and she even coaxes Perkins into his most convincing show of heterosexual arousal.

Still under contract, Jane follows Logan east to rehearse *There Was a Little Girl*. But when the play closes after only sixteen Broadway performances, and it's clear that *Tall Story* is a nonevent, Logan decides to sell Jane's contract to producer Ray Stark. She persuades him to let her

---

* "The subject of fat is almost an obsession with me," Logan said in 1953. "I hate it to such a degree that it affects my attitude toward the world." See *The New Yorker*, 4/4/1953, 38.

buy it instead. She spends years working off the debt, and parsing the nightmare with her analyst.

∽

In 1962, Warner Bros. tests Peter for the lead in *PT 109*, the story of John Kennedy's World War II heroism. Future president, young Fonda—it's a passing of the torch, a laundering of history, and a commercial hook. So Peter fumbles it as badly as he can. On the day of the heavily publicized test, he balks at speaking with the expected broad Boston accent. Finally he agrees, but the test is a catastrophe. Word goes out that young Fonda is a prima donna, and Jack Warner personally vetoes his casting.

The picture flops, so Peter breaks even. But it's a losing game. As a misfit trying to fit a system he despises, he inhabits the juvenile inanities of *Tammy and the Doctor* and the antiwar broodings of *The Victors* (both 1963) with equal vacancy. Even playing a role with psychic relevance, Peter doesn't come across: As a suicide in *Lilith* (1964), he funnels a prissy performance through prop eyeglasses. Conceivably, he's defeated in the latter film by the pressure of depicting an illness similar to the one that killed his mother; certainly, his technique is incapable of transmitting the fear the scenario raises in him.

Despite it all, the Hollywood establishment is prepared to accept Peter Fonda as its own. And so it goes for a bit, as he works his way down from a princeling's perch to the mediocre middle folds of show business. He fathers a girl, Bridget, in 1964, and a boy, Justin, two years later, works on his television résumé, and collects the perks of his profession (tennis court, swimming pool, cars, extra cars). So what if he gets into crashes, plays with guns, has untreated manic depression? If he holds steady, someday he'll star in his own series as a dedicated teacher, or doctor, or detective, or lawyer. That will be canceled after two seasons, and he'll graduate to being a guest murderer on *Columbo*. He'll live.

But he will not play his part in history. Hollywood is set to transform itself, for a brief stretch, from a dominion of aging hacks to a place where experiment and nerve are the currency; where fringe visions of

American darkness and dislocation are entertained, and something like real people observed; where myths are rewritten and new kinds of horseshit patented: a transformation to be called—pompously, but not unreasonably—"the Hollywood Renaissance."

American film is primed for rebirth, with Henry Fonda's son as its star-child.

∽

Back at the Actors Studio, Jane finds her next Svengali in Greek-born actor-director Andréas Voutsinas—a gifted theater man, and, in Henry's estimation, "a parasite." He crafts her image and molds her moves for roughly three years, with spotty results: On Broadway, a respectable success (1960's *Invitation to a March*) is followed by a perfect disaster (1962's *The Fun Couple,* placed by Walter Kerr among "the five worst plays of all time").

As for Jane's films in this period, none is a big hit, but a few are attention-getters. Save for the retro tearjerker *In the Cool of the Day* (1963), they are broadly comic, and Jane often overexerts in a Method eagerness to *act out*. But Jane Fonda is clearly her own creation, whatever the influence of her gurus. In *Walk on the Wild Side* (1962), she uses costar Laurence Harvey's stiffness as a cat uses a scratching post; in *The Chapman Report* (1962), she overflows a shallow character by implying more life than it can hold. Better is *Period of Adjustment* (1962), a Tennessee Williams comedy in which she plays a hysterical southern bride close to parody, threatening to go too far—but threat, we now see, threat of the unexpected and of the too-much, is part of her magnetism.

Singly, these early movies are pointless; together, they are a mosaic of something fresh and different. Jane recalls the beauties of classic screwball comedy, but her neurosis and toughness are up to the minute. She is a sexy jungle of mixed-up modern selfhood, and a new kind of woman on the screen.

In early interviews, she credits psychoanalysis with showing her the truth about herself and her upbringing. She attributes her decision to enter her father's profession not to talent but to her own "neurotic drive." Actors, she says, are "more neurotic and selfish and insecure than the average person," and "are not likely to be particularly good parents."

Anticipating the art and politics of the new decade, Jane is attempting to expose the fiction, strip the stage. Henry appears unaffected by her criticisms, but those who know him know he buckles with each blow. "It breaks his heart," says Susan Blanchard, remarried now, but still close to the kids. "When she makes remarks about him as a father, he dies, he dies."

∞

The range of Henry's films in the middle and late 1960s gives the appearance of diversity, but it is really surrender—to virtually any project that will pay him to show his face. He'll say his agents are to blame, but Henry would rather make a bad movie than no movie at all. So his marginal works multiply, the follies and trivia of an actor still major enough to command salary and billing, yet shoehorned by necessity into the lucrative genre of the instant—sex romp, comic Western, crime drama, spy thriller, battle spectacular, family frolic.

Sex. The 1964 *Sex and the Single Girl* is chiefly about Tony Curtis seducing Natalie Wood with a series of fatuous deceptions, and secondarily about Fonda, as a panty-hose mogul, repeatedly fighting and reuniting with Lauren Bacall. Coscenarist Joseph Heller recalls, "Natalie Wood didn't want to do the picture, but she owed it to Warner Bros. on a three-film deal. And Tony Curtis needed the money to settle a divorce. That's what I like best about the movie industry: the art and idealism."

Western. As an aging cowpuncher in 1965's *The Rounders,* Henry has a nice drunk scene, and shows a talent for rising sleepily from a bunk, crossing to a table, picking up a rooster, and tossing it out a door. The movie lacks subtlety or beauty, but it has a soul, and deserves better from MGM than to become the bottom of a double bill with *Get Yourself a College Girl,* starring Mary Ann Mobley and Chad Everett.

A Big Hand for the Little Lady (1966) is an Old West poker showdown with a passel of old-time actors and a plot twist as unforeseeable as the Rocky Mountains. Also in this class of fossil goes a later dried bone, *The Cheyenne Social Club* (1970), which reunites Fonda and Jimmy Stewart. Stewart inherits a whorehouse, and the two mangy cowboys must clean up and become businessmen. The stars will not rouse themselves to states of excitation, but why should they? "It's like working with the Statue of Liberty and the Washington Monument," says director Gene Kelly—meaning it as a compliment.

Cop. As an owlish academic turned lawman, coordinating the hunt in, and for, *The Boston Strangler* (1968), Fonda is less a man than a fusty bookish vapor emanating from a brown suit. It's conceivably his dullest performance. Somewhat more vigorous as the New York Police commissioner in Don Siegel's *Madigan,* released later in 1968, he is stranded by a script that shifts emphasis from the hero of Richard Dougherty's fine novel *The Commissioner* to the detective Madigan (Richard Widmark). Fonda admires the novel, but the film's switch from character study to crime drama leaves his star turn as impressively empty as a bank vault.

Spy. In *The Dirty Game* (1965)—an anthology-style espionage thriller—he is a double agent trying to stay alive in a "safe" room. Mordant in the fashionable manner of le Carré, the segment features an unconvincing though agonized performance from Fonda. The whole seedy package is smuggled into heartland drive-ins with something called *Macabro,* "a camera-viewing of strange festivals and fetishes around the world."

War. Like a tank, the big-budget war movie heaves into the 1960s, spewing oil and crushing the tender buds of art. A claque of financiers assembles a spectacular, *Battle of the Bulge,* about the last great German offensive of World War II, and familiar faces situate it among macho endurance tests from *The Longest Day* and *The Great Escape* to *The Dirty Dozen* and *Kelly's Heroes.* Rendered odd by a bad dye job and remote by his own dullness, Fonda resents both the assignment and himself for fitting it. But money is on the table and the agents natter and Henry sighs, Ah, what the hell: It's all the same indignity—*Sex and the Single Girl* with testes instead of tits.

In contrast, Otto Preminger's *In Harm's Way* (1965), about the navy's response to Pearl Harbor, is military melodrama done with clarity and feeling. Fonda's admiral is a fleeting figure brought on at intervals to scold John Wayne's incorrigible captain, and their scenes are strangely touching. Wayne is visibly pained (he is soon to lose a lung to the cancer that will one day kill him), and the gaze of the crisp, healthy Fonda upon the Duke's ailing bulk bespeaks the rugged love that exists between old campaigners.

Years before, their friendship had broken over the blacklist. Now their interactions are enriched by admiration, acceptance, age, regret, with the ethic of manliness honored and mortality evoked without pity or poetry. Fonda's smiles at Wayne, stifled manfully and recessed in the jaw, are as dry and sincere as unwept tears.

∽

Jane met Roger Vadim in Paris in late 1957. She was not yet twenty; he was a decade older, notorious as filmmaker and rake. *And God Created Woman*, his succes de scandale of a year before, had made Brigitte Bardot into the sex goddess of the decade. Director and star were married, but theirs was an open arrangement, and Vadim lived in the opening. Jane was running with a fast crowd; the director materialized as one would-be seducer among many, and she found him "perverse" and "hateful."

In the fall of 1963, Jane returns to France to work with director René Clément on *Les Félins,* a flashy, murky pulp thriller. Vadim has meanwhile made more films, and consolidated something like a style: gauzy, coy, a boudoir aesthetic framed around his wife or mistress of the moment. The films have taste, design, and dessicated wit, but tend to be empty-headed and emotionally shallow.

He and Jane meet again, but as different people, with new, chic credentials. Deferring marriage in favor of a shack-up, they go on to produce some of the funniest, sexiest twaddle to come from Europe in this decade. *La Ronde* (1964), a remake of Max Ophüls's *comédie d'amour*, is as fragrant and inviting as bedsheets in a fancy bordello, and more fun than any previous Vadim film. Is Jane—though just one of the numerous players—the key that unlocks and admits warmth into his voyeuristic frame? *La Curée* (1965) follows, a melodrama about a woman's affair with her stepson; in the last shots of Jane's mascara-stained face, she again draws from Vadim a new species of feeling.

Moving with Vadim into a country house outside Paris, Jane finds she must adjust to his code of marital conduct. Accustomed to being bent by men into unnatural poses, she swings along with her husband's request for threesomes, while in the press evincing blissful satisfaction with her new life. Asked how Vadim has changed her, Jane says, "I'm much more relaxed now." How is the analysis progressing? "Oh, I gave that up—I was traveling so much that I didn't have time. And when I did have time, I found I didn't need it anymore."

In August 1965, they marry (partly, Jane confesses, to soothe her father's sense of propriety) and become a celebrity couple, envied and chastised. Though rumors circulate of their "sophisticated" ways, their self-presentation is candid, playful, and far from depraved. While Jane removes her clothes for Vadim's camera, she will not allow them to be removed for her: Displayed bare-bottomed on a Times Square billboard for *La Ronde,* she moves to have the necessary undergarment painted on. Likewise, when *Playboy* publishes nude photos taken surreptitiously on the set of *La Curée,* she sues the Bunny empire for $17.5 million.

A daughter, Vanessa, is born in 1968. A novel called *The Exhibitionist*—a *Valley of the Dolls* knockoff written by a pseudonymous *Newsweek* journalist—becomes a best-seller, teasing airport idlers with its story of promiscuous starlet Merry Houseman, daughter of a manly, melancholy, many-times-married Hollywood idol.* Soon after the baby arrives, Vadim directs Jane in *Barbarella,* their most notorious collaboration. Wearing space drag and plashing platinum wig, her breasts

---

* Offended by its gamut of sex scenes, from incest to lesbianism to rape, Bennett Cerf—chairman of Random House, and a friend of Henry—refused to publish the novel. Though the book's narrative only distantly parallels the Fonda family saga, Henry was encouraged to consider suing for defamation; he declined, telling Cerf, "I don't have time for nonsense like that." See Henry Guthrie, *The Exhibitionist* (New York: Fawcett, 1968 [1967]); *Time,* 10/27/1967 (available at http://w.w.w.time.com/time/magazine/,article/0,9171,841150,00html); *San Antonio Express-News,* 1/16/1972.

encased in plastic, Jane lands on the covers of both *Life* ("Fonda's Little Girl") and *Penthouse* ("The Kinkiest Film of the Year").

Daring yet wholesome, Jane is one of those few to whom this breathtaking zeitgeist seems to organically belong. But—surprise—it is mostly illusion. Bulimic, insecure, she has little sense of what she is. Like Frances, she strains to justify her husband's selfish absences, while growing more depressed and body-fixated. As the sweet life starts to pall, she finds Henry haunting her regrets. "I'd so much wanted to do better than my dad at marriage," Jane will later say.

∽

Hitting his changes fast and rough, Peter scores his first transformation in the summer of 1966. After being off the big screen for a year and a half, he breaks out in *The Wild Angels,* a high-octane "wheeler" from a low-rent studio, inspired by the Hell's Angels motorcycle cult.

It is no great shakes as art, nor is Peter's performance as gang leader Heavenly Blues a masterwork of depth. But the movie is raw and right just now, and Peter as its main face glows with mystique. Though denounced as trash, the movie makes millions, defines a new audience, and glamorizes modern outlaw style, with a star disturbingly suggestive of the young Henry Fonda reincarnated as a lissome thug in Beatle mop and Nazi cross.

Things have changed, within him and without him. In his year of invisibility, Peter has had a series of experiences that take him to the lower layers of the decade's glamour, where persistently he finds a face looking back at him. His own face: the face of the lost boy.

Peter meets Eugene McDonald III, nicknamed "Stormy," at the University of Omaha. Heir to a Zenith Radio fortune estimated at thirty million dollars, Stormy is handsome, sensitive, and frequently depressed, with one parent who is dead and the other absent: Peter's mirror image. The two build an uncommonly close bond, what Peter calls "a complicity in music, humor, ideals, and principles." Brothers in romance and rebellion, they even devise, only half in jest, the scenario for a suicide pact.

On February 3, 1965, the mirror cracks. Stormy is found in a rented Tucson house with a bullet in the back of his head and his wrists slashed. There are oddities to the apparent suicide: No note is found, and forensics suggests the body has been moved before authorities arrived. An inquest is held, with a distraught Peter among the witnesses. Though the coroner's jury finds that Stormy died in the presence of a person or persons unknown, no charges are brought. Peter feels he knows the truth: His mirror image has taken the same escape as his mother, and as Bridget Hayward. For a while, he feels more affinity with the dead than with the living.

Soon after Stormy's death, Peter experiments with LSD. The result is a sensory freak-out, leading to the same breakthrough soon to be claimed by many an acid initiate: cosmic consciousness. Having tripped, he says in 1967, "I know where I am on this planet."

He's tripped several times by late August 1965, when through the intercession of the Byrds' Jim McGuinn and David Crosby he meets the Beatles. Concluding their second American tour, the Fab Four are taking their rest in a hillside mansion on stilts in the wilds north of Beverly Hills. Music plays, pot smoke is on the breeze, and Playboy Bunnies offer relaxation in private rooms. As John Lennon will later recall, "The sun was shining and the girls were dancing and the whole thing was beautiful and Sixties."

But as the day lengthens and the sun goes burnt orange, things turn, in McGuinn's words, "morbid and bizarre." Acid comes out. Its takers loll in an empty sunken tub. After a while, George Harrison says he feels as though he's dying. Peter flashes on his ten-year-old self—and perhaps on Stormy, gone just a few months. "I know what it's *like* to be dead," he whispers back.

Lennon is nearby, growing paranoid. He is a bright, rebellious boy with a distant father and dead mother; Peter's utterance takes him close to an edge he would rather avoid. "You're making me feel like I've never been born," he moans. Those who would transform must first disintegrate: The mysteries and pains of the sixties might be summed up in this one exchange. Out of it, Lennon will write "She Said She Said," a highlight of the Beatles' 1966 *Revolver* album, with Peter as the spectral agitator "she" to Lennon's bewildered "I."

By the time he resurfaces in *The Wild Angels,* then, our rebel has seen the fear that is at the basis of both suicide and rebirth; glimpsed the glories these times offer for ambitious young artists; and imbued the Beatles' grooves with Fonda ghosts. In lysergic intimacy with the world's foremost pop group, Peter has discovered, and handed on, a psychic connection between his generation's mass odyssey and the lonesome road of the motherless child.

∽

Henry tries. As his offspring bait him in the press, the drift of the day goes against many of his own inclinations, and millions of others his age hold to an increasingly bitter set of authoritarian faiths, Henry makes gestures across the generation gap.

But an aspect of his creative stagnation is that the gestures are evasive and foolish. *Generation*, by novice playwright William Goodhart, offers Fonda as Jim Bolton, a Chicago adman with a drinking problem and an unhappy marriage, who visits his pregnant daughter and her beatnik husband in Greenwich Village. The daughter means to have a natural childbirth at home; Bolton conceives a series of clumsy schemes to redirect the birth into a sterile hospital.

Opening in October 1965, the play runs well into the next spring. It lets the star flex comic muscles seldom used, and affords audiences the rare view of Fonda having fun onstage. Notices are above average, albeit in a dismal season, but the play is little more than a breakneck sitcom. Not that we should assume Fonda was after anything but a mildly topical hit. *Generation* is the paltriest piece of theater he has fronted since *Blow Ye Winds*, but it logs more performances than his last two shows combined, and on that level is a ringing success.

On either side of the play are family films that outdo it in duplicity. *Spencer's Mountain,* a bucolic fancy about the travails of a Wyoming logging clan, is released in 1963, just before the revolt of white middle-class American youth becomes a matter of significance. Yet its views of character and context are retrieved from 1930s Hollywood, and even its star detests it for setting "the movie business back twenty years."

Showing none of the plain observation and character nuance of *The Waltons*, the successful TV series to which it will lead, the film offsets domestic verities with labored leers about burgeoning bosoms, sex practices between bull and cow, et cetera. We are repeatedly assured that the Spencer couple's loins have not gone pruney with age, and one slam-bang comic moment has wicked Pa smacking feisty Ma's upraised behind—a gesture more affectionate than anal rape, though almost equally distasteful.

In *Yours, Mine and Ours* (1968), Fonda costars with Lucille Ball in a comedy based on the Beardsleys, minor media curiosities in the mid-1950s: A navy pilot with ten children meets a Navy nurse with eight, and the families merge into a megafamily. In the eyes of at least one of its stars, the picture is a corrective to the explicit subjects and styles of contemporary movies. "They've gone too far now," Lucille Ball says, "and we are all so satiated with the extremes, with what they call reality. I refuse to admit this degradation is reality." She adds, in those endearing tobaccinated tones, "I'm also getting tired of mini-skirted beauties running the world."

Far from guileless, the movie has an agenda—the assertion of mega-family values against the claims of the counterculture.* But *Yours, Mine and Ours* is less honest than the youth-oriented exploitation movies it means to counteract. We wonder why Lucy, opposing the miniskirt oligarchy, goes through the film wearing thickly painted lips and false lashes that curl over her eyes like fried spiders; we ask how traditional morals are advanced by a screenplay sprinkled with, in Renata Adler's words, "all sorts of sleazy dirty lines, and coy bedroom scenes and smiley, hesitant conversations about puberty."

Henry has tried. But vehicles like these can only trivialize generational

---

* Nor is it coincidence that Henry narrated, around the same time, a TV documentary called *The Really Big Family*, about a week in the life of a middle-class Seattle couple with eighteen children.

divides. Fonda has aligned himself with every lame comedian, reactionary pundit, and trendy academic laboring to reduce the debates of the day—over war, rights, family and society, the understanding of history—to terms so banal that the issues behind them might as well not exist.

∽

Depressed at home, on the screen Jane vaults ahead of her peers—even though Hollywood cannot put her across as Vadim does. There's more of her comic juice in one minute of *La Ronde* than in all of the excruciating *Cat Ballou* (1965); more of her sexiness in a frame of *La Curée* than in the feeble romps *Sunday in New York* (1963), *Any Wednesday* (1966), and *Barefoot in the Park* (1967). Jane cannot redeem these movies, but she batters their boundaries, straining upward from the waist as her narrow legs transport her efficiently from spot to spot, twisting or flapping her exasperated hands.

In drama she is equally watchable, and equally wasted. She mostly just wanders intensely through Arthur Penn's small-town sex opera *The Chase* (1966), while Otto Preminger's *Hurry Sundown* (1967) is memorable mostly for the scene of Jane kneeling before her impotent saxophone-playing husband and sensuously blowing his . . . horn. Sardonic wolf whistles are heard across the land.

Back in France, *Barbarella* pushes Vadim's boudoir aesthetic and the couple's creative synergy to the final frontier. Sent on an interstellar mission by the French-accented President of the Universe—Jane's father and husband in one?—the titular vixen braves monsters, revolutionaries, and bondage kink to triumph through sheer purity of spirit. The movie is bad, but Jane has such quick responses to the dangers and debauches around her—"such a panic in the eyes"—that she can embody innocence while mocking it: Her knack for the put-on leaves Vadim's in the shade.

Barbarella Jane becomes a popular poster image, erotic icon of pubertal bedrooms and Vietnam base camps. And radical Jane will have no choice, two years on, but to renounce her: Liberation ideology in its militant phase has no place for Barbarella's zero-gravity striptease, her cosseted cleavage, or her sense of humor. Later, Jane will mellow on her alter ego, and allow that other, subtler kinds of liberation may thrive in an exploitation movie, even one with the sickly smell of pot fumes and poured plastic.

But here in 1968, the picture is a dead end. To make it, Jane has refused two of the most significant female roles Hollywood has ever offered—*Bonnie and Clyde* and *Rosemary's Baby*. Her creative drift has been toward camp, and the thing she has had with Vadim is all but over. There will be just one more film between them—a segment of the 1968 Edgar Allan Poe omnibus *Histoires extraordinaires,* whose odd, atmospheric Vadim contribution has Jane engaging in crypto-incestuous horseplay with brother Peter.

Vadim has reached the limits of his vision, whereas Jane feels her outer shell melting, and a hunger artist emerging. Already skinny, in slavery to diet and Dexedrine, she starves herself further to play Gloria, an end-of-tether loser in *They Shoot Horses, Don't They?* It is a break from Vadim, from Europe, from her performing past: a rebirth.

Peopled by castoffs of the Hollywood dream, Horace McCoy's 1935 novel had used the dance marathon as a Depression-era metaphor for life, and telegraphed the message: It's all fixed. (Much like certain protonoirs of that period, a few starring Henry Fonda.*) The movie, directed by Sydney Pollack, is keyed to a different kind of American depression, with the novel's despair inflated to hysteria. But it is something rare—a large, powerful popular entertainment founded in real darkness and turmoil, a film that will not cop out to affirmation: an avatar of New Hollywood.

It belongs to Jane. She dives deep and comes up yet again as a new kind of female star, haggard yet glamorous, burned-out yet lividly sensitive. She has never been more in command of every muscle and flutter;

---

* As a screenwriter for hire, McCoy had cowritten two of Henry's early vehicles—*The Trail of the Lonesome Pine* and *Wild Geese Calling*.

her character's extremes are paced and apportioned by technique. Muffled at first, the panic in her eyes comes alive as the marathon drags on and death draws near.

The new depth of Jane's acting seems inseparable from what the part finally asks of her—to act out a suicide. Frances's ghost cannot be far away. Gloria gazes off the Santa Monica pier and says she wants out. Beside her is a failed screenwriter, young and dim but good-hearted (Michael Sarrazin). Gloria presses a gun on the boy, and Jane goes for broke. Gloria begs to be killed, and Jane drops the last defense separating her, and us, from the character's humiliation and defeat.

And then, the virtually unprecedented in an American movie: The girl gets her death wish. The gun goes off and Jane's head tilts delicately, all cynicism and contempt expelled, in her eyes a wondering. And this, the new Hollywood movie says, is our happy ending, our best shot at rebirth. *Bang.*

For a while after *Horses,* Jane vanishes. Reappearing in late 1969 to promote the picture, she is equally eager to discuss herself, and to set some things straight. "My father is a fantastic man," she says. "As you grow older you understand how difficult it is to be a parent. In spite of all that has been written, I never hated my father. I was fighting for my own identity."

∽

Roger Corman, king of American International Pictures—skid row studio, exploitation factory, and the unlikely garden containing seeds of Hollywood's renaissance—wants to test the motorcycle market. He has a bare-bones script in which a Hell's Angel, the Loser, is shot by cops. "Busted out" of the hospital by his buddies, the Loser dies, and his funeral at a country church becomes an orgy of desecration, complete with Nazi flag and gang rape on the altar. At the end, leader Blues has an epiphany of emptiness: "I blew it all for the Loser." Blues digs his buddy's grave as the cops close in.

There's not much to it—except for straightforward style, moral neutrality, and great timing. *The Wild Angels* costs $360,000, and within a year earns $6 million, to become AIP's most profitable production ever.

Angels is key for tapping into the nihilism that is the shadow of sixties affirmation. An engine-age Western shot from the side of the marauding gang rather than the besieged town, it finds a new audience, one that wants cheap thrills, fast machines, and violent defiance of authority—that wants to feel *power,* and the thrill of righteous wreckage. Peter's sullenness expresses both the waste and the lure of this pop nihilism; his own defiance finds focus in the romance of failure.

Blues is trapped in the moment, and doubt, like the Loser's grave, is a void that has only just opened. *The Wild Angels* drops a hint, one that Peter pockets and preserves, even if the audience misses it entirely: "I blew it all for the Loser."

∽

Henry is also working on a new kind of Western—minimal, grubby, defeatist. Thanks to the 1960s, the revisionist Western is viable as a minor investment for major studios, and Fonda, alone among the erstwhile cowboy icons, fits the cut of the new variant.

As John Wayne's Western roles grow more colorful and fantastic, Henry's shrink to something smaller than life-sized. *Welcome to Hard Times, Stranger on the Run* (both 1967), and *Firecreek* (1968) offer him the chance to do unlikely, uningratiating work at the margins of attention; they cast him as, in turn, coward, outcast, and criminal; and they assert a claim on existential relevance at a time when veneration is deadening his nerves, killing his desire to care.

As leader of a criminal gang in *Firecreek,* Henry limns a fine sadness and a jaded ease, but the other actors showboat and the director declares his allegiance to formula. In Don Siegel's no-frills *Stranger on the Run,* Fonda's alcoholic drifter, fingered for a killing, is pursued, beaten, bounced about like a figure in a shooting arcade. Henry has never appeared more wretched or pitiable: Silently screaming from a shot of whiskey, his limbs protesting their every exertion, this most elegant of actors makes a marvel of his character's ability to remain upright. But while the concept is gutsy, the product is only so much prop plywood around Fonda's trembling center. Simply that these films are notable does not make them very good: Like the men who make them, they are grizzled and sardonic and have false teeth.

In *Welcome to Hard Times,* adapted by writer-director Burt Kennedy from E. L. Doctorow's novel, a frontier town is invaded by a mute psychopath who lays waste to everything, leaving a few scarred survivors to rebuild. "Well I have seen the elephant," someone in the novel says as the climax nears; and Fonda's Will Blue—a horrified witness turned reluctant sheriff—looks as though he sees that great ghost around every corner. Moving like an older, slower Wyatt Earp, but without the skill or cunning, he feels his way through a timid man's desperate efforts to remain among the living.

Fonda the actor goes away disappointed, regretful that the attempt, which he'd hoped would yield another *Ox-Bow Incident,* "didn't come off." By which he means it didn't go far enough. It remains for other films to draw lines and dare outrages in the coming years, to explicitly link the myths of the Old West to the realities of now. But these early anti-Westerns at least wonder about such salient matters as heroism, conquest, and community, and respond to a new mood of doubt in the mainstream audience.

Henry *is* the mainstream: He believes in America. But he doubts it, too. And he has much to doubt just now, because he—like John Wayne, like Jimmy Stewart, like all of Old Hollywood—supports America's war in Vietnam.

∽

In 1966, Peter is involved in two incidents with police. In June, LAPD narcotics officers acting on a tip find several marijuana plants under cultivation at a house in the suburb of Tarzana. Peter Fonda's signature is on the telephone contract; so he, along with three other men, is charged with possession. And on November 26, three days before the trial begins, he is briefly taken into police custody during the Sunset Strip riots, a series of weekend clashes between police and youngsters stemming from the city's imposition of a curfew.

During the trial in Los Angeles Superior Court, Henry, wearing stubble grown for *Firecreek,* takes the stand to testify on his son's behalf. Conceivably, his appearance is what saves Peter from prison, given the strength of the circumstantial case. The jury fails to reach a verdict on his charge, though it convicts one of his codefendants; before releasing Peter, Judge Mark Brandler delivers a stern lecture: "Make the most of this opportunity by leading a useful and productive life so that your wife, children, and illustrious father will never again be ashamed or humiliated by you."

Such comeuppance could mean ruin for Peter—the new wild angel of shock cinema dressed down by a judge, defended by establishment Dad. But our rebel presses on. His next film, *The Trip,* again directed by Roger Corman (from a script by Jack Nicholson), attempts to recreate the totality of an LSD experience, with Peter chasing the lysergic in quest of revelation. The film brags on its authenticity, but it turns out that LSD perception closely resembles imagery drawn from a Fellini festival, painted in candy colors and punched up with bad jazz-pop.

In February 1968, *Esquire* runs an article on Peter by Rex Reed. Taking the sun on his Beverly Hills patio, his bullet wound visible as a four-inch scar, Peter is full of anger, self-pity, and foolish schemes. There is much monologue about his loneliness growing up, and his mortification at adult hands. He voices his desire to make movies "without all the big-studio shit" and pitches two pornographic concepts, one based on a Beatles song, the other—to be directed by Vadim!—on the Fonda family.

Prominent in the spray of verbiage are Peter's stinging remarks about Henry. The themes, expectedly, are silence ("Nobody told me the truth about my mother. . . . My father won't even talk to me about *today,* so he's not gonna talk about yesterday. There are too many yesterdays for him to get into") and absence ("My father was never around, he never speaks any fucking words to me, he never said a bloody goddam thing"). But even at his most bilious, Peter wants to forgive. "Now I know," he says of his father, "that all in all he saved me."

The interview is a cathartic, Peter will tell Sheilah Graham soon after, and has the effect of improving communications between himself
and his father. Something of this catharsis—and a mature acceptance
that not all wisdom resides in the fancies of youth—may have worked
itself into Peter's new project. Presently filming on locations across the
American South, it is neither the Beatle porn nor the Fonda porn, nor
any porn at all.

"It's called *Easy Rider*," Peter says. "It's about what's happening
today, young and old."

∽

After World War II, Henry is a proponent of global disarmament and
multilateralism. Then the line between principled restraint and imperial
intervention is blurred by JFK, whose administration is fascinated with
assassination and foreign adventure. Kennedy's domino theory rational-
izes the U.S. presence in Vietnam, and the liberal-intellectual establishment buys in.

Doing his part, Henry hosts, in 1962, an installment of *The Big Picture,* a series of propaganda films about the army's role in international
conflict. His episode is a tribute to the Special Forces, aka the Green
Berets, soon to be made famous in a hit single and a John Wayne movie.
"Recent headlines have spotlighted such areas as Laos, Vietnam, and
of course Cuba," Fonda says. "We have to be able to meet this kind of
threat, and to help others to meet it. And we intend to."

The picture is bigger, and the battle bloodier, by late 1966, when
Henry narrates *To Save a Soldier,* an ABC-TV documentary about the
evacuation and treatment of wounded troops. Overcome by the raw
footage, he has difficulty recording his voice-overs: "The experience was
that strong," he says. "The camera moves right in on the soldier's face
before the operation begins . . . and this man looks like he's going to die.
The scene really tears you apart." Perhaps this eyeful of patriotic gore
fortifies his belief in the war; perhaps it inspires the first of his doubts.

Soon after, he is invited by the USO on a "handshake tour" of the
war zone. For three weeks in April 1967, Fonda meets and poses for

photos with hundreds of GIs. The same month, Gen. William Westmoreland tells President Johnson that the conflict is at a "crossover point," and Martin Luther King, Jr., links the civil rights and antiwar movements in an address at New York's Riverside Church.

Back home, Henry sounds less than steadfast. "I'm still a liberal," he says. "[B]ut you can't be there and come away and not at least feel, well, obviously we should be there and the job is being done and it's a good job." His diagnosis of the real problem—that continuous peace rallies and antiwar protests will only make the war last longer—seconds the logic of hawk pundits and war presidents.*

By chance, another prominent American visits South Vietnam at the same time. On April 17, after returning, Richard Nixon says, "The irony is that marchers for peace prolong the war." Politics make strange bedfellows, but has Henry "I'm still a liberal" Fonda ever imagined himself in this ménage à trois—Duke Wayne on one side, Tricky Dick on the other, himself in the middle, arm in arm on the road to Saigon?

∽

Many circumstances converge to test Henry's commitment to the American mission as now defined—chiefly, the newfound radicalism of his daughter.

Jane's is one of the gutsiest public transformations of the era. She enters the fight after the bone-breaking battles of the 1968 Democratic National Convention, the Weathermen's Days of Rage, and Ronald Reagan's violent clampdown on the streets of Berkeley. The issues are neither few nor simple: Not just antiwar and Black Power protesters but also advocates for women's liberation, the American Indian Movement, gay liberation, and other movements are jostling for space on the street and the front page.

Feeling the necessities of the moment, Jane Fonda takes her leap and

---

* In his autobiography, Fonda says he was hesitant to accept the USO invitation because he didn't agree with the war (*FML*, 292–93); but at the time, his support of U.S. policy was quite clear.

risks career, comfort, safety, Dad's last portion of patience. Why? She recalls a mosaic of formative moments: an encounter with hippie dropouts in Big Sur; an awareness, while in France, of student protest; a trip to India; an Alcatraz Indian woman on the cover of a New Left magazine; first meetings with Black Panthers and embittered young soldiers; her reading of Jonathan Schell's *The Village of Ben Suc,* a nonfiction account of what happened there.

Her first radical act is to lie down in the provost's office at the Fort Lewis military reservation near Tacoma, Washington, as part of an attempted Indian occupation. It is March 1970, and her first arrest. Upon their release, she and the other protesters agitate at nearby Fort Lawton, and are ejected; the next day, through her attorney, Warren Commission debunker Mark Lane, Jane files suit for civil rights infringement against Defense Secretary Melvin Laird.

Like many from privileged backgrounds, Jane finds that activism simplifies her life and clarifies her identity. She separates from Vadim, and replaces her gay French duds and luxe hairstylings with somber, androgynous outfits and a battle-ready shag cut. Throughout 1970, she crisscrosses the country, participating in strikes, exhorting and leafleting, getting arrested, and otherwise sculpting an identity as straight America's latest pain in the ass.

On November 3, passing through Cleveland's Hopkins International Airport, Jane is detained by customs agents, who find a large volume of pills in her luggage. An agent attempts to place her under arrest, and there is a disturbance. The pills, it's reported, comprise more than a hundred vials containing two thousand capsules of unknown content, in addition to prescription Dexedrine, Compazine, and Valium. Jane is charged with smuggling and assault, though she claims the mystery pills are vitamins. She pleads not guilty and requests a jury trial, Mark Lane again serving as her attorney; but charges are dropped when the drugs are found to be, indeed, vitamins. (Jane has obtained them, ironically, at her father's behest, and through his physician.)

The accumulation of arrests and antagonisms finally breaks Henry's self-control. He begins referring to Jane as "my alleged daughter," and tells her privately that, should he suspect her of subversion, he will report her to the FBI. Interviewed in the wake of the Cleveland episode, Henry fills Earl Wilson's newspaper column with blank lines in place of an obscene three-word phrase beginning with "crock":

> My daughter makes statements that she's glad to have been in jail because so many wonderful people have been in jail! That's a————! That's not my daughter's opinion, it's Mark Lane's and he's a————! . . .
>
> All of us that love her, Peter and I and everybody, hope she isn't going to let herself be destroyed.

∞

In September 1967, Peter is autographing a still from *The Wild Angels,* showing himself and costar Bruce Dern standing before their bikes in silhouette. The figures speak to him with psychic precision: Blues and the Loser, the lost boy and his accomplice. And the larger vision: a modern Western, with motorcycles in place of horses.

Peter asks Dennis Hopper, a bit player in *The Trip,* to be his costar and director. The Kansas-born Method actor, a veteran of both mainstream Hollywood and fringe exploitation, has never directed a film. He and Peter develop a treatment, titled *The Losers,* about cocaine dealers biking to Florida. American International declines to finance it, but when superstar satirist Terry Southern lends it his name and counsel, independent producers Bob Rafelson and Bert Schneider consent to seed a budget of $360,000 to make the retitled project—*Easy Rider.*

Shooting begins in New Orleans in February, with an unfinished script, ragtag crew, and director zonked on power and substances; three months of location shooting follow. Revising scenes daily, Peter and Hopper find their characters: Wyatt, controlled, wounded; and Billy, pugnacious, pleasure-seeking. A third character emerges—an alcoholic lawyer and liberal redneck, played by Jack Nicholson, working for union scale. The narrative, a series of encounters between freaks and straights on American back roads, is suffused with Peter's desolation and Hopper's paranoia.

Easy Rider is the hit of the May 1969 Cannes Film Festival, but no one is prepared for its impact upon reaching America the following month. Some observers invest its arrival with millennial weight, while others dismiss it as youth-stroking fantasy. Peter and Hopper are anointed oracles of youth; Nicholson gets an Oscar nod and a ticket to the stratosphere. The picture grosses forty million dollars and joins the small group of films that have expressed something essential about these difficult times.

Easy Rider is full of grace notes and irreducible thrills: the bikers climbing an L.A. freeway with Steppenwolf on the track; razor-flicking flash-forwards to an indistinct near future; Peter asking "How's your joint, George?" in such a friendly tone. Land and atmosphere are palpable, the feel of heat and dust, shade and water. Death runs through the rock score like the river of the final frames. Beneath everything is a legacy of direct violence and ambiguous meaning inherited from the Western. The filmmakers catch the breath of the frontier—that ghost country all around us—give it the snap of contemporary danger, and put it to a pop pulse.

Peter's performance is passive bordering on posthumous, yet it bears comparison to his father's work. Peter too is the soulful center of a Ford-like community of oddballs; his is the gaze around which an inspired director frames a vision. It is this still center that distinguishes *Easy Rider* from all youth cinema before it. Conceivably, the movie might exist without Henry Fonda in its genes, but it would be something else entirely—would be a glorified *Hell's Angels on Wheels*.

Peter explodes his own placid surface just once, when Wyatt experiences a death trip in a rainy New Orleans graveyard. Towering above Saint Louis Cemetery #1, a tight maze of crypts abutting a ghetto, is a tomb bequeathed to the city by its Italian Society: a sitting woman with her hand upraised. Reluctantly, Peter obeys his director's command to climb the monument and sit in the woman's lap. Hopper, retrieving his Method training through sheets of wine and speed, calls from below: She's your mother. Talk to her.

Peter does, and soon breaks down, sobbing into the cold face and empty eyes. It is embarrassing and uncomfortable, a primal scene: The camera finds the lost boy in the arms of his dead mother, arms as cold as the grave, attempting his own rebirth.

It doesn't happen—or at least we don't witness it. Only the effort. But this is one gauge of the New Hollywood as *Easy Rider* and other films will define it: Scenes may happen without completing or culminating. Life flows past, the frame catching only pieces, and new movies will require of audiences a new openness to obscurity and chance. The magic will be in the catching, and resolutions may dangle out of reach, or suggest themselves as the ghosts of a thousand possibilities.

Or they may be cut off completely, as in life. *Easy Rider*'s money shot is the bikers' execution on a country road—shotgun blast, cycle leaping over meadow like a riderless horse, and exploding. For Peter, it is the longed-for suicide pact and romantic gesture, the lost boy and his accomplice blasting through, together—after which they are simply gone, like Frances, like Bridget Hayward, like Stormy McDonald. The only residue lies in the burning wound, the perspective pulling back like the trailing off of memory, the goneness of life.

"We blew it," Wyatt says in the frontier firelight, just before the end. Peter ad-libs the line, knowing it is cryptic but feeling right with it, and he fights Hopper to retain it as the film's closest thing to a statement.

The words could fit any point in American history when the great goal had slipped away, after seeming close enough to touch. Like the day after Lincoln was killed; or the day someone first realized the 1960s had ended on the abortion of so many rebirths, that time had run out before culmination was reached and transformation achieved. A thousand possibilities were blown, and they blow now in the dust of a country that—in *Easy Rider* and in the films that follow from it—is suddenly more open, inexplicable, fast, and random than movies have ever allowed it to be.

∽

Early in 1968, Henry receives an offer from an Italian director he has never heard of. The director's name is Sergio Leone, and he has been after Fonda for years.

Between 1964 and 1966, Leone loosed on Europe three Westerns— *A Fistful of Dollars, For a Few Dollars More,* and *The Good, the Bad and the Ugly*—that blew the genre open. They propose floridly Italian actors in Spanish locations as Americans in the Old West. Actors mug and sweat; guns go off like cannons; Ennio Morricone's music suggests Wagner on the hoof. The photographic vistas are enormous, the humor broad and killings innumerable, the films explosive and altogether new.

After Leone's "*Dollars* trilogy" mopped up at the Italian box office, United Artists secured American distribution and staged a staggered U.S. release. The bet paid off: White middle-aged American men were enraptured, and the little-known Clint Eastwood, as Leone's unnamed hero, became a star.

Now the spaghetti Western rules, and Leone's success earns him a deal with Paramount, an all-star cast, and the use of John Ford's Monument Valley. A sheaf of scenes is assembled, something about a woman, a bandit, the railroad, revenge. . . . Well, what does story matter? Leone is a big-picture man. For casting, he is certain of just one thing—Fonda, on whom he has been fixated since the late 1940s, when Ford Westerns flickered on the flyspecked screens of cinema societies in postwar Rome.

In early 1964, Leone submitted the script of *A Fistful of Dollars* to Henry's agents. The agents responded that their client would never consider such a role as this "Man with No Name." (They gave him *The Rounders* instead.) The next year, Leone envisioned his elusive idol as the Man's quick-drawing ally in *For a Few Dollars More.* Again, the answer was no. (*Battle of the Bulge.*) But now Leone is going Hollywood, and Henry's (new) agents advise him to jump aboard the mad Italian's money train.

Disliking the script, Fonda goes to Eli Wallach, a friend since *Mister Roberts.* As the Mexican bandit of *The Good, the Bad and the Ugly,*

Wallach has lately delivered the performance of a career, and he gives Henry the lowdown: Leone commands an invigorating, anarchic set; shoots "from sunup to sundown"; has "some kind of magical touch." He urges Fonda to do the picture.

Doing it will mean weeks of shooting on Spanish plains and back in Monument Valley, endless mountings and dismountings of horses, eating dust and baking in the sun, all in service to a director who speaks no English and whose set is a noisy chaos. Henry is sixty-three. He hates chaos and distrusts horses.

After a genial meeting with Leone and a comprehensible script revision, Fonda watches the *Dollars* trilogy. The films win him over: "I thought they were funny and entertaining in every possible way." At last Leone has his Fonda.

But what role will Henry play in this movie, so grandly titled *C'era una volta il West* ("Once upon a time, there was the West")? Leone's large belly tingles as he lays it out: Noble Fonda will be the villain and deadly king snake of the piece—a man called Frank, whose first act in the film is to kill a child.

Something inside Fonda tingles right back.

He reports to the Cinecittà set in Rome in March 1968 wearing a bushy mustache, heavy eyebrows, and dark contact lenses. Leone erupts: The Fonda face is what he has paid for—unwhiskered mouth and blue eyes. Thirty years before, John Ford had molded his star's face into Lincoln's; now, Leone desires the face that has been molded by those intervening decades. In a reverse of Fonda's first great screen transformation, the director will strip the face to its sunburned surface. For the first time, we will see it in all its age, complexity, and beauty.

"This Leone fellow," Henry will say when filming is finished. "He seems to get right inside your head, making you think differently, react to situations as never before and perform as you've never performed in the past. I've done things for him that I once would have backed away from."

Thus influenced, he will achieve closer communion with the ghost that lives in his acting than he ever has, or ever will again.

∽

When *Klute* appears in June 1971, Jane Fonda is reborn as a quintessential woman of the new decade. The performance is a further innovation in screen acting, as cogent a contribution to cultural life as Bogart's detective or Brando's brute. Directed by Alan J. Pakula, *Klute*—about a New York prostitute shadowed by both an investigator and a killer—is attuned to moods of quiet and trembling in the heart of the city. The look suggests noir, but the audience has a new sense that character arises less from plot contrivance than from inspiration and accident.

Jane's Bree Daniels exists, as few screen characters do. Take the scene in which, smoking grass in her silent apartment, she sings herself a formal hymn about marching with God. The song is retrieved, like Peter's cemetery scene, from memory—it was sung in chapel at the Emma Willard School—and Jane inserts it on impulse. Yet the need to sing the song is Bree's, and it places us in the room with her. We cannot say where the song comes from, or why it should haunt us.

Bree's scenes with her therapist are improvised by Jane. In a monologue that builds from cliché to breakthrough, Bree articulates her need to self-destruct. At the same time, Jane sounds the gap between herself and her father—Henry's compulsion to honor limits, and her own to push them. As she approaches insight, her hands grip the air, her energy intensifies, her eyes pin the thing in place. Bree, the character, finally goes too far—speaks the truth of herself before knowing what to do with it—and Jane, the actor, presses her fists to her mouth, as if that could take it all back.

The performance is a freehand masterpiece painted in air, the more impressive for having been alchemized out of chaos and in the face of terrific scorn, both public and private.

But scorn only propels her. In February 1971, she is present at the Winter Soldier hearings, a gathering of GIs, who relate horrors witnessed and committed in Vietnam. She cofounds a satirical musical revue, FTA ("Fuck the Army"), as an alternative to Bob Hope shows, and shoots a film with radical French auteur Jean-Luc Godard. In the fall, FTA plays

at army outposts and off-base coffeehouses before touring U.S. installa-
tions along the Pacific Rim. Around this time, Jane introduces her father
to a group of antiwar GIs; their accounts from the quagmire place a deep
wedge between Henry and the war he has so equivocally backed.

In the midst of this, she manages to be Oscar-nominated for *Klute*.
Hearing the news, Jane seeks Henry's advice—they are speaking again—
and when her name is called, she accepts the prize with what may be the
briefest speech ever given by a recipient in the acting categories: "There's
a great deal to say, but I'm not going to say it tonight. Thank you."

The words, she grants, are her father's, pretty much verbatim: In
Fonda style, a moment primed for excess is cooled with restraint, yet
filled with implications. The award is a miracle of discernment in the
muddled and myopic history of the Oscars; Jane is dignified and impressive. Middle America, innately respectful of televised awards, must
acknowledge her.

Then she goes, in the eyes of millions, finally and irrevocably too far.
In July 1972, Jane makes her infamous trip to Hanoi. She has heard
reports that American planes are bombing dikes in the Red River Delta
of North Vietnam. The collateral effect of these strikes, White House
strategists project, will be to flood the surrounding rice paddies and
cause widespread starvation. Nixon denies the bombing; Jane's goal is
to gather evidence.

Partly at the encouragement of antiwar activist Tom Hayden, encountered a few months before, Jane flies to Hanoi as an invited guest. One
day, her hosts lead her to an antiaircraft gun in a training area; asked to
sit in the gunner's seat, she does. She then grips the gun's controls, the
barrel pointing skyward, and laughs. A photo is taken. Others seem to
show Jane applauding and serenading the North Vietnamese. The
photogs cannot believe their luck, the tour guides' heads spin with the
propaganda possibilities, and Jane does not realize what has happened.

On July 14, she makes the first of ten broadcasts, transmitted over
Radio Hanoi and within earshot of both fighting troops in the south
and captured prisoners in the north. She lauds the North Vietnamese
and indicts the bankruptcy of the government and culture of the United

States. She asks servicemen to question their mission, urges the adoption of the North Vietnamese peace plan, and equates Nixon with the war criminals of Germany and Japan. Jane doesn't foresee that the crimes she has come to expose will be overshadowed by her own fawning regard of a brutal regime; nor does she win converts by contending that captured U.S. pilots testifying to torture in North Vietnam are "liars, hypocrites and pawns."

She has force-fed Middle America something it cannot swallow. Pundits release a spew of Archie Bunkerisms, one suggesting the name Jane be forever synonymous with betrayal, "to convey the impression of a female Judas goat." Treason hearings are launched in the House of Representatives and the Justice Department. Maj. Ted Gostas, a POW in Hanoi, recalled being made by his captors to read the text of one of Jane's broadcasts. "I felt betrayed," he said.

> I had seen a movie years ago when Henry was young. It was about *Drums on the Mohawk* or something. You know, "Leatherstocking" stuff. Well, Henry ran away from Indians chasing him with tomahawks. They poop out and he gets safely to reinforcements. How often I thought of that in prison.

There's a certain heroism in going too far for the right reasons, and a certain cruelty. In exposing Nixon's lies, Jane has done damage to the men at his mercy; in opposing the war, she has helped to marginalize the radical resistance. For the damage to individuals, Jane will apologize many times. For the damage to the movement, nothing may really be blamed, perhaps, but cycles of passion and backlash, a momentum of events beyond individual control.

But for any act of magnitude, there are innumerable results. Another is that Henry Fonda admits to a change of heart on Vietnam, and on Jane's politics generally. In January 1973, he attends her wedding to Tom Hayden, and three years later he supports Hayden's bid for the California Senate against incumbent John V. Tunney. In March 1974, hours after opening on Broadway as Clarence Darrow, Henry hosts a benefit for Jane's action group, the Indochina Peace Campaign. And in his autobiography he says, very simply, "She's been vindicated. That war was obscene."

But Jane will always carry the mark of the dangerous woman. In the 2004 presidential race, her name will be used to discredit Senator John Kerry, a Vietnam veteran and passing acquaintance.* Publicizing her memoir the following year, Jane will be spit on by a veteran. In 2010, an American woman recruiting Muslim extremists via the Internet will use the alias "Jihad Jane." And unto eternity, the urinals in certain U.S. Army latrines will be decorated with pictures of Jane: target practice for the troops.

In the 1960s and 1970s, Jane transformed herself to fit the sexual and political extremes of husbands who magnified qualities she admired in her father. That left people asking how strong a personality she really had. Henry observed, as far back as 1961, that if Jane "goes out with a liberal, the next day she spouts his philosophy, but I doubt that she realizes what it means." But in the years from 1969 to 1972—her most fruitful and extreme, as artist and activist—her quest has been to discover for herself, often alone and scorned, what it means. That has been the point of all these changes and risks, these demands on self and society, and they have left not just the daughter but the father—and the country they both love—changed forever.

∽

"We blew it" is the obvious or hidden accusation in the films that crown the Hollywood Renaissance: *The Wild Bunch, Little Big Man, Five Easy Pieces, Zabriskie Point, McCabe and Mrs. Miller, Mean Streets, The Parallax View, Chinatown, Shampoo, The Missouri Breaks*, and of course the *Godfather* movies. *We came this close to something—the truth, a*

---

* Jane and Kerry knew each other from the Winter Soldier hearings, but a photo supposedly showing the two together at an early 1970s antiwar rally proved to be a fake.

clean getaway, our American dream—and we blew it. Easy Rider strikes the perfect theme for a country that has become a Roman circus of conquest and cholesterol, dark parades and bad dreams.

As for Peter, he does not blow it: He makes it. *Easy Rider* earns his fortune, turns Hollywood upside down, and stands as a film. These matters achieved, he returns to being a journeyman, albeit one with aura. He directs *The Hired Hand* (1971), a Western, and *Idaho Transfer* (1973), an ecological cautionary tale. The first is a picture-poem of great beauty, the second a perversely compelling experiment in monotony. Both are classic "We blew it" stories, and so low-key that they go all but unnoticed by critics or audiences. He then returns to drive-in roots with entertaining redneck hits like *Dirty Mary Crazy Larry* (1974), *Race with the Devil* (1976), and *Fighting Mad* (1979).

Latter days show Peter at ease with the limits placed on him by heredity and history. He has worked prodigiously, and is as likely to plug a nostalgia-begging anthology of sixties pop as he is to give a first-rate performance in *The Limey* (1999), which contains one scene—a self-dramatizing reverie about the great decade, delivered to a clueless concubine barely out of her teens—as good as any he has played.

There is no wrapping up the story of a father and son, but if our purpose has been to draw reflective traces from tandem journeys, one or two remain. As a beekeeper in *Ulee's Gold* (1997), Peter channels Henry's middle-aged modes of speech and movement into his warmest acting since *The Hired Hand*. He has never been more submerged in an imaginative projection of his father—the cussedness and courage, the stone-ground love—yet he has seldom seemed more natural on the screen. His Ulee is both performance and séance.

Wanda Nevada (1979), a Disneyesque ball of corn, is the last film Peter has directed, and the only one in which he and his father appear together. As an ancient prospector, Henry comes on to the tune of "Clementine" and delivers two or three lines. Wearing a baseball cap, goggles, and great mangy beard, he looks half man, half horsefly. But the walk is unmistakable, as are the up-tilted triangular nose and the husked-out voice snapping sentences into middle western word clusters.

Between takes, Peter shows Dad the porpoises he has lately had tattooed on his shoulder. Henry is so aghast, he is unable to speak. Really, now—after all that has come and gone between them? Apparently, Omaha propriety never dies; it only waits to be offended.

But Peter smiles. "He doesn't want to talk about them," he says of Dad and the porpoises. "God bless him."

∽

Once Upon a Time in the West is such an odd film. So estranged from earthly reality it could be occurring on the moon, its mythic confrontation between avenger and criminal nonetheless meshes with the temporal conflicts of the late 1960s. This epic Western should have nothing to do with Vietnam and student protests, or with Henry Fonda and his offspring, yet it does. *Once upon a time*: Why can't the time be a hundred years ago, or right now?*

Jill (Claudia Cardinale), a New Orleans prostitute just wed to a desert entrepreneur, arrives in Sweetwater, Arizona, to find her new family massacred and herself the inheritor of a desirable property; she is watched over by Cheyenne, a fugitive accused of the murders (Jason Robards). Meanwhile a stranger with a harmonica (Charles Bronson) patiently contrives a showdown with a veteran gunman, Frank (Fonda). The stranger and the fugitive forge an alliance while the gunman engages in cat and mouse with his employer, Morton (Gabrielle Ferzetti), a railroad tycoon desperate to secure the widow's property and reach the Atlantic Ocean before he succumbs to cancer.

But the plot is only an excuse for actors and identities to walk the same spaces and regard each other as if they have met before—which they have: across the story, across the genre, across time. From its first shots—three assassins materializing in three doorways—to its last image

---

* During the filming, Robert Kennedy was assassinated. Mickey Knox, who wrote the movie's English dialogue, recalls Fonda's "rare show of emotion" at the news—one way in which the outside world of political murder and social chaos contributed to the alchemy of this masterpiece. See Mickey Knox, *The Good, the Bad and the Dolce Vita: The Adventures of an Actor in Hollywood, Paris, and Rome* (New York: Nation, 2004), 265.

of figures receding in smoke drifts, this is a haunted work. The harmonica-blowing stranger is pure phantom; Cheyenne is all flesh. Jill—brutalized, stripped of frills to become earth mother of the new West—is the only character to be absorbed rather than defeated by time.

Frank is the most haunted of them all. Strong, fast, and ruthless, he appears omnipotent. But he is repeatedly outmaneuvered by those who see further ahead than he, or further back. His destiny is to understand finally that he is not omnipotent at all but answerable, in blood, to the demand of the past.

Frank's passage has poignancy because he is not a soulless psychopath, but a master of cruel necessity who, in another life, might have been president. Leone restores to Fonda the physical magnificence he has lacked since the great Ford films; we've lost sight of how *ordinary* this beautiful man has been made to look by a legion of prosaic camera hacks. Liberated and challenged by Leone's wide screen, Henry dominates it with the virility of an aging conqueror.

From this come moments that are revelatory. When Frank coerces sex from Jill on a bed suspended from ropes in a cave—a scene so lulling and disturbing—Fonda shows a gift for malevolent eroticism. Elsewhere, Frank, betrayed by an inept spy, places a cheroot in his mouth. He lowers his face to light it, draws smoke as if savoring the taste of punishment, and flicks a look at the spy from under his hat brim. *There he is*—the killer that Leone's eyes saw in Fonda long ago. This is the Man with No Name.

Fonda performs as if feeling his physical tools and sensual powers in a new way. Part of Leone's magic is to get, as Henry puts it, "in back of your mind, back of your eyes"—to enable actors to see themselves differently. So Fonda luxuriates in his own prowess as never before. Observing Morton's death crawl, Frank spits a long sluice of tobacco and reholsters his gun: The spit is like a cobra's kiss, the holstering sexual, as Fonda feels all the mechanics of muscle and arranges them in a flow that is visually liquid and sensually pleasing.

We've never seen this before: Henry is having sex with himself. And the sex is great.

ᵔᵕ

The film is concerned with time, and with generations. Frank's first act is to kill a small boy with a warm smile and a single shot to the heart; his last, to be killed by another boy—the stranger, a grown version of the boy whose brother died at Frank's hands.

There is a moment when fear of the past first creeps into Frank's heart. Captured at gunpoint, the stranger is tied up in Morton's train car. He insinuates responsibility for the deaths of Frank's men. The killer approaches warily, removes the stranger's hat. Fonda comes eye to eye with Bronson, another actor of deep inwardness who regards the present as if across vast plains of the past.

"Who are you?" Frank asks.

"Dave Jenkins."

Fonda's cheeks sag; the cheroot dips in his mouth. Degrees of warmth and of life drain from his face.

"Dave Jenkins dead a long time ago," says Frank.

The stranger smiles, not smugly. His smile is as sweet as the sweetest memory.

"Calder Benson."

Frank's skin drops slacker. The voice breaks.

"What's *your* name?" he all but pleads. "Benson's dead too."

"You should know, Frank, better than anyone. You killed them."

That cuts the trance. Frank slaps the stranger three times hard—smashing that smile, reasserting the present over the past, his own power over a ghost's. And buys himself a bit more time.

There is no fathoming this brief scene. Its otherworldliness comes from Bronson's immovable stare, deflecting all irony and disbelief; the eerie wailings on the sound track; the precise editing, keyed to the shared heartbeat of the two men. But it comes mostly from the Fonda close-up, and the impossible delicacy of his responses. For a few seconds, he is a Münch painting come to life. Our eyes cannot grasp the fear he expresses, nor can our words describe its depth, except to say we are seeing a man who sees a ghost.

Only a showdown—that western ritual, which in this decade has been acted out for real on many stages, many streets, between armies of bodies—will settle the debts of the past. The stranger is haunted by the memory of a blurred figure approaching in slowed motion. In the moments before the last draw, the memory returns, the blur clarifies, and out of the past steps Henry Fonda—thirty years younger, sexy and swaggering, eyes ablaze with youthful depravity, looking like Abe Lincoln crossed with Satan.

"He comes from the depths of the image," Leone says, "just as he comes from the lower depths of memory." And so the positions of that first encounter between stranger and killer are reversed: Frank is now the ghost, the stranger his witness. Young Frank pulls out a harmonica. His smile goes ugly as he says, "Keep your lovin' brother happy," and shoves the bar in a boy's mouth. The boy is the stranger, and his wrists are bound. On his shoulders stands a man, bound as well, and around the man's neck is a noose, suspended from a stone arch at the center of Monument Valley.

All the combined magics of Leone and Fonda—director's audacity, actor's force and symbolism—come to bear. Beyond the arch in the far distance is a great burst of sun and cloud, a spreading miasma, as if the spirits of this hallowed valley were rioting in the sky. Morricone's operatic accompaniment climbs, shrieks, rains thunder; quick cuts go from sobbing boy to cursing brother to smiling killer. The boy pitches forward as the brother's legs fly out of sight. The harmonica drops and dust covers the boy's head. The music dissolves in the tolling of bells, and we perceive that one of the deepest Fonda themes has been turned inside out. He is the voyeur of his own crime: *He* is the man with the noose.

No symbol lies deeper in Fonda's art than the hanging rope, and no reversal could be, at this climax of a career, more powerful. It is the last, darkest revisioning of Fonda as the noble man who understands the will to murder, of the father as a man who would destroy his children.

The tolling bell and swirling dust carry us back to the present—to the crack of the stranger's gun and the killer's spin as he is hit. Frank staggers, crumples slowly, shot in the heart: a small, secret vengeance from the murdered boy of the first massacre. He squints into the sun, and gasps for the last time: "Who are you?"

The stranger rips off the harmonica as if pulling out his own heart. He shows it to Frank—the last witnessing—and pushes it in his mouth. Finally naked before the past that has been stalking him, buckling under its gathering weight, Frank remembers everything. Nods, accepts. Exhales and falls.

Time has slain the father. Death and memory join in the last breath.

∽

Released in the spring of 1969, *Once Upon a Time in the West* is a hit with European cineastes and Marxists. Its relevance to radical politics is intuited by the Parisian students, veterans of the historic strike of the previous May, who line up to see it. In the United States, however, it passes like a phantom ship in the night. Cut by nearly an hour—just too long, Paramount feels, with not enough bullet ballet—it will nonetheless be ridiculed for its excessive length and ragged continuity.

Other reasons may be adduced for this neglect. *Once Upon a Time in the West* appears just weeks behind *Easy Rider; They Shoot Horses, Don't They?* will follow a few months later. Why should anyone think that the American imagination will be taken by this long, dusty Italian horse opera? The New Hollywood is busy being born, and the Fonda kids are more to the point.

By any reckoning, *Easy Rider* and *They Shoot Horses* are important films. But next to the Leone-Fonda achievement, they are as nothing. It will be Henry's triumph—or simply the fruit of his endurance—to have finally outdistanced his progeny in the race to creative transformation. For *Once Upon a Time in the West* is, in addition to what director John Boorman calls "both the greatest and the last Western," the finest film Henry Fonda has made, with a performance at least the equal of any he has given.

Transformation is in the eyes: how we see the world, how we are seen by it. And the performance of Frank, for all that it involves Fonda's complete being, lives in his eyes. Eyes that have gone weary in these confounding days when children have revolted, politics have failed, and all the action has seemed to be occurring in someone else's America. Eyes that have nonetheless remained alive, desirous, cunning, and that now, on Leone's desert floor, are so dead they appear transparent, ageless, cleansed of the past—as if to be born again.

11

The Old Man Himself

Sometimes a Great Notion

Four summers before his death, Henry Fonda makes a last visit to the little six-room house where he was born. In 1966, he had financed moving the house from the corner of West Division Street in Grand Island to the Stuhr Museum of the Prairie Pioneer, just outside of town.

Twelve years later, Lew Cole, the museum's public relations director, will describe Fonda's visit.

"He quietly walked through each of the rooms, studying details of the furniture, walls and floors. Then he came to the bedroom where he was born. He stood looking at the brass bed for several minutes with a distant gaze.

"Then he said, 'That's enough,' and walked out the door."

༓

Shapes, faces, colors.

∽

As Henry Stamper in *Sometimes a Great Notion,* the film of Ken Kesey's novel about an Oregon logging family, Fonda delivers a full-throated, foul-tempered voice from a face bristly enough to scour pots. Aged sixty-five and playing a decade older, he has never seemed less a specter, more a solid piece of natural matter.

For the location shoot in the summer of 1970, Henry rents a house on the dunes near the Columbia River with his wife, Shirlee, and daughter Amy. Raised by Susan Blanchard, Amy is now in her late teens; she has kept to her schoolwork and avoided public notice. Days off the set, father and daughter walk, talk, fish, and sift the sand for agates.

The other actors love Fonda as children love the towering, enduring tree of their summers. Paul Newman, who is both starring and directing, claims *The Farmer Takes a Wife* was the first movie he ever saw. "Henry has always held a very special place in my heart," he says. "I don't think it's any exaggeration to say that I'm just as much in awe of him today as I was then—if not more so."

Late in the movie, the Newman character is chain-sawing a tree trunk. It splits, spins, and crashes down on Henry Stamper. He is rushed to emergency, his arm dangling. The limb is lost, but the old man hangs on. Flat on his back, eyebrows shooting up like puffs of weed, Fonda writhes in pain.

"Don't you believe 'em," he says.

Newman asks who.

"*Them.* They're trying to put me in the grave. I'm not even close . . ."

Suddenly the face collapses. Old Stamper moans inconsolably.

"*Oh, Lor-dee, Lorrrr-deeeeeeee. Son of a bitch!*"

Fonda has never made anything like this sound before: the wail of a man fighting off death. Performance blurs with existence, and it is almost too real to bear.

But if the man has glimpsed death, the artist has seized that vision to render it as a masterstroke. Fonda's cry is controlled, rich, a Shake-spearean rattling of the soul.

The rest of the film may be forgotten; this sound, never.

∽

The former Shirlee Mae Adams has been at Henry's side, unobtrusively, for the latter half of the 1960s. Entrusted by divorcing parents to an Illinois orphanage at the age of four, she spent her youth in study and prayer, but on coming of age, she has pursued the worldly occupations of flight attendant and fashion model. Shirlee is thirty years old and comfortable on the margins of the spotlight when Henry meets her in late 1962, at the premiere of *The Longest Day*.

She claims, like Frances before her, never to have seen Henry's mov-ies. Yet she too is taken by the handsome stranger, and single-minded in her pursuit: "It took me six months to track him down," she says.

In the summer of 1963, as Henry films *The Best Man,* Shirlee is a frequent guest at his Beverly Hills rental; Walter Winchell reports the couple's "midnightly trysts" at PJ's, a Hollywood rock 'n' roll club. The next summer, between shooting *The Rounders* in Arizona and *In Harm's Way* in Hawaii, they share the guesthouse at 10050 Cielo Drive in Bel Air—soon to be one of America's most infamous addresses. In the fall, they are seen together at Broadway shows. By this time, columnists are pointing out that Shirlee, nearly thirty-three, is on the cusp of mandatory retirement for airline "stews." On December 3, 1965, they are wed—at Fonda's instigation—in the chambers of Justice Edwin Lynde in Mine-ola, New York.

Trim, well-assembled, adroit yet unimposing, Shirlee has the not-yet-formed nose of an adolescent girl, and her smile defines *pert*. Of Henry's wives, she is the only one whose manner suggests no hidden agenda or dark inner world. She presents an image of health, youth, the good life; yet she is concerned with social ills, and works extensively for charities around greater Los Angeles. She is eager for people to get along, proud to be a helper, and her clearest ambition is to serve and support Henry. "I have tried to make Fonda the central pivot of my life," she says, sharing her predecessors' habit of calling Henry by his last name. When they meet, she is a beautiful young thing for Henry to sport on his arm. As years pass and his infirmities set in, she becomes an ideal combination of lover, caregiver, and domestic administrator.

This will be by far the longest-lived of Fonda's marriages, perhaps because it achieves the best balance between emotional feeling and psychic dependency. Shirlee, like Frances and Afdera, may desire a father surrogate; unlike them, she doesn't seek to be abused or controlled. Her manner is vivacious and wholesome, but no one leaves an orphanage soft. Fiercely protective of family and home, she shields Henry from excessive press attention in his difficult last years. Shirlee's toughness is also a necessary self-defense throughout the marriage, as the dark rages of Fonda's middle age morph into the manifold quirks and irritations of an ailing old man.

"He's complex and difficult," Shirlee says. "But I'm not easy either."

For the first time Henry has a wife willing, for reasons of her own, to place him ahead of everything else. That is not always what he wanted in a wife, but it is what he needs now.

∽

In early 1967, Fonda purchases a nine-acre estate at 10744 Chalon Road, snug in the green, shaded windings of Bel Air. The forty-year-old, 9,400-square-foot house is a sprawling hacienda of white brick and Spanish tile, with exposed rafters, large windows, and cavernous rooms. Later, after it is furnished in Fonda style, hung with paintings, and festooned with overgrown plants, the home's rustic opulence will remind one visitor of "a fancy new Mexican restaurant."

Henry and Shirlee take occupancy in 1969. After twenty years, he's had enough of Manhattan's noise, push, and vertical glamour. In Bel Air's expansive warrens of wealth, the only sounds to break the hush are a car powering up a hill, or the motorized tools of landscaping crews. As the neighborhood gathered cachet in the late 1940s, the actor Clifton Webb called it "a delightful acreage . . . a Forest Lawn of the living."

Henry is hardly ready for the cemetery, but the move is an easing into twilight years, as evidenced in an increased dedication to restful and solitary hobbies. He continues to paint, and takes up needlework, particularly crewel embroidery. The dozens of fruit trees on the back nine allow him to resume his second life as a farmer. And he discovers bees. The retired battalion chief of the Alhambra Fire Department, hired to neutralize a hive found under the eaves, presents the dead husk to Fonda. Interest piqued, he takes out a subscription to the *American Bee Journal,* masters the apiarist's eccentric art, and soon is home-bottling his own brand of honey—Henry Fonda's Bel Air Hive.

There are still plenty of ways to get stung in the golden land. In the late 1960s, Southern California garners a reputation as America's locus of moral decadence and radical violence. Drugs, sex, Satan, and politics are in the witches' brew, and straight America is nervous. In August 1969, just as the Fondas are settling in on Chalon Road, five people are slaughtered at the nearby Cielo Drive estate—now owned by director Roman Polanski and his wife, actress Sharon Tate—where they'd summered in 1964. One of the dead, Jay Sebring, is a Hollywood hairdresser noted as an innovator in male styling. Henry, a client, attends Sebring's funeral five days after the murders.

Our man is also singed by the political flames of the moment. On October 17, 1970, Fonda plans to speak at a campaign rally for Representative John V. Tunney in the largely Mexican-American area of East Los Angeles. A riot following an antiwar rally in the neighborhood weeks before has left three people dead. Tunney has come, he says, to "establish a dialogue," but his speech is quickly drowned out by protesters. Things turn ugly; Tunney and Fonda retreat as an angry crowd descends on their car.

A spokesman for the Chicano Moratorium Committee claims Tunney—a Democrat running for Senate against Republican and former actor George Murphy—had come to East L.A. only "to try to buy votes with free beer and with Mexican flag buttons with his name on them." Henry is not injured in the melee; only shaken, perhaps, by the distance between days once defined by Tom Joad and now by César Chávez. In six years, he will be supporting his son-in-law, Tom Hayden, against Tunney in the California Senate race.

∞

On the whole, though, he appears happier—and certainly healthier—for the changes. His skin regains luster, and he looks well preserved even beside a much younger wife. The trim, monochrome suits of the urban gentleman are replaced by mod western gear; anyone glancing up at the right moment may spot Henry Fonda in his black Mercedes sports coupe, waiting to turn onto Sunset Boulevard.

He fights to retain each atom of physical command. Rising every morning before six, he sits in the sauna, then does sit-ups on a slanting board. He rides a stationary bicycles, takes megavitamins, and drinks a high-protein milk shake with lecithin powder and a raw egg. Gossip says he's had cosmetic surgery. Evidently performed sometime in late 1970, it is only a touch-up: "I had a little eye work done," Henry is quoted as saying when asked how he stays so young-looking.

It sounds cheesy, but what of it? A movie career is a devil's bargain, and something inside him has known that from the beginning.

Time again to make payments on the bargain. In 1970, he signs as pitchman for the General Aniline and Film Corporation (GAF), doing commercials for vinyl flooring and View-Master slide machines. The contract, specifying eleven TV spots per year, requires two weeks of work and is rumored to be worth $250,000. Sales rise in response to the ads, and Henry is seen to have legitimized a new market for established stars—soon even Laurence Olivier will be endorsing Kodak cameras.

In this guise Fonda evolves a bit further as image and presence—less man, more symbol. Columnist Bob MacKenzie describes the odd phenomenon of watching Fonda walk into a kitchen to appraise a woman's floors. He's got no reason to be there, other than that he is Henry Fonda, arbiter of all he surveys. He "belongs wherever he chooses to amble," MacKenzie accepts, "and his judgment of a kitchen floor or a pearl-handled six-shooter is obviously the judgment of the final authority."

The commercials are absurd, but brief. They move product and create work. And as Henry says, "A good commercial is better for a person than a bad movie."

∽

Or a bad TV show. ABC announces in April 1970 that Fonda will star in *The Smith Family,* slated for the fall. He'll play Chad Smith, an LAPD detective sergeant with a wife and three children; the stories "will touch on today's gap between generations and the problems of today's youth in their attempt to remodel the world."

Henry's still trying.

Though he claims to be intrigued by its focus on a cop's domestic life, the show's real attraction is the cut-and-paste production method patented by executive producer Don Fedderson. "The Fedderson System," previously tested on two hit family shows built around older male stars— *My Three Sons,* with Fred MacMurray, and *Family Affair,* with Brian Keith—simply involves shooting all of the star's scenes up front in a two-month burst, then filming the remainder in his absence.

Fonda, seduced by money and ease into believing the result will be more than the sum of its detachable parts, films fifteen episodes in October and November, and promotes the show hard. "The scripts were all completed," he says, "the money and ownership were right, but most importantly I believed in the characters and the concept of the show. . . . All the cast and crew are excited because we feel it will not only be successful but good. Very good."

With Janet Blair costarring as the wife and Ronnie Howard as the older son, *The Smith Family* debuts in January 1971 as a midseason replacement. "Henry Fonda stars as Chad Smith . . . a man you'll like," *TV Guide*'s ad vaguely assures. Response to the show is blandly positive; rather like the homemaker in the GAF commercial, viewers look up to find that Henry Fonda has wandered in to admire their floors.

The Smith Family is bad. Very bad. Structure is split between domestic scenes with a laugh track and cop scenes so listless they make *Dragnet* look like *Brigadoon.* Henry sulks through on fatherly forbearance, with smiles that resemble dyspeptic grimaces. "There is nothing here that really lifts the spirit," says the Associated Press critic. "The wish is that this show had been done with more style, more insight, more wit, more guts, and had more meat and bones to it."

By season's end, early ratings have plummeted, along with Henry's enthusiasm: He declines to publicize the second season at all. But what about the domestic life of a cop, the belief, the excitement—? "He does it for money," TV writer Lawrence Laurent declares.

On September 15, season two premieres to the sound of crickets. ABC pulls *The Smith Family* at midseason, and cancels it after the first of the year.

∽

The theater has changed since Henry's heyday. The thing now is to provoke the audience with nudity and noise, radical exhortation and Total Experience. He notes the shift but is uncertain what to do about it.

Lately, most of his theatrical juice has gone into the Plumstead Playhouse, a company cofounded in 1968 by Martha Scott, Robert Ryan, and Henry to showcase established and emerging stars in classic American plays. Named after the first professional theater in America, the nonprofit production company boasts, on paper if not always onstage, such worthies as Mildred Dunnock, Godfrey Cambridge, Roddy McDowall, John McGiver, and Estelle Parsons; but Henry becomes its most visible exponent.

Our Town and *The Front Page* are announced as Plumstead's first offerings. Henry will play the Stage Manager in the former, a reporter in the latter. "We might fall on our puss," he admits as rehearsals begin, but it must be money he is thinking of losing, since the creative risk is far from awesome. To some, even the performers look bored. Journalist Jane Wilson studies the *Our Town* cast in a midtown rehearsal space in the summer of 1968. "Stifling boredom filled this room," she writes. "What fun, these movie stars had thought, to spend innocent autumnal weeks as the Plumstead Players at a homey theater on Long Island, how cleansing to get back to the root of the matter, back to basic American theater. But now, as they waded through Thornton Wilder's archetypal corn, some of the first flush of enthusiasm had clearly worn off."

That doesn't prevent Plumstead's *Our Town* from being a reasonable success. Opening at the Mineola Theatre in September, it goes to Broadway in November 1969, and has a short run in Los Angeles early the next year. Like *Generation,* though, it is only a successful waste of time for Henry. It shows he can still fill seats, and draw moisture even from the gimlet eyes of theater critics. But it has not been a play to draw revelations from an actor, or stir new life in an audience.

It may be his portrayal of the Stage Manager—addressing the audience, watching the young wed and the old die—that sparks Fonda's notion of a one-man show on the theme of parents and children. Assembled, to Henry's design, by writer-director Sid Stebel, incorporating cuttings from Socrates, Shakespeare, Thoreau, O'Neill, Bob Dylan, and others, *Fathers vs. Sons* premieres in April 1970 at the Joslyn Art Museum in Omaha. Later in the year, Fonda takes the evening—now called *Fathers Against Sons Against Fathers*—on a brief tour of regional theaters. As well as a meditation on filial themes, Fonda conceives of it as a cheap, portable annuity for his late years.

He has not been so variously and vigorously involved in theater since the University Players. But everything is a revival or a rehash: He is working hard merely to stay in place. In December 1971, he directs an all-star production of *The Caine Mutiny Court-Martial* in Los Angeles; simultaneously, the Plumstead Playhouse readies its staging of Saroyan's *The Time of Your Life,* with Henry headlining a cast that includes Jane Alexander, Strother Martin, and Richard Dreyfuss. Opening at the Kennedy Center in Washington, D.C., in January 1972, the show goes on a national tour, which occupies Fonda through the spring and summer.

But the Saroyan play is less robust than the Wilder, its revival even more superfluous. "Seen now, in a new context," writes the Long Beach critic, "the play seems vapid, pointless, and pretentious. Since the play has not changed, apparently we have."

∽∾

Yet hidden between these safe, sober endeavors is Henry's sole venture into anything resembling radical theater. He's sent a play entitled *The Trial of A. Lincoln* in late 1970, soon after its premiere in Hartford, Connecticut. Penned by white playwright James Damico, the piece combines racial politics with Pirandello illusion to dramatize black urban anger. It also calls upon Fonda to portray the ghost of the historical figure with whom he is most dearly associated—not the jackleg youth, but the sallow sage of Brady's portraiture.

Set in the basement of an urban police department, the play begins as courtroom drama: A modern-day black militant has labeled Lincoln a racist, and the president's risen spirit charges libel. Finally, in the Pirandello twist, the ghost trial is revealed as a setup, a mechanism by which police administrators have sought to defuse racial tensions in the force.

With this part, Henry constructs obvious arcs to the past—by playing his young Lincoln at a later age, and by walking in the proximate steps of George Billings. Yet those arcs, begun so long ago, end squarely in the present day, with the Great Emancipator interrogated and judged by a new, Pantherized black militancy.

This drama of racial confrontation will have its unlikely reopening in Arizona, then travel to Los Angeles and Detroit. Already in the cast are Billy Dee Williams as the militant and Moses Gunn as his defender—two black actors well known in New York but not in the provinces. Fonda signs on as the company's brand name and joins rehearsals in January 1971.

The part is a stern physical challenge, with rehearsals lasting as long as twelve hours. Fonda self-applies layers of heavy makeup; onstage, he wears four-inch lifts and trains his legs to walk on what amount to small stilts. Henry says he finds the play "very provocative, very powerful"; asked how audiences will respond, he sounds almost eager for controversy. "We have no idea what the reaction will be. When we play it in Detroit, for instance, it could very well provoke riots."

Response to the March 27 preview in Tucson is mixed but excited; the local reviewer finds that "a hurried poll among Saturday night's audience indicated a favorable reaction." There are a handful of walkouts at the opening in Phoenix two nights later, but the play is praised as "one of the most explosive statements of the black cause in modern drama." Fonda's presence is valued, though he is seen to be primarily the catalyst for larger discussions: "The performance is superb, but largely window dressing."

The play then goes to Los Angeles, where in a drastically edited version it is called "the most thoroughly entertaining new play in years." But Henry's personal reviews are again variable. To one critic, he "possesses wit, warmth, and true spirit," while another believes he "plays Lincoln a bit stiffly, even stuffily."

The Trial of A. Lincoln moves on to Detroit. No riots. Yet something upsets Fonda's faith in the production, and word leaks that it will not be going to Broadway after all. Reportedly, he is troubled by disagreements over the text. Fonda having a well-developed sense of his own marquee value, it may nettle him to be overshadowed by the play's issues, his costars, or both; maybe he is depressed by his middling reviews.

Anyway, he is out of the show—just that abruptly. He resumes his previous obligations, and never discusses the play again; it's almost as if it had been a passing delirium. Meanwhile, as the producers scramble to find Henry's replacement, the playwright is said to be doing another major revision.

To date, *The Trial of A. Lincoln* has never been staged in New York.

∽

It will be almost two years before Fonda receives the script that effectively settles every qualm, his and ours, about what he should be doing in the theater right now. *Clarence Darrow* conjoins nostalgia and challenge. It is another ghost trial; a bridge between past and present forms of American radicalism; and a one-man show that works.

Based on Irving Stone's biography, the play is the work of David Rintels, a TV writer whose notable previous credit is the controversial legal drama *The Defenders*. Reading it in the fall of 1973, Fonda has doubts. The shapeless text runs well over three hours; he's uncertain of his ability to physicalize the bullish, overweight attorney; and he has verbally committed himself to a new Edward Albee play, *Seascape*.

But in reading the Stone book, Darrow's autobiography, and courtroom transcripts, Henry comes alive to his subject. Like most Americans, he recalls little of Clarence Darrow beyond the landmark defenses—of Socialist Eugene V. Debs; child-killers Nathan Leopold and Richard Loeb; and science teacher John T. Scopes, defendant in the Tennessee "Monkey Trial." "I didn't know about his fights for labor," Fonda says, "for the eight-hour day, for the poor, the blacks, or his own nightmarish trial on a charge of buying off a jury, for which he was acquitted."

He finds commonality with the "Old Lion." Both men revere their fathers, leave small towns for the big city, are lonesome liberals in conservative outlands. Both have passed in and out of cultural favor: As Leslie Fiedler writes, Darrow, after becoming a folk hero, had by the early 1920s "begun to look like yesterday's liberal, the provincial and slightly ridiculous spokesman for the not-quite-enlightened middlebrows." Yet repeatedly he'd jolted the populist nerves of the country despite public doubt, powerful opposition, and his own misanthrophy; always he strove to be, in Stone's memorable phrase, "as great as his cause."

∞

For Fonda, it's a familiar challenge, but in a new costume and a new era. How to make this man live? How to render his true size to the Americans who have forgotten him, or never really knew him?

Henry's insecurity manifests, as it had in the 1950s, in a need to establish dominion over his stage. The monologue continues to be unwieldy, and Henry decides he doesn't trust the judgment of the director hired by producers Mike Merrick and Don Gregory. Soon the entire enterprise is, in his mind, hopeless, a folly. He threatens to quit unless major changes are made, not just to the play but to its direction. Desperate, Rintels and Merrick place a call to producer John Houseman.

He's an inspired choice. Houseman has been the legend behind the legend since the 1930s, when he produced the early triumphs of Orson Welles and the Mercury Theatre. In Hollywood, he has helmed a number of prestigious projects by eccentric directors. He has known Fonda distantly since 1946, when at RKO they discussed a Herman Mankiewicz script called *That Girl from Memphis,* recalled by the producer as "some sort of sexy Western." Years later, Houseman produced Jane's bathetic *In the Cool of the Day,* and he next met Henry in January 1968, when directing an all-star CBS telecast from Ford's Theatre in Washington, D.C.

After viewing a *Darrow* rehearsal, Houseman conferences with star, writer, and producers. He feels that, with trims and tryouts, the play could produce one of Fonda's great performances. While not keen on displacing the director, he agrees to step in.

Henry requires minimal direction anyway. "My main use to him as a director," Houseman will later write, "lay simply in my being out front and supplying him with a trustworthy, living mirror in which he was able to see his own reflection and check the truth of his performance." Reasonable resemblance between actor and lawyer is achieved with body padding, a slash of hair across the forehead, and a pair of suspenders. Henry sleeps in his stage clothes to get the wrinkles right; Rintels continues to prune the text; Houseman calibrates stage blocking and lighting cues. Harmony is slowly, methodically reached between ego and art.

Clarence Darrow is previewed in Louisville, with Henry's voice amplified by a radio mike (a first for him). From there it goes to Chicago, Washington, D.C., Cleveland, and Philadelphia. Reviews are outstanding. "Fonda is doing something incredible here," Earl Wilson reports from Chicago. A Washington reviewer calls the performance "the accumulation of all that Fonda has learned through the years as an actor"; another lauds his "Olympian feat" of acting in a play that is "an epic love poem to a man."

The acclaim continues after the play moves to Broadway's Helen Hayes Theatre on March 26, 1974. "It would be difficult to think of praise too high," writes Clive Barnes in the *New York Times.* "If Clarence Darrow was not like this, he should have been."

The five-week run sells out, and beginnings are seen of a virtual Darrow cult. "People seem to have a compulsion to tell me what this show meant and did to them," Henry says. Tour dates are scheduled for the western United States, running through late August. A television special is planned, and requests for command performances come in from around the world. Years later, Henry's Darrow will still be sought by the cultural ministries of nations as far-flung as South Africa, Australia, and the USSR.

$$\backsim$$

In the shower of glories, a few worthy doubts are raised. John Simon points out that Fonda, though a great actor, has never starred in a great play. Why has he never challenged himself against the modernist mysteries of Brecht, Pirandello, or Lorca; the grinding Nordic tragedies of Ibsen, Strindberg, or O'Neill; or indeed the classics of Molière and Shakespeare? Simon fears that Henry's preference for the certitudes of community-theater staples like Saroyan and Wilder—and, not so implicitly, *Darrow* itself—will commend him to theatrical history only as "the great interpreter of the second-rate."

Columnist Jeffrey Hart notes a "curious current phenomenon, in which assorted actors are scoring big hits by impersonating well-known American personalities out of the past"—aside from Fonda, these include Hal Holbrook as Mark Twain, and James Whitmore as Harry Truman.* "No doubt all this reflects the general 'nostalgia' boom," Hart figures; but it "may also be part of the 'Americanism' mood attendant upon the Bicentennial and strengthened by frustration abroad."

But *Clarence Darrow* as it airs on television—and presumably as it is seen by audiences at its hundreds of stage performances—is far from a simplistic piece of Americana. Nor is it free of incredible demands upon Fonda the actor, despite its not being a great play, or necessarily a play at all.

Fonda enters a set that is both courtroom and law office, backed by a nighttime cityscape. As Darrow, he moves slowly, his lips set in frowning resolve, his hand feeling respectfully the wooden railing of the jury box.

---

* Whitmore had already given Will Rogers the solo treatment, and William Windom would soon portray war correspondent Ernie Pyle in a one-man show.

Romance in the ruins: with Afdera Franchetti, Rome, late 1955, soon after they met. *(Photofest)*

And five years later: the faces say it all. *(Jerry Ohlinger's)*

"The somnambulistic quality of a bad dream": *The Wrong Man* (1957). *(Photofest)*

On set with Hitchcock and Jimmy Stewart. "I bought a story called *Rear Window*," said Josh Logan in 1955. "We were going to shoot it in one of the apartment districts in New York, with Henry Fonda making it in the daytime while he appeared in *Roberts* at night. But then I got involved in other matters." *(Photofest)*

The holdout: as Juror No. 8 in *12 Angry Men* (1957). *(Jerry Ohlinger's)*

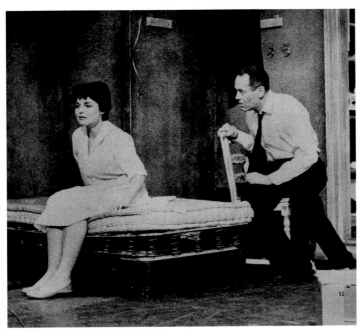

Opposite Anne Bancroft in *Two for the Seesaw* (1958). Playwright William Gibson called the production "the most odious experience of my life." *(Photofest)*

The Deputy (1959), costarring Allen Case. "The thought of having an annuity from the residuals is very satisfying," Fonda said. *(Jerry Ohlinger's)*

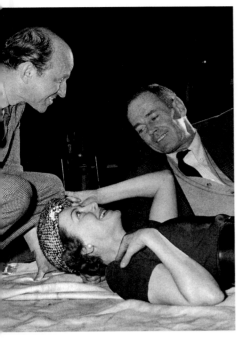

Rehearsing *A Gift of Time* (1962) with costar Olivia de Havilland and director Garson Kanin. Peter's telegram to Henry on opening night: "Get out there and kill yourself." *(Photofest)*

Pod person: *Advise and Consent* (1962). *(Photofest)*

Egghead: *The Best Man* (1964), with Cliff Robertson and Kevin McCarthy.
(Photofest)

President: shooting *Fail-Safe* (1964) with director Sidney Lumet. *(Photofest)*

The Fondas at Grand Central Terminal during filming of Jane's *Sunday in New York* (1963). *(Photofest)*

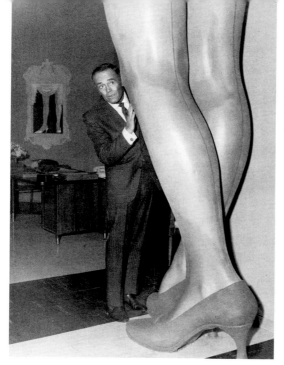

Lost in the sixties: as a panty-hose mogul in *Sex and the Single Girl* (1964)...

...as a spy in
The Dirty Game
(1966)...

...as a widower in *Yours, Mine and Ours* (1968, with Louise Troy)...

...and as a cop in *Madigan* (1968, with James Whitmore, left). *(Jerry Ohlinger's)*

With Shirlee at a charity function, c. 1966. "Fonda is definitely a loner," she said. "I love people and I love parties.... I force him to go." *(Photofest)*

In his East 74th Street town house, mid-1960s. *(Photofest)*

"Now that you've called me by name..." Sergio Leone (in white hat at right) directing *Once Upon a Time in the West*, spring 1968. *(Photofest)*

The virility of an aging conqueror: as Frank in *Once Upon a Time in the West* (1969). *(Photofest)*

Henry and kids after a performance of *Our Town*, December 1969. *(Photofest)*

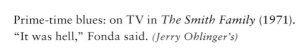

Prime-time blues: on TV in *The Smith Family* (1971). "It was hell," Fonda said. *(Jerry Ohlinger's)*

Fonda gave this 1969 pencil drawing, *Third Floor Rear*, to an Albuquerque family whose daughter was a production assistant on *My Name Is Nobody*. *(Photofest)*

Clarence Darrow (1974). His last great performance. *(Jerry Ohlinger's)*

Leaving Lenox Hill Hospital after his pacemaker operation, May 7, 1974. *(Photofest)*

Elizabeth Taylor, Warren Beatty, and Lauren Bacall were among those who rushed to Washington, D.C., for the late 1977 opening of *First Monday in October,* costarring Jane Alexander (back row, far left). *(Photofest)*

"The loons! The loons!"
With Jane and Katharine
Hepburn in *On Golden
Pond* (1981). *(Photofest)*

The Best Actor, March 30, 1982. "I
don't want it because I don't believe in
it," Fonda had once said of the
Oscars. Hearing his name, he burst
into tears. *(ITV/Rex USA)*

Darrow makes jokes. They are corny, Rotary Club standards. He describes hitting a baseball as a boy, grips the imaginary bat and points to the sky, and we fear that nostalgia may drape like sweet old linen over our violent history.

At a certain point, Darrow makes another joke. It is not crucial which one—it might be different for different watchers—except that now you laugh. There has been a cumulative rhythm to Fonda's ramble, acumen in Darrow's homilies. Nixon is invoked without being named, and a sense impressed of how alike our eras are, with Darrow the spirit of a rueful native intelligence transcending time. Your laugh is rich and you feel suddenly free—free to believe in the ideal, the humor, the hero. Yes, along with its criminals and liars, pollution and poison, America contains *this, too.*

And Fonda has you. He leads you past nostalgia into a recounting of forgotten crimes committed by Americans against Americans, capital against workers, strong against weak: the evils, readily translatable to our own or any time, of "evil men—men who are themselves criminals." He makes the crimes and their consequences live by miming Darrow's interactions with a gamut of crooks and victims. He defines the stakes with Darrow's angry description of conditions in tenements housing Pullman railway employees. He incarnates the spirit of resistance by shouting the cry of striking laborers at club-swinging police:

"Don't you know what day this is? It's the Fourth of July—*Independence Day!*"

Of all actors, perhaps only Fonda, with his exact nuances—querulous expression, tone of outrage and amazement, the forward lean of his body into the living dark—could make that rebuke ring and sting, like some primal piece of democratic rhetoric.

He does so much with this monologue. He combines his country's nostalgic wish with its radical capability. He demonstrates that revolt is not a sixties aberration but a patriotic tradition. He conjures anew the American night, the ghosts of dead men and women, lost children, murderers, and heroes who move about in it. He brings that hush down upon his stage and his audience.

Not least or simplest, Fonda infuses Darrow with himself, their two histories mingling, so that we feel the actor's investment in the lawyer's statement of self: "I know my life. I know what I have done. My life has not been perfect; it has been human, too human. I have tried to help in the world. I have not had malice in my heart. I have done the best I could."

Clarence Darrow is Henry Fonda's last foray into the American dark, that night of crime and brutalized ideal where he finds his country and his hero, the mob and the man; where he casts out demons and raises the dead; where he reaches into himself, and past himself; and where, in the impassioned voicing of doubt, he awakens us to a belief we thought lost. He is as great as his cause.

∽

In the summer of 1969, *The Cheyenne Social Club* is shooting at a ranch near Santa Fe. This is the kind of hot, dry country that saps younger men, yet Henry Fonda has been bragging to reporters about his health—passed a preshoot physical "with flying colors."

One day, though, he has difficulty breathing. He is taken from the set to Bataan Memorial Methodist Hospital. His diagnosis is first reported as influenza. This is later changed to a "respiratory condition."

At the time, no one says "heart attack"; no one says "cancer"; no one says anything. No one but Fonda, who, according to a nurse, says on entering the hospital, "I'm just a tired old man, and I want to be left alone."

∽

He has always treated his body as a skilled shootist treats a beautiful rifle: He knows it was made to be used, but he is wise enough to keep it clean. Alcohol, tobacco, and other abuses are in moderation, just enough to grease the action. But time corrodes, elements weather, and well-tooled mechanisms may simply, suddenly fail.

On April 23, 1974, a month into *Darrow*'s Broadway run, Henry collapses in his dressing room after a performance. The next morning, he is admitted to Lenox Hill Hospital, said to be suffering from exhaustion. Henry confesses to having felt winded lately. "I suddenly found myself out of breath one day," he says. "I'm a great walker and I had to stop twice on my way to do a radio spot to help the Red Cross raise money. I mentioned it to my doctor, who sent me to a specialist. He told me: 'You're fibrillating.' "

Suddenly, he is unconscious on a dressing room floor. He wakes up wearing an oxygen mask in a hospital bed. Around him are shapes and faces. There are wires on his skin, tubes in his veins, and a monitor displaying the jumps of his heart.

Outside the hospital, Shirlee tells the gathered press that Henry "isn't really sick . . . they put him in the hospital because that's the only place you can keep this man down. He doesn't know what rest is."

He focuses on breathing, and letting the shapes form into people. Three days pass with nothing but an announcement that *Darrow*'s remaining New York performances have been canceled. The hospitalization continues into May. The upcoming dates in Boston are likewise canceled.

Then it's decided that a temporary pacemaker will be installed in Henry's chest. The backstage collapse, it seems, was not exhaustion, but oxygen loss due to an irregular heartbeat. His heart is in a badly weakened state—the almost certain result of a nonstop work and travel schedule sustained over four decades, combined with a lifetime's accumulated stresses and suppressed emotions.*

Fonda joins the company of William O. Douglas and Peter Sellers, who are among the celebrated recent recipients of the pacemaker, a device pioneered in 1960 by William M. Chardack, a cardiac surgeon working at a VA hospital in Buffalo, New York. A small box with a thin wire carrying electrical impulses is implanted near the heart, and its signals

---

* There may also have been a genetic component: The younger of Henry's two sisters, Herberta, died after two open-heart surgeries. See *Syracuse Herald-Journal,* 9/5/1969.

are transmitted to the muscles of the heart's lower region to regulate pulse and blood flow. Early pacemakers were carried outside the body in a shoulder holster, and malfunctioned frequently; updated devices are more rugged, and as of 1975, some 200,000 Americans have them.

Henry is fitted with the newest model, designed by physicists at Johns Hopkins and powered with rechargeable nickel-cadmium cells. A visitor, invited by Fonda to feel the device beneath his skin, describes it as "a hard spot on his chest, the size of a child's wooden block." A wall-plugged charger is held to the chest with a Velcro vest, emitting a beep until it is correctly placed, at which time the charging begins. "Once a week," Fonda will explain a year after the implantation, "I have a little recharge—flip it on, read, nap, or do needlepoint."

He leaves Lenox Hill on May 7, returning two weeks later for an adjustment of the device. On the twenty-second, he is sent home to Bel Air. *Darrow*'s scheduled engagements are postponed indefinitely.

We've entered the next phase of Henry's life, and the first of his death.

∽

Just weeks later, he is back playing Darrow at the Huntington Hartford Theatre in L.A. "The veteran of fifty years on stage and film showed no visible loss of strength, spirit, or imaginative genius," writes one critic. "We cannot sit through Henry Fonda's one-man triumph of dramatic craftsmanship in *Clarence Darrow* without being profoundly impressed by Darrow the man and Fonda the actor. Both were, and are, giants of our age." Adela Rogers St. Johns—daughter of the attorney who defended Darrow in his 1912 bribery trial—writes, "A most incredible and soul-shaking thing has befallen me. I [have] seen—a spectre, an appearance as plain as ever Hamlet saw his father or Lady Macbeth saw Banquo. Moreover, it was a ghost of solid flesh . . ."

Henry spends two evenings in a New York studio taping the television version of *Darrow*. It cuts twenty-two minutes from the play and adds six feet to the length of the stage, but otherwise it is a direct transfer of the theater experience. "The only difference from doing it as a play," Henry says, "was that I was vaguely aware there were four cameras somewhere in the darkness." Directed by John Rich, presented by Norman Lear and IBM, the show airs on NBC on September 4.

Henry gets another checkup, and relaxes for the rest of the year. Then, the TV special having renewed interest in the play, *Darrow* returns to Broadway on March 3, 1975, this time at the Minskoff Theatre. Henry forgoes matinees, and his health continues to improve. Greeting a visitor to his town house, he runs up and down the stairs as proof of his stamina. Tour dates are lined up through mid-May.

The tour completed, Henry plays Adm. Chester Nimitz in the World War II epic *Midway*. In July, after just a few weeks off, he and Shirlee depart for London, where *Darrow* begins a ten-week stand at the Piccadilly Theatre. Opening night is a triumph, with multiple curtain calls; moved by the reception, Fonda tells the audience that to play the West End is "every American actor's dream." Though he's reported to be incensed at the nine-dollar charge for top seats, his is the hottest ticket in town.

"An entertainment that uplifts the spirit in a darkening world," says the *Daily Express*. "It takes one noble man to play another. Henry Fonda is that man."

He's making up for lost time. The pacemaker is a miraculous new tool in life extension, and Fonda is prominent among its success stories. Soon the American Heart Association will name him its Man of the Year.

∽

In early 1976, X-rays show a tumor near Henry's lung. He checks into Cedars-Sinai Medical Center in Los Angeles, and on March 17 undergoes his second surgery in two years.

The operation lasts seven and a half hours. Thought at first to be beneath the right lung, the tumor is instead found to be growing from the right side of the diaphragm—some of which must be removed, though the lung is spared. Doctors will later report that the tumor in Fonda's abdomen, though it is benign, "had grown to the size of two grapefruits within a four-month period."

The surgery has meant the cancellation of *Darrow*'s projected college tour,* but Henry's recovery looks promising. Then it goes sour. Perhaps other X-ray omens are found. His release is delayed, and more college dates go by the board. Finally, on April 13, he is sent home, though without a clean bill of health. He spends the next several weeks recuperating under clouds of uncertainty.

Whispers of cancer begin to circulate. They intensify after Fonda flies back to New York on June 14 for a scheduled checkup. In Hollywood, rumors of illness can be every bit as damaging to perception and career as illness itself. Henry is furious at the rumors, and unbowed by the physical setback.

"I'm not afraid," he assures an interviewer. "I'm optimistic that I will lick this."

But he will not say what "this" is.

∽

Most of Fonda's late pictures are of no importance to the man himself; most are not good and were probably not meant to be good. Projects as dumb or desiccated, cynical or saccharine as *The Serpent* and *Ash Wednesday* (both 1973) may be justified at least on the grounds that they keep our man active, his joints moving and his assets liquid.

The first is an espionage thriller with many snaky hisses on the sound track and many dour spooks walking endless corridors; Fonda plays the director of the CIA, and though he is physically there, he really could care less. *Ash Wednesday* is a soap opera with Elizabeth Taylor as a woman undergoing plastic surgery, and Henry as her tycoon husband. Otherwise trashy and ghoulish, it contains a fine Fonda portrait of a wealthy stud gone to seed, whose response to his wife's stunning new face combines romantic regret, clinical admiration, and bemusement at her naïve faith that mere cosmetics could ever touch his cold mind or selfish heart.

---

* TV comedy host Steve Allen, it was announced, would replace Fonda on the tour. Requests for refunds would be honored. See *Athens Messenger,* 3/21/1976.

Fonda is an august presence in several World War II movies. As Cardinal Schuster in a film about Mussolini, *The Last Four Days* (1974), his nonplussed expression and sepulchral outline hold firm against Rod Steiger's gross overacting. He reveals creditable emotion as a military man with two sons in action in the international production *The Biggest Battle* (1978), but the film is unworthy of him. *Midway* (1976) is a war spectacular in the long tradition, more coherent and exciting than usual, though unwittingly racist: The American actors savor their salty dialogue and esprit de corps, while the Japanese players, including the great Toshiro Mifune, are like robots exchanging binary code.

Elsewhere, Henry settles into the inevitability of playing men aware of their age, whereby he may convey on-screen the fear of death he will never quite admit in life. *My Name Is Nobody* (1973) is a spoof on the spaghetti Western genre, which has by now peaked. (Sergio Leone is the film's executive producer, as well as prime target of its parody.) As a famed gunslinger brought out of retirement by an overzealous young gun, Fonda is dignified—too dignified: Either he isn't in on the movie's joke or he doesn't think it's funny.

He's far looser in *The Great Smokey Roadblock* (1977), despite its having been shot in the wake of his tumor surgery and cancer scare—and the fitting of an earpiece that compensates for an estimated 40 percent hearing loss. Fonda is Elegant John, an independent trucker who escapes from a hospital ward, hijacks his rig, and transports a crew of prostitutes cross-country. Affectionate and sloppy, the movie has a mid-seventies vibe of being an agreeable shambles. "There's a bit of *Easy Rider* in it," Henry says, accurately.

Encountering a subculture of longhaired freaks and dropouts, no judgment or superiority in his style, Fonda gives perhaps the liveliest, warmest performance of his last decade. He convincingly throws a much younger, stronger man across a room, and looks on his leading lady with pleasure. But the scenes that stick longest are John's nightmares of loss and wandering, from which he wakes to bodily torment. In one scene, he stumbles, clutching his burning chest, into the woods to splash water on his face. He sags to his knees, sobbing in the moonlight reflecting off the stream. We think of Eddie's long-ago death in a haunted wood.

∽

If his film work is increasingly tangential, Henry's presence on TV is inescapable. In 1973, he and Maureen O'Hara star in a remake of Steinbeck's *The Red Pony,* which sparks debate when its graphic footage of a foal's birth is censored by NBC. The same year, he headlines ABC's *The Alpha Caper,* a drab leeching on the fads for heist pictures and lovable crooks, and consents to figurehead *The Henry Fonda Special,* a "unique blend" of music, comedy, and sports with Lee Trevino, Leslie Uggams, Sammy Davis, Jr., Don Knotts, Foster Brooks, and other guests.

In return for Norman Lear's production of the *Darrow* special, Henry plays himself in *Maude,* and hosts an anthology of *All in the Family* clips. Incarnating Douglas MacArthur in the Korean War docudrama *Collision Course* (1976), he gives a straightforward reading of a man who "represented everything I don't stand for." He walks through haughty patrician roles in two period miniseries, *Captains and the Kings* (1976) and *Roots: The Next Generation* (1979). He turns up in PSAs for hearing aids and the Boy Scouts.

When narration is needed for anything from an FDR documentary to *The World of the Beaver,* Henry is there. When old friends are feted at American Film Institute galas and Dean Martin Celebrity Roasts, he is there. When Hollywood throws a party on the anniversary of the Jewish homeland (*The Stars Salute Israel at 30*), he is there.

Rumor says he is mulling over a regular show based on *The Red Pony.* A Clarence Darrow series is likewise proposed. Most alarming, though, is a concept called *O. W. Street,* projected as a Movie of the Week and series pilot. It would star Fonda as a Texas sheriff and criminology professor hired as captain of detectives in a large California city. "Sounds like a tossed salad of Barnaby Jones, Hec Ramsey and Cannon," one observer concludes. The star is reportedly on board, but the show never materializes, and America is spared the weekly experience of Henry Fonda stealing Buddy Ebsen's thunder.

∽

Disaster movies are a backlash phenomenon. Alienated from the dark visions and small defeats of post–*Easy Rider* Hollywood, the mass audience looks again to spectacle and star, and surrenders to the engineering of movies as thrill rides. It also seeks a popular genre to mock its fear of widespread collapse—economic, environmental, social: Films like *The Poseidon Adventure, Earthquake,* and *The Towering Inferno* are delirious wastes of money and resource in a time of inflation, pollution, and shortage.

Henry Fonda spends the late 1970s hip-deep in disaster. His first forays come in 1977, with *Tentacles,* an Italian-made *Jaws* rip-off (octopus in place of shark); and *Rollercoaster,* which at least has sense enough to literalize the disaster movie as a clanking contraption run amok. In 1979 come *Meteor* and *City on Fire,* Henry cashing in as president and fire chief, respectively.

Biggest and baddest of all is *The Swarm,* Irwin Allen's 1978 follow-up to *Poseidon* and *Inferno.* Exploiting fears of African killer-bee migration, the picture is a harvest of shame. Playing an entomologist, Fonda is confined, for no reason, to a squeaky wheelchair. After much brow furrowing in the lab, he injects himself with an experimental antisting serum; it fails. Fonda suffers a long, sweaty cardiac arrest and, at the moment of death, hallucinates, ludicrously, a godlike killer bee.

Is this any way for a man to die—or for Henry to relive his own heart attack?

∽

Among the dead—that is, unmade—projects of this period, three have unusual potential. *A House Divided* is a family saga set during the American Revolution; it is intended to star all three Fondas, and to appear in time for the bicentennial. Screenplay drafts come and go, and so does the bicentennial. In December 1979, a columnist reports Henry's claim that Jane is negotiating with Hallmark to produce it as a TV miniseries. As a result, the greeting-card company is inundated with angry letters from

Jane's detractors, and the company's president issues a hurried clarification: Hallmark does have a Revolutionary War drama in development, but it is not the Fondas', and he doesn't know who gave Henry that impression. Coup de grâce.

A story about black fighter pilots in World War II, *Com-TAC 303* is announced in June 1977 as forthcoming from Pinnacle Productions, starring Billy Dee Williams, Greg Morris, and Chad Everett, with Henry in a cameo as an air force general. Shooting begins in the Mojave Desert, but is shut down after two and a half weeks when Gulf + Western, owners of Paramount Pictures, withdraws financing. At that point the project, according to a spokesman, is inactive; though the other stars may return if filming resumes, it's known that Fonda is "involved with other commitments and is not now available."

The Journey of Simon McKeever is a 1949 novel by Albert Maltz about an elderly man, mangled by arthritis, who hitchhikes from Sacramento to Glendale seeking a cure. Previous attempts have been made to film it, first with Walter Huston, later with Spencer Tracy. A revival of the property, starring Fonda, is announced in April 1978. But progress stalls, the star is sidetracked and falls ill, and the chance passes.

It's a loss, because McKeever could have been a great Fonda character. Simon is seventy-three and lives meagerly in a nursing home; his wife and child are long dead. He is a workingman with a vivid imaginative life, his hike an often hair-raising picaresque through post–New Deal itinerant America. Like *Appointment in Samarra*—that other phantom film—*Simon McKeever* offers Henry Fonda a gift of story and understanding, a narrative key to his contemporary fears. Yet the visions are so different: O'Hara's novel is about a young man's surrender to hopelessness, Maltz's about an old man's resistance to it:

> It was not the sheer fact of growing old that McKeever ever had minded. There was a rhyme and a reason to that, like night and day. . . . The only thing he did fear [was] the horror of having to lie twisted and helpless in bed, endlessly, day and night, without func-

tion or purpose, while life passed him by. When a man was like that he was nothing, he was . . . garbage.

∽

The American Film Institute announces Henry Fonda as the recipient of its sixth annual Lifetime Achievement Award. Among those attending the ceremony in Beverly Hills on March 1, 1978, are friends from every phase of his career—Omaha, Falmouth, Hollywood, Broadway.

An edited version of the ceremony airs on CBS on March 15. It is a typical glitzy affair—canned intros, hacked-up clips, celebrities looking around to see who else is there—but there's a richness of feeling, and a few affecting speakers. Jimmy Stewart admits that he voted Henry Best Actor for *The Grapes of Wrath* over himself, for *The Philadelphia Story;* but then, he'd also voted for Landon, Willkie, and Dewey. Richard Burton imagines Fonda taking a tour of Welsh valleys around 1925 and meeting Mother Burton, "a very beautiful woman." John Wayne speaks briefly but movingly from a scratchy throat and chest filled with cancer: Tonight all rifts are mended.

But Henry is the highlight of his own evening. He has been sitting through tribute and testimonial, with broad smile and infinite patience, at a banquet table with Shirlee, his children, and his grandchildren. Now he takes the podium to give thanks and to deliver—eloquently, with great wit and restraint, without notes or teleprompter—a coherent summing up.

In these later years, William Brace Fonda has emerged as the hero of his son's memories. Henry references him often in interviews, and identifies with Clarence Darrow's veneration of his own father. William will be the phantom figurehead of Henry's autobiography. At the AFI tribute, Henry admits that "Dad" wouldn't have approved of all that his son has done, but guesses he would be proud tonight. He then relates a story we've heard before, though not from Henry's own mouth.

Prompted by his friend, local actress Dorothy Brando, he began stooging and stagehanding at the Omaha Community Playhouse. It was the summer of 1925 and for a college dropout with plausible prospects in the dull but sustaining professions of the middle class, the theater was held to be a frivolity at best, an indecency at worst: a cut above the carnival circuit, perhaps. For Henry, it meant risking the esteem of his father, "a man I not only respected but whose approval I needed." Yet the twenty-one-year-old was too dazzled and excited by this newfound world of creativity and chance to stay away, and throughout his first season at the Playhouse, he performed any and every task the stage managers would toss him—painting, pulling, hammering, hanging.

Meanwhile paying his dues to Dad and the daylight world, young Henry landed a job with the Retail Credit Company. Only then did Gregory Foley, Playhouse director and competing father figure, ask Henry to star in the season opener, *Merton of the Movies.*

"When I announced this at home," Fonda tells the AFI audience, "my dad was appalled, and he made it very clear that he felt that it was a lot of nonsense. I had a good job, it was a chance of advancement, and he wasn't going to dream of letting me jeopardize this."

A fierce argument ensued between father and son, ending only when Herberta Fonda stepped in, forcing the warriors to opposite corners. In defiance, Henry accepted the role and sealed his fate. Throughout the weeks of rehearsal, he and his father observed an icy distance, avoiding each other's company and exchanging few words.

"When we did meet, he gave me the silent treatment. It was a *towering* silence. And the message was clear—that once I forgot this foolishness and concentrated on a business career, he would resume communication."

But when opening night arrived, the Fondas were in full attendance. They watched Henry earn his first standing ovation, the first of so many to come. After, he went home to join his waiting family—uncertain of what his reception would be.

Dad was sitting in Dad's chair, behind his newspaper. So I joined my mother and my sisters, who immediately tried to outdo each other with superlatives, until Harriet began to say something that sounded as though it *might* become a criticism.

And Dad's paper came down. And he said, "Shut up, he was perfect."

I guess . . . I guess that's the best notice I ever got.

Over forty-years and innumerable telling, Henry has held close this moment of triumph, his memory polishing it like a precious stone. And here, close to the end, he knows the extent to which he is describing not just his father but also himself. His life, on one level, has been about defying his father's wishes; on another, about the fulfillment of his example: the hiddenness, the damning silence, finally the love that would conceal itself for fear of being seen. He and the ghost are one.

∽

During the AFI tribute, there are a few seconds of video from a performance of *First Monday in October*—Henry's latest play, recently closed after ten weeks at the Eisenhower Theatre in Washington, D.C. The Jerome Lawrence–Robert E. Lee comedy has Fonda as a Supreme Court justice and old-line liberal modeled on William O. Douglas, and Jane Alexander (daughter of Thomas "Bart" Quigley, a childhood friend and Falmouth colleague of Henry's) as a newly appointed, more conservative justice. The two wrangle on points of law and social policy, pornography and free speech, and shout and jostle each other into romantic positions. Deep into the play, the Fonda character is stricken with a heart attack.

The play's reviews are only tepid, but Henry—doubtless drafting a bit on the gust of the Darrow triumph—is again crowned king of the American theater, and upholder of the democratic liberalism that seems, ever more these days, a piece of nostalgia prized mostly by playwrights and theater critics. But those moments of vagrant video indeed show a Henry Fonda still in command of the theater, that ancient space and darkness. His voice is clear, his body active. Fonda onstage, even at this late hour, is a man alive, a physical force.

There is standing room only at the Eisenhower. On October 3, 1978, the play reopens on Broadway at the Majestic Theatre; after five weeks, it moves to the ANTA Playhouse, where it closes on December 9. Again, critics belittle the play while extolling the actor. The UPI reviewer feels that even at seventy-three, Fonda "looks twenty years too young for the part. He moves beautifully onstage and, if his vocal range is limited, he does wonders with it."

"There he is," Walter Kerr writes, "rock-solid, instinctively and irre-mediably erect, a shaft of steel holding the stage in place—and the audi-ence magnetized—while the bits and pieces of [the play] threaten to drift into the orchestra pit. . . . And his fortitude doesn't simply come from the fact that this time he's playing a man who prides himself on his mulish stubbornness. We at last realize, as we watch him stand his ground, that he has always played this man, that he is in fact this man."

Fonda's various illnesses are in remission, but the adrenaline of per-formance gives a false impression of his overall health. "I'm in good shape," he says during the Majestic run, "though I have to take it easy physically. I'm not allowed even to do isometric exercises. I can't carry anything heavy. I keep getting skinnier."

∽

In March, *First Monday* begins a month's residence at the Huntington Hartford, Henry tending his bees, gardens, and fruit trees between per-formances. On March 29, he takes the play to the Blackstone Theatre in Chicago, with Eva Marie Saint replacing Jane Alexander. The run is slated for seven weeks.

A week and a half in, Fonda is lying in bed. He has been limping spo-radically for weeks. Now he stretches, and feels his hip joint pop loose. He tries to rise; his body will not let him.

Doctors at Michael Reese Hospital diagnose him with inflammatory arthritis of the left leg. He is admitted for a week's observation. The Chicago run is finished.

Five days later, Henry checks back into Cedars-Sinai Medical Center in L.A. Two separate operations are performed, the first to relieve the inflammation in his hip, the second to remove an obstruction in his prostate. The latter, it's found, is a tumor. Cancerous.

Good catch: The tumor is removed, and the prostate is otherwise clean. Within a day, Henry is ambulatory and "in excellent spirits." He leaves the hospital two days later, with rest and recuperation ordered. Further engagements of *First Monday* are canceled.

∞

Since 1974, one of the stories of Henry Fonda's life has been the story of his cancellations. But sick as he has been, he cannot bear to be unproductive. Since he began this career, productivity has been his mode and his compulsion. Now more than ever it is his ally against uselessness, his palliative against pain, the diversion that allows him to claim he doesn't mind growing old: "I don't have much time to think about it."

There is still so much left to produce.

There are the light duties, the little paychecks and why nots. He adds cameos to disaster movies, and another to *Fedora,* Billy Wilder's inscrutable revisitation to the themes of *Sunset Blvd.*: As "President of the Academy," Fonda confers an Oscar on an aging actress and gives a creepy, smiling, unlifelike rendition of himself. In 1978, an album of his readings from *The Grapes of Wrath* is released; another, based on *The Ox-Bow Incident,* follows the next year. In late 1979, he tapes brief video intros for a PBS series, *The American Short Story.*

There is a play by Preston Jones, *The Oldest Living Graduate,* that comes in the mail; its producers want Henry to star as a World War I veteran and graduate of a Texas military academy. Henry says why not, and on April 7, 1980, he performs in a live telecast from Southern Methodist University in Dallas. Once the wearisome staginess of the piece is accepted, Fonda is quite hilarious, and his energy jumps in exchange with first-rate actors like Cloris Leachman, George Grizzard, and Harry Dean Stanton. The play then runs briefly at the Wilshire Theatre in Beverly Hills; Jane and Peter attend a performance on Henry's seventy-fifth birthday.

There is one big movie left—ample budget, full crew, location shoot—the one big movie his doctors will allow him lately. In August and September, he is on Big Squam Lake, in New Hampshire, shooting *On*

Golden Pond, from a play by Ernest Thompson; Jane has purchased it for them to make together. Opposite Henry is Katharine Hepburn, his iconic equal, and an actress he has never had occasion to meet until now.

There are many pictures to paint. In early 1973, a painting called *Ripening*—two tomatoes on a flaking windowsill in the sun—is bought by industrialist Norton Simon for $23,000 at Shirlee's "Neighbors of Watts" auction. Dealers take note, and in October 1974, Henry is the subject of a solo exhibit at L.A.'s Windsor Gallery. His canvases multiply in these convalescent years, and they soon grace celebrity foyers across Hollywood: It is homespun chic to own a Fonda. His paintings are compared to Andrew Wyeth's—detailed yet plain, very American and seemingly literal, but sensual and intense: Stare long enough, and the plainness vibrates.

There is always honey to be drained from the hives—Henry's bee count is up to 400,000. There are the acres to see to, the gardens and trees that have always yielded so bountifully to his patient hands and organic compost. From the garden at Chalon Road come corn, zucchini, lettuce, string beans; Henry hand-delivers his surplus to neighbors like Jimmy Stewart. He has also done well with apple trees, "apples so tart," he says proudly, "they make your eyes pucker."

∽

"My father loved to farm," Henry recalls in May 1980. "We had chickens at home, and I guess that's where I've gotten that from. It seems to be part of the Midwestern way that I've never been able to shake from me."

He's been sitting with a writer lately, talking into a tape recorder for a book about his life. He's been remembering things like that—the chickens, his father, Omaha.

∽

He is admitted to the Intensive Care Unit at Cedars-Sinai on December 8 for tests involving a new pacemaker medication. He remains there almost two weeks.

The hospital announces on the nineteenth that he will leave in a few days. But something changes, and Henry, despite being listed in fair to satisfactory condition, is held for further observation.

Eventually he feels better, and on Christmas, after sixteen days in the hospital, he returns home. "I'm not going down the chimney yet," Henry promises. But it will be, he allows, "a quiet Christmas."

∽

The feeble, bony-legged bastard will not quit. A few days into January, he begins rehearsals for yet another new play, Lanny Flaherty's *Showdown at the Adobe Motel,* about the reunion of two elderly rodeo stunt riders in a run-down lodge off a Dallas highway. Between days, he flies to Omaha for a celebration in his honor at the Community Playhouse. Perhaps he tells his friends there he'll see them again.

Showdown opens at the Hartman Theater Company in Stamford, Connecticut, on February 10. Henry is almost never offstage. The *New York Times*'s Frank Rich finds poignancy in Henry's playing his true age onstage: "He walks in a stooped posture, leaning heavily on a cane"; his voice resembles "a distant radio signal."

The cane works as a prop, but the stoop is for real. As are the ebbing, quavering tones, and the deliberation with which Henry must manipulate his limbs. Many in the audience and backstage are distracted from the performance by their own fear that Fonda will collapse; indeed, a doctor warns Shirlee that if Henry isn't taken home, he might die on the stage.

The play ends with the star alone, in a chair, looking at the baby he holds in his arms. From out in the hushed dark, Rich sees Fonda's face change from the ravaged, spotted countenance of an old man into "a peaceful, childlike death mask."

Henry struggles through twenty-four performances. On March 1, 1981, he takes his last bow and leaves his last stage. Bent, agonized, and on his feet.

∽

The Academy of Motion Picture Arts and Sciences announces on March 29 that Henry Fonda will receive a special award, "in recognition of his brilliant accomplishments and enduring contribution to the art of motion pictures," to be presented by Robert Redford on the following night's Oscar telecast. The president-elect of the United States, Ronald Reagan, as "a former member of the industry," has also been invited to appear, via taped message.

The following afternoon, while entering the presidential limousine outside the Washington Hilton, Reagan is shot by John Hinckley. The Oscar show is delayed by one night. Reagan, conscious and stabilized after touch-and-go surgery, insists that his message run as scheduled. He watches from bed as his prerecorded likeness greets the nation and blesses the event, and Henry Fonda treads lightly on weakened legs to address a monumental ovation, a collective fare-thee-well.

The convergence is apt, even poetic: two men long connected by lines of fate, each at death's door as they bookend the Oscars with twin emotional climaxes. But one is receding into twilight, the other just beginning his time in the sun.

Reagan circles back to us, a smiling, abiding ghost. It is no accident that his moment arrives just now. He is corrective to the recrimination and self-disgust that have characterized America, its psyche and culture, since the 1960s. He is Hollywood Man, tall in the saddle and shooting movie quotes from the hip. He incarnates the conservative wish for an earlier, nobler (and whiter) America, with a revitalized belief in the American exceptionalism that Fonda's watchful, dark-minded, representative man hated on instinct and opposed in action.

It can seem as though Reagan has been standing behind Fonda all these years, waiting patiently for him, and the liberalism he represents, to age out. He was born six years after Henry, also in the Middle West. He got into movies on the death of a Fonda friend. The two were social acquaintances throughout the 1940s, when Reagan ascended to the presidency of the Screen Actors Guild. *She's Working Her Way Through College*, a 1952 remake of *The Male Animal*, stars Reagan as Professor John Palmer, a rewrite of Fonda's Tommy Turner. Three years later, Reagan, as host of *General Electric Theater*, introduced Fonda's TV movie *Clown*.

But if he has always held Henry's coat as an actor, politically Reagan has triumphed at every point. He was on the winning side in the HUAC–Hollywood episode. In 1966, he challenged incumbent Edmund G. Brown for the California governor's office, and in 1970, he defended it against State Assemblyman Jesse Unruh; Fonda supported the Democrats, and they lost decisively.

Ten years later, the day after Reagan's presidential landslide, Henry said this: "I'm desolate. I think it is a worse tragedy than Milhous Nixon." He amplified this the following year. Reagan is "talking a language that people haven't heard for a long time and it impresses them. *I* listen to a Reagan speech and want to throw up!"

The president, assuming he is aware of these sentiments, will bear no obvious grudge: Among the first responses to Fonda's death will be a gracious statement from the Oval Office. But such magnanimity costs Reagan nothing, for he knows his influence on the American quest will finally dwarf any exerted or even dreamed of by Henry Fonda. These coming years will be his, and he's been waiting for them a long time—ever since the night Ross Alexander blew his brains out in Beverly Hills.

∽

On April 6, 1981, Henry enters Sharp Memorial Hospital in San Diego for an exploratory heart catheterization. A month later, he is back at Cedars-Sinai for a "diagnostic evaluation of his long-term cardiac condition."

The evaluation results in another heart surgery. Henry spends his seventy-sixth birthday in the ICU, receiving sedation. On May 20, his pacemaker is replaced, his condition listed as satisfactory.

He is discharged June 8. For the next three months, he tries his best to rest, while consulting on the manuscript of his autobiography; sitting for a long interview with journalist Lawrence Grobel; and awaiting the release of the film he and Jane shot in New Hampshire the previous summer.

∽

More and more now, he sits in his chair and drifts. In the kitchen, or in the bedroom near the plants. Sleeps, wakes; goes in and out of other realms of seeing.

Drifts. Jane senses he is "already gone from us on some level."

∽

Fonda: My Life reaches stores in time for Christmas. It's a curious production: Though billed as autobiography, it is Fonda's life "as told to" playwright Howard Teichmann, with the actor placed in the third person. Both Jane and Peter will challenge the book in coming years for its selective arrangement of facts, its illusion of candor.

It is self-serving and self-acquitting at many points, and so stylistically drab that it might have been designed for the exact purpose of discouraging any future interest in its subject. Many celebrity names are dropped in the book, many backstage stories told, but there is little fresh dirt and the dish is not deep. Still, sales are good and critics respectful, with Jonathan Yardley of the *Washington Post* one of the few to pay the higher respect of straight talk. "Badly written, adulatory, fatuous," he calls the book. Nonetheless it should be read: "This is Henry Fonda speaking and that is enough."

Simultaneously, the Grobel interview appears in *Playboy* magazine. It is the longest and most revealing talk Fonda has ever given in print, though it often recapitulates—and contradicts—stories told in the book. Both book and interview serve as publicity satellites for Henry's film with Jane and Kate Hepburn, which now shapes up as a major hit of the holiday season.

On Golden Pond premieres at the Motion Picture Academy Theater in Beverly Hills on November 18. Henry is too ill to attend, but Jane holds a brief press conference beforehand, saying, "He's here in spirit. This is perhaps his last film and it may be his best."

She can hardly say otherwise. In shooting the picture with her father, Jane has achieved some degree of catharsis; as one of its producers, she hopes it will make money. And though it will not deserve mention alongside Henry Fonda's best pictures, as a crowd-pleaser it cannot miss. By the time it opens nationwide on January 22, *On Golden Pond* has already been sanctified as a classic, a symphony of senior sentiment, and Henry Fonda's last great film.

∞

As the loving husband, sadistic father, and sly curmudgeon Norman Thayer, Henry pauses to regard several photos of himself as a young man. In one, he holds baby Jane and stands next to Frances. Except that for the purposes of fiction, Jane is Norman's daughter, Chelsea, and Frances, through retouching, becomes a young Katharine Hepburn as his wife, Ethel.

As Fonda studies his younger self, then his seventy-five-year-old face in a mirror, the frisson is unrelated to the character he plays. It's created instead by the phenomenon of an actor-icon projecting mortal awareness in real time. Call him "Norman Thayer," but Henry Fonda is in fact playing, really for the first time, himself—his own iconicity, his own decrepitude and nearness to death. No matter how conscientiously he attempts to embody Norman, with Norman's unique set of thoughts and worries, Fonda will spend the film cogitating on his own extinction.

But that's why we've bought the ticket—to see these actors portray themselves as we have come to understand them: Katharine Hepburn, clenched, efficient, indomitable; Jane Fonda, aerobicized woman and frustrated daughter; Henry Fonda, harsh parent and dying man. Everything that is supposed to make *On Golden Pond* powerful relies on the audience's perception of these actors, their offscreen crises and accrued personae. Without them, the movie would neither make a fortune nor become beloved: Imagine Gregory Peck as Norman, Angela Lansbury as Ethel, and Faye Dunaway as Chelsea, and imagine a movie no one would remember.

On Golden Pond delivers the goods. Scenes between Jane and Henry have an edge, produced by the daughter's palpable terror of her father; they are not exactly dramatic, but they are as compelling as any confessional. Hepburn and Fonda attack Ernest Thompson's precious dialogue with the industry and hardheadedness of woodpeckers. And it is difficult for even the cynical to resist the story's primal pull, its canniness.

But *On Golden Pond* asks its audience to passively consume sentiment rather than actively engage in feeling. Only Fonda's performance of misanthropy signals contradiction, complication—life. Not that he undermines the melodrama: In the clinches, he goes mushy and delivers the goods. But he also makes the most out of Norman's horrible cussedness, his flat determination to treat his daughter like garbage and go to the grave unchanged.

Given that his physical means are so withered, and director Mark Rydell so uninterested in what cannot be plainly shown, Henry can work only very little of the hidden into the performance. Hiddenness becomes a matter of obfuscating costume (Norman's eyeglasses and fishing hat), and revelation lies in the anxiety organic to the face of a dwindling man who will never quite be ready to die. Age diminishes nuance in Fonda's face, but it exposes fear more nakedly than ever. Every smile is a stay against desperation, and the eyes struggle for purchase on a world that is turning unreal.

On Golden Pond is the second-biggest Hollywood moneymaker of 1981 (after *Raiders of the Lost Ark*), and probably the biggest, even with inflationary adjustments, of Henry's career. A large part of that success can be attributed to its frank embrace of morbid sentimentality, but it can be attributed as well to Fonda's refusal to pretend he is eating sugar rather than sucking a lemon. Were he less abrasive, the audience's collective skin would crawl up the theater wall. Yet there's enough leeway for viewers to read Norman's spitefulness as the ditherings of a geezer who, under his crust, is as lovable as the drunken lynchers of *Young Mr. Lincoln*.

As always, the audience is free to turn each of Henry Fonda's refusals into an affirmation—free to accept his appearance of sincerity, and feel a bit safer with its fears.

∽

Darkness, when it comes, comes quickly. Heart troubles recur in late September, leaving Henry weakened. Throughout October and into

November, he remains at home; one of his few journeys outside is to a private studio screening of his and Jane's movie.

He refuses at first to reenter the hospital, despite his worsening condition—a stubbornness common to frequently ill people who have decided enough is enough. Jane is on his side, but Shirlee insists. On November 16, Henry agrees to reenter Cedars-Sinai. The stated cause is minor—readjustment of his heart medication—but the days drag on and Henry remains bedridden. Thanksgiving comes and goes. By the end of the month, his release date is still undetermined. As *On Golden Pond* opens to widespread worship, the speculation is that he may spend the rest of the year in his hospital bed.

∽

Christmas passes, and New Year's.

He is sent home in early January. A few weeks later, accepting Henry's award for Best Performance as an Actor in a Motion Picture—Drama at the Golden Globes, Shirlee says things are looking up: "He's getting well, he's painting, he's walking with a cane." But Shirlee, some feel, has been in denial for a long time.

∽

March arrives. As predicted by literally everyone, Henry receives the Oscar as the year's Best Actor. He and Shirlee are watching at home when Sissy Spacek, the previous year's Best Actress, announces his name. "He just burst into tears," Shirlee says.

Jane is on hand to make the acceptance. Upon leaving the stage, she hurries to Chalon Road with her husband and children and presents the award to her father. As wire photos are taken of Henry holding his Oscar, a succession of visitors is allowed in, one at a time, to offer congratulations. Fonda remains seated, swathed in sweaters, blankets, and a thick beard, which he vows he won't shave until he gets well.

"This makes me feel very happy," he says in a high, quiet voice. Though wan, he promises he is "feeling better all the time."

After the pictures have been taken and congratulations given, Shirlee asks everyone to allow her husband some rest. "He's still a very sick man."

No doubt Henry has recognized some of his visitors, with others little more to him than shapes and faces, phantoms floating and smiling on waves of color.

∽

"Some days he seems fine," Shirlee tells an interviewer. "On others, he kind of fades. I just have to play it by ear, hour by hour."

A nurse sees Henry five days a week, and Shirlee has a cot near his bed. "If he wants something," she says, "he asks for it graciously, and he always has a word of thanks."

∽

On July 8, Henry is back at Cedars-Sinai, this time for treatment of a urinary-tract infection and further adjustment of his medication. He is discharged on the twenty-fourth, and he spends the next sixteen days at home. They are the last he will spend outside a hospital.

∽

Periods of relative lucidity alternate with days of disconnection, times when his mind leaves the land of the floating faces.

West, past the mountains to the sky, orange and blue. East, where lies Omaha, where lie the graves of his mother and father.

∽

He is rehospitalized on August 8 for further unspecified heart treatments.

Three days later he is reported stable and in intensive care. Shirlee, Jane, and Peter are with him. Hospital spokesman Larry Baum says any life-prolonging measures will be determined by the family and doctors, when and if they become necessary.

∽

Shapes, faces, colors.

∽

News items on his condition appear daily. The media are on death watch.

Three days after reentering the hospital, Henry takes a turn for the worse. His condition is downgraded to serious. He is fading fast. Yet he remains conscious and responsive.

∽

Drifts.

Story's almost over.

But I have seen the elephant.

∽

The shape leans over him and smiles. The face asks how he feels. He says he is fine. He says he feels no pain.

∽

Henry dies at 7:55 on the morning of August 12, 1982. The certified cause is cardiorespiratory arrest—"respiratory failure brought on by heart disease." Shirlee is at his bedside; Jane and Peter are en route to the hospital.

Later that day, wife and children gather outside the Chalon Road house for a brief announcement to the press.

"He had a good night," Shirlee says. "He talked with all of us and he was conscious at all times. He woke up this morning, he sat up, and just stopped breathing."

∽

Obituaries are run on the late news, and statements of tribute heard from Barbara Stanwyck, Charlton Heston, Bette Davis, Lucille Ball, Jane Alexander, David Rintels, and others. Cedars-Sinai is flooded with calls from admirers wishing to send flowers and condolences. "People really loved him," says a hospital spokeswoman.

From President Reagan come these words:

Nancy and I were deeply saddened to learn of Henry Fonda's passing today. Henry Fonda was a true professional, dedicated to excel-
lence in his craft, whose skill and precision as an actor entertained
millions. Throughout his long and distinguished career Henry Fonda
graced the screen with a sincerity and accuracy which made him a legend. We will miss Henry and extend a deep sympathy to his family.

In the USSR, the government paper *Izvestia* reports the death of "a
noted American actor." *Corriere della Sera* of Milan, Italy's largest daily
newspaper, remembers Fonda as "a democratic figure in the jungle of the
movie world." *La Stampa* of Turin calls him a "civil and proud hero."

"I've just lost my best friend," Jimmy Stewart says.

∽

A week later, the contents of Henry's will—executed on January 22,
1981—are announced. It bequeaths $200,000 to daughter Amy Fonda
Fishman, with the remainder of the estate and all personal effects going
to Shirlee. The stipulation is made that, should Shirlee die within ninety
days, the estate will go to the Omaha Community Playhouse. No bequests are made to Jane or Peter, on presumption of their financial independence.

Henry's eyes will be donated to the Manhattan Eye Bank.

As for burial or funeral services, there will be none. Henry Fonda has
specified, in the plainest language, that his bodily remains be "promptly
cremated and disposed of without ceremony of any kind."

∽

In a fragment titled "The Old Man Himself," dated 1891, Walt Whitman held forth:

Walt Whitman has a way of putting in his own special word of
thanks, his own way, for kindly demonstrations, and may now be

considered as appearing on the scene, wheeled at last in his invalid chair, and saying, *propria persona,* Thank you, thank you, my friends all. . . . One of my dearest objects in my poetic expression has been to combine these Forty-Four United States into One Identity, fused, equal, and independent. My attempt has been mainly of suggestion, atmosphere, reminder, the native and common spirit of all, and perennial heroism.

One of the last projects Henry Fonda considers, we're told by one researcher, is a solo show about Walt Whitman. Picture it—Henry, "wheeled at last in his invalid chair," wearing the full beard of his final months. The blue eyes have lost their focus, yet they appear winsome, content on other visions: shapes, faces, colors. He is winding down, like a tough old animal or exquisite timepiece, but he has long outlived his father to become what George Billings impressed him as being—the old man in the shawl, who wept tears of history into his beard.

How would Fonda have rehearsed his Whitman? In the mirror? In his mind? Who would his Whitman have been—the song-poet of democracy, or the lusty bard of the meadows? And what passages would he have chosen? Studying the preface to *Leaves of Grass,* scanning the words with the rheumy eyes and ivory fingers of the old man himself, would Henry have lingered on these lines—

Past and present and future are not disjoined but joined. The greatest poet forms the consistence of what is to be from what has been and is.

—or these—

He drags the dead out of their coffins and stands them again on their feet.

—or these?

He says to the past, Rise and walk before me that I may realize you.

12

Omaha, 1919

Will Brown

It was hours past sundown, but the Omaha sky on September 28, 1919, was bright with light: The Douglas County Courthouse was burning.

Starting in the afternoon, a mob of thousands had been laying siege to the building with stones, bricks, and Louisville Sluggers. Some had begun firing guns at the windows. Eventually, the mob had penetrated the courthouse and taken over the ground-floor rotunda, driving police and other city employees to the upper stories. The lines of a nearby service station were tapped, and the first floor sprayed with gasoline. Someone lit the first match.

The courthouse held the county jail, and the mob was demanding the surrender of a prisoner—a forty-one-year-old black laborer, Will Brown, under arrest for raping a white girl. In his courthouse office, Omaha's mayor, Edward P. Smith, had been trying to contact government officials and secure federal troops. As yet, no aid had arrived. In a show of resistance to the mob, Smith had refused to leave his office, but finally the fire made it unsafe to stay.

Near eleven o'clock, the mayor emerged on the eastern steps to plead restraint and reason. But few could hear him.

Suddenly, a gunshot cut the din of voices.

"He shot me," someone screamed—and fingers were pointing at Smith, whose hands were empty.

The mob converged on the mayor, forced him to the corner, got a rope around his neck, and, tossing the free end over a traffic light, tried to hang him.

∽

In late 1918, thousands of black veterans had returned from the war, dressed proudly in the uniforms they had earned. Cheap automobiles and rail travel offered hope of mobility to poor families trapped in racist backwaters, and northward migration, as John Hope Franklin wrote, "spread like wild fire among Negroes. . . . It was estimated that by the end of 1918 more than one million Negroes had left the South." They left for the urbanized North and Middle West to survive, but also because they felt possibilities opening for the first time in their lives.

But often, what they found on reaching cities like Chicago, Kansas City, and Omaha was bigotry in new forms. Labor unions resented having to share a job market already crowded with foreign immigrants. The Klan, exploiting the feeling, spread its tentacles to the Middle West. In the overlap of economics and mass migration, America grew rank with racial violence, usually expelled upon blacks spuriously charged with crimes against whites.

Racial terror was widespread in the spring of 1919. Race riots in Philadelphia, Washington, D.C., and Chicago left hundreds dead in July alone. In Ellisville, Mississippi, John Hartfield was publicly burned at a predetermined hour, his mob execution announced ahead of time in the local paper. A number of lynching victims had served in the war. The murders were almost always preceded by drawn-out acts of torture, and medieval horrors committed by ordinary citizens became daily news. Writer-activist James Weldon Johnson looked on that sea-son of blood and gave it the only name that fit: "Red Summer."

∞

Omaha had been Nebraska's chief beneficiary of the northward migra-tion, more than doubling its black population since 1910. The integra-tion had not always gone easily, as striking white meatpackers were replaced by newly arrived black workers. An educated, activist black middle class was developing, but free intermingling occurred only in the bars and brothels of the city's interracial underground.

Then, on September 28, at the climax of Red Summer, the mob lit up the Douglas County Courthouse and demanded Will Brown. At a win-dow over the courthouse square, Henry Fonda, age fourteen, stood be-side his father, William, and watched.

"It was so horrifying," Henry would recall near the end of his life. "When it was all over, we went home."

∞

Three days earlier, Agnes Loebeck, a white girl who gave her age as nine-teen, had filed a police report, claiming she'd been sexually assaulted by a gun-wielding black man on a street in South Omaha. The next day, Will Brown—identified as "an itinerant meatpacker" from Cairo, Illinois—was picked up on an anonymous tip, arrested, identified, and jailed.

The case was simple, yet it wasn't. Whispers went round that Loebeck and Brown knew each other, in more than a passing way; that Brown had spurned her for another white woman; that a jealous Loebeck was taking her revenge. Brown was allowed a brief consultation with a black lawyer, H. J. Pinkett, who observed that the prisoner was hobbled by rheumatism—casting doubt on the feats of strength and speed attributed to him.

Men of power in Omaha saw the chance to exploit the case, for rea-sons that had little to do with the direct defense of white supremacy. John Gunther's curious floating allusion to the city's "lack of effective civic leadership" had its origins in this period, when the town was run by a ruthless political machine that made Omaha, in the words of a 1919 report in the black journal *The Crisis,* "perhaps the most lawless of any city of its size in the civilized world."

∽

Running the machine was a gambler named Tom Dennison, who had been in charge of graft in the vice-rich Third Ward since the 1890s. His front man was Omaha's mayor, James Dahlman, known as "Cowboy Jim"—likewise a gambler, drinker, giver and taker of bribes, and for all that a protégé of Nebraska's own William Jennings Bryan, presidential candidate and the era's paragon of Christian piety. In their corner was the *Omaha Daily Bee,* most outspoken of the city's three dailies, founded by Edward Rosewater in 1871. Conservative, Republican, and pro-Dennison, the paper was also antilabor and antiimmigrant—despite Rosewater's being a native of Czechoslovakia, real name Rossenwasser.

Dahlman ran essentially unopposed for a decade, and Dennison's "sporting district," centered at Harney and Sixteenth streets, just blocks from the courthouse, thrived. But after statewide prohibition passed in 1916, the rhetoric of reform led to city laws that cut into Dennison's power. Two years later, Dahlman was ousted by Democrat and reform candidate Edward P. Smith.

Ed Smith appointed as police commissioner fellow reformer J. Dean Ringer, who instructed his men to raid Dennison's houses. Smith also embraced the NAACP, whose Omaha chapter was founded on his watch. Such tolerance endeared him neither to the police nor to white laborers angry at black migrants who had taken their jobs during a recent meat-packers' strike.

Dennison formed the strategy of subverting Smith by exploiting racial tension. Between June and September, the *Daily Bee* published twenty-one separate allegations of assaults on women; twenty of the claimants were white, with sixteen assailants identified as black. It also reported copiously on racial attacks around the country, giving them an alarmist, retributive spin: The riot in Washington, D.C., Omahans were informed, had begun as "retaliation for recent attacks by blacks on white women."

The paper also ran Chief of Police (and Dennison appointee) Marshal Eberstein's warning to an NAACP gathering that if "the good colored people" of Omaha did not aid in the apprehension of "the negroes responsible for the numerous recent assaults on white women," a deadly riot of the kind lately seen in East St. Louis, Illinois, might well occur in Omaha.

When Agnes Loebeck's charges hit the city room at the *Daily Bee,* someone there may have paused to feel the weight of the moment: Red Summer had come to town.

∽

Two afternoons later, a group of youths gathered outside a school in South Omaha and began marching to the jail. En route, adults, both men and women, joined in; by the time it reached the courthouse—protected by a meager ring of thirty policemen—the mob numbered in the thousands.

They began by shattering all the windows on the first two floors and storming the doors. Inside were forty-five additional policemen; when the main entrance was breached and the rioters took the rotunda, the officers retreated up the stairs. By this time, stones had been replaced with guns. Police at the third- and fourth-floor windows returned fire, killing a sixteen-year-old rioter in the rotunda, as well as a businessman a block away. A young man was seen riding a white horse in and out of the square, flashing a rope and exhorting the rioters.

Around eight-thirty, the ground floor was set afire. When fire wagons appeared, the crowd prevented them from entering the square; firefighters were forced back, and their hoses severed. City employees scrambled to higher floors. Some were seen phoning their families to say good-bye.

Near eleven, Mayor Smith emerged and shouted his appeal. A pamphlet printed locally soon after the riot described the next several minutes:

> The crowd surged toward the mayor. He fought them. One man hit
> the mayor on the head with a baseball bat. Another slipped the

noose of a rope around his neck. The crowd started to drag him away.

"If you must hang somebody, then let it be me," the mayor gasped. . . .

He was carried to Sixteenth and Harney Streets. There he was hanged to a metal arm of a traffic signal tower.

Mayor Smith's body was suspended in the air when State Agent Ben Danbaum drove a high-powered automobile into the throng right to the base of the signal tower. In the car with Danbaum were City Detectives Al Anderson, Charles Van Deusen and Lloyd Toland. They grasped the mayor's body. Russell Norgard, 3719 Leavenworth Street, untied the noose. The detectives brought the mayor to Ford Hospital. There he lingered between life and death for several days, finally recovering.

It was the same basic American scene that *Young Mr. Lincoln* would, twenty years later, seek to mythify and make right. But that was Springfield, 1839, in the sheltering darkness of fable. In Omaha, 1919, in the real American night, nothing worked out that way.

∽

No utterance is attributed to Will Brown in any account of the Omaha riot, save one. To the sheriff, he is supposed to have shouted: "I am innocent, I never did it, my God I am innocent."

The police herded well over a hundred shackled prisoners—male and female, white and black—to the roof, which gave threat of collapsing. There the police decided on their last resort. The females were allowed to exit the courthouse safely, but the males were told to get ready to run. Led by the cops, they charged down the stairs and were met by the mob. The consensus account is that the prisoners, not the police, were responsible for the final surrender of the victim.

Will Brown was stripped and beaten—castrated as well, one historian claims, and there is no particular reason to disbelieve it. He was then dragged down the stairs to the south entrance. There his hands were tied and he was beaten further. He may have been dead even before the rope went around his neck.

Men scaled a ladder to the top of a lamppost at the intersection of Eighteenth and Harney. The other end of the rope was thrown over, and those on the sidewalk grabbed it and pulled. Will Brown's body flew skyward, and as it spun, shooters riddled it with bullets. It was then tied to the rear of a car and dragged with raucous ceremony for four blocks, to the corner of Seventeenth and Dodge. A bonfire was built, and the body thrown on top. As it blackened to char, photographs were taken, men and boys jostling for position, their faces aglow in the flames.

Eventually, the burned thing was again tied to a car and dragged through the downtown streets. No record reveals what then became of it—where its parts were found, who disposed of them and how.

By "it," we refer to the body, not the man. Will Brown was long gone.

∽

Lt. Col. Jacob Wuest, commander of nearby Fort Omaha, belatedly dispatched over two hundred army troops. One company was stationed at the hanging corner, and another at the center of "Colored Town," Omaha's black community. The next day, the city was placed under martial law. Whites were told they would be arrested if found with guns; blacks were simply ordered not to leave their homes.

In a joint investigation by army and city officials, over one hundred men were charged with crimes ranging from disturbing the peace to murder. The investigation quickly focused on a plausible set of local suspects—among them, the brother and friends of Agnes Loebeck. In November, a grand jury blamed "a certain Omaha newspaper" for its smear campaign against the Smith administration, and asserted that the riot was "premeditated and planned." Lt. Col. Wuest's superior, Maj. Gen. Leonard Wood, likewise concluded that accountability rested with "'the old criminal gang' . . . and one newspaper."

Not one of the grand jury's 120 indictments was acted upon. According to an Omaha railway official quoted in the *New York Times*, two thousand blacks fled the city by train within days of the riot. Ed

Smith ran in the next election, holding to his reform principles; opposing him was Cowboy Jim Dahlman. Invoking the courthouse siege as proof of Smith's unfitness to lead, Dahlman regained the mayor's office, holding it until his death in 1930. Smith died the same year, having retired from public life. Tom Dennison passed on four years later, wealthy and feted throughout the state.

With the Omaha lynching, the lid was off populist racism in Nebraska. In 1921, the state's first Klan klavern was founded in Lincoln, and within two years, the KKK was active not just in the capital city but also in Omaha, Fremont, York, Grand Island, Hastings, North Platte, and Scotts Bluff.

∞

In the years before his death, Henry Fonda's witnessing of Will Brown's lynching is regularly adumbrated in interviews and feature stories. It becomes a part of his template biography, along with the heartland boyhood, heroic roles, suicidal wife, and controversial offspring. Henry tells the story in his autobiography, and in the late Grobel interview. The lynching is invariably cited in obituaries, and after he is gone, both Peter and Jane reference it as a key to their father's concern for social justice.

But Fonda seems not to have spoken publicly about the event before 1974, when he mentions it in connection with *Clarence Darrow*—which begins with a similar anecdote from the life of its subject. He describes it most fully on November 1, 1975, as a guest on Norman Parkinson's BBC chat show during the London run of the Darrow play.

Parkinson runs a clip: the lynch mob scene from *Young Mr. Lincoln*. He suggests the scene might have been especially meaningful to Fonda: Didn't he himself watch, as a child, a man being lynched?

Fonda says yes, he did, and begins to tell the story. His father had come home after a day at the printing office, and told his family about the mob that was growing at the center of town.

After supper he put me in the car with him, and we drove back downtown. And it was very unusual for me for my dad to be taking

me, at my age, and turning lights on and unlocking doors and going up the stairs. . . . It's not like doing it in the daytime. I remember those physical things and walking across this empty office to a
window that overlooked the courthouse square. This was where
the riot was happening.

My father never talked about it. He never preached about it. We
both just were observers. And I watched an out-of-control mob of
several hundred men . . . drag a young black boy out of the jail in
the courthouse. Overpowered the sheriff to get him out. Strung him
up on a lamppost. Riddled him with bullets. Dragged him around
back of a car, something like that. The *mayor* . . . they damn near
lynched the *mayor*. That's how out of control these . . . these bas-
tards can get, you know.

Fonda returns to the scene in the Lincoln film. He wonders, as Lincoln
had, how men who read the Bible, who were raised on Christ and pretend fealty to the highest morality, could commit such acts. Still there is
no answer. Only the question; only the memory of the question.

"I'll never forget it," Henry says.

His father has imprinted him with a memory the weight of which
will be his lifelong gift and burden. The darkness, the quiet, the odd
sense of ceremony, an approach both solemn and ordinary: climbing
stairs, unlocking a door. Something is opening before him in the dark.
The boy is admitted to knowledge, knowledge he can never not remember, knowledge as horrible as any there is: Mobs kill, people disappear,
and there is murder in the American night.

∽

Parkinson asks Fonda why his father would have made him witness
such a thing.

"He never told me," Fonda replies, "but I would like to think he
realized it would be a lesson. I had to grow up and move away from
Omaha to appreciate that my father was a liberal Democrat in a hotbed

of Republican reactionaries. That's Omaha. And Nebraska still is. That's another reason I feel you're lucky to have the parents—"

Fonda stops, inarticulate when speaking of himself, and as himself. He shifts to the skin of his character, and, as he has always done, lets his character speak for him.

"Clarence Darrow says it in this play. He was brought up right."

∽

What Fonda never said, though he probably knew it, was that Will Brown's was not the first lynching at the Douglas County Courthouse. In October 1891, a five-year-old white girl claimed she was molested by a black man named George Smith. A mob formed. The sheriff was abducted and restrained. Smith was removed from the jail, beaten, dragged, and hanged from a trolley wire at the corner of Seventeenth and Harney—at which point, a newspaper report claims, "a shout from ten thousand throats rent the air."

The lynching of Will Brown twenty-eight years later, eerily similar in outline, was the return of a hell with which Omahans were familiar. William Fonda would have been a boy of twelve when George Smith was killed. Did he see it? Was he made to see it by his father? Might Grandpa Nike and young William even have been among the mob?

Such questions are pebbles down the deepest well: We let them fall without hope of hearing the answer. But something happened to make Henry's father "a liberal Democrat in a hotbed of Republican reactionaries," and we can be certain that William Fonda was thinking of the past as well as the present when he took Henry downtown, mounted dark stairs, unlocked an empty room, went to a window, and made his son witness the inevitable in silence.

∽

It is important to understand, or at least imagine, how the Will Brown lynching affected Fonda. This is why it has been recounted in detail, and why we have avoided countenancing it until now. The event is a specific outrage, a unique obscenity, but it also implies—or seems to—much about the man whose life and work we have traced.

It suggests the seeds of so much sorrow, anger, and solitude in Fonda. It justifies his distrust of patriotic rhetoric, and his certainty that democracy was fearsome in the hands of mendacious men and bigoted mobs. It explains his projection of himself into lynching scenarios, whether as savior, victim, or finally villain, and his insistence on memories, ghosts, and obligations. It traces his own hiddenness to that of his father, and his own fine, deep, natural silence to the silence of a dark room, a night of fear, and an act of witnessing.

We may postulate at length about what the lynching symbolizes. But Will Brown was not a symbol, and against the facts of his murder, postulations matter very little. Yet we hope to take *something* when we go—if only an idea. Thus, the thought that the story of the lynching would explain not just how Will Brown died but how Henry Fonda lived. That, like fire in the night, it would illuminate men's faces.

But here is the twist: It won't. At most it is a context, a history, a memory. All we may claim is that it happened, and all we may justifiably imagine is that a boy witnessed it, remembered it, and carried it with him through all the years of a long, difficult, meaningful, magnificent American life—until he too was dead, his bones burned, his body released from all pain, all memory, ashes to ashes.

Epilogue

Douw Jellis Fonda's
tombstone. Caunawagha
Cemetery, Fonda, New York.

History can be measured in many ways. Here are two:
Not long after this book was begun, Henry Fonda turned 100.
The centenary was honored by the United States Postal Service, which
made Fonda the subject of the eleventh stamp in its Legends of Hollywood series. A press release was issued, summing up the actor's significance in terms that had for decades comprised his standard tribute.

Henry Fonda typically played thoughtful men of integrity, and was
indelibly associated with the American characters he portrayed,
among them young Abe Lincoln, lawyer Clarence Darrow, marshal
Wyatt Earp and, in what many consider his finest performance, the
dispossessed farmer Tom Joad in *The Grapes of Wrath*. As an actor,
Fonda was noted for his seeming naturalness and ease, an illusion
he worked hard to convey, and his distinctively flat Midwestern
accent.

Someone labored over that paragraph, trying to truthfully summarize a life and its meanings in a space too small to breathe in. The attempt has honor, if not elegance. Combine it with the stamp itself—a nice lifelike painting of Fonda circa 1941, looking right at you, as handsome as Hopsie in a blue suit and tie—and you have one measure of history: an official measure, declared in civil tongue and placed in the civic space. It is meant for the museum, the time capsule, the permanent record, and so is made with permanence in mind. It may be polite and evasive, but within its limits it is not false.

In upstate New York, where Fonda's ancestors settled after fleeing Europe, there's a cemetery in the small town that was named for the family. No sign heralds it; the town itself, one in a long line of off-thruway villages damaged by recession, can appear, on some days, all but empty. Yet the cemetery, dominated by trees taller than any in dreams, looks down from the top of a hill on mountain valleys to the south, farm fields to the west, and damned if it isn't a living place.

Among the dozens of Fondas buried there is Douw Jellis, victim of Iroquois scalpers in 1780. His stone, so old that it looks primeval, can barely be read; its colors are those of earth and extreme age. To the touch, it feels like any organic thing planted in the same soil for hundreds of years: mossy and moist, cool and rough. The silence of the hilltop is absolute, the monumentality of the trees intimidating, the sense of being an interloper powerful and less than pleasant. The Fonda cemetery is a place one respects instantly, and is not unhappy to leave.

This is another measure of history, one that renders us inarticulate and immobile, small and uncertain; one too great for that civic space that is the size of a postage stamp and the length of a press release. Where the first is about the usable image, the recognizable ideal, the other is about ghosts.

Somewhere in between the two is where we have found Henry Fonda, if we can say we have found him at all.

∽

His place in the American pantheon is secure. For as long as we read, we will read Emerson and Whitman, Hawthorne, Poe, and Hemingway; and as long as the dreams of the movie screen exert any grip on us, Henry Fonda will be there, as keen and fixated a witness as they to our quest, our tumult, and our crimes.

Like those artists with whom he properly belongs, Fonda refused America's cheapest promises and most destructive myths. He was a man who acted as though there was a certain kind of life he was obliged to live, some long-ago death he was bound to honor. He was an American another American could claim as one's own, with greater pride because he was no saint or simpleton, but broad and deep, at once nobleman and son of a bitch. One would need to both defend and question his behavior, to take stock of the lives he damaged as well as those he strengthened, and wonder how much the bad finally mattered against the good; how much the private sins of one difficult man, whose motives were often a mystery even to himself, negated the great values to which he gave living expression.

Those values were an interwoven set of assumptions, stances, and skepticisms, and they belonged to an individualistic, fair-minded American, one who believed in the complexity of the ordinary; whose eyes told him that life was a terror and a tragedy; who felt arrogance was folly and power the weapon of bullies; who demanded an ethical accounting of his country, his fellows, himself. Who often failed, as man and artist, to meet that accounting, but who walked and talked so as to feel justified in the eyes of the dead—as if they were his true audience, his invisible watchers and unseen judges.

These were the values that for fifty years he acted out on the country's movie screens, and that would remain alive, one hoped, somewhere on the screen of its memory—even in the first years of a new century, when it seemed more and more as if those values had been *buried* alive, existing as little but a nagging recollection, a despised and unfashionable form of patriotic conscience.

Watching him over the past decade, one has been stunned by the relevance of his critique of America, his persistence in seeing the ghost—his own, and ours. In a time when the best lack all conviction and the worst are full of passionate intensity, one has been moved by Fonda's belief, and by his refusal. It's been worth attending to him in these bad years, times when the values he turned into behaviors have been trumpeted to the skies, while lying so dead on the ground that it has been a daily struggle to remember, or conceive of, an America in which they might have existed at all.

But he's still there: Look and listen. When we feel our memories weakening, our sense of the past dissolving, we may look at him. We may look at Henry Fonda and begin to remember, as he remembers.

Notes

For books included in the selected bibliography, publication information is found in that section. Dates in brackets refer to the year of original publication. The following abbreviations are used:

FML   *Fonda: My Life*
PB   *Playboy* interview
MLSF   *My Life So Far*
DTD   *Don't Tell Dad: A Memoir*
NBN   *Never Before Noon: An Autobiography*

PROLOGUE

2   "majesty and trash": John Berryman, *Stephen Crane: A Critical Biography* (New York: Cooper Square Press, 2001 [1950]), xiii.

2   "I suppose": Steinbeck, *America and Americans*, 224.

1. SPRINGFIELD, 1839

8   "This scene": Peter Handke, *Short Letter, Long Farewell* (New York: Farrar, Straus and Giroux, 1974), 115.

8   "A jack-legged young lawyer": *FML*, 127; see also McBride, 302.

9   read most of the Lincoln books: *FML*, 125.

9   he was named in Hollywood columns: *Sheboygan Press*, 10/23/1935.

9   "It's like playing Jesus": Curtis Lee Hanson, "Henry Fonda: Reflections on Forty Years of Make-Believe," in *Playing to the Camera: Film Actors Discuss Their Craft*, ed. Bert Cardullo et al. (New Haven: Yale University Press, 1998), 213.

10   "What the fuck": *FML,* 127.

10   The film, shot mostly around Sacramento: See http://www.imdb.com/title/
     tt0032155/locations; *Oakland Tribune,* 4/16/1939.

10   "I first saw this film": Eistenstein, 139–49.

11   "one of the most dramatic": Thomas Dixon, Jr., *The Clansman* (New York:
     Doubleday, Page, 1905), ii.

11   "Like writing history": *Village Voice Film Special,* 11/30/1993.

11   *The Birth of a Nation* grossed: ibid.

11   Henry Brocj: *The Crisis,* June 1916, 87.

11   "If the people": *Oxford American* 56 (2007): 119.

11   "would play Ku Klux Klan": O'Hara, 109.

12   Appearing as one of Griffith's Klan riders: McBride, 81.

12   Ford dissolves: Dan Ford, *Pappy: The Life of John Ford* (Englewood Cliffs, NJ:
     Prentice Hall, 1979), 139.

14   Ann Rutledge: Wilson, *Honor's Voice,* 115–18.

15   "He mourned her loss": Schurz, 58.

15   "A highly dubious business": Vidal, *United States,* 666.

15   "symbolic significance": Wilson, *Honor's Voice,* 125.

15   "I never seen a man": ibid., 120.

16   "showed that in mourning": Alvarez, 126.

17   "a gaze of cosmic reproaches": Eisenstein, 149.

18   "is that of Lincoln as": McBride, 303.

19   "preparing himself": Graham Greene, *Graham Greene on Movies: Collected Film
     Criticism 1935–1940*, ed. John Russell Taylor (New York: Simon & Schuster,
     1972), 242.

2. THE ELEPHANT AND THE BLACK DOG

21   "One of Mr. Fonda's": Springer, 54.

21   *Fonda,* from the Latin: http://www.fonda.org/stories.htm#Origins.

21   "was one of the leaders": ibid.

21   Dutch reform movement: Newman, 573–85.

21   at around 1628: Ross and Ross, 83.

22   Douw   Jellis: http://wc.rootsweb.ancestry.com/cgi-bin/igm.cgi?op=GET&db
     =amfonda&id=ind00295.

22   "on the rapids": Sherman Williams, *Stories from Early New York History* (New
     York: Scribner's, 1906), 299.

22   "venerable old David": Bonney, 83.

22   "house   was   plundered":   http://wc.rootsweb.ancestry.com/cgi-bin/igm.cgi?op
     =GET&db=amfonda&id=ind00295.

22   "At midnight June 30, 1863": http://www.fonda.org/stories.htm#Ten Eyck.

23   "I had orders to spare nothing": ibid.

23   the Burlington & Missouri River Railroad: www.kancoll.org/books/andreas_ne/railroad/railroad-p4.html#BMRR.

23   William... was born there in 1879: http://www.fonda.org/notables.htm.

23   William married: http://knol.google.com/k/will-johnson/henry-jaynes-fonda/4hmquk6fx4gu/14#.

23   "ordinary American people": Brough, 21.

25   "great highway" of westward migration: Mattes, 23.

25   At first, the departed: ibid., 87.

25   crosses marking their graves: ibid., 82.

26   "he believed deeply": Hofstadter, 36.

26   "a general need for Americans": Shortridge, 9.

26   "This is America": Gunther, 274.

26   "To curse a farm": Wills, 308.

27   the city of Omaha: Bristow, 1, 83–92.

27   "On Saturday nights": Walker D. Wyman, "Omaha: Frontier Depot and Prodigy of Council Bluffs," *Nebraska History Magazine* 17 (1936): 143–54.

27   "a great place for aggressive hijinks": Gunther, 255.

27   "Dr. Roeder reports": http://www.stuhrmuseum.org/virtualtour/fonda.htm.

29   "ornamental shade trees": J. Sterling Morton and Albert Watkins, *History of Nebraska; From the Earliest Explorations of the Trans-Mississippi Region* (Lincoln, NE: Western Publishing and Engraving Co., 1918); available at http://www.usgennet.org/usa/ne/topic/resources/OLLibrary/MWHNE/mwhne000.htm.

29   nickelodeon: *High Point Enterprise,* 10/30/1976.

29   Orpheum Theatre: William Kalush and Larry Sloman, *The Secret Life of Houdini: The Making of America's First Superhero* (New York: Simon & Schuster, 2006), 81; Nebraska State Historical Society (http://www.nebraskahistory.org/publish/publicat/timeline/astaire_fred.htm). Later in life, Henry claimed to have been pulled up on stage once as Houdini's assistant. See: *Kingsport Times-News,* 2/23/1975.

29   Minnie Stout: U.S. Census Report, Omaha, Douglas County, NB, 1910; available at www.ancestry.com.

29   "To have seen *the elephant*": Albert Barrére, ed., *A Dictionary of Slang, Jargon and Cant* (London: Ballantyne Press, 1889), 344.

30   "the popular symbol": Mattes, 61.

30   The Fondas were Christian Scientists: *FML,* 21; *PB,* 106.

30   Mark Twain attacked: Mark Twain, *Christian Science* (New York: Oxford University Press, 1997 [1907]). Willa Cather and Georgine Milmine, *The Life of Mary Baker G. Eddy and the History of Christian Science* (Lincoln: University of Nebraska Press, 1993 [1909]).

30 "as if they were caused": *DTD,* 64, 116.

31 "an angelic woman": Brough, 8.

31 "Everything he did was": Anita Summer, "Famous Men Remember: 'The Little Things' About My Father's Greatness," *Family Circle,* 6/15/1975, 6.

31 "I was always trying to find out": Norman, 87.

31 "biological vulnerability": *MLSF,* 35.

31 "black dog": Anthony Storr, *Churchill's Black Dog and Other Phenomena of the Human Mind* (New York: HarperCollins, 1997).

33 "I had no ambition to be": Ross and Ross, 85.

34 "It was a nightmare": ibid.

34 "I didn't dare look up": ibid.

34 the Retail Credit Company: ibid.

35 "writers, various kinds of activists": Chansky, 2.

35 "To raise the drama": http://www.omahaplayhouse.com/history.aspx.

35 "Like other reform activities": Chansky, 3.

35 "Most Little Theatre workers": ibid.

36 "Shut up": Cole and Farrell, 10.

3. A TIME OF LIVING VIOLENTLY

39 "I pride myself": *Waterloo Evening Courier,* 2/24/1926.

39 He sees, by his account: *FML,* 35; *PB,* 104.

40 Bette Davis: *FML,* 35–36. Davis relates the incident in Charlotte Chandler, *The Girl Who Walked Home Alone: Bette Davis, A Personal Biography* (New York: Simon & Schuster, 2006), 117–19, though curiously not in her autobiography, *The Lonely Life* (New York: Putnam, 1962).

41 *The Barker:* Ross and Ross, 86.

41 "a high, strangulated sob": Logan, 21.

41 "some odd human animal": ibid.

42 Elmer: ibid., 27–28.

42 "Several years ago": Houghton, 109.

42 "[Now] he was aware": ibid., 120.

43 He spends the winter months: Sweeney, 169–74; *FML,* 54–55, 58–59.

43 "stimulating plays": *New York Times,* 1/8/1935.

44 "She intrigued me": Hayward, 185. See also Houghton, 84.

44 *The Devil in the Cheese:* Hayward, 185–86.

45 "By the time I am thirty-five": Collier, 31.

45 "cream": *FML,* 91.

45 "Hank was much in love": Houghton, 161.

45 "Fonda": Brough, 43.

46 marriage license: Brooke Hayward Papers, Billy Rose Theatre Division of the New York Public Library for the Performing Arts.

46 Fonda initially objects: Houghton, 240.

46 "They fought so terribly": Brough, 37.

46 the two marry: rector's receipt, Brooke Hayward Papers.

48 Jed Harris: Martin Gottfried, *Jed Harris: The Curse of Genius* (Boston: Little, Brown, 1984), 145–46.

48 divorce proceedings: unedited transcript of HF's 1975 interview with Brooke Hayward (hereafter given as Hayward interview transcript), Brooke Hayward Papers.

48 stranger in a Christian Science reading room: *FML,* 66–67.

49 "unable to give the role": *New York Times,* 1/2/1960.

49 Death comes: ibid.

50 She dies only nine months: *New York Times,* 10/19/1960.

50 His first sex had been: *FML,* 29.

52 "is made to look delighted": Haskell, 150.

52 head shot: Brooke Hayward Papers.

52 "Casa Gangrene": *FML,* 70–71; Brough, 52.

53 "stooging": Hayward interview transcript.

53 Inspector Enderby: *Portsmouth Herald,* 9/6/1932.

53 "a sentimental romance": *Barnard Bulletin,* 10/21/1932.

53 *Forsaking All Others:* www.ibdb.com/production.php?id=11729.

53 *Love Story:* Sweeney, 176.

53 *All Good Americans:* *FML,* 77; www.ibdb.com/production.php?id=11804.

53 Mr. Goldfarb: *FML,* 73.

54 "a potpourri": *New York Times,* 2/22/1985.

54 "Finances had to be pooled": *Piqua Daily Call,* 5/4/1934.

55 "lacks pace": "The Theatre: New Play in Manhattan," *Time,* 3/2/1934; available at www.time.com/time/magazine/article/0,9171,747250,00.html.

55 "a fairly witty": *San Antonio Daily News,* 4/1/1934.

55 March through July 1934: http://www.ibdb.com/production.asp?ID=11849.

55 Dwight Deere Wiman: *FML,* 84–85.

56 Henry introduces Hayward: Hayward interview transcript.

56 "Hayward has the agent's habit": Margaret Case Harriman, "Profiles: Hollywood Agent," *The New Yorker,* 7/11/1936, 24.

56 "It wasn't my ambition": *FML,* 85; Hayward, 134–35.

57 Walter Wanger: Bernstein.

57 Wanger would introduce Siegel: Bernstein, 163; David Weddle, *"If They Move . . . Kill 'Em!": The Life and Times of Sam Peckinpah* (New York: Grove, 1994), 109, 116.

58 "a fine and daring producer": Bernstein, 123.

58 "a daring experimenter": ibid., 128.

58 "one of the fanciest": Otis Ferguson, *The Film Criticism of Otis Ferguson* (Philadelphia: Temple University Press, 1971), 265.

58 "I could go back": Hayward, 135.

58 Henry will not recall him warmly: *PB*, 118.

58 Joel McCrea or Gary Cooper: Cole and Farrell, 21.

58 loan-out fee: *FML*, 95.

58–59 star gets approval: Bernstein, 112.

59 "I had no ambition": *PB*, 118.

59 *The President Vanishes*: Bernstein, 97.

60 "Wouldn't he be wonderful": Roberts and Goldstein, 44.

60 "He was patently ideal": Brough, 58.

60 the good sense to compliment Connelly: *FML*, 87.

61 "a manly, modest performance": Cole and Farrell, 21.

61 "an extraordinarily simple": ibid.

61 "will be transferred": *Syracuse Herald*, 11/8/1934.

61 warned by the director, Victor Fleming: *FML*, 97–98.

62 dies in Omaha: *Lincoln Star*, 10/8/1934. To make it worse, the notice identifies Herberta's son as "Harry Fonda of New York." See also FML, 88–89.

63 Henry rents a bungalow with Jimmy Stewart: *FML*, 99–102; Michael Wilmington, "Small-Town Guy," *Film Comment*, March–April 1990, 52.

63 Martin bomber: *FML*, 99.

64 Ross Alexander and Aleta Freel: ibid., 96.

64 Freel shoots herself: *San Antonio Express*, 12/8/1935.

64 "The day following": *Waterloo Daily Courier*, 12/10/1935.

64 Ronald Reagan: Ronald Reagan, *Reagan: A Life in Letters*, ed. Kiron K. Skinner, Annelise Anderson, and Martin Anderson (New York: Free Press, 2003), 30–31.

65 "a generation of favorites": Thomson, *The Whole Equation*, 154.

66 "Youth is a time": Houghton, 259.

4. THE BIG SOUL

67 "The only actor of the era": Baldwin, 21.

67 "first conscious calculation": ibid., 28.

67 Shirley Ross: *Middlesboro Daily News*, 10/31/1935; http://www.imdb.com/name/nm0743841/; *FML*, 98.

69 "Henry Fonda says it is": *San Mateo Times*, 3/21/1936.

69 "One of the most personable": Cooke, ed., 72.

69 He lodges at: HF to Sullavan, 7/1/1936, Brooke Hayward Papers.

69   She is related by marriage: *New York Times,* 8/24/1936.

70   "an alcoholic": Andersen, 23.

70   "a part-time poet": Guiles, 4.

70   paranoid schizophrenic: *MLSF,* 25.

70   She claimed to have been molested: ibid., 26.

70   Clare Boothe: Andersen, 24.

71   "descend on Wall Street": *MLSF,* 28.

71   an impatient Frances suggesting to Brokaw: Guiles, 4.

71   cash bequest: *FML,* 119.

71   yearly income in excess: *New York Times,* 11/9/1935.

71   "When a woman": Guiles, 4.

71   "I've always gotten": *MLSF,* 37.

72   "Dearest Peggy": HF to Sullavan, 7/1/1936, Brooke Hayward Papers. (Dating contradicts sources that say HF did not leave for England until 7/10.)

73   "THEY'LL BE MARRIED": *Lowell Sun,* 8/24/1936.

73   a reception: *New York Times,* 9/9/1936; *FML,* 118.

73   "blundering fool": HF to Sullavan, 9/9/1936, Brooke Hayward Papers.

73   The wedding: *New York Times,* 9/17/1936.

74   "Mrs. Robert Kane": *Waterloo Sunday Courier,* 10/4/1936.

74   Fonda admits that he has begun to secede: *FML,* 120.

77   "expressed certain feelings": Kael, *Kiss Kiss Bang Bang,* 49–50.

79   "I was barely aware": *PB,* 102.

80   "In a way": Baldwin, 25.

80   "And because they were lonely": Steinbeck, *The Grapes of Wrath,* 264.

80   "The right to be let alone": Samuel Warren and Louis Brandeis, "The Right to Privacy," *Harvard Law Review,* 12/15/1890, 193.

80–81   "the America of the murders and rapes": Wilson, *Literary Essays and Reviews of the 1930s and 40s,* 519.

82   *Blockade* (1938): Bernstein, 129–32.

82   "The story does not attempt": John Walker, ed., *Halliwell's Film Guide 1994* (New York: HarperCollins, 1994), 137.

83–84   "I have read a book": *Port Arthur News,* 1/21/1940.

84   was sold, days after publication: *Fresno Bee,* 4/21/1939.

84   "The shadow": Steinbeck, *The Grapes of Wrath,* 187.

84   "Maybe all men": ibid., 33.

85   "an organization of the unconscious": ibid., 135.

85   "They's stuff": ibid., 236–37.

85   "people in flight": ibid., 166.

5. WAYS OF ESCAPE

93 "Death in the guise": Percy, 313.

94 she especially wants a boy: Andersen, 28; *MLSF,* 41.

94 leaping with excitement: *FML,* 121.

95 provision written into: *FML,* 122–23.

95 "Dad was so emotionally distant": *MLSF,* 50.

95 "Protestant rages": ibid.

95 "We were all afraid": Brough, 80.

95 "children, operations": Kiernan, 20; Anderson, 28–29.

95 "quarantined": *FML,* 124.

96 Bell Telephone: Hayward interview transcript.

96 purchase the property: *FML,* 133; *MLSF,* 49.

96 "in increments": *DTD,* 8.

96 "a bare hill": Hayward interview transcript.

96 "In those days": Hayward, 138.

96 "Probably the most carefully planned home": Marva and Lloyd Shearer, "The Fondas' Formula for Successful Living," *House Beautiful,* July 1948, 40.

97 the styling of the house: Ross and Ross, 93.

97 she retreats for three weeks: Andersen, 32; *FML,* 134.

97 he left his virginity: Gussow, 11.

98 "a little melodrama": ibid., 57.

98 "would transform himself": Custen, 227.

99 "divided allegiance": Gussow, 21.

99 "Henry Fonda is fast becoming": *Syracuse Herald,* 11/20/1939.

100 "We intend to follow": Gussow, 84.

100 "one casting decision": Custen, 233.

100 recounting their meeting: *FML,* 128–29.

101 "I know I'm bad": *Ogden Standard-Examiner,* 7/7/1940.

105 "certainly not entertainment": Custen, 273.

105 "high pressure salesmanship": *Syracuse Herald-Journal,* 7/14/1943.

106 "Did you ever hear": Clark, 146–47.

107 "What is the conscience": ibid., 66–67.

108 "I'll be glad": ibid., 309.

108 "I was a typical eager beaver": *PB,* 118.

108 staged fight: *Galveston Daily News,* 12/5/1941.

108 Whether Roosevelt foresaw: Costello, 607–8; Vidal, *The Last Empire,* 448–56, 457–65.

108 "shared disbelief": Costello, 608.

109 "an escape": Axel Madsen, *William Wyler: The Authorized Biography* (New York: Crowell, 1973), 258.

109   "He was genuinely patriotic": *MLSF,* 51.

110   "I'd like to be with the fellows": *Charleston Gazette,* 8/25/1942.

110   "Without the usual Hollywood fanfare": ibid.

110   "It has been my desire": *Wisconsin State Journal,* 8/25/1942.

111   "I won World War II": *FML,* 138.

111   Henry finishes third in the class: F. S. Crosley to Lt. Cmdr. H. V. Bird, 8/25/1943, HF's military file.

111   on the USS *Satterlee*: *FML,* 143.

111   sworn in as a lieutenant: ibid., 144.

112   joint intelligence among the service branches: James D. Marchio, "Days of Future Past: Joint Intelligence in World War II," *Joint Forces Quarterly* (Spring 1996): 116–23.

112   "should have had experience": Crosley to Bird, 8/25/1943, HF's military file.

113   "demonstrates officer-like qualities": ibid.

113   "[I]t has been determined": ibid.

113   "there was a favorable atmosphere": Melville C. Branch, *Planning and the Human Condition: Conceptual Development, Prospective Conclusions* (Lincoln, NE: Writer's Showcase, 2002), 13.

113   company's drill instructor: *FML,* 144.

113   "Lieutenant (junior grade) Fonda": Cmdr. E. K. Zitzewitz, Officer Fitness Report, 11/2–12/23/1943, HF's military file.

113   graduates fourth: Crosley to Bird, 8/25/1943, HF's military file.

113   "That impressed": *PB,* 120.

113   USS *Curtiss*: Dictionary of American Naval Fighting Ships, available at www.history.navy.mil/danfs/c16/curtiss.htm.

115   "Officers pored over": Thomas, 155.

115   "our doctor has had to order him": *Del Rio News-Herald,* 3/15/1945.

115   "Lieutenant Fonda": *El Paso Herald-Post,* 4/23/1948.

116   "How many of us would have been killed": Terkel, 47.

116   "It was an eerie sight": *FML,* 158.

117   "keen intelligence": memo, Office of U.S. Pacific Fleet, Commander Marianas, 8/18/1945, HF's military file.

117   "operating in the Southern Ryukyus Islands": Office of Public Information report; available at www.usscurtiss.com.

117   on shore leave: *FML,* 158.

117   *Enola Gay*: Timothy Luke, *Museum Politics: Power Plays at the Exhibition* (Minneapolis: University of Minnesota Press, 2002), 25.

118   Fonda knows, though not clearly: FML, 159.

118   "sort of took me back": *PB,* 120.

118   an estimated 140,000 people: Douglas Holdstock and Frank Barnaby, *Hiroshima and Nagasaki: Retrospect and Prospect* (London: Frank Cass, 1995), 2.

118   receiving the Bronze Star: *Council Bluffs Nonpareil,* 8/13/1945; *Stars and Stripes,* 8/14/1945.

118   *The Navy Hour:* Sweeney, 219–20.

118   resigns his commission: Acting Secretary of the Navy Thomas S. Gates, Jr., to HF, 12/11/1953, HF's military file.

119   "Reactions to combat stress": Michael Sturma, *The USS Flier: Death and Survival on a World War II Submarine* (Lexington: University of Kentucky Press, 2008), 154.

120   "Peter lost it": *PB,* 120.

120   "Mrs. Henry Fonda is off": *San Antonio Light,* 11/10/1944.

120   "Mrs. Henry Fonda": ibid., 12/18/1944.

120   affairs while Henry was at war: *FML,* 155.

121   a man named Joe: *MLSF,* 23–24.

121   the man recalled by Peter: *DTD,* 10.

121   Frances begins administering the household: *FML,* 173.

121   Barbara Thompson: *Dunkirk Evening Observer,* 7/14/1943; *Lima News,* 7/14/1943; *Nevada State Journal,* 7/14/1943; *Yuma Daily Sun,* 7/14/1943; *Lowell Sun,* 7/15/1943; *Port Arthur News,* 7/15/1943; *Ogden Standard-Examiner,* 7/16/1943; *Sheboygan Press,* 7/20/1943; *Modesto Bee,* 9/7/1943; *Long Beach Independent,* 10/5/1943; *Williamsport Gazette and Bulletin,* 10/20/1943; *Yuma Daily Sun,* 12/3/1946.

123   "my father began having affairs": *MLSF,* 50.

123   quoted an anonymous friend: FML, 121.

124   "They say his domestic affairs": *Wisconsin State Journal,* 8/28/1945.

124   "angrily [denying] the divorce": *Uniontown Morning Herald,* 9/26/1945.

124   Louella Parsons says: *Modesto Bee,* 11/10/1945.

124   "lies in the fertilizer": *Berkshire Evening Eagle,* 7/3/1948.

124   "was seriously into making": *DTD,* 16.

124   "the hottest": *Ironwood Daily Globe,* 10/21/1946.

124   April through June of 1946: McBride, 435.

125   "I screamed and yelled": *DTD,* 28–29. See also *FML,* 173–74.

125   "In those days": *FML,* 167.

125   stories of routine transgressions: *DTD,* 13–14. See also *FML,* 167.

125   "a very difficult man": *DTD,* 17.

125   "Death in the guise": This and subsequent quotes from the book are from Percy, 313–14.

6. A SORT OF SUICIDE

128 *Fort Apache*: Wills, 175–76; William Darby, *John Ford's Westerns: A The-matic Analysis, with a Filmography* (Jefferson, NC: McFarland, 1996), Chapter 6.

129 "mythopathic moment": Herr, 47–48.

132 Tigertail pasture: *FML,* 171–72; *DTD,* 20–21.

132 has gotten Fox to increase: Dennis McDougal, *The Last Mogul: Lew Was-serman, MCA, and the Hidden History of Hollywood* (New York: Da Capo, 2001 [1998]), 117.

134 "I look forward": *Ironwood Daily Globe,* 10/21/1946.

134 "the Burbank of Brentwood": *Statesville Daily Record,* 1/11/1947.

134 "Deftly, she tried": *Joplin Globe,* 7/29/1947.

134 "a city slicker": *Ogden Standard-Examiner,* 9/21/1947.

135 "the wonderman of the musical stage": E. J. Kahn, Jr., "Profiles: The Tough Guy and the Soft Guy—II," *The New Yorker,* 4/11/1953, 65.

135 Here it is, he says: Logan, 207; *FML,* 4.

136 "I was": Gay Talese, *Fame and Obscurity* (New York: Dell, 1986), 104.

137 *Mr. Roberts* previews: Logan, 212.

137 "a gilt-edged investment": *Nevada State Journal,* 2/13/1948.

137 "There were too many curtain calls": Logan, 216.

137–38 "standing on their seats": *PB,* 123.

138 The next day's critical acclaim: Logan, 216; *Uniontown Morning Herald,* 3/9/1948; *Cumberland Sunday Times,* 2/22/1948; John Lardner, "Roberts for President," *The New Yorker,* 2/28/1948, 48.

138 "bettering by several thousand": Leggett, 398.

138 Antoinette Perry Award: *New York Times,* 3/29/1948.

138 Atkinson will estimate: *New York Times,* 5/21/1950.

139 "He always wanted": E. J. Kahn, Jr., "Profiles: The Tough Guy and the Soft Guy—I," *The New Yorker,* 4/4/1953, 62.

140 "He'll never be seduced": ibid., 61–62.

140 Heggen has told Logan: Logan, 207.

140 "There are people": Heggen, 211.

141 Both are: Leggett, 279.

141 "feeling, carried since his teens": ibid., 315.

141 "feeling selfish": *Uniontown Morning Herald,* 3/9/1948.

142 By April, a house: *Wisconsin State Journal,* 4/9/1948.

142 Pecksland Road: Brough, 101.

142 destroyed in the worst brush fire: *FML,* 277–78; *Long Beach Independent,* 11/7/1961.

142 Jane evokes Charles Addams: *MLSF,* 9.

142 "musky, attic-like": *DTD*, 36.

142 "unknown darkness": ibid., 41.

142 Peter contracts pneumonia: *DTD*, 38, 42; *Portland Press Herald*, 7/30/1949.

142 "Dad asked me": *MLSF*, 10. See also *FML*, 187–88.

143 Henry moves to the nearby town: *Portland Press Herald*, 7/30/1949.

143 he buys each of his kids: *Logansport Press*, 3/5/1948.

143 "She began to feel": *FML*, 188.

143 "there": *DTD*, 38.

143 Frances informs him: *FML*, 190.

143 Austen Riggs Center: www.austenriggs.org. See also Lawrence S. Kubie, M.D., *The Riggs Story: The Development of the Austen Riggs Center for the Study and Treatment of the Neuroses* (New York: Paul D. Hoeber, 1960).

144 "special hotels": Chesler, 34.

144 Margaret Sullavan will experience: Hayward, 19.

144 "Perhaps": Chesler, 35.

145 Susan Blanchard: Collier, 79–80.

146 becomes engaged: ibid., 79.

146 disturbed by the approach of grandmotherhood: *FML*, 195.

146 "floating" kidney: Guiles, 33.

147 Tom Heggen's body is found: *New York Times*, 5/20/1949.

147 "I do know": Logan, 253.

147 "I don't much like": Leggett, 283.

147 He was earning: *New York Times*, 5/20/1949.

148 "The most terrible enemy": Heggen and Logan, 159–60.

148 "They just cut me": Guiles, 33.

149 "my better half": ibid., 34.

149 socializing at the Stork Club: *Aiken Standard and Review*, 7/6/1949.

149 asks her for a divorce: *FML*, 195–96.

150 "The shock of Hank": *DTD*, 43.

150 "I could see": Sylvia Plath, *The Bell Jar* (New York: Bantam, 1972 [1971]), 104–5.

150 she has a new will: Guiles, 40.

150 lapses into psychosis: *FML*, 197–98; *MLSF*, 15.

150 Frances returns to Riggs: FML, 198.

150 Pan gives birth: *Joplin Globe*, 12/14/1949.

150 "Pan lost her baby": Collier, 79.

151 "She seemed all right": *DTD*, 43.

151 "as soon as it is legally possible": *New York Journal American*, 12/29/1949.

151 Kilgallen has gotten the scoop: Guiles, 37.

151 Craig House: *FML*, 199–200.

151 Zelda Fitzgerald: Matthew J. Bruccoli, *Some Sort of Epic Grandeur: The Life*

of *F. Scott Fitzgerald,* 2nd rev. ed. (Columbia: University of South Carolina Press, 2002 [1981]), 361.

151   "I wanted to do everything": Plath, 105.

151   improvements in her condition: *FML,* 202.

151   Frances takes a day trip home: *DTD,* 44.

152   "I'm very sorry": *San Mateo Times,* 4/15/1950.

152   suicide verdict is summarily entered: *Salt Lake Tribune,* 4/15/1950.

152   ashes interred: www.findagrave.com/cgi-bin/fg.cgi?page=gr&GRid=9795853.

152   "She was making a wonderful recovery": *San Mateo Times,* 4/15/1950.

153   Brooke Hayward's insistence: Hayward, 18.

153   "Probably": *PB,* 122.

153   his own sober decision: *FML,* 205–6.

153   "too numb": *PB,* 122.

153   "apparently killed herself": *San Mateo Times,* 4/15/1950.

153   "pale with fatigue": *Kingston Daily Freeman,* 4/15/1950.

153   "He was even sharper": ibid.

153   performance is essentially identical: *FML,* 206.

153   "He went on": Norman, 86.

153   "I think he didn't know": ibid.

154   "When [Fonda]": Collier, 83.

154   "Men commit actions": Chesler, 48.

154   "immediate trigger": *FML,* 208.

154   "in a mood": ibid.

154   "arranged this solution": ibid., 209.

154   Dr. Knight: *Clinician and Therapist: Selected Papers of Robert P. Knight,* ed. Stuart C. Miller (New York: Basic Books, 1972), includes recollections by colleagues Erik Erikson and Margaret Brenman-Gibson, and a portrait of the doctor by his neighbor and patient Norman Rockwell.

155   "disposes of an estate": *Kingsport Times,* 5/11/1950.

155   "a tactless woman": Sheilah Graham, *Confessions of a Hollywood Columnist* (New York: Bantam, 1970 [1969]), 225.

155   "It was just a bore": *PB,* 122.

7. THE RIGHT MAN

159   "'In the middle of the journey'": Alvarez, 169.

159   suburb of Darien: *Bridgeport Sunday Post,* 9/9/1951.

160   four-story brownstone: *Olean Times Herald,* 9/6/1950.

161   a custody bid: *MLSF,* 78.

161   guardianship: *Traverse City Record-Eagle,* 7/3/1950.

161   shoots himself in the abdomen: *MLSF,* 72–73; *DTD,* 51–56.

161   "very favorable condition": *Idaho State Journal,* 1/8/1951.

162   Jane has her doubts: *MLSF,* 73.

162   Henry believes him: *PB,* 128.

162   "No one ever talked": *DTD,* 46.

162   "She remained cool": *Lowell Sun,* 1/8/1951.

162   torn knee cartilage: *Cedar Rapids Gazette,* 10/4/1950.

163   "was almost unable to go on speaking": *Olean Times Herald,* 11/6/1950.

163   "This is my first tour": *Wisconsin State Journal,* 3/6/1951.

163   snowstorm: *Madison Capitol Times,* 3/20/1951.

163   "If I get a chance": *Cedar Rapids Gazette,* 3/26/1951. See also *Council Bluffs
        Nonpareil,* 3/26/1951; *Wisconsin State Journal,* 3/26/1951.

164   "I don't feel it": Logan, 262–63; *FML,* 217–18.

164   "had become so identified": E. J. Kahn, Jr., "Profile: The Tough Guy and the
        Soft Guy—I," *The New Yorker,* 4/4/1953, 62.

165   "will charge $8": *San Mateo Times,* 9/21/1951.

165   advance ticket sale: *Uniontown Evening Standard,* 12/20/1951.

165   show sells out: *Marion Star,* 11/3/1951.

166   "absorbing and generally entertaining": *Nevada State Journal,* 11/16/1951.

166   Potter: Hayward interview transcript.

166   Kazan: ibid.

166   "feeling that I was cheating": ibid.

166   "an honest second act": *FML,* 222.

166   The notices are glumly approving: Osborn, dust jacket.

167   "deep beneath the waters": John P. Marquand, *Point of No Return* (New
        York: Bantam, 1952 [1949]), 492.

167   "There was nothing to explain": ibid., 458–59.

167   "*A single light*": Osborn, 139.

168   "My life has been peppered": *FML,* x.

168   the tour in Baltimore: *Cedar Rapids Gazette,* 12/14/1952.

168   "is not the greatest play": *Oakland Tribune,* 4/8/1953.

168   he rejects: *FML,* 226; *Cedar Rapids Gazette,* 7/12/1953; *Sheboygan Press,*
        5/28/1954; *Waterloo Daily Courier,* 7/9/1954.

169   three options he is given: *FML,* 227.

170   "One-nighters": *Bradford Era,* 10/2/1953.

170   headquarters of the American Federation of Musicians: *San Antonio Express,*
        9/4/1953; *Joplin Globe,* 10/3/1953.

170   to cede partial rights: Callow, 225.

171   "What do you know": ibid., 227.

171   "I consider Fonda": http://theatreisterritory.com/tag/charles-nolte.html. Nolte
        had previously played a crew member in *Mister Roberts.*

172 Henry Fonda has "the gift": *El Paso Herald-Post,* 11/5/1953.

172 advance Broadway ticket sale: *Cedar Rapids Gazette,* 12/2/1953.

172 "and is eager": *Oakland Tribune,* 10/16/1953.

172 "aloof": *Lowell Sun,* 12/9/1953.

172 "What direction?": *Charleston Gazette,* 12/10/1953.

172 "[We're] just one happy family": *Charleston Gazette,* 12/14/1953.

172 "At least five people": ibid.

172 "I got into a slight squabble": *Tucson Daily Citizen,* 1/16/1954.

172 putting his fist through a door: *Nevada State Journal,* 10/27/1953.

172 acclaim across the board: *Chillicothe Constitution-Tribune,* 1/30/1954.

173 "one of the great shows": *Uniontown Morning Herald,* 1/27/1954.

173 "a throat-grabbing chunk": *Waterloo Daily Courier,* 7/9/1954.

173 "I am in that near-comatose state": *Beckley Post-Herald,* 3/3/1954.

173 "Queeg deserved better": Wouk, *The Caine Mutiny Court-Martial,* 128.

173 "the toughest scene": *Corpus Christi Caller-Times,* 2/21/1954.

174 cries onstage: *FML,* 228.

174 Caribbean locations: *Portland Press-Herald,* 9/11/1948.

175 "homosexual": McBride, 543–44.

175 Brando's involvement: *Albuquerque Journal,* 2/19/1954.

175 "who has aged": ibid.

175 "Bullshit!": *FML,* 230.

175 "I had no intention": *Long Beach Independent,* 7/30/1954.

176 "an Irish": McBride, 547.

177 "screw up": ibid., 548.

177 Fonda feels a blow: Norman, 88; PB, 123.

177 Ford appears at Henry's door: Norman, 89.

177 "Just a great actor": Ford interview on Criterion Collection DVD of *Young Mr. Lincoln.*

178 Ward Bond: McBride, 550.

178 "I despised that film": ibid., 552.

179 half of all American homes: Whitfield, 153.

179 thirty-nine episodes: www.tv.com/shows/henry-fonda-presents-the-star-and-the -story/season/?season=all.

179 "appalling to see an actor": *Waterloo Daily Courier,* 7/27/1959.

180 "I am an actor": *Valparaiso Videlio-Messenger,* 7/22/1954.

180 "vast wasteland": Newton N. Minow, *Equal Time: The Private Broadcaster and the Public Interest* (New York: Atheneum, 1964), 45.

180 "secret ambition": *News Television and Radio Guide* (Lima, OH), 3/12/1955.

180 "I want to do the picture": *Portsmouth Herald,* 11/10/1954.

180 eighty thousand dollars: *News Television and Radio Guide* (Lima, OH), 3/12/1955.

182 "astoundingly restrictive": *DTD,* 78, 85.

182 Susan admits to being fearful: Norman, 91.

183 "Don't cry": ibid., 71.

183 "probably the biggest movie": *El Paso Herald Post,* 5/23/1955.

183 David O. Selznick and Mike Todd: ibid.

183 The movie will have: ibid.

183 six million dollars: ibid.

184 "You understand, don't you": Brough, 124.

184 Henry finds his daily pages: *Oakland Tribune,* 10/27/1959.

184 "If I'd seen it": *Lebanon Daily News,* 8/2/1956.

184 "It was as if we were": Norman, 90.

185 granted a divorce decree: *Newport News,* 12/8/1955; *Long Beach Independent,* 5/3/1956.

186 Anita Ekberg: *Salt Lake Tribune,* 5/24/1959; *NBN,* 8; Collier, 99.

186 Venice Film Festival: *Humboldt Standard,* 8/27/1955.

186 "laughing" with Italian starlet Loren Pastini: *San Antonio Light,* 10/27/1955.

186 She and Henry meet: *NBN,* 2.

186 "There was something pure": ibid.

186 "barbaric and primeval": ibid., 30.

187 Augusto Torlonia: "Italy: Lord of the Earth," *Time,* 7/4/1949; available at www.time.com/time/magazine/article/0,9171,888539,00.html.

187 "Eurotrash": *DTD,* 109.

187 Franchetti history: *NBN,* 43–44, 116–17.

187 beaten by her brutish brother: ibid., 43.

188 she had inspired: Carlos Baker, *Ernest Hemingway: A Life Story* (New York: Scribner's, 1969), 486.

188 "She's a character": *PB,* 127.

189 "sad and boring": *NBN,* 34.

8. THE WRONG MAN

190 O'Hara: *FML,* 4.

190 current reading: Henry Fonda, "My Current Reading," *Saturday Review of Literature,* 7/31/1948, 29.

191 "in the old days": John O'Hara to H. N. Swanson, 9/29/1963; O'Hara to Swanson, 2/5/1965; Swanson to O'Hara, 3/18/1969. Contents synopsized in the Calendar of the John O'Hara Letters to H. N. Swanson, 1955–1970, Penn State University Archives, available at www.libraries.psu.edu/digital/speccolls/Findin gAids/oharaswanson.frame.html.

192 Hitchcock: Patrick McGilligan, *Alfred Hitchcock: A Life in Darkness and Light*

(San Francisco: HarperCollins, 2004), 535. See also Devin McKinney, "The Right Man," *The Believer,* March/April 2008, 13, 27.

192 "the somnambulistic quality": Herbert Brean, "A Case of Identity," *Life,* 6/19/1953, 97.

192 Hitchcock reckoned this a misjudgment: François Truffaut, *Hitchcock* (New York: Simon & Schuster, 1967), 177–83.

194 scissoring her eyes: *FML,* 254.

194 villa on the Mediterranean: *FML,* 256–57; *DTD,* 107–14.

195 "a dentist's waiting room": *NBN,* 53.

195 realistic oil studies: *Abilene Reporter-News,* 1/5/1962.

195 "renting period": *DTD,* 120.

195 amount of business logged: *Oakland Tribune,* 7/10/1956; *Abilene Reporter-News,* 6/31/1956; *Austin Daily Herald,* 10/17/1956; *Fresno Bee,* 9/13/1956; *Long Beach Independent,* 2/28/1957.

195 "Medics are warning": *Burlington Daily Times-Herald,* 10/22/1956.

196 "Each achievement": *NBN,* 74.

196 Southwest Airways: Hayward, 69.

196 Oklahoma oil: *Ada Evening News,* 11/15/1953.

196 independent production deal: *New York Times,* 2/11/1955.

197 never star in a TV series: *Long Beach Independent,* 4/28/1957.

197 "save a dollar": *Connellsville Daily Courier,* 1/4/1960.

197 handpicked by the star: *Kittanning Leader-Times,* 6/22/1959.

197 "looked so startlingly": *Oakland Tribune,* 9/16/1959.

197 "I guess he doesn't plan": ibid.

199 "underwritten": Gibson, 21.

199 "Start it rolling": ibid., 24–25.

199 a quarter of it Fonda's own money: ibid.

199 Henry is miscast as Jerry: ibid., 57.

200 When Henry meets Dr. Brenman-Gibson: ibid., 108.

200 "with a fixed": ibid., 36.

200 "zest and fine realism": *Corpus Christi Times,* 12/6/1957.

200 a nauseous Bancroft: Gibson, 106.

201 shouting at the playwright: *FML,* 263; Gibson, 107; Henry Fonda and Glenn Loney, "In the Words of Henry Fonda," *Cue,* 12/20/1969, 12.

201 "the most odious experience": Gibson, 107.

201 "the birth of a star": *Mansfield News-Journal,* 1/25/1958.

201 selling his quarter share: *Winnipeg Free Press,* 9/27/1965.

201 "can't stomach Hollywood": *Long Beach Independent,* 5/28/1957.

203 "I imagine if we could hear": Anderson, *Silent Night, Lonely Night,* 34.

203 "excessively verbose": *New York Times,* 12/4/1959.

203 "that I find this talky": *San Mateo Times,* 12/22/1959.

205   Gena Rowlands: *Elyria Chronicle-Telegram*, 11/8/1960.

205   "I was discovering myself": *NBN*, 107.

205   "the father I never had": ibid., 174.

205   "If it had been maybe ten years later": Norman, 94.

205   "Just the slightest of slaps": *NBN*, 72.

205   "if he had done it more often": ibid.

206   "completely friendly": *Fresno Bee*, 3/16/1961.

206   "I can only reproach myself": *Long Beach Independent*, 3/16/1961.

206   she and a traveling companion: *New York Times*, 8/1/1966; *Bridgeport Post*, 8/1/1966; *Bucks County Courier-Times*, 11/10/1966; *Bridgeport Telegram*, 11/11/1966.

207   rented a Bel Air house: *Albuquerque Journal*, 6/29/1961.

207   "I made my first picture": *Corpus Christi Caller-Times*, 9/10/1961.

208   "the greatest acting challenge": *Cumberland Sunday Times*, 11/26/1961.

208   "about a writer": *Greeley Tribune*, 12/18/1961.

210   "to the radiologist's": *Corpus Christi Times*, 3/16/1962.

210   "We talked": *Mansfield News-Journal*, 1/28/1962.

210   rudiments of the classical guitar: ibid.

210   "that the theatre": *New York Times*, 3/4/1962.

210   "is a long time to watch": *Bridgeport Post*, 1/30/1962.

211   "party" block: ibid.

211   "Lael!": Kanin, 75–77.

212   "I love you": ibid., 150.

212   "just the God damnedest": Springer, 38.

212   Critics too are uncertain: ibid.; *New York Times*, 2/23/1962; *Time*, 3/2/1962, available at www.time.com/time/magazine/article/0,9171,939893,00.html; Harold Clurman, *The Collected Works of Harold Clurman: Six Decades of Commentary on Theatre, Dance, Music, Film, Arts and Letters*, ed. Marjorie Loggia and Glenn Young (New York: Applause, 2000), 475; *Oakland Tribune*, 3/11/1962.

212   covered with bruises: *Anderson Daily Bulletin*, 3/28/1962.

212   a film version is rumored: *Salina Journal*, 6/15/1962.

214   A small item appears: *San Mateo Times and Daily News Leader*, 10/31/1935.

214   Another version of the same incident: *Galveston Daily News*, 11/16/1935.

9. NEW FRONTIER AND HIDDEN AGENDA

217   vital center: Arthur Schlesinger, Jr., *The Vital Center: The Politics of Freedom* (Boston: Houghton Mifflin, 1949).

218   "in the air": William Safire, *Safire's Political Dictionary* (New York: Oxford University Press, 2008), 465–66.

218 "tracked the trajectory": Hoberman, 117.

219 "political party": California Voter Registry, Los Angeles City Precinct No. 1674; available at www.ancestry.com.

219 Anti-Nazi League: Charles J. Maland, *Chaplin and American Culture: The Evolution of a Star Image* (Princeton: Princeton University Press, 1991), 162.

219 "the most prominent manifestation": ibid.

219–20 Vittorio Mussolini, Leni Riefenstahl: *Corpus Christi Times*, 11/30/1938; *Salt Lake Tribune*, 12/1/1938; *Las Vegas Daily Optic*, 12/2/1938; *Kalispell Daily Inter-Lake*, 1/7/1939.

220 "a front for the Communist Party": Larry Ceplair and Steven Englund, *The Inquisition in Hollywood: Politics in the Film Community, 1930–1960* (Champaign: University of Illinois Press, 2003), 109.

220 "challenging it to substantiate": *Logansport Press,* 8/18/1938.

220 "lack of funds": Ceplair and Englund, 110–11.

221 "'Red' really means": Leslie Fiedler, *An End to Innocence: Essays on Culture and Politics* (Boston: Beacon, 1966 [1955]), 13.

221 spies inside the U.S. government: see R. Bruce Craig, *Treasonable Doubt: The Harry Dexter White Spy Case* (Lawrence: University Press of Kansas, 2004); Allen Weinstein and Alexander Vassiliev, *The Haunted Wood: Soviet Espionage in America—The Stalin Era* (New York: Random House, 1999); and *Report of the Commission on Protecting and Reducing Government Secrecy* (Washington, D.C.: U.S. Government Printing Office, 1997), A-37.

221 "many fine people": Ronald Reagan, *An American Life* (New York: Simon & Schuster, 1999), 114.

221 an FBI informant: Friedrich, 320.

221 Committee for the First Amendment: John Cogley, *Report on Blacklisting—I: Movies* (New York: Fund for the Republic, 1956), 6.

222 "The accused men": Stefan Kanfer, *A Journal of the Plague Years* (New York: Atheneum, 1973), 79.

222 "It was a sorry performance": Friedrich, 326.

222 "of what in the United States": Greil Marcus, *The Manchurian Candidate* (London: British Film Institute, 2002), 61.

222 Edward Dmytryk: Nicholas Christopher, *Somewhere in the Night: Film Noir and the American City* (New York: Shoemaker & Hoard, 2006), 76.

223 Larry Parks: Randy Roberts and James S. Olson, *John Wayne, American* (New York: Free Press, 1995), 346.

224 Jane Fonda will later criticize: *MLSF,* 67.

225 become a bitter detractor: *PB,* 136.

225 *Ike from Abilene: Uniontown Evening Standard,* 6/6/1952.

225 a public defection: *Harrisburg Daily Register,* 10/13/1952.

225 "Eisenhower seems to have": Steinbeck, *America and Americans,* 222.

225 HUAC hearings: Stephen E. Ambrose, *Nixon: The Education of a Politician, 1913–1962,* vol. 1 (New York: Simon & Schuster, 1988), 157–60.

226 "she had spurned": ibid., 209.

226 antilynching bill: Zoe Trodd, ed., *American Protest Literature* (Cambridge: Harvard University Press, 2006), 279–80.

227 Gahagan, Downey, Boddy: Ambrose, 209–10.

227 symphony of smear: Herbert S. Parmet, *Richard Nixon and His America* (Boston: Little, Brown, 1990), 186.

227 "Long after Watergate": ibid.

228 "Such fuckin' lies": *PB,* 136.

228 "can be seen": Feeney, 52–53.

228 "If you ever saw": ibid., 92.

229 "It is the sum": *Barnard Bulletin,* 10/27/1952.

230 cross-country fund-raiser: *Charleston Gazette,* 10/7/1956; *Austin Daily Herald,* 10/17/1956.

230 "Henry Fonda looked": *Butte Montana Standard,* 10/28/1956.

232 "intimately": *PB,* 136.

232 "is withdrawn": Vidal, *United States,* 799.

232 Puerto Rican houseboy: *Syracuse Post-Standard,* 7/31/1963.

233 high campaign gear: *Provo Daily Herald,* 7/14/1960; *Oxnard Press-Courier,* 6/28/1960; *Long Beach Independent,* 9/17/1960; *Oxnard Press-Courier,* 9/30/1960; *Hayward Daily Review,* 10/27/1960; *Florence Morning News,* 11/2/1960. Fonda's PT-109 ad is at http://www.livingroomcandidate.org/commercials/1960/henry-fonda.

234 *The Ed Sullivan Show:* *Syracuse Post-Standard,* 2/11/1961.

234 National Cultural Center: Alice Goldfarb Marquis, *Art Lessons: Learning from the Rise and Fall of Public Arts Funding* (New York: Basic Books, 1995), 55.

234 the president will thank him: *New York Times,* 5/20/1962.

234 "a registered Republican": Sarris, *Confessions of a Cultist,* 52.

235 Alger Hiss trial: Fiedler, *An End to Innocence,* 3–24; Whitfield, 27–31; Allen Weinstein, *Perjury: The Hiss-Chambers Trial* (New York: Knopf, 1978).

235 Ronald Reagan: Edward M. Yager, *Ronald Reagan's Journey: From Democrat to Republican* (Lanham, MD: Rowman & Littlefield), 98.

236 "There is something a bit wicked": Andrew Sarris, "Film Fantasies, Left and Right," *Film Culture* (Fall 1964): 34.

237 based on Stevenson and Nixon: *Burlington Daily Times-News,* 10/24/1963.

237 "a couple of lines": *Auburn Citizen-Advertiser,* 8/30/1963.

238 will likewise vanish: Marcus, 61.

239 "Gentlemen, the president": John Baxter, *Stanley Kubrick: A Biography* (New York: Carroll & Graf, 1997), 189–91.

239   "I'm beginning to *feel*": *San Antonio Light,* 3/19/1963.

239   sitting in a dentist's chair: *FML,* 284.

239   The courage of life: *John F. Kennedy, Profiles in Courage—50th Anniversary Edition* (New York: HarperCollins, 2006 [1956], 225.

240   "What makes it a 'Western' ": Kael, *Kiss Kiss Bang Bang,* 42.

240   "Long before he even suspected": Joseph Heller, *Catch-22* (New York: Dell, 1974 [1961]), 85.

240   Democratic Study Group: Julian E. Zelizer, *On Capitol Hill: The Struggle to Reform Congress and Its Consequences, 1948–2000* (New York: Cambridge University Press, 2004), 104.

241   Paulsen special: *Ogden Standard-Examiner,* 10/21/1968.

241   "a reasonably tall": Norman Mailer, *Miami and the Siege of Chicago* (New York: Signet, 1970 [1969]), 122.

242   "There is a poverty": Norman Mailer, *St. George and the Godfather* (New York: Signet, 1973 [1972]), 22.

242   "an absence of rich greeting": ibid., 107.

245   read by JFK: Hoberman, 66–67.

246   "more muted": Greil Marcus, *Invisible Republic: Bob Dylan's Basement Tapes* (New York: Holt, 1997), 207.

10. HE NOT BUSY BEING BORN

250   "I've made lots of westerns here": *Fort Walton Beach Playground Daily News,* 9/19/1966.

251   "*running in the streets*": Vincent Bugliosi and Curt Gentry, *Helter Skelter* (New York: Norton, 1994 [1974]), 392 (italics in original).

251   a party is held: *Syracuse Herald-Journal,* 6/28/1966.

251   "Were he never": Peter Bogdanovich, "Homage to Hank," *New York Times,* 7/3/1966. See also Bogdanovich's *Who the Devil Was in It: Conversations with Hollywood's Legendary Actors* (New York: Random House, 2005), 300–317.

252   Louis Jean Heydt: *Fresno Bee,* 1/30/1960.

252   "You're going to fall behind": Kiernan, 120–21.

252   *The Country Girl:* FML, 238–39.

253   she pretends that her father: Brough, 127.

253   Lee Strasberg: Ross and Ross, 99; *The American Weekly,* 2/19/1961.

253   "such a panic": Kiernan, 89.

253   She has spent: *MLSF,* 99, 107–8.

253   "a bit of a romp": Ross and Ross, 95.

253   "counter-need": ibid., 99.

253   "somewhere inside yourself": ibid.

254   "Difficult and very sensitive": Al Aronowitz, "America's Answer to Bardot: The Young Jane Fonda," at http://www.blacklistedjournalist.com/ column63index.html. This is a forty-thousand-word expansion of Aronowitz's profile "Lady Jane," *The Saturday Evening Post*, 3/23/1963.

254   "a no-good": *DTD*, 93–94.

254   his certainty of adult conspiracy: Reed, 208.

254   "not part of this system": *DTD*, 99.

254   "a rare combination": "Life Guide," *Life*, 12/1/1961, 27.

254   Susan Brewer: *DTD*, 120–21.

254   unknown Warren Beatty: David Thomson, *Warren Beatty and Desert Eyes: A Life and a Story* (New York: Vintage, 1988 [1987]), 70.

254   "I don't know what the Method is": Aronowitz, "America's Answer to Bardot."

255   "will *act out*": Norman Mailer, *Marilyn: A Biography* (New York: Grosset & Dunlap, 1973), 108.

255   "Analysis": *New York Times,* 7/16/1967.

255   "a Kafkaesque nightmare": *MLSF,* 128.

255   She persuades him: Kiernan, 138.

256   *PT 109*: *DTD*, 160–61; Hoberman, 57–58.

257   "a parasite": *FML*, 287.

257   "the five worst plays": Guiles, 112.

257–58   "neurotic drive": *Pasadena Independent*, 2/13/1961.

258   "more neurotic and selfish": ibid.

258   "are not likely to be": ibid.

258   "It breaks his heart": Aronowitz.

258   "Natalie Wood didn't want": Joseph Heller, "*Playboy* Interview," *Playboy*, June 1975, 72.

258   *Get Yourself a College Girl*: Springer, 212.

258   "It's like working": *Aniston Star*, 12/14/1969.

259   "a camera-viewing of strange festivals": *Des Moines Register*, 9/18/1966.

260   "perverse" and "hateful": Thomas Thompson, "A Place in the Sun All Her Own," *Life*, 3/29/1968, 72.

261   request for threesomes: *MLSF,* 154–55.

261   "I'm much more relaxed": *Kingston Daily Gleaner*, 2/1/1965.

261   they marry: *Burlington Daily Times-News*, 8/16/1965.

261   Times Square billboard: *Lowell Sun*, 3/10/1965.

261   *Playboy* publishes nude photos: *Albuquerque Journal*, 8/27/1966.

261   "I'd so much wanted": *MLSF,* 211.

262   Peter meets Eugene McDonald III: *DTD*, 130. In *FML*, Peter claims they met at Westminster, the boarding school Peter attended in Connecticut (256).

262   "a complicity": *San Mateo Times*, 2/26/1965.

262   Brothers in romance and rebellion: *Arizona Daily Star*, 2/12/1965; *Cedar Rapids Gazette*, 3/5/1964; *DTD*, 188, 190.

263   Peter feels he knows the truth: *DTD*, 195.

263   "I know where I am": Reed, 205.

263   "The sun was shining": G. Barry Golson, ed., *The Playboy Interviews with John Lennon and Yoko Ono* (New York: Playboy, 1981), 152.

263   "morbid and bizarre": Steve Turner, *A Hard Day's Write: The Stories Behind Every Beatles Song* (New York: HarperCollins, 1994), 111.

265   "the movie business": *FML*, 283.

265   "They've gone too far": *Lowell Sun*, 8/5/1967.

265   "all sorts of sleazy": Renata Adler, *A Year in the Dark: A Year in the Life of a Film Critic 1968–1969* (New York: Berkley, 1971 [1969]), 147.

267   *Bonnie and Clyde* and *Rosemary's Baby*: Kiernan, 208.

268   "My father is a fantastic": *San Antonio Express*, 12/19/1969.

269   earns $6 million: *Oakland Tribune*, 10/1/1967.

270   "Well I have seen": E. L. Doctorow, *Welcome to Hard Times* (New York: Random House, 1960), 22.

270   "didn't come off": *Hayward Daily Review*, 8/25/1966; *Oakland Tribune*, 10/27/1967.

270   In 1966, Peter is involved: *DTD*, 227–36. See also *Albuquerque Tribune*, 6/21/1966; *Syracuse Post-Standard*, 11/28/1966; *Tucson Daily News*, 11/28/1966.

271   takes the stand to testify: *Long Beach Independent*, 12/3/1966; *Fresno Bee*, 12/13/1966.

271   "Make the most": *Syracuse Post-Standard*, 12/28/1966.

271   "without all the big-studio shit": Reed, 216.

271   pornographic concepts: ibid., 217.

271   "Nobody told me": ibid., 208.

271   "My father was never": ibid., 219.

271   "Now I know": ibid.

272   The interview is a cathartic: *Independent Star-News*, 4/7/1968.

272   "It's called *Easy Rider*": ibid.

272   "Recent headlines": www.archive.org/details/gov.archives.111-tv-547.

272   "The experience was that strong": *Ogden Standard-Examiner*, 10/23/1966.

272–73   "handshake tour" of the war zone: *FML*, 292–93; *Van Nuys News*, 4/16/1967; *Anderson Daily Bulletin*, 5/5/1967; *Panama City News*, 7/31/1967.

273   "I'm still a liberal": *New York Times*, 7/16/1967.

273   His diagnosis of the real problem: *Troy Record*, 4/17/1967.

274   Jonathan Schell's nonfiction account: *MLSF*, 195–96.

274   her first arrest: *Mansfield News Journal*, 4/20/1971; *Walla Walla Union-Bulletin*, 3/17/1970.

274 Jane is detained: *MLSF,* 261–63. See also *Coshocton Tribune,* 11/3/1970; *Alton Evening Telegraph,* 11/4/1970; *Danville Times,* 11/5/1970; *Elyria Chronicle-Telegram,* 11/10/1970.

274 vitamins: *MLSF,* 261; *FML,* 310.

275 "my alleged daughter": *New York Times,* 10/18/1970.

275 he will report her: *FML,* 302.

275 "My daughter makes statements": *Bucks County Courier-Times,* 1/29/1971.

275 The figures speak to him: *DTD,* 241; Lee Hill, *Easy Rider* (London: British Film Institute, 1996), 10–11.

275 He and Peter develop: Details on the creation, financing, and filming of *Easy Rider* are from: Peter Biskind, *Easy Riders, Raging Bulls: How the Sex-Drugs-and-Rock 'n' Roll Generation Saved Hollywood* (New York: Touchstone, 1999 [1998]), 61–72; *DTD,* 252–81; Hoberman, 190–97; Hill, 15–29.

276 The picture grosses: Biskind, 74.

276 rainy New Orleans graveyard: *DTD,* 256–58.

278 he has been after Fonda: Frayling, 134.

278 United Artists secured: Richard T. Jameson, "Something to Do with Death: A Fistful of Sergio Leone," *Film Comment,* March 1973, 8.

278 Leone submitted the script: Frayling, 134, 183.

278 goes to Eli Wallach: *FML,* 306.

279 "from sunup to sundown": Frayling, 225.

279 "some kind of magical touch": ibid., 224.

279 "I thought they were funny": *Dialogue on Film* 3, no. 2 (November 1973): 14.

279 wearing a bushy mustache: ibid.

279 "This Leone fellow": *Big Spring Herald,* 11/16/1969.

280 The song is retrieved: *MLSF,* 90.

280 Winter Soldier hearings: ibid., 259–60.

280 FTA: *Madison Capital Times,* 2/18/1971.

281 Jane introduces her father: *FML,* 302.

281 "There's a great deal to say": *MLSF,* 279.

281 planes are bombing dikes: ibid., 287–88. See also William M. Hammond, *Public Affairs: The Military and the Media, 1968–1973* (Washington, D.C.: U.S. Government Printing Office, 1996), 577–78.

281 Jane's goal is to gather evidence: *MLSF,* 290.

281 encouragement of antiwar activist Tom Hayden: ibid., 290–91.

281 Jane flies to Hanoi, photos: ibid., 290–321. See also U.S. Government document *H.R. 16742: Restraints on Travel to Hostile Areas* (available at www.wintersoldier.com/index.php?topic=FondaHanoi); Carol Burke, *Camp All-American, Hanoi Jane, and the High-and-Tight: Gender, Folklore, and Changing Military Culture* (Boston: Beacon, 2004).

281 "liars, hypocrites and pawns": *MLSF,* 327.

282 "to convey the impression": *Morgantown Post*, 4/26/1973.

282 "I felt betrayed": Guiles, 243.

282 change of heart on Vietnam: *Eureka Times-Standard*, 11/1/1972.

282 he attends her wedding: *Long Beach Independent*, 1/22/1973.

282 he supports Hayden's bid: *Oakland Tribune*, 12/29/1975.

283 Henry hosts: *Billings Gazette*, 4/5/1974.

283 "She's been vindicated": FML, 301.

283 John Kerry, a Vietnam vet and passing acquaintance: CNN.com, 2/12/2004 (available at www.cnn.com/2004/ALLPOLITICS/02/11/ elec04.prez.kerry .fonda/); SFGate.com, 2/20/2004 (available at http://articles.sfgate.com/2004 -02-20/news/17414203_1_anti-war-rally-photo-agency-separate-photo).

283 spit on by a veteran: People.com, 4/21/2005 (available at www.people.com/ people/article/0,,1052328,00.html).

283 "Jihad Jane": washingtonpost.com, 3/10/2010 (available at www.washington post.com/wp-dyn/content/article/2010/03/09/AR2010030902670.html).

283 latrines will be decorated: Bruce Cumings, *Dominion from Sea to Sea: Pacific Ascendancy and American Power* (New Haven: Yale University Press, 2009), 408.

283 "goes out with a liberal": *Lima News*, 9/11/1961.

285 "He doesn't want to talk": *Elyria Chronicle-Telegram*, 9/9/1978.

286 "in back of your mind": *Pasadena Star-News*, 5/26/1968.

288 "He comes from the depths": Frayling, 298.

289 Parisian students: ibid., 300.

289 cut by nearly an hour: Jameson, "Something to Do with Death," 10.

289 "both the greatest": Frayling, 299.

11. THE OLD MAN HIMSELF

291 Fonda makes a last visit: *Seguin Gazette-Enterprise*, 8/13/1982.

292 For the location shoot: *San Antonio Express-News*, 1/10/1971.

292 "Henry has always had": *Burlington Times-News*, 8/5/1970.

293 Shirlee Mae Adams: FML, 281–82.

293 Henry meets her in late 1962: *Syracuse Post-Standard*, 1/15/1966. In FML (279), HF claims Shirlee was his date at the premiere.

293 "It took me six months": *Syracuse Post-Standard*, 1/15/1966.

293 In the summer of 1963: FML, 284.

293 "midnightly trysts": *San Antonio Light*, 10/7/1963.

293 The next summer, between shooting: *Casa Grande Dispatch*, 5/20/1964; *Kokomo Morning Times*, 8/24/1964.

293 10050 Cielo Drive: FML, 285.

293 they are seen together at Broadway shows: *Galveston News*, 11/17/1964.

293 cusp of mandatory retirement: *San Antonio Express,* 12/9/1964.

293 they are wed: *FML,* 289–91; *Newport Daily News,* 12/4/1965.

293 works extensively for charities: *Long Beach Independent,* 3/12/1973; *Salina Journal,* 5/31/1974.

293–94 "I have tried": *Salina Journal,* 5/31/1974.

294 "He's complex": *Chicago Daily Herald,* 3/30/1981.

294 estate at 10744 Chalon Road: *Des Moines Register,* 2/2/1967; http://www .realtor.com/property-detail/10744-Chalon-Rd_Los-Angeles_CA_90077_ 3b8ae001?source=web); *Aniston Star,* 2/22/1970.

294 "a fancy new Mexican restaurant": Don Bachardy, *Stars in My Eyes* (Madison: University of Wisconsin Press, 2000), 185.

294 "a delightful acreage": John Bainbridge, "Mr. Belvedere and Mr. Webb," *Life,* 5/30/1949, 50.

295 crewel embroidery: Jeff Stafford, "Starring Henry Fonda," cgi.tcm.turner. com/MONTH_SPOTS/00/09/fonda2.html.

295 fruit trees on the back nine: *Winnipeg Free Press,* 3/21/1979.

295 discovers bees: *Winnipeg Free Press,* 3/1/1978; *Indiana Evening Gazette,* 6/28/1980.

295 Bel Air Hive: *Indiana Evening Gazette,* 6/28/1980.

295 Jay Sebring: *Tri-City Herald,* 5/23/1965.

295 Sebring's funeral: *Bridgeport Post,* 8/14/1969.

295 John V. Tunney: *Long Beach Independent,* 10/18/1970; *Fresno Bee,* 10/19/ 1970.

296 supporting his son-in-law: *Oakland Tribune,* 12/29/1975; *Winnipeg Free Press,* 1/29/1976.

296 his black Mercedes: *Aniston Star,* 2/22/1970.

296 He rides a stationary bicycle: *San Antonio Express-News,* 1/10/1971; *Victoria Advocate,* 10/30/1969.

296 cosmetic surgery: *Pasadena Star-News,* 3/29/1973.

296 "I had a little eye work": *Oakland Tribune,* 3/8/1975.

296 pitchman for General Aniline and Film Corporation: *Salina Journal,* 10/ 23/1974.

296 legitimized a new market: *Pacific Stars and Stripes,* 2/22/1974.

296 "belongs wherever he chooses to amble": *Oakland Tribune,* 1/21/1971. The floor-wax spot is on YouTube (www.youtube.com/watch?v=VBQuT0s1tNk), as is Fonda's commercial for the View-Master, costarring a nine-year-old Jodie Foster (www.youtube.com/watch?v=q5QGd-0X3bg&feature=related).

297 "A good commercial": *Pacific Stars and Stripes,* 2/22/1974.

297 *The Smith Family: Fresno Bee,* 5/24/1970.

297 "will touch on today's gap": ibid.

297 claims to be intrigued: *Portsmouth Times,* 12/21/1970.

297 "The Fedderson System": *Gettysburgh Times*, 4/25/1970.

297 films fifteen episodes: *Fresno Bee*, 10/25/1970; *Cedar Rapids Gazette*, 2/21/1971.

297 "The scripts were all completed": *Cedar Rapids Gazette*, 1/10/1971.

298 "There is nothing": *Lowell Sun*, 1/21/1971.

298 "He does it": *Tucson Daily Citizen*, 6/15/1971.

298 ABC pulls *The Smith Family*: *Sheboygan Press*, 11/17/1971 and 1/6/1972.

298 Plumstead Playhouse: Julie Baumgold, "Starting Small with Big Names," *New York*, 9/30/1968, 58–59.

298 such worthies: *San Antonio Light*, 8/11/1968; Springer, 40.

298 "We might fall": Baumgold, 58.

298 "Stifling boredom": *San Antonio Express-Times*, 11/17/1968.

299 *Our Town*: Springer, 40–41.

299 Assembled to Henry's design: ibid., 41.

299 premieres in April 1970: *Cedar Rapids Gazette*, 4/2/1970.

299 a cheap, portable annuity: Springer, 41.

299 production of *The Caine Mutiny Court-Martial*: Sweeney, 190.

299 readies its staging: *Bucks County Courier-Times*, 11/17/1971; *Pocono Record*, 11/22/1971; *Oakland Tribune*, 1/13/1972.

299 Opening at the Kennedy Center: *Des Moines Register*, 1/17/1972; *Long Beach Independent*, 2/2/1972.

299 "Seen now": *Long Beach Independent*, 3/23/1972.

300 premiere in Hartford: *Waterloo Sunday Courier*, 5/3/1970.

300 the piece combines: ibid.; *Tucson Daily Citizen*, 4/7/1971; *Van Nuys Valley News*, 4/11/1971.

300 will have its unlikely reopening: *Hutchinson News*, 2/20/1971.

300 Already in the cast: *Tucson Daily Citizen*, 4/7/1971.

300 Fonda signs on: *Tucson Arizona Republic*, 3/27/1971.

300 The part is a stern: ibid.

300 "very provocative": ibid.

300 preview in Tucson: *Tucson Arizona Republic*, 3/29/1971.

300 "a hurried poll": ibid.

300–01 handful of walkouts: *Tucson Daily Citizen*, 4/7/1971.

301 "one of the most explosive": ibid.

301 "the most thoroughly entertaining": *Van Nuys Valley News*, 4/11/1971.

301 "possesses wit": ibid.

301 "plays Lincoln a bit stiffly": *Long Beach Independent*, 4/9/1971.

301 he is troubled: *Tucson Arizona Republic*, 6/11/1971.

301 Meanwhile, as the producers scramble: ibid.

301 David Rintels: http://www.imdb.com/name/nm0725766/.

301 Reading it in the fall of 1973: *Albuquerque Tribune*, 10/4/1973.

301 Fonda has doubts: *Salina Journal*, 3/26/1974.

302 *Seascape*: FML, 313; *Long Beach Independent*, 4/28/1974.

302 But in reading: *Pacific Stars and Stripes*, 4/4/1974.

302 "I didn't know": *Lincoln Sunday Journal and Star*, 9/1/1974.

302 "begun to look like": Leslie Fielder, *The Collected Essays of Leslie Fielder*, vol. 1 (New York: Stein & Day, 1971), 436.

302 "as great as his cause": Stone, 133.

302 doesn't trust the judgment: *FML*, 313; *Columbus Telegram*, 4/13/1974; Houseman, *Final Dress*, 578.

302 place a call to producer John Houseman: *FML*, 314; *Columbus Telegram*, 4/13/1974.

302 *That Girl from Memphis*: Houseman, *Front and Center*, 181.

302 Ford's Theatre: Houseman, *Final Dress*, 334.

303 he agrees to step in: ibid., 518.

303 "My main use to him": ibid., 578.

303 Henry sleeps in his stage clothes: *Long Beach Independent*, 2/24/1974.

303 previewed in Louisville: Houseman, *Final Dress*, 519.

303 From there it goes to Chicago: ibid.

303 "Fonda is doing something incredible": *Columbus Telegram*, 4/13/1974.

303 "the accumulation": *Frederick News-Post*, 3/1/1974.

303 "Olympian feat": *Oakland Tribune*, 2/19/1974.

303 the play moves to Broadway: *Lebanon Daily News*, 3/28/1974.

303 "It would be difficult": *New York Times*, 5/27/1974.

303 The five-week run sells out: *Long Beach Independent*, 4/28/1974.

303 "People seem to have a compulsion": *Elyria Chronicle-Telegram*, 9/4/1974.

303 tour dates: *Long Beach Independent*, 4/28/1974.

303 A television special: ibid.

303 Henry's Darrow will still be sought: *Elyria Chronicle-Telegram*, 10/22/1978.

304 "the great interpreter of the second-rate": John Simon, "Failures of Nerve," *New York*, 4/8/1974, 84.

304 "curious current phenomenon": *Coshocton Tribune*, 5/31/1975.

305 "evil men": Rintels, 22.

305 "Don't you know": ibid., 20.

306 "I know my life": ibid., 48–49.

306 a ranch near Santa Fe: *Albuquerque Tribune*, 7/24/1969.

306 "with flying colors": *Victoria Advocate*, 10/30/1969.

306 Bataan Memorial: *Albuquerque Tribune*, 7/11/1969.

306 reported as influenza: *Annapolis Evening Capital*, 7/10/1969.

306 "a respiratory condition": *Albuquerque Tribune*, 7/11/1969.

306 "I'm just a tired old man": *Annapolis Evening Capital*, 7/10/1969.

306 Henry collapses: *Bucks County Courier-Times*, 4/26/1974.

306   admitted to Lenox Hill: ibid.

307   "I suddenly found myself": *Kingsport Times-News*, 2/23/1975.

307   "isn't really sick": *Bucks County Courier-Times*, 4/26/1974.

307   The hospitalization continues: *Oakland Tribune*, 5/3/1974.

307   dates in Boston are likewise canceled: *Newport Daily News*, 5/2/1974.

307   temporary pacemaker will be installed: *Oakland Tribune*, 5/3/1974.

307   irregular heartbeat: *Newport Daily News*, 5/2/1974.

307   William O. Douglas and Peter Sellers: *Parade*, 9/28/1975.

307   a device pioneered in 1960: ibid.

308   Henry is fitted with the newest model: ibid.

308   "a hard spot on his chest": *Bennington Banner*, 5/27/1975.

308   A wall-plugged charger: *Parade*, 9/28/1975.

308   "Once a week": ibid.

308   He leaves Lenox Hill: *Florence Morning News*, 5/8/1974; *Abilene Reporter-News*, 5/19/1974.

308   he is sent home to Bel Air: *Pasadena Star-News*, 5/21/1974.

308   *Darrow*'s scheduled engagements are postponed: *Colorado Springs Gazette Telegraph*, 5/18/1974.

308   "The veteran of fifty years": *Pasadena Star-News*, 6/17/1974.

308   "A most incredible": *Las Cruces Sun-News*, 9/4/1974.

308   television version of *Darrow*: *Long Beach Independent*, 9/1/1974.

308   It cuts twenty-two minutes: ibid.; *Charleston Daily Mail*, 9/4/1974.

308   "The only difference": *Clovis News-Journal*, 9/3/1974.

309   Henry gets another checkup: *Newcastle News*, 9/20/1974.

309   *Darrow* returns to Broadway: *Kingsport Times-News*, 2/23/1975.

309   Henry forgoes matinees: *Clovis News-Journal*, 9/3/1974.

309   he runs up and down the stairs: *Kingsport Times-News*, 2/23/1975.

309   Tour dates are lined up: ibid.

309   Henry plays Adm. Chester Nimitz: *Danville Bee*, 6/4/1975.

309   *Darrow* begins a ten-week stand at the Piccadilly: *Winnipeg Free Press*, 7/18/1975.

309   "every American actor's dream": *Naples Daily News*, 8/10/1975.

309   he's reported to be incensed: *Winnipeg Free Press*, 7/18/1975.

309   "An entertainment that uplifts": *Des Moines Register*, 7/18/1975.

309   will name him its Man of the Year: *Las Cruces Sun-News*, 7/11/1975.

309   X-rays show a tumor: *Long Beach Independent*, 3/15/1976.

309   He checks into Cedars-Sinai: ibid.

309   undergoes his second surgery: *Helena Independent Record*, 3/18/1976.

309   "had grown to the size": ibid.

310   cancellation of *Darrow*'s projected college tour: *Long Beach Independent*, 3/16/1976.

310   Henry's recovery looks promising: *Logansport Pharos-Tribune & Press*, 3/23/
      1976.

310   His release is delayed: *Canandaigua Daily Messenger*, 4/7/1976.

310   more college dates go by the board: *Mansfield News Journal*, 3/24/1976; *Water-
      loo Courier*, 3/25/1976.

310   on April 13, he is sent home: *Oakland Tribune*, 4/13/1976.

310   Fonda flies back to New York on June 14: *Long Beach Independent*, 6/14/1976.

310   Henry is furious at the rumors: ibid.

310   "I'm not afraid": *Oakland Tribune*, 5/13/1976.

311   40 percent hearing loss: *Chicago Daily Herald*, 5/11/1980. See also *FML*, 323.

311   "There's a bit of *Easy Rider*": *Cedar Rapids Gazette*, 11/21/1976.

312   Henry's presence on TV: *Bridgeport Post*, 3/17/1973; *Long Beach Independent*,
      4/20/1973; *Albuquerque Tribune*, 12/29/1975; *Great Bend Daily Tribune*,
      2/2/1970; Sweeney, 210, 212, 214; *Pasadena Star-News*, 4/10/1973; *San Mateo
      Times*, 8/10/1974; *New Castle News*, 9/20/1974.

312   *O. W. Street*: *Salt Lake Tribune*, 10/25/1973.

312   "Sounds like a tossed salad": ibid.

313   *A House Divided*: *Salina Journal*, 6/15/1975; *Kingsport Times-News*, 2/23/1975;
      Pacific Stars and Stripes, 2/4/1976 and 12/26/1979; *Lowell Sun*, 7/14/1976.

314   *Com-TAC 303*: *Brownsville Herald*, 6/19/1977; *Colorado Springs Gazette Tele-
      graph*, 10/1/1977; "Future of Movie About Black Pilots Remains in Doubt," *Jet*,
      10/13/1977, 19.

314   "involved with other commitments": "Future of Movie About Black Pilots
      Remains in Doubt," *Jet*, 10/13/1977, 19.

314   first with Walter Huston, later with Spencer Tracy: *Winnipeg Free Press*,
      3/21/1979. See also Bernard F. Dick, *Radical Innocence: A Study of the Holly-
      wood Ten* (Lexington: University of Kentucky Press), 96.

314   A revival of the property: *Blytheville Courier News*, 4/27/1978.

314   progress stalls: *Winnipeg Free Press*, 3/21/1979.

314   "It was not the sheer fact": Albert Maltz, *The Journey of Simon McKeever*
      (New York: Avon, 1979 [1949]), 22.

315   The American Film Institute announces: *Des Moines Register*, 10/30/1977.

315   an edited version of the ceremony: *The American Film Institute Salute to
      Henry Fonda* (Castle Vision Video, 1978). The AFI tributes are no longer avail-
      able due to licensing issues.

316   "was a *towering* silence": ibid.

316   modeled on William O. Douglas: Sweeney, 193; *FML*, 326.

316   daughter of Thomas "Bart" Quigley: *FML*, 326.

317   standing room only: *Winnipeg Free Press*, 3/1/1978.

317   the play reopens: *Elyria Chronicle-Telegram*, 10/22/1978; http://www.ibdb.com/
      production.php?id=3791.

317   "looks twenty years": *Galveston Daily News,* 10/19/1978.

317   "There he is": *Hutchinson News,* 10/20/1978.

317   "I'm in good shape": *Elyria Chronicle-Telegram,* 10/22/1978.

317   residence at the Huntington Hartford: *Winnipeg Free Press,* 3/21/1979.

317–18   Blackstone Theatre in Chicago: *Indiana Evening Gazette,* 4/14/1979.

318   hip joint pop loose: *FML,* 331–32.

318   diagnose him with inflammatory arthritis: *Indiana Evening Gazette,* 4/14/1979; *Pacific Stars and Stripes,* 4/16/1979.

318   Henry checks back into Cedars-Sinai: *Huntington Daily News,* 4/16/1979; *Indiana Evening Gazette,* 4/19/1979; *Casa Grande Dispatch,* 4/20/1979; *Syracuse Herald-Journal,* 4/21/1979.

318   obstruction in his prostate: *Tyrone Daily Herald,* 4/21/1979.

318   "in excellent spirits": *Indiana Evening Gazette,* 4/14/1979.

318   He leaves the hospital: *Syracuse Herald-Journal,* 4/21/1979.

318   engagements of *First Monday* are canceled: ibid.

318   "I don't have much time": *Chicago Daily Herald,* 5/11/1980.

318   *Grapes* and *Ox-Bow* recordings: *The Grapes of Wrath* (Caedmon TC 1570); *The Ox-Bow Incident* (Caedmon TC 1620).

319   he performs in a live telecast: Sweeney, 203.

319   The play then runs: *Doylestown Daily Intelligencer,* 5/16/1980.

319   Big Squam Lake: *Winnipeg Free Press,* 9/2/1980.

319   a painting called *Ripening*: *Long Beach Independent,* 3/27/1973; *FML,* 346–47.

319   Windsor Gallery: *Anderson Daily Bulletin,* 9/25/1974.

319   compared to Andrew Wyeth's: *Lima News,* 12/15/1969.

319   bee count is up to 400,000: *Chicago Daily Herald,* 5/11/1980.

319   From the garden: *Hutchinson News,* 10/26/1977.

319   "apples so tart": *Winnipeg Free Press,* 3/1/1978.

320   "My father loved to farm": *Chicago Daily Herald,* 5/11/1980.

320   He is admitted to the ICU: *Annapolis Evening Capital,* 12/18/1980.

320   held for further observation: *Kingston Daily Gleaner,* 12/19/1980; *Gettysburg Times,* 12/20/1980.

320   he feels better: *Annapolis Evening Capital,* 12/23/1980.

320   he returns home: *Syracuse Post-Standard,* 12/25/1980.

320   "I'm not going": ibid.

320   rehearsals for yet another new play: *Syracuse Herald-Journal,* 1/8/1981.

320   he flies to Omaha: *Salina Journal,* 12/18/1980; *Logansport Pharos-Tribune,* 1/13/1981.

320   *Showdown* opens: Sweeney, 35.

320   "He walks in a stooped posture": *New York Times,* 2/13/1981.

321   a doctor warns Shirlee: *People,* 4/12/1982, 32.

321   Henry struggles through: Sweeney, 35.

321   On March 1: ibid.

321   "in recognition of": *Galveston Daily News,* 3/29/1981.

321   "a former member": ibid.

321   Reagan is shot: *New York Times,* 3/31/1981.

321   insists that his message run: *Logansport Pharos-Tribune,* 4/1/1981.

322   The two were social acquaintances: A 10/3/1946 UPI photo showing HF, Reagan, and others during a SAG strike talk can be seen at http://www.upi.com/topic/Henry_Fonda/.

322   Edmund G. Brown: *Bridgeport Post,* 10/3/1966.

322   Jesse Unruh: *Cedar Rapids Gazette,* 7/19/1970.

322   "I'm desolate": *Doylestown Daily Intelligencer,* 11/7/1980.

322   "talking a language": *PB,* 138.

323   enters Sharp Memorial: *Syracuse Post-Standard,* 4/11/1981; *Waterloo Courier,* 4/14/1981.

323   "diagnostic evaluation": *Annapolis Evening Capital,* 5/13/1981.

323   another heart surgery: *Winnipeg Free Press,* 5/16/1981; *Salina Journal,* 5/17/1981; *Waterloo Courier,* 5/18/1981.

323   pacemaker is replaced, his condition listed as satisfactory: *Winnipeg Free Press,* 5/22/1981.

323   He is discharged: *Syracuse Herald-Journal,* 6/9/1981.

323   "already gone from us": *MLSF,* 440.

323   Jane and Peter will challenge: *DTD,* 116; *MLSF,* 15.

323   "Badly written": *Washington Post,* 10/28/1981.

324   *On Golden Pond* premieres: *Elyria Chronicle-Telegram,* 11/19/1981.

324   "He's here in spirit": ibid.

324   opens nationwide on January 22: http://www.imdb.com/title/tt0082846/releaseinfo.

325   second-biggest Hollywood moneymaker of 1981: http://www.boxofficemojo.com/yearly/chart/?yr=1981&p=.htm.

326   Heart troubles recur: *Frederick Post,* 11/12/1981.

326   private studio screening: *Monessen Valley Independent,* 4/6/1982.

326   He refuses at first: *Winnipeg Free Press,* 11/13/1981.

326   Jane is on his side, but Shirlee insists: *People,* 4/12/1982, 32.

326   Henry agrees to reenter Cedars-Sinai: *Syracuse Herald-Journal,* 11/17/1981; *Galveston Daily News,* 11/18/1981.

326   Thanksgiving comes and goes: *Aiken Standard,* 11/25/1981; *Salina Journal,* 11/30/1981.

326   may spend the rest of the year: *Doylestown Daily Intelligencer,* 12/16/1981.

326 "He's getting well": *Syracuse Herald-American*, 1/30/1982.

326 has been in denial: *MLSF*, 442.

327 He and Shirlee are watching: *Frederick News*, 3/30/1982; *Gettysburg Times*, 3/31/1982.

327 "He just burst": *Frederick News*, 3/30/1982.

327 presents the award to her father: ibid.; *MLSF*, 438–39.

327 "This makes me feel": *Frederick News*, 3/30/1982.

327 "feeling better all the time": ibid.

327 "He's still a very sick": ibid.

327 "Some days he seems fine": *People*, 4/12/1982, 32.

327 back at Cedars-Sinai: *Gettysburg Times*, 7/10/1982.

327 He is discharged: *Indiana Gazette*, 7/24/1982.

328 He is rehospitalized: *Doylestown Daily Intelligencer*, 8/11/1982.

328 Three days later: *Winnipeg Free Press*, 8/12/1982; *Tyrone Daily Herald*, 8/12/1982.

328 He is fading: *Winnipeg Free Press*, 8/12/1982.

328 Henry dies: *Frederick Post*, 8/12/1982.

328 "respiratory failure": ibid.

329 Shirlee is at his bedside: ibid.

329 Jane and Peter are en route: *MLSF*, 443; *DTD*, 452.

329 "He had a good": *Frederick Post*, 8/12/1982.

329 statements of tribute: ibid.; *New York Times*, 8/13/1982; *Chicago Daily Herald*, 8/13/1982; *Galveston Daily News*, 8/13/1982.

329 Cedars-Sinai is flooded: *Galveston Daily News*, 8/14/1982.

329 "People really loved him": ibid.

329 "Nancy and I": *New York Times*, 8/13/1982.

329 "a noted American actor": This and subsequent newspaper tributes are quoted in *Galveston Daily News*, 8/14/1982.

329 "I've just lost": *MLSF*, 445.

329 Henry's will: *Stars and Stripes*, 8/22/1982. HF's Last Will and Testament is available at http://livingtrustnetwork.com/estate-planning-center/last-will-and-testament/wills-of-the-rich-and-famous/last-will-and-testament-of-henry-fonda.html.

330 eyes will be donated: *Seguin Gazette-Enterprise*, 8/13/1982.

330 "promptly cremated": HF's Last Will and Testament.

330 "Walt Whitman has": Walt Whitman, *Walt Whitman, Poetry and Prose*, ed. Justin Kaplan (New York: Library of America, 1982), 1344.

330 solo show about Walt Whitman: Sweeney, 37.

330 *Past and present*: This and subsequent lines from the preface to *Leaves of Grass* in *Walt Whitman, Poetry and Prose*, 13.

12. OMAHA, 1919

332 Starting in the afternoon: *Omaha's Riot in Story and Picture* (available at http://historicomaha.com/riot.htm).

333 "spread like wild fire": John Hope Franklin, *From Slavery to Freedom: A History of American Negroes,* 2nd ed. (New York: Knopf, 1956), 464–65.

333 John Hartfield: Robert Whitaker, *On the Laps of Gods: The Red Summer of 1919 and the Struggle for Justice that Remade a Nation* (New York: Random House, 2008), 47.

333 lynching victims had served in the war: ibid., 47, 54.

334 its black population: Michael L. Lawson, "Omaha, A City of Ferment: Summer of 1919," *Nebraska History* (Fall 1977): 415.

334 "It was so horrifying": *PB,* 104.

334 Agnes Loebeck: *Omaha Daily Bee,* 9/27/1919.

334 Whispers went round: "The Real Causes of Two Race Riots," *The Crisis,* December 1919, 56.

334 hobbled by rheumatism: Lawrence Harold Larsen, *Upstream Metropolis: An Urban Biography of Omaha and Council Bluffs* (Lincoln: University of Nebraska Press, 2007), 219.

334 "lack of effective civic leadership": Gunther, 255.

335 "perhaps the most lawless": "The Real Causes of Two Race Riots," 56.

335 Tom Dennison, James Dahlman, Edward Rosewater: Orville D. Menard, "Tom Dennison, the *Omaha Bee,* and the 1919 Omaha Race Riot," *Nebraska History* 68 (1987): 153; Federal Writers' Project, 230; Bristow, 93.

335 Smith also embraced the NAACP: Mark Robert Schneider, *"We Return Fighting": The Civil Rights Movement in the Jazz Age* (Boston: Northeastern University Press, 2002), 33.

335 white laborers angry at black migrants: ibid.

335 twenty-one separate allegations: See Nicolas Swiercek, "Stoking a White Backlash: Race, Violence, and Yellow Journalism in Omaha, 1919," paper presented at the Third Annual James A. Rawley Conference in the Humanities, 4/12/2008 (available at http://digitalcommons.unl.edu/historyrawleyconference/31/).

335 racial attacks: *Omaha Daily Bee,* 7/30/1919, 7/12/1919, and 6/27/1919.

335 "retaliation for recent attacks": *Omaha Daily Bee,* 7/22/1919.

336 "the good colored people": *Omaha Daily Bee,* 3/18/1919.

336 a school in South Omaha: *Omaha's Riot in Story and Picture.*

336 a young man was seen: Menard, 159.

336 "The crowd surged": *Omaha's Riot in Story and Picture.*

337 "I am innocent": Menard, 159.

337 castrated as well: Larsen, 222.

338 "a certain Omaha newspaper": Menard, 161.

338 "premeditated and planned": ibid., 164.

338 "'old criminal gang'": ibid, 162.

338 120 indictments: Stephen L. Wilburn, "The Omaha Riot of 1919," *The Nebraska Lawyer* (December 1999/January 2000): 59.

338 two thousand blacks fled: Walter C. Rucker and James N. Upton, *Encyclopedia of American Race Riots* (Westport, CT: Greenwood, 2007), 488.

339 KKK was active: Donald R. Hickey, Susan A. Wunder, and John R. Wunder, *Nebraska Moments* (Lincoln: University of Nebraska Press, 2007), 199.

339 Norman Parkinson's BBC chat show: The broadcast is included on the Criterion Collection DVD of *Young Mr. Lincoln*.

341 George Smith: *Lincoln Evening News,* 10/10/1891; *New York Times,* 10/20/1891.

EPILOGUE

343 "Henry Fonda": United States Postal Service, Stamp News Release No. 05-025, 5/20/2005 (available at www.prnewswire.com/news-releases/henry-fonda-joins-us-postal-service-legends-of-hollywood-stamp-series-54483847.html.

Selected Bibliography

Dates in parentheses refer to the year of original publication.

Allen, Frederick Lewis. *The Big Change: America Transforms Itself, 1900–1950*. New York: Perennial, 1969 (1952).

Alvarez, A. *The Savage God: A Study of Suicide*. New York: Norton, 1990 (1971).

Andersen, Christopher. *Citizen Jane: The Turbulent Life of Jane Fonda*. New York: Henry Holt, 1990.

Anderson, Robert. *Silent Night, Lonely Night*. New York: Random House, 1960.

Baldwin, James. *The Devil Finds Work*. New York: Dial, 1976.

Beidler, Philip D. *The Good War's Greatest Hits: World War II and American Remembering*. Athens: University of Georgia Press, 1998.

Bernstein, Matthew. *Walter Wanger, Hollywood Independent*. Minneapolis: University of Minnesota Press, 1994.

Bess, Michael. *Choices Under Fire: Moral Dimensions of World War II*. New York: Vintage, 2008 (2006).

Black, Gregory D. *Hollywood Censored: Morality Codes, Catholics, and the Movies*. New York: Cambridge University Press, 1994.

Bogdanovich, Peter. *John Ford*. Berkeley: University of California Press, 1978.

Bonney, Catharina Van Rensselaer. *A Legacy of Historical Gleanings*. Vol. 1. Albany, NY: J. Munsell, 1875.

Bristow, David. *A Dirty, Wicked Town: Tales of 19th Century Omaha*. Caldwell, ID: Caxton Press, 2000.

Brough, James. *The Fabulous Fondas*. London: Star, 1975 (1973).

Callow, Simon. *Charles Laughton: A Difficult Actor*. New York: Fromm International, 1997 (1987).

Chansky, Dorothy. *Composing Ourselves: The Little Theatre Movement and the American Audience*. Carbondale: Southern Illinois University Press, 2004.

Chesler, Phyllis. *Women and Madness.* New York: Avon, 1973 (1972).

Clark, Walter Van Tilburg. *The Ox-Bow Incident.* New York: Scribner's, 1940.

Cole, Gerald, and Wes Farrell. *The Fondas.* New York: St. Martin's Press, 1984.

Collier, Peter. *The Fondas: A Hollywood Dynasty.* New York: Putnam's, 1991.

Cooke, Alistair, ed. *Garbo and the Night Watchmen.* New York: McGraw-Hill, 1971 (1937).

Costello, John. *The Pacific War 1941–1945.* New York: Perennial, 2002 (1982).

Creigh, Dorothy Weyer. *Nebraska: A History.* New York: Norton, 1977.

Custen, George F. *Twentieth Century's Fox: Darryl F. Zanuck and the Culture of Hollywood.* New York: Basic Books, 1997.

Doherty, Thomas. *Pre-Code Hollywood: Sex, Immorality, and Insurrection in American Cinema, 1930–1934.* New York: Columbia University Press, 1999.

Dougherty, Richard. *The Commissioner.* New York: Doubleday, 1962.

Eisenstein, Sergei. *Film Essays and a Lecture by Sergei Eisenstein.* Edited by Jay Leyda. New York: Praeger, 1970.

Evans, Thomas W. *The Education of Ronald Reagan: The General Electric Years and the Untold Story of His Conversion to Conservatism.* New York: Columbia University Press, 2006.

Farber, Manny. *Negative Space: Manny Farber on the Movies.* New York: Da Capo, 1998 (1971).

Federal Writers' Project (Works Progress Administration). *Nebraska: A Guide to the Cornhusker State.* New York: Viking, 1939.

Feeney, Mark. *Nixon at the Movies: A Book About Belief.* Chicago: University of Chicago Press, 2004.

Fonda, A. Mark. "Descendants of Jellis Douw Fonda (1614–1659)." www.fonda.org.

Fonda, Afdera. *Never Before Noon: An Autobiography.* New York: Weidenfeld and Nicholson, 1986.

Fonda, Henry, as told to Howard Teichmann. *Fonda: My Life.* New York: New American Library, 1981.

———. "*Playboy* Interview." *Playboy,* December 1981: 95–138.

Fonda, Jane. *My Life So Far.* New York: Random House, 2005.

Fonda, Peter. *Don't Tell Dad: A Memoir.* New York: Hyperion, 1998.

Frayling, Christopher. *Sergio Leone: Something to Do with Death.* London: Faber and Faber, 2000.

Friedrich, Otto. *City of Nets: A Portrait of Hollywood in the 1940's.* Berkeley: University of California Press, 1997 (1986).

Fussell, Paul. *Wartime: Understanding and Behavior in the Second World War.* New York: Oxford University Press, 1989.

Gailey, Harry A. *The War in the Pacific: From Pearl Harbor to Tokyo Bay.* Novato, CA: Presidio, 1995.

Galbraith, John Kenneth. *The Great Crash—1929.* New York: Mariner, 2003 (1955).

Gibson, William. *Two for the Seesaw and The Seesaw Log.* New York: Knopf, 1959.

Goldstein, Norm, and the Associated Press. *Henry Fonda.* New York: Holt, Rinehart and Winston, 1982.

Goodhart, William. *Generation.* New York: Doubleday, 1966.

Gregory, James Noble. *American Exodus: The Dust Bowl Migration and the Okie Culture in California.* New York: Oxford University Press, 1989.

Greene, Graham. *The Power and the Glory.* New York: Bantam, 1968 (1940).

———. *Graham Greene on Film.* New York: Simon & Schuster, 1972.

Guiles, Fred Lawrence. *Jane Fonda: The Actress in Her Time.* New York: Pinnacle, 1983 (1982).

Gunther, John. *Inside U.S.A.* New York: New Press, 1997 (1947).

Gussow, Mel. *Don't Say Yes Until I Finish Talking: A Biography of Darryl F. Zanuck.* New York: Pocket Books, 1972 (1971).

Haskell, Molly. *From Reverence to Rape: The Treatment of Women in the Movies.* New York: Holt, Rinehart and Winston, 1974.

Hayward, Brooke. *Haywire.* New York: Knopf, 1977.

Heggen, Thomas. *Mister Roberts.* Cambridge: Riverside Press, 1946.

Heggen, Thomas, and Joshua Logan. *Mister Roberts: A Play.* New York: Random House, 1948.

Herr, Michael. *Dispatches.* New York: Discus, 1980 (1977).

Hoberman, J. *The Dream Life: Movies, Media, and the Mythology of the Sixties.* New York: New Press, 2003.

Hofstadter, Richard. *The American Political Tradition and the Men Who Made It.* New York: Vintage, 1989 (1948).

Houghton, Norris. *But Not Forgotten: The Adventure of the University Players.* New York: William Sloane Associates, 1951.

Houseman, John. *Front and Center.* New York: Simon & Schuster, 1979.

———. *Final Dress.* New York: Simon & Schuster, 1983.

Johnson, Will. "Chairpotato Presents: Henry Jaynes Fonda." http://knol.google.com/k/will-johnson/henry-jaynes-fonda/4hmquk6fx4gu/14#. 2007-09.

Kael, Pauline. *Kiss Kiss Bang Bang.* Boston: Little, Brown, 1968.

———. *5001 Nights at the Movies.* New York: Henry Holt, 1991.

Kanin, Garson. *A Gift of Time.* New York: Random House, 1962.

Kerbel, Michael. *Henry Fonda.* New York: Pyramid, 1975.

Kiernan, Thomas. *Jane: An Intimate Biography of Jane Fonda.* New York: Putnam's, 1973.

Knight, Robert P. *Clinician and Therapist: Selected Papers of Robert P. Knight.* Edited by Stuart C. Miller. New York: Basic Books, 1972.

Leggett, John. *Ross and Tom.* New York: Penguin, 1975 (1974).

Levin, Ira. *Critic's Choice.* New York: Random House, 1961.

Logan, Joshua. *Josh: My Up and Down, In and Out Life.* New York: Delacorte, 1976.

Marcus, Greil. *The Manchurian Candidate*. London: British Film Institute, 2002.

Marston, Daniel, ed. *The Pacific War Companion: From Pearl Harbor to Hiroshima*. London: Osprey, 2005.

Mattes, Merrill J. *The Great Platte River Road: The Covered Wagon Mainline via Fort Kearny to Fort Laramie* (3rd rev. ed.). Lincoln: University of Nebraska Press, 1987 (1969).

McBride, Joseph. *Searching for John Ford: A Life*. New York: St. Martin's Press, 2001.

McElvaine, Robert S. *The Great Depression: America, 1929–1941*. New York: Three Rivers, 1993.

Mordden, Ethan. *Medium Cool: The Movies of the 1960s*. New York: Knopf, 1990.

Newman, Albert Henry. *A Manual of Church History*. Vol. 2, *Modern Church History (A.D. 1517–1903)*. Philadelphia: American Baptist Publication Society, 1903.

Norman, Barry. *The Film Greats*. London: Futura, 1985.

O'Hara, John. *Appointment in Samarra*. New York: Random House, 1934.

Omaha's Riot in Story and Picture. Omaha, NE: Education Publishing, 1919. http://www.historicomaha.com/riot.htm.

Osborn, Paul. *Point of No Return*. New York: Random House, 1952.

Parmet, Herbert S. *Richard Nixon and His America*. Boston: Little, Brown, 1990.

Percy, Walker. *The Second Coming*. New York: Washington Square, 1981 (1980).

Reed, Rex. *Do You Sleep in the Nude?* New York: Signet, 1969 (1968).

Rintels, David. *Clarence Darrow: A One-Man Play*. New York: Doubleday, 1975.

Roberts, Allen, and Max Goldstein. *Henry Fonda: A Biography*. Jefferson, NC: McFarland & Co., 1984.

Ross, Lillian, and Helen Ross. *The Player: A Profile of an Art*. New York: Limelight, 1984.

Sarris, Andrew. *The American Cinema: Directors and Directions 1929–1968*. New York: Dutton, 1968.

———. *Confessions of a Cultist: On the Cinema, 1955–1969*. New York: Touchstone, 1971 (1970).

Schindler, Colin. *Hollywood in Crisis: Cinema and American Society 1929–1939*. London: Routledge, 1996.

Schurz, Carl. *Abraham Lincoln: A Biographical Essay*. Edited by Truman Howe Bartlett. New York: Houghton Mifflin, 1907.

Shenk, Joshua Wolf. *Lincoln's Melancholy: How Depression Challenged a President and Fueled His Greatness*. New York: Houghton Mifflin, 2005.

Shortridge, James R. *The Middle West: Its Meaning in American Culture*. Lawrence: University of Kansas Press, 1989.

Siegel, Don. *A Siegel Film: An Autobiography*. London: Faber and Faber, 1993.

Somers, Henry. *A Subway Ride to the Pacific*. Victoria, BC: Trafford, 2004.

Springer, John. *The Fondas: The Films and Careers of Henry, Jane and Peter Fonda*. New York: Citadel, 1970.

Steinbeck, John. *The Grapes of Wrath*. New York: Random House, 1939.

———. *America and Americans, and Selected Nonfiction*. New York: Random House, 2002.

Stokes, Melvyn. *D. W. Griffith's The Birth of a Nation: A History of "The Most Controversial Motion Picture of All Time."* New York: Oxford University Press, 2007.

Stone, Irving. *Clarence Darrow for the Defense*. New York: Bantam, 1958 (1941).

Sweeney, Kevin. *Henry Fonda: A Bio-Bibliography*. Westport, CT: Greenwood Press, 1992.

Terkel, Studs. *"The Good War": An Oral History of World War II*. New York: New Press, 2004 (1984).

Thomas, Evan. *Sea of Thunder: Four Commanders and the Last Great Naval Campaign 1941–1945*. New York: Simon & Schuster, 2006.

Thomas, Tony. *The Films of Henry Fonda*. Secaucus, NJ: Citadel, 1983.

Thomson, David. *The New Biographical Dictionary of Film*. New York: Knopf, 2002.

———. *The Whole Equation: A History of Hollywood*. New York: Vintage, 2006 (2004).

Thompson, Ernest. *On Golden Pond: A Play*. New York: Dodd, Mead, 1979.

Tosches, Nick. *Dino: Living High in the Dirty Business of Dreams*. New York: Delta, 1999 (1992).

Vidal, Gore. *United States: Essays 1952–1992*. New York: Broadway Books, 2001 (1993).

———. *The Last Empire: Essays 1992–2000*. New York: Vintage, 2002 (2001).

Watkins, T. H. *The Hungry Years: A Narrative History of the Great Depression in America*. New York: Henry Holt, 2000 (1999).

Wellman, William A. *A Short Time for Insanity: An Autobiography*. New York: Hawthorn, 1974.

Wertenbaker, Lael Tucker. *Death of a Man*. New York: Random House, 1957.

Whitfield, Stephen J. *The Culture of the Cold War*. Baltimore: Johns Hopkins University Press, 1991.

Wills, Garry. *John Wayne's America*. New York: Touchstone, 1998 (1997).

Wilson, Douglas L. *Honor's Voice: The Transformation of Abraham Lincoln*. New York: Knopf, 1988.

Wilson, Edmund. *Patriotic Gore*. New York: Farrar, Straus and Giroux, 1961.

———. *The American Earthquake*. New York: Anchor, 1964 (1958).

———. *Literary Essays and Reviews of the 1930s and 40s*. New York: Library of America, 2007.

Wouk, Herman. *The Caine Mutiny*. New York: Dell, 1968 (1951).

———. *The Caine Mutiny Court-Martial*. Garden City, NY: Doubleday, 1954.

Zanuck, Darryl F. *Memo from Darryl F. Zanuck: The Golden Years at Twentieth Century–Fox*. Edited by Rudy Behlmer. New York: Grove, 1993.

Fonda on Film, Stage, and Television

FILMS

The Farmer Takes a Wife. 1935. Fox Film Corporation. Director: Victor Fleming. Producer: Winfield R. Sheehan. Screenplay: Edwin J. Burke, from play by Frank B. Elser and Marc Connelly, from novel *Rome Haul*, by Walter D. Edmonds. Cinematographer: Ernest Palmer. Cast: Janet Gaynor, Henry Fonda, Charles Bickford, Slim Summerville, Jane Withers, Andy Devine, Roger Imhof, Margaret Hamilton, Sig Ruman, John Qualen.

Way Down East. 1935. Fox Film Corporation. Director: Henry King. Producer: Winfield R. Sheehan. Screenplay: Howard Estabrook and William Hurlbut, from play by Lottie Blair Parker. Cinematographer: Ernest Palmer. Cast: Rochelle Hudson, Henry Fonda, Slim Summerville, Edward Trevor, Margaret Hamilton, Russell Simpson, Andy Devine, Spring Byington.

I Dream Too Much. 1935. RKO. Director: John Cromwell. Producer: Pandro S. Berman. Screenplay: James Gow and Edmund North, from story by Elsie Finn and David G. Wittels. Cinematographer: David Abel. Cast: Lily Pons, Henry Fonda, Eric Blore, Osgood Perkins, Lucien Littlefield, Lucille Ball, Mischa Auer, Paul Porcasi, Scott Beckett.

The Trail of the Lonesome Pine. 1936. Paramount. Director: Henry Hathaway. Producer: Walter Wanger. Screenplay: Grover Jones, adapted by Harvey Threw and Horace McCoy, from novel by John Fox, Jr. Cinematographers: Robert Bruce and Howard Greene. Cast: Sylvia Sidney, Fred MacMurray, Henry Fonda, Fred Stone, Nigel Bruce, Beulah Bondi, Robert Barrat, George "Spanky" McFarland, Fuzzy Knight.

The Moon's Our Home. 1936. Paramount. Director: William A. Seiter. Producer: Walter Wanger. Screenplay: Isabel Dawn and Boyce DeGaw, from novel by Faith Baldwin (additional dialogue by Dorothy Parker and Alan Campbell). Cinematographer: Joseph A. Valentine. Cast: Margaret Sullavan, Henry Fonda, Charles Butterworth, Beulah Bondi, Henrietta Crosman, Walter Brennan, Dorothy Stickney, Lucien Littlefield, Margaret Hamilton.

Spendthrift. 1936. Paramount. Director: Raoul Walsh. Producer: Walter Wanger. Screenplay: Walsh and Bert Hanlon, from story by Eric Hatch. Cinematographer: Leon Shamroy. Cast: Henry Fonda, Pat Paterson, Mary Brian, George Barbier, Edward Brophy, Richard Carle, J. M. Kerrigan, Spencer Charters.

You Only Live Once. 1937. United Artists. Director: Fritz Lang. Producer: Walter Wanger. Screenplay: Gene Towne, from story by C. Graham Baker. Cinematographer: Leon Shamroy. Cast: Sylvia Sidney, Henry Fonda, Barton MacLane, Jean Dixon, William Gargan, Jerome Cowan, Charles "Chic" Sale, Margaret Hamilton, Warren Hymer, John Wray.

Wings of the Morning. 1937. Twentieth Century–Fox/New World. Director: Harold D. Schuster. Producer: Robert T. Kane. Screenplay: Thomas J. Geraghty, from story by Donn Byrne. Cinematographer: Ray Rennahan. Cast: Annabella, Henry Fonda, Leslie Banks, Stewart Rome, Irene Vanbrugh, Harry Tate, Mark Daly, John McCormack.

Slim. 1937. Warner Bros. Director: Ray Enright. Producer: Samuel Bischoff. Screenplay: William Wister Haines, from his novel. Cinematographer: Sid Hickox. Cast: Pat O'Brien, Henry Fonda, Stuart Erwin, Margaret Lindsay, J. Farrell MacDonald, Dick Purcell, Joseph Sawyer, Craig Reynolds, John Litel, Jane Wyman.

That Certain Woman. 1937. Warner Bros. Director-producer: Edmund Goulding. Screenplay: Goulding. Cinematographer: Ernest Haller. Cast: Bette Davis, Henry Fonda, Anita Louise, Ian Hunter, Donald Crisp, Hugh O'Connell, Katharine Alexander, Minor Watson, Sidney Toler.

I Met My Love Again. 1938. United Artists. Directors: Joshua Logan and Arthur Ripley. Producer: Walter Wanger. Screenplay: David Hertz, from novel *Summer Lightning,* by Allene Corliss. Cinematographer: Hal Mohr. Cast: Joan Bennett, Henry Fonda, Louise Platt, Alan Marshal, Dame May Whitty, Alan Baxter, Dorothy Stickney, Tim Holt.

Jezebel. 1938. Warner Brothers. Director: William Wyler. Producers: Wyler, Henry Blanke, and Hal B. Wallis. Screenplay: Clements Ripley, Abem Finkel, and John Huston, from play by Owen Davis. Cinematographer: Ernest Haller. Cast: Bette Davis, Henry Fonda, George Brent, Margaret Lindsay, Donald Crisp, Fay Bainter, Richard Cromwell, Henry O'Neill, Spring Byington, John Litel, Gordon Oliver.

Blockade. 1938. United Artists. Director: William Dieterle. Producer: Walter Wanger. Screenplay: John Howard Lawson and James M. Cain (uncredited). Cinematographer: Rudolph Maté. Cast: Madeleine Carroll, Henry Fonda, Leo Carrillo, John Halliday, Vladimir Sokoloff, Robert Warwick, Reginald Denny, Peter Godfrey, William B. Davidson, Katherine DeMille, Fred Kohler.

Spawn of the North. 1938. Paramount. Director: Henry Hathaway. Producer: Albert Lewin. Screenplay: Jules Furthman and Talbot Jennings (uncredited), from story by Barrett Willoughby. Cinematographer: Charles Lang, Jr. Cast: George Raft, Henry Fonda, Dorothy Lamour, Akim Tamiroff, John Barrymore, Louise Platt, Lynne Overman, Fuzzy Knight, Vladimir Sokoloff.

The Mad Miss Manton. 1938. RKO. Director: Leigh Jason. Producer: P. J. Wolfson. Screenplay: Philip G. Epstein, from story by Wilson Collison. Cinematographer: Nicholas Musuraco. Cast: Barbara Stanwyck, Henry Fonda, Sam Levene, Frances Mercer, Stanley Ridges, Whitney Bourne, Vickie Lester, Ann Evers, Catherine O'Quinn, Hattie McDaniel, Miles Mander, John Qualen, Grady Sutton.

Jesse James. 1939. Twentieth Century–Fox. Director: Henry King. Producer: Darryl F. Zanuck. Screenplay: Nunnally Johnson. Cinematographers: George Barnes and W. H. Greene. Cast: Tyrone Power, Henry Fonda, Nancy Kelly, Randolph Scott, Henry Hull, Slim Summerville, J. Edward Bromberg, Brian Donlevy, John Carradine, Donald Meek, John Russell, Jane Darwell, Charles Tannen.

Let Us Live. 1939. Columbia. Director: John Brahm. Producer: William Perlberg. Screenplay: Anthony Veiller and Allen Rivkin, from story by Joseph F. Dinneen. Cinematographer: Lucien Ballard. Cast: Maureen O'Sullivan, Henry Fonda, Ralph Bellamy, Alan Baxter, Stanley Ridges, Henry Kolker, George Lynn, George Douglas.

The Story of Alexander Graham Bell. 1939. Twentieth Century–Fox. Director: Irving Cummings. Producer: Darryl F. Zanuck. Associate Producer: Kenneth Macgowan. Screenplay: Lamar Trotti, from original story by Ray Harris. Cinematographer: Leon Shamroy. Cast: Don Ameche, Loretta Young, Henry Fonda, Charles Coburn, Gene Lockhart, Spring Byington, Sally Blane.

Young Mr. Lincoln. 1939. Twentieth Century–Fox. Director: John Ford. Producer: Darryl F. Zanuck, Associate Producer, Kenneth Macgowan. Screenplay: Lamar Trotti. Cinematographers: Bert Glennon, and Arthur Miller (uncredited). Cast: Henry Fonda, Alice Brady, Marjorie Weaver, Arleen Whelan, Eddie Collins, Pauline Moore, Richard Cromwell, Donald Meek, Judith Dickens, Eddie Quillan, Spencer Charters, Ward Bond.

Drums Along the Mohawk. 1939. Twentieth Century–Fox. Director: John Ford. Producer: Darryl F. Zanuck. Screenplay: Lamar Trotti and Sonya Levien, from novel by Walter D. Edmonds. Cinematographers: Bert Glennon and Ray Rennahan. Cast: Claudette Colbert, Henry Fonda, Edna May Oliver, Eddie Collins, John Carradine, Dorris Bowdon, Jessie Ralph, Arthur Shields, Robert Lowery, Roger Imhof, Francis Ford, Ward Bond, Kay Linaker, Russell Simpson.

The Grapes of Wrath. 1940. Twentieth Century–Fox. Director: John Ford. Producers: Nunnally Johnson and Darryl F. Zanuck. Screenplay: Johnson, from novel by John Steinbeck. Cinematographer: Gregg Toland. Cast: Henry Fonda, Jane Darwell, John Carradine, Charley Grapewin, Dorris Bowdon, Russell Simpson, O. Z. Whitehead, John Qualen, Eddie Quillan, Zeffie Tilbury, Frank Sully, Frank Darien, Darryl

Hickman, Shirley Mills, Roger Imhof, Grant Mitchell, Charles D. Brown, John Arledge, Ward Bond.

Lillian Russell. 1940. Twentieth Century–Fox. Director: Irving Cummings. Producer: Darryl F. Zanuck. Screenplay: William Anthony McGuire. Cinematographer: Leon Shamroy. Cast: Alice Faye, Don Ameche, Henry Fonda, Edward Arnold, Warren William, Leo Carrillo, Helen Westley, Ernest Truex, Nigel Bruce, Joe Weber, Lew Fields.

The Return of Frank James. 1940. Twentieth Century–Fox. Director: Fritz Lang. Producer: Darryl F. Zanuck. Screenplay: Sam Hellman. Cinematographer: George Barnes. Cast: Henry Fonda, Gene Tierney, Jackie Cooper, Henry Hull, John Carradine, J. Edward Bromberg, Donald Meek, Eddie Collins, George Barbier, Russell Hicks.

Chad Hanna. 1940. Twentieth Century–Fox. Director: Henry King. Producers: Nunnally Johnson and Darryl F. Zanuck. Screenplay: Johnson, from novel *Red Wheels Rolling,* by Walter D. Edmonds. Cinematographers: Ernest Palmer and Ray Rennahan. Cast: Henry Fonda, Dorothy Lamour, Linda Darnell, Guy Kibbee, Jane Darwell, John Carradine, Roscoe Ates, Ben Carter, Frank M. Thomas, Frank Conlan.

The Lady Eve. 1941. Paramount. Director: Preston Sturges. Producer: Paul Jones. Screenplay: Sturges, from story "The Faithful Heart," by Monckton Hoffe. Cinematographer: Victor Milner. Cast: Barbara Stanwyck, Henry Fonda, Charles Coburn, Eugene Pallette, William Demarest, Eric Blore, Melville Cooper, Martha O'Driscoll, Janet Beecher, Robert Greig.

Wild Geese Calling. 1941. Twentieth Century–Fox. Director: John Brahm. Executive Producer: Darryl F. Zanuck. Producer: Harry Joe Brown. Screenplay: Horace McCoy, from novel by Stewart Edward White. Cinematographer: Lucien Ballard. Cast: Henry Fonda, Joan Bennett, Warren William, Ona Munson, Barton MacLane, Russell Simpson, Iris Adrian, James C. Morton, Paul Sutton, Mary Field, Stanley Andrews.

You Belong to Me. 1941. Columbia Pictures. Director: Wesley Ruggles. Producer: Ruggles. Screenplay: Claude Binyon, from story by Dalton Trumbo. Cinematographer: Joseph Walker. Cast: Barbara Stanwyck, Henry Fonda, Edgar Buchanan, Roger Clark, Ruth Donnelly, Melville Cooper, Ralph Peters, Maude Eburne, Renie Riano, Ellen Lowe, Mary Treen, Gordon Jones, Fritz Feld, Paul Harvey.

Rings on Her Fingers. 1942. Twentieth Century–Fox. Director: Rouben Mamoulian. Producer: Milton Sperling. Screenplay: Ken Englund, from story by Robert Pirosh and Joseph Schrank. Cinematographer: George Barnes. Cast: Henry Fonda, Gene Tierney, Laird Cregar, John Shepherd, Spring Byington, Frank Orth, Henry Stephenson, Marjorie Gateson, George Lessey, Iris Adrian, Harry Hayden.

The Male Animal. 1942. Warner Bros. Director: Elliott Nugent. Producer: Hal B. Wallis. Screenplay: Julius J. and Philip G. Epstein, from play by James Thurber and Elliott Nugent. Cinematographer: Arthur Edeson. Cast: Henry Fonda, Olivia de Havilland,

Joan Leslie, Jack Carson, Eugene Pallette, Herbert Anderson, Hattie McDaniel, Ivan F. Simpson, Don DeFore, Jean Ames, Minna Phillips, Regina Wallace.

The Magnificent Dope. 1942. Twentieth Century–Fox. Director: Walter Lang. Producer: William Perlberg. Screenplay: George Seaton, from original story by Joseph Schrank. Cinematographer: Peverell Marley. Cast: Henry Fonda, Lynn Bari, Don Ameche, Edward Everett Horton, George Barbier, Frank Orth, Roseanne Murray, Marietta Canty, Hobart Cavanaugh, Hal K. Dawson.

Tales of Manhattan. 1942. Twentieth Century–Fox. Director: Julien Duvivier. Producers: Boris Morros and S. P. Eagle (Sam Spiegel). Screenplay: Edmund Beloin, Ben Hecht, Ferenc Molnár, Donald Ogden Stewart, Samuel Hoffenstein, Alan Campbell, Ladislas Fodor, László Vadnay, László Görög, Lamar Trotti, Henry Blankfort, and William Morrow. Cinematographer: Joseph Walker. Cast: Charles Boyer, Rita Hayworth, Ginger Rogers, Henry Fonda, Charles Laughton, Edward G. Robinson, Paul Robeson, Ethel Waters, Eddie "Rochester" Anderson, Thomas Mitchell, Eugene Pallette, Cesar Romero, Gail Patrick, Roland Young, Marion Martin, Elsa Lanchester, Victor Francen, George Sanders, James Gleason, Harry Davenport, J. Carrol Naish.

The Big Street. 1942. RKO. Director: Irving Reis. Producer: Damon Runyon. Screenplay: Leonard Spigelgass, from story "Little Pinks," by Runyon. Cinematographer: Russell Metty. Cast: Henry Fonda, Lucille Ball, Barton MacLane, Eugene Pallette, Agnes Moorehead, Sam Levene, Ray Collins, Marion Martin, William T. Orr, George Cleveland, Vera Gordon, Ozzie Nelson.

Immortal Sergeant. 1943. Twentieth Century–Fox. Director: John M. Stahl. Producer: Lamar Trotti. Screenplay: Trotti, from novel by John Brophy. Cinematographer: Arthur Miller. Cast: Henry Fonda, Maureen O'Hara, Thomas Mitchell, Allyn Joslyn, Reginald Gardiner, Melville Cooper.

The Ox-Bow Incident. 1943. Twentieth Century–Fox. Director: William A. Wellman. Producer: Lamar Trotti. Screenplay: Trotti, from novel by Walter Van Tilburg Clark. Cinematographer: Arthur Miller. Cast: Henry Fonda, Dana Andrews, Mary Beth Hughes, Anthony Quinn, William Eythe, Henry Morgan, Jane Darwell, Matt Briggs, Harry Davenport, Frank Conroy, Marc Lawrence, Paul Hurst, Victor Kilian, Chris-Pin Martin, Willard Robertson, Ted North, Francis Ford, Margaret Hamilton.

My Darling Clementine. 1946. Twentieth Century–Fox. Director: John Ford. Producer: Samuel G. Engel. Screenplay: Engel and Winston Miller, from story by Sam Hellman, from book *Wyatt Earp: Frontier Marshal,* by Stuart N. Lake. Cinematographer: Joe MacDonald. Cast: Henry Fonda, Linda Darnell, Victor Mature, Cathy Downs, Walter Brennan, Tim Holt, Ward Bond, Alan Mowbray, John Ireland, Roy Roberts, Jane Darwell, Grant Withers, J. Farrell MacDonald, Russell Simpson, Francis Ford, Mae Marsh.

The Long Night. 1947. RKO. Director: Anatole Litvak. Producers: Robert and Raymond Hakim, and Litvak. Screenplay: John Wexley, from story by Jacques Viot. Cinematographer: Sol Polito. Cast: Henry Fonda, Barbara Bel Geddes, Vincent

Price, Ann Dvorak, Howard Freeman, Moroni Olsen, Elisha Cook, Jr., Queenie Smith, David Clarke, Charles McGraw.

The Fugitive. 1947. Argosy-RKO. Director: John Ford. Producers: Ford and Merian C. Cooper. Screenplay: Dudley Nichols, from novel *The Power and the Glory,* by Graham Greene. Cinematographer: Gabriel Figueroa. Cast: Henry Fonda, Dolores del Rio, Pedro Armendáriz, J. Carrol Naish, Leo Carrillo, Ward Bond, Robert Armstrong, John Qualen.

Daisy Kenyon. 1947. Twentieth Century–Fox. Director-producer: Otto Preminger. Screenplay: David Hertz, from novel by Elizabeth Janeway. Cinematographer: Leon Shamroy. Cast: Joan Crawford, Dana Andrews, Henry Fonda, Ruth Warrick, Martha Stewart, Peggy Ann Garner, Connie Marshall, Nicholas Joy, Art Baker.

On Our Merry Way (aka *A Miracle Can Happen*). 1948. United Artists. Directors: King Vidor and Leslie Fenton. Producers: Benedict Bogeaus and Burgess Meredith. Screenplay: Laurence Stallings, from original story by Arch Oboler, John O'Hara, and Lou Breslow. Cinematographers: Gordon Avil, Joseph Biroc, Edward Cronjager, and John F. Seitz. Cast: Paulette Goddard, Burgess Meredith, James Stewart, Henry Fonda, Harry James, Dorothy Lamour, Victor Moore, Fred MacMurray, William Demarest, Hugh Herbert, Charles D. Brown, Eduardo Ciannelli, Betty Caldwell, Dorothy Ford, Carl Switzer.

Fort Apache. 1948. Argosy-RKO. Director: John Ford. Producers: Ford and Merian C. Cooper. Screenplay: Frank S. Nugent, from story "Massacre," by James Warner Bellah. Cinematographer: Archie Stout. Cast: John Wayne, Henry Fonda, Shirley Temple, Pedro Armendáriz, Ward Bond, George O'Brien, Victor McLaglen, Anna Lee, Irene Rich, Dick Foran, Guy Kibbee, Grant Withers, Jack Pennick, Ray Hyke, Movita, Miguel Inclán, Mary Gordon, Philip Keiffer, Mae Marsh, Hank Worden, John Agar, Francis Ford.

Jigsaw. 1949. United Artists. Director: Fletcher Markle. Producers: Edward J. and Harry Lee Danziger. Screenplay: Markle and Vincent McConnor, from story by John Roeburt. Cinematographer: Don Malkames. Cast: Franchot Tone, Jean Wallace, Myron McCormick, Marc Lawrence, Winifred Lenihan, Betty Harper, Hedley Rainnie, Walter Vaughan, George Breen, Robert Gist, Hester Sondergaard. Uncredited cameos: Leonard Lyons, Marlene Dietrich, Henry Fonda, John Garfield, Burgess Meredith, Everett Sloane.

Mister Roberts. 1955. Warner Bros. Directors: John Ford and Mervyn LeRoy. Producer: Leland Hayward. Screenplay: Frank S. Nugent and Joshua Logan, from play by Thomas Heggen and Logan, from Heggen's novel. Cinematographer: Winton Hoch. Cast: Henry Fonda, James Cagney, William Powell, Jack Lemmon, Betsy Palmer, Ward Bond, Phil Carey, Nick Adams, Perry Lopez, Ken Curtis, Robert Roark, Harry Carey, Jr., Pat Wayne, Frank Aletter, Tiger Andrews, Fritz Ford, Jim Moloney, Buck Kartalian, Denny Niles, Francis Connor, William Hudson,

Shug Fisher, Stubby Kruger, Danny Borzage, Harry Tenbrook, Martin Milner, Gregory Walcott.

War and Peace. 1956. Paramount. Director: King Vidor. Producers: Dino De Laurentiis and Carlo Ponti. Screenplay: Vidor, Bridget Boland, Robert Westerby, Mario Camerini, Ennio De Concini, Ivo Perilli, Gian Gaspare Napolitano, and Mario Soldati, from novel by Leo Tolstoy. Cinematographer: Jack Cardiff. Cast: Audrey Hepburn, Henry Fonda, Mel Ferrer, Vittorio Gassman, Herbert Lom, Oscar Homolka, Anita Ekberg, Helmut Dantine, Tullio Carminati, Barry Jones, Milly Vitale, Lea Seidl, Anna Maria Ferrero, Wilfred Lawson, May Britt, Jeremy Brett, Patrick Crean, John Mills.

The Wrong Man. 1956. Warner Bros. Director-producer: Alfred Hitchcock. Screenplay: Maxwell Anderson and Angus MacPhail, from story by Anderson. Cinematographer: Robert Burks. Cast: Henry Fonda, Vera Miles, Anthony Quayle, Harold J. Stone, John Heldabrand, Doreen Lang, Norma Connolly, Lola D'Annunzio, Robert Essen, Dayton Lummis, Charles Cooper, Esther Minciotti, Laurinda Barrett, Nehemiah Persoff, Kippy Campbell, Richard Robbins, Peggy Webber, Barry Atwater, Henry Beckman, Bonnie Franklin, Werner Klemperer.

12 Angry Men. 1957. United Artists. Director: Sidney Lumet. Producers: Henry Fonda and Reginald Rose. Screenplay: Reginald Rose, from his teleplay. Cinematographer: Boris Kaufman. Cast: Henry Fonda, Lee J. Cobb, Ed Begley, E. G. Marshall, Jack Warden, Jack Klugman, Edward Binns, Joseph Sweeney, Martin Balsam, George Voskovec, John Fiedler, Robert Webber.

The Tin Star. 1957. Paramount. Director: Anthony Mann. Producers: William Perlberg and George Seaton. Screenplay: Dudley Nichols, from story by Barney Slater and Joel Kane. Cinematographer: Loyal Griggs. Cast: Henry Fonda, Anthony Perkins, Betsy Palmer, Michel Ray, Neville Brand, John McIntire, Mary Webster, Peter Baldwin, Richard Shannon, Lee Van Cleef, James Bell, Howard Petrie, Russell Simpson, Hal K. Dawson.

Stage Struck. 1958. RKO. Director: Sidney Lumet. Producer: Stuart Millar. Screenplay: Ruth and Augustus Goetz, from play *Morning Glory,* by Zoe Akins. Cinematographers: Maurice Hartzband and Franz Planer. Cast: Henry Fonda, Susan Strasberg, Joan Greenwood, Herbert Marshall, Christopher Plummer, Daniel Ocko, Pat Harrington, Jr., Frank Campanella, John Fiedler, Patricia Englund, Jack Weston.

Warlock. 1959. Twentieth Century–Fox. Director-producer: Edward Dmytryk. Screenplay: Robert Alan Aurthur, from novel by Oakley Hall. Cinematographer: Joe MacDonald. Cast: Richard Widmark, Henry Fonda, Anthony Quinn, Dorothy Malone, Dolores Michaels, Wallace Ford, Tom Drake, Richard Arlen, DeForest Kelley, Regis Toomey, Vaughn Taylor, Don Beddoe, Whit Bissell, Frank Gorshin, L. Q. Jones, Gary Lockwood, Joe Turkel.

The Man Who Understood Women. 1959. Twentieth Century–Fox. Director-producer: Nunnally Johnson. Screenplay: Johnson, from novel *The Colors of the Day,* by Romain Gary. Cinematographer: Milton R. Krasner. Cast: Leslie Caron, Henry Fonda, Cesare Danova, Myron McCormick, Marcel Dalio, Conrad Nagel, Edwin Jerome, Bern Hoffmann, Harry Ellerbe, Frank Cady, Ben Astar.

Advise and Consent. 1962. Columbia. Director-producer: Otto Preminger. Screenplay: Wendell Mayes, from novel by Allen Drury. Cinematographer: Sam Leavitt. Cast: Franchot Tone, Lew Ayres, Henry Fonda, Walter Pidgeon, Charles Laughton, Don Murray, Peter Lawford, Gene Tierney, Burgess Meredith, Eddie Hodges, Paul Ford, George Grizzard, Inga Swenson, Paul McGrath, Will Geer, Edward Andrews, Betty White, Malcolm Atterbury, J. Edward McKinley, Bill Quinn, Tiki Santos, Raoul De Leon, Tom Helmore, Hilary Eaves, Rene Paul, Michele Montau, Raj Mallick, Russ Brown, Janet Jane Carty, Chet Stratton, Larry Tucker, John Granger, Sid Gould, Irv Kupcinet.

The Longest Day. 1962. Twentieth Century–Fox. Directors: Ken Annakin, Andrew Marton, and Bernhard Wicki. Producer: Darryl F. Zanuck. Screenplay: Romain Gary, James Jones, David Pursall, Jack Seddon, and Cornelius Ryan, from Ryan's book. Cinematographers: Jean Bourgoin and Walter Woititz. Cast: Eddie Albert, Paul Anka, Arletty, Jean-Louis Barrault, Richard Beymer, Hans Christian Blech, Bourvil, Richard Burton, Wolfgang Büttner, Red Buttons, Pauline Carton, Sean Connery, Ray Danton, Irina Demick, Fred Dur, Fabian, Mel Ferrer, Henry Fonda, Steve Forrest, Gert Fröbe, Leo Genn, John Gregson, Paul Hartmann, Peter Helm, Werner Hinz, Donald Houston, Jeffrey Hunter, Curt Jürgens, Alexander Knox, Peter Lawford, Fernand Ledoux, Christian Marquand, Dewey Martin, Roddy McDowall, Michael Medwin, Sal Mineo, Robert Mitchum, Kenneth More, Richard Münch, Edmond O'Brien, Leslie Phillips, Wolfgang Preiss, Ron Randell, Madeleine Renaud, Georges Rivière, Norman Rossington, Robert Ryan, Tommy Sands, George Segal, Jean Servais, Rod Steiger, Richard Todd, Tom Tryon, Peter van Eyck, Robert Wagner, Richard Wattis, Stuart Whitman, Georges Wilson, John Wayne, Richard Dawson, Frank Finlay.

How the West Was Won. 1963. MGM. Directors: John Ford, Henry Hathaway, and George Marshall. Producer: Bernard Smith. Screenplay: James R. Webb. Cinematographers: William H. Daniels, Milton Krasner, Charles Lang, Jr., and Joseph LaShelle. Cast: Carroll Baker, Lee J. Cobb, Henry Fonda, Carolyn Jones, Karl Malden, Gregory Peck, George Peppard, Robert Preston, Debbie Reynolds, James Stewart, Eli Wallach, John Wayne, Richard Widmark, Brigid Bazlen, Walter Brennan, David Brian, Andy Devine, Raymond Massey, Agnes Moorehead, Harry Morgan, Thelma Ritter, Mickey Shaughnessy, Russ Tamblyn, Spencer Tracy, Ken Curtis, Jay C. Flippen, Jack Lambert, John Larch, Cliff Osmond, Harry Dean Stanton, Karl Swenson, Lee Van Cleef, William Wellman, Jr.

Spencer's Mountain. 1963. Warner Bros. Director-producer: Delmer Daves. Screenplay: Daves, from novel by Earl Hamner, Jr. Cinematographer: Charles Lawton. Cast: Henry Fonda, Maureen O'Hara, James MacArthur, Donald Crisp, Wally Cox, Mimsy Farmer, Virginia Gregg, Lillian Bronson, Whit Bissell, Hayden Rorke, Kathy Bennett, Dub Taylor, Hope Summers, Ken Mayer, Bronwyn Fitzsimmons, Barbara McNair, Larry D. Mann, Robert "Buzz" Henry, James O'Hara, Victor French, Michael Greene, Med Flory, Ray Savage, Mike Henry, Gary Young, Michael Young, Veronica Cartwright.

The Best Man. 1964. MGM. Director: Franklin J. Schaffner. Producers: Stuart Millar and Lawrence Turman. Screenplay: Gore Vidal, from his play. Cinematographer: Haskell Wexler. Cast: Henry Fonda, Cliff Robertson, Edie Adams, Margaret Leighton, Shelley Berman, Lee Tracy, Ann Sothern, Gene Raymond, Kevin McCarthy, Mahalia Jackson, Howard K. Smith, John Henry Faulk, Richard Arlen, Penny Singleton, George Kirgo, George Furth, Anne Newman, Mary Lawrence, H. E. West, Michael MacDonald, William R. Ebersol, Gore Vidal.

Fail-Safe. 1964. Columbia. Director: Sidney Lumet. Producers: Charles H. Maguire and Max E. Youngstein. Screenplay: Walter Bernstein, from novel by Eugene Burdick and Harvey Wheeler. Cinematographer: Gerald Hirschfeld. Cast: Dan O'Herlihy, Walter Matthau, Frank Overton, Ed Binns, Fritz Weaver, Henry Fonda, Larry Hagman, William Hansen, Russell Hardie, Russell Collins, Sorrell Booke, Nancy Berg, John Connell, Frank Simpson, Hildy Parks, Janet Ward, Dom DeLuise, Dana Elcar.

Sex and the Single Girl. 1964. Warner Bros. Director: Richard Quine. Producer: William T. Orr. Screenplay: Joseph Heller and David R. Schwartz, from book by Helen Gurley Brown. Cinematographer: Charles Lang. Cast: Tony Curtis, Natalie Wood, Henry Fonda, Lauren Bacall, Mel Ferrer, Fran Jeffries, Leslie Parrish, Edward Everett Horton, Larry Storch, Stubby Kaye, Howard St. John, Otto Kruger, Max Showalter, William Lanteau, Helen Kleeb, Sheila Stephenson [MacRae], Count Basie.

The Rounders. 1965. MGM. Director: Burt Kennedy. Producer: Richard E. Lyons. Screenplay: Kennedy, from novel by Max Evans. Cinematographer: Paul C. Vogel. Cast: Glenn Ford, Henry Fonda, Sue Ane Langdon, Hope Holiday, Chill Wills, Edgar Buchanan, Kathleen Freeman, Joan Freeman, Denver Pyle, Barton MacLane, Doodles Weaver, Allegra Varron, Casey Tibbs, Warren Oates.

In Harm's Way. 1965. Paramount. Director-producer: Otto Preminger. Screenplay: Wendell Mayes, from novel by James Bassett. Cinematographer: Loyal Griggs. Cast: John Wayne, Kirk Douglas, Patricia Neal, Tom Tryon, Paula Prentiss, Brandon De Wilde, Jill Haworth, Dana Andrews, Stanley Holloway, Burgess Meredith, Franchot Tone, Patrick O'Neal, Carroll O'Connor, Slim Pickens, James Mitchum, George Kennedy, Bruce Cabot, Barbara Bouchet, Tod Andrews, Larry Hagman, Henry Fonda, Hugh O'Brian.

The Dirty Game (aka *Secret Agents*). 1966. American International. Directors: Christian-Jaque, Werner Klingler, Carlo Lizzani, and Terence Young. Producer: Richard Hellman. Screenplay: Philippe Bouvard, Jacques Gaborie, Christian-Jaque, Jo Eisinger, and Jacques Remy. Cinematographers: Richard Angst, Erico Menczer, and Pierre Petit. Cast: Henry Fonda, Robert Ryan, Vittorio Gassman, Annie Girardot, Bourvil, Robert Hossein, Peter van Eyck, Maria Grazia Buccella, Mario Adorf, Jacques Sernas, Georges Marchal, Wolfgang Lukschy, Klaus Kinski.

Battle of the Bulge. 1965. Warner Bros. Director: Ken Annakin. Producers: Milton Sperling and Philip Yordan. Screenplay: Yordan, Sperling, and John Melson. Cinematographer: Jack Hildyard. Cast: Henry Fonda, Robert Shaw, Robert Ryan, Dana Andrews, George Montgomery, Ty Hardin, Pier Angeli, Barbara Werle, Charles Bronson, Hans Christian Blech, Werner Peters, James MacArthur, Karl-Otto Alberty, Telly Savalas, Steve Rowland.

A Big Hand for the Little Lady. 1966. Warner Bros. Director-producer: Fielder Cook. Screenplay: Sidney Carroll, from teleplay by Reginald Rose. Cinematographer: Lee Garmes. Cast: Henry Fonda, Joanne Woodward, Jason Robards, Paul Ford, Charles Bickford, Burgess Meredith, Kevin McCarthy, Robert Middleton, John Qualen.

Welcome to Hard Times. 1967. MGM. Director: Burt Kennedy. Producers: David Karr and Max E. Youngstein. Screenplay: Kennedy, from novel by E. L. Doctorow. Cinematographer: Harry Stradling, Jr. Cast: Henry Fonda, Janice Rule, Keenan Wynn, Janis Paige, John Anderson, Warren Oates, Fay Spain, Edgar Buchanan, Aldo Ray, Denver Pyle, Michael Shea, Arlene Golonka, Lon Chaney, Jr., Royal Dano, Elisha Cook, Jr., Paul Fix.

Firecreek. 1968. Warner Bros/Seven Arts. Director: Vincent McEveety. Producer: Philip Leacock. Screenplay: Calvin Clements, Sr. Cinematographer: William H. Clothier. Cast: James Stewart, Henry Fonda, Inger Stevens, Gary Lockwood, Dean Jagger, Ed Begley, Jay C. Flippen, Jack Elam, James Best, Barbara Luna, John Qualen, Louise Latham.

Madigan. 1968. Universal. Director: Don Siegel. Producer: Frank P. Rosenberg. Screenplay: Howard Rodman and Abraham Polonsky, from novel *The Commissioner,* by Richard Dougherty. Cinematographer: Russell Metty. Cast: Richard Widmark, Henry Fonda, Inger Stevens, Harry Guardino, James Whitmore, Susan Clark, Michael Dunn, Steve Ihnat, Don Stroud, Sheree North, Warren Stevens, Raymond St. Jacques, Bert Freed, Harry Bellaver.

Yours, Mine and Ours. 1968. United Artists. Director: Melville Shavelson. Producer: Robert F. Blumofe. Screenplay: Shavelson and Mort Lachman. Cinematographer: Charles F. Wheeler. Cast: Lucille Ball, Henry Fonda, Van Johnson, Louise Troy, Sidney Miller, Tom Bosley, Nancy Howard, Walter Brooke, Tim Matheson, Gil Rogers, Nancy Roth, Gary Goetzman, Morgan Brittany.

The Boston Strangler. 1968. Twentieth Century–Fox. Director: Richard Fleischer. Producer: Robert Fryer. Screenplay: Edward Anhalt, from book by Gerold Frank. Cinematographer: Richard H. Kline. Cast: Tony Curtis, Henry Fonda, George Kennedy, Mike Kellin, Hurd Hatfield, Murray Hamilton, Jeff Corey, Sally Kellerman, William Marshall, George Voskovec, Leora Dana, Carolyn Conwell, George Furth, Richard X. Slattery, William Hickey, James Brolin, Dana Elcar, Carole Shelley.

Once Upon a Time in the West. 1969. Paramount. Director: Sergio Leone. Producer: Fulvio Morsella. Screenplay: Leone and Sergio Donati. Cinematographer: Tonino Delli Colli. Cast: Claudia Cardinale, Henry Fonda, Jason Robards, Charles Bronson, Gabriele Ferzetti, Keenan Wynn, Frank Wolff, Woody Strode, Jack Elam, Al Muloch, Lionel Stander, Paolo Stoppa.

Too Late the Hero. 1970. Cinerama. Director-producer: Robert Aldrich. Screenplay: Aldrich and Lukas Heller. Cinematographer: Joseph Biroc. Cast: Michael Caine, Cliff Robertson, Ian Bannen, Harry Andrews, Ronald Fraser, Denholm Elliott, Lance Percival, Percy Herbert, Patrick Jordan, Henry Fonda.

The Cheyenne Social Club. 1970. National General. Director-producer: Gene Kelly. Screenplay: James Lee Barrett, from novel by Davis Grubb. Cinematographer: William H. Clothier. Cast: James Stewart, Henry Fonda, Shirley Jones, Sue Ane Langdon, Elaine Devry, Robert Middleton, Arch Johnson, Dabbs Greer, Jackie Russell, Jackie Joseph, Sharon DeBord, Richard Collier, Charles Tyner.

There was a crooked man . . . 1970. Warner Bros. Director-producer: Joseph L. Mankiewicz. Screenplay: David Newman and Robert Benton. Cinematographer: Harry Stradling, Jr. Cast: Kirk Douglas, Henry Fonda, Hume Cronyn, Warren Oates, Burgess Meredith, John Randolph, Lee Grant, Arthur O'Connell, Martin Gabel, Alan Hale, Jr., Victor French, Claudia McNeil, Bert Freed, Jeanne Cooper, Barbara Rhoades, Gene Evans.

Sometimes a Great Notion. 1970. Universal. Director: Paul Newman. Producer: John C. Foreman. Screenplay: John Gay, from novel by Ken Kesey. Cinematographer: Richard Moore. Cast: Paul Newman, Henry Fonda, Lee Remick, Michael Sarrazin, Richard Jaeckel, Linda Lawson, Cliff Potts, Sam Gilman, Lee de Broux, Jim Burk, Roy Jenson, Joe Maross, Roy Poole, Charles Tyner.

The Serpent (aka *Flight from Moscow*). 1973. AVCO Embassy. Director-producer: Henri Verneuil. Screenplay: Verneuil and Gilles Perrault. Cinematographer: Claude Renoir. Cast: Yul Brynner, Henry Fonda, Dirk Bogarde, Philippe Noiret, Michel Bouquet, Virna Lisi, Guy Tréjan, Elga Andersen, Marie Dubois, Nathalie Nerval, André Falcon, Robert Party, William Sabatier, Robert Alda.

Ash Wednesday. 1973. Paramount. Director: Larry Peerce. Producer: Dominick Dunne. Screenplay: Jean-Claude Tramont. Cinematographer: Enno Guarnieri. Cast: Elizabeth Taylor, Henry Fonda, Helmut Berger, Keith Baxter, Maurice Teynac, Margaret Blye, Monique van Vooren, Henning Schlüter, Dino Mele.

My Name is Nobody. 1973. Titanus/Universal. Director: Tonino Valerii. Producer: Fulvio Morsella. Screenplay: Ernesto Gastaldi, story by Fulvio Morsella and Ernesto

Gastaldi, from idea by Sergio Leone. Cinematographer: Giuseppe Ruzzolini. Cast: Terence Hill, Henry Fonda, Jean Martin, R. G. Armstrong, Piero Lulli, Mario Brega, Marc Mazza, Karl Braun, Leo Gordon, Steve Kanaly, Geoffrey Lewis.

The Last Four Days (aka *Last Days of Mussolini*). 1974. Paramount/Aquila Cinematografica. Director: Carlo Lizzani. Producer: Enzo Peri. Screenplay: Lizzani and Fabio Pittorru. Cinematographer: Roberto Gerardi. Cast: Rod Steiger, Franco Nero, Lisa Gastoni, Lino Capolicchio, Giuseppe Addobbati, Andrea Aureli, Bruno Corazzari, Manfred Freyberger, Henry Fonda, Franco Balducci.

Midway. 1976. Universal. Director: Jack Smight. Producer: Walter S. Mirisch. Screenplay: Donald S. Sanford. Cinematographer: Harry Stradling, Jr. Cast: Charlton Heston, Henry Fonda, James Coburn, Glenn Ford, Hal Holbrook, Toshiro Mifune, Robert Mitchum, Cliff Robertson, Robert Wagner, Robert Webber, Ed Nelson, James Shigeta, Christina Kokubo, Monte Markham, Biff McGuire, Christopher George, Kevin Dobson, Glenn Corbett, Gregory Walcott, Edward Albert, Pat Morita, Dabney Coleman, Erik Estrada, Tom Selleck.

The Great Smokey Roadblock. 1977. Mar Vista. Director: John Leone. Producer: Allan F. Bodoh. Screenplay: Leone. Cinematographer: Edward R. Brown. Cast: Henry Fonda, Eileen Brennan, Austin Pendleton, Robert Englund, Dub Taylor, John Byner, Susan Sarandon, Melanie Mayron, Leigh French, Gary Sandy, Valerie Curtin.

Tentacles. 1977. American International. Director-producer: Ovidio G. Assonitis. Screenplay: Steven W. Carabatsos, Tito Carpi, and Jerome Max. Cinematographer: Roberto D'Ettore Piazzoli. Cast: John Huston, Shelley Winters, Bo Hopkins, Henry Fonda, Delia Boccardo, Cesare Danova, Alan Boyd, Sherry Buchanan, Franco Diogene, Claude Akins.

Rollercoaster. 1977. Universal. Director: James Goldstone. Producer: Jennings Lang. Screenplay: Richard Levinson and William Link. Cinematographer: David M. Walsh. Cast: George Segal, Richard Widmark, Timothy Bottoms, Henry Fonda, Harry Guardino, Susan Strasberg, Helen Hunt, Dorothy Tristan, Harry Davis.

The Biggest Battle (aka *Battle Force*). 1978. National Cinematigrafica. Director: Umberto Lenzi. Producer: Mino Loy and Luciano Martino. Screenplay: Lenzi and Cesar Frugoni, from story by Lenzi. Cinematographer: Federico Zanni. Cast: Helmut Berger, Samantha Eggar, Giuliano Gemma, John Huston, Stacy Keach, Ray Lovelock, Aldo Massasso, Venantino Venantini, Ida Galli, Orson Welles, Henry Fonda, Rik Battaglia.

The Swarm. 1978. Warner Bros. Director-producer: Irwin Allen. Screenplay: Stirling Silliphant. Cinematographer: Fred J. Koenekamp. Cast: Michael Caine, Katharine Ross, Richard Widmark, Henry Fonda, Richard Chamberlain, Olivia de Havilland, Lee Grant, Ben Johnson, José Ferrer, Patty Duke, Slim Pickens, Bradford Dillman, Fred MacMurray, Cameron Mitchell.

Fedora. 1979. Lorimar. Director-producer: Billy Wilder. Screenplay: I. A. L. Diamond and Wilder. Cinematographer: Gerry Fisher. Cast: William Holden, Marthe Keller,

Hildegard Knef, José Ferrer, Frances Sternhagen, Mario Adorf, Stephen Collins, Henry Fonda, Michael York, Arlene Francis.

Wanda Nevada. 1979. United Artists. Director: Peter Fonda. Producers: Dennis Hackin and Neal Dobrofsky. Screenplay: Hackin. Cinematographer: Michael Butler. Cast: Peter Fonda, Brooke Shields, Fiona Lewis, Luke Askew, Ted Markland, Severn Darden, Paul Fix, Henry Fonda.

City on Fire. 1979. AVCO Embassy. Director: Alvin Rakoff. Producer: Claude Héroux. Screenplay: Jack Hill, David P. Lewis, and Céline La Frenière. Cinematographer: René Verzier. Cast: Barry Newman, Susan Clark, Shelley Winters, Leslie Nielsen, James Franciscus, Ava Gardner, Henry Fonda, Jonathan Welsh, Hilary Labow, Richard Donat.

Meteor. 1979. American International. Director: Ronald Neame. Producers: Arnold Orgolini and Theodore Parvin. Screenplay: Stanley Mann and Edmund H. North. Cinematographer: Paul Lohman. Cast: Sean Connery, Natalie Wood, Karl Malden, Brian Keith, Martin Landau, Trevor Howard, Richard Dysart, Henry Fonda, Joseph Campanella.

On Golden Pond. 1981. Universal. Director: Mark Rydell. Producer: Bruce Gilbert. Screenplay: Ernest Thompson, from his play. Cinematographer: Billy Williams. Cast: Katharine Hepburn, Henry Fonda, Jane Fonda, Doug McKeon, Dabney Coleman, William Lanteau.

SELECTED STAGE WORK

The Game of Love and Death. November 25, 1929, Guild Theatre. Director: Rouben Mamoulian. Producer: Theatre Guild. Writer: Romain Rolland, translation by Eleanor Stimson Brooks. Cast: Claude Rains, Alice Brady, Frank Conroy, Clinton Corwin, Frank De Silva, William Earle, Anita Fugazy, Charles Henderson, Lizbeth Kennedy, Otto Kruger, Robert Norton, Sidney Paxton, Henry Fonda.

I Loved You Wednesday. October 11, 1932, Sam H. Harris Theatre. Director: Worthington Miner. Producer: Crosby Gaige. Writers: Molly Ricardel and William Du Bois. Cast: Henry Bergman, Humphrey Bogart, Jean Briggs, Mary Alice Collins, Frances Fuller, Harry Gresham, Guy Hamilton, Ken Harvey, Henry Fonda.

New Faces. March 15, 1934, Fulton Theatre. Director: Elsie Janis. Producer: Charles Dillingham. Music: Warburton Guilbert, Donald Honrath, Martha Caples, James Shelton, and Morgan Lewis. Lyrics: Viola Brothers Shore, Nancy Hamilton, and June Sillman. Book: Leonard Sillman. Cast: Reeder Boss, Imogene Coca, Frances Dewey, Henry Fonda, Dorothy Kennedy Fox, Hildegarde Halliday, Nancy Hamilton, Billy Haywood, Louise Lynch, Beverly Phalon, Edith Sheridan, Leonard Sillman, Roger Stearns, Charles Walter, O. Z. Whitehead.

The Farmer Takes a Wife. October 30, 1934, 46th Street Theatre. Director: Marc

Connelly. Producer: Max Gordon. Writers: Frank B. Elser and Connelly, from novel *Rome Haul,* by Walter D. Edmonds. Cast: June Walker, Henry Fonda, Wylie Adams, Walter Ayres, Joe M. Fields, Ruth Gillmore, Margaret Hamilton, Frank Knight, Mabel Kroman, Lewis Martin, Kate Mayhew, Mary McQuade, Bert J. Norton, Joseph Sweeney.

Blow Ye Winds. September 23, 1937, 46th Street Theatre. Director-producer: Arthur Hopkins. Writer: Valentine Davies. Cast: Henry Fonda, Helen Murdoch, Edgar Barrier, James Clairton, Blaine Cordner, Doris Dalton, Blair Davies, James Doody, Albert Hayes, Harry Hermsen, Linda Lee Hill, Mary Rockwell.

Mister Roberts. February 18, 1948, Alvin Theatre. Director: Joshua Logan. Producer: Leland Hayward. Writers: Thomas Heggen and Logan, from novel by Heggen. Cast: Henry Fonda, William Harrigan, Robert Keith, David Wayne, Tiger Andrews, Robert Baines, Fred Barton, Joe Bernard, Jocelyn Brando, John Campbell, Ellis Eringer, Murray Hamilton, Steven Hill, Marshall Jamison, John Jordan, Mikel Kane, Bob Keith, Jr., Lee Krieger, John "Red" Kullers, Rusty Lane, Harvey Lembeck, Karl Lukas, Joe Marr, Ralph Meeker, Walter Mullen, Jack Pierce, James Sherwood, Len Smith, Jr., Casey Walters.

Point of No Return. December 13, 1951, Alvin Theatre. Director: H. C. Potter. Producer: Leland Hayward. Writer: Paul Osborn, from novel by John P. Marquand. Cast: Henry Fonda, Phil Arthur, Frances Bavier, Heywood Hale Broun, Madeleine Clive, Frank Conroy, John Cromwell, Leora Dana, Susan Harris, Pitt Herbert, Katherine Hynes, James Jolley, Colin Keith-Johnston, Madeleine King, James MacDonald, Davis Roberts, Bartlett Robinson, Robert Ross, Keith Russell, Harriet Selby, Patricia Smith.

The Caine Mutiny Court-Martial. January 20, 1954, Plymouth Theatre. Director: Charles Laughton. Producer: Paul Gregory. Writer: Herman Wouk, from his novel *The Caine Mutiny.* Cast: Henry Fonda, John Hodiak, Lloyd Nolan, Russell Hicks, Herbert Anderson, Larry Barton, Paul Birch, Jim Bumgarner, Stephen Chase, Richard Farmer, Eddie Firestone, Robert Gist, John Huffman, T. H. Jourdan, Charles Nolte, Richard Norris, Ainslie Pryor, Greg Roman, Pat Waltz.

Two for the Seesaw. January 16, 1958, Booth Theatre. Director: Arthur Penn. Producer: Fred Coe. Writer: William Gibson. Cast: Henry Fonda, Anne Bancroft.

Silent Night, Lonely Night. December 3, 1959, Morosco Theatre. Director: Peter Glenville. Producer: Playwrights' Company. Writer: Robert Anderson. Cast: Barbara Bel Geddes, Henry Fonda, Bill Berger, Peter De Visé, Eda Heinemann, Lois Nettleton.

Critic's Choice. December 14, 1960, Ethel Barrymore Theatre. Director-producer: Otto Preminger. Writer: Ira Levin. Cast: Henry Fonda, Billie Allen, Virginia Gilmore, Murray Hamilton, Eddie Hodges, Georgann Johnson, Mildred Natwick.

A Gift of Time. February 22, 1962, Ethel Barrymore Theatre. Director: Garson Kanin. Producer: William Hammerstein. Writer: Kanin, from book *Death of a Man,* by Lael Tucker Wertenbaker. Cast: Olivia de Havilland, Henry Fonda, Joseph Campanella, Lucretia Gould, Leslye Hunter, John MacKay, Gary Morgan, Marian Seldes, Rufus Smith, Guy Sorel, Leo Bloom, Guy Danfort, Kris Davis, Virginia Downing, Ann Draper, Alex Easton, Daniel Evan, Sol Frieder.

Generation. October 6, 1965, Morosco Theatre. Director: Gene Saks. Producer: Frederick Brisson. Writer: William Goodhart. Cast: Henry Fonda, A. Larry Haines, Sandy Baron, Don Fellows, Richard Jordan, Holly Turner.

Clarence Darrow. March 26–April 23, 1974, Helen Hayes Theatre; March 3–22, 1975, Minskoff Theatre. Director: John Houseman. Producers: Mike Merrick and Don Gregory. Writer: David W. Rintels, from book *Clarence Darrow for the Defense,* by Irving Stone. Cast: Henry Fonda.

First Monday in October. October 3–November 12, 1978, Majestic Theatre; November 14–December 9, 1978, ANTA Playhouse. Director: Edwin Sherin. Producers: The John F. Kennedy Center for the Performing Arts and the Plumstead Theatre Society. Writers: Jerome Lawrence and Robert E. Lee. Cast: Jane Alexander, Henry Fonda, Larry Gates, Ron Faber, Carol Mayo Jenkins, Patrick McCullough, John Newton, Alexander Reed, P. J. Sidney, Tom Stechschulte, John Stewart, Eugene Stuckmann, Earl Sydnor.

Showdown at the Adobe Motel. February 2, 1981, Hartman Theater Company (Stamford, CT). Director-producer: Edwin Sherin. Writer: Lanny Flaherty. Cast: Henry Fonda, Arthur E. Lund, Cecilia Hart.

SELECTED TELEVISION WORK

The Decision at Arrowsmith. July 11, 1953. CBS. *Chrysler Medallion Theatre* (live). Director: Ralph Nelson. Producer: William Spier. Teleplay: Tad Mosel, from novel by Sinclair Lewis. Cast: Henry Fonda, Diana Douglas, Juano Hernandez.

Clown. March 27, 1955. CBS. *General Electric Theater.* Director: James Neilson. Producer: Henry Fonda. Teleplay: Mel Goldberg and Richard Collins, from book by Emmett Kelly. Host: Ronald Reagan. Cast: Henry Fonda, Dorothy Malone, James Flavin, Barry Kelley, James McCallion, Gus Schilling, Billy Barty.

The Petrified Forest. May 30, 1955. NBC. *Producers' Showcase* (live). Director: Delbert Mann. Producer: Fred Coe. Teleplay: Tad Mosel, from play by Robert Sherwood. Cast: Humphrey Bogart, Lauren Bacall, Henry Fonda, Paul Hartman, Jack Warden, Richard Jaeckel, Natalie Schafer, Richard Gaines, Jack Klugman, Joseph Sweeney, Steven Ritch, Dick Elliott.

The Deputy. September 1959–July 1961. NBC. Creators: Norman Lear, Roland Kibbee. Producers: Henry Fonda, William Frye, and Michael Kraike. Cast: Henry Fonda, Allen Case, Wallace Ford, Betty Lou Keim, Read Morgan.

Henry Fonda and the Family. February 6, 1962. CBS. Director: Bud Yorkin. Producers: Yorkin and Norman Lear. Teleplay: Lear and Toni Koch. Cast: Henry Fonda, Cara

Williams, Carol Lynley, Dick Van Dyke, Paul Lynde, Verna Felton, Flip Mark, Michael J. Pollard, Dan Blocker.

Tissue of Hate. February 26, 1963. NBC. *The Dick Powell Show.* Director: Marc Daniels. Teleplay: Tony Barrett. Host: Charles Boyer. Cast: Henry Fonda, Polly Bergen, Gloria Vanderbilt, John Larkin, Eduard Franz, Elisabeth Fraser, Liam Sullivan.

Stranger on the Run. October 31, 1967. NBC. *NBC Tuesday Night at the Movies.* Universal. Director: Don Siegel. Producer: Richard E. Lyons. Screenplay: Dean Reisner, from story by Reginald Rose. Cast: Henry Fonda, Anne Baxter, Michael Parks, Dan Duryea, Sal Mineo, Lloyd Bochner, Michael Burns, Bernie Hamilton.

The Smith Family. January 1971–June 1972. ABC. Director: Herschel Daugherty. Producer: Don Fedderson. Cast: Henry Fonda, Janet Blair, Darleen Carr, John Carter, Ron Howard, Charles McGraw, Michael-James Wixted.

The Red Pony. March 18, 1973. NBC. *Bell System Family Theatre.* Omnibus/Universal. Director: Robert Totten. Producer: Frederick H. Brogger and James Franciscus. Screenplay: Totten and Ron Bishop, from novel by John Steinbeck. Cast: Henry Fonda, Maureen O'Hara, Ben Johnson, Jack Elam, Clint Howard, Julian Rivero, Lieux Dressler, Roy Jensen, Richard Jaeckel, Woodrow Chambliss, Rance Howard.

The Alpha Caper. October 16, 1973. ABC. Silverton/Universal. Director: Robert Michael Lewis. Producers: Aubrey Schenck and Harve Bennett. Screenplay: Elroy Schwartz. Cast: Henry Fonda, Leonard Nimoy, James McEachin, Larry Hagman, Elena Verdugo, John Marley, Noah Beery, Jr., Tom Troupe, Woodrow Parfrey, Vic Tayback, Kenneth Tobey, James B. Sikking.

Collision Course: Truman vs. MacArthur. January 4, 1976. ABC. *ABC Theatre.* Director: Anthony Page. Producers: Stan Margulies and David L. Wolper. Screenplay: Ernest Kinoy. Cast: Henry Fonda, E. G. Marshall, Lucille Benson, Lee Kessler, Lloyd Bochner, Ward Costello, Andrew Duggan, Russell Johnson, John Larch, John Randolph, Barry Sullivan, Priscilla Pointer, Howard Hesseman.

Home to Stay. May 2, 1978. CBS. Time Life Films. Director: Delbert Mann. Producers: Donald W. Reid, David Susskind, and Frederick Brogger. Screenplay: Suzanne Clauser, from novel *Grandpa and Frank,* by Janet Majerus. Cast: Henry Fonda, Kristen Vigard, Michael McGuire, Frances Hyland, David Stambaugh.

The Oldest Living Graduate. April 7, 1980. *NBC Live Theatre.* Director: Jack Hofsiss. Producer: Gareth Davis. Executive producer: David W. Rintels. Teleplay: Preston Jones, from his play. Cast: Henry Fonda, Cloris Leachman, George Grizzard, John Lithgow, Harry Dean Stanton, Penelope Milford, David Ogden Stiers, Timothy Hutton, Allyn Ann McLerie.

Gideon's Trumpet. April 30, 1980. CBS. *Hallmark Hall of Fame.* Producer: Robert H. Justman. Director: Robert Collins. Producers: David W. Rintels and John Houseman. Screenplay: Rintels, from book by Anthony Lewis. Cast: Henry Fonda,

José Ferrer, John Houseman, Fay Wray, Sam Jaffe, Dean Jagger, Nicholas Pryor, William Prince, Lane Smith, Dolph Sweet.

Summer Solstice. December 30, 1981. ABC. Director: Ralph Rosenblum. Producer: Stephen Schlow. Screenplay: Bill Phillips. Cast: Henry Fonda, Myrna Loy, Stephen Collins, Lindsay Crouse, Patricia Elliott, Marcus Smythe.

Acknowledgments

My gratitude goes first, as ever, to Kathy—for everything, and for everything else.

I'm indebted to the staffs of the National Personnel Records Center in St. Louis; the Museum of Television and Radio in New York; the New-York Historical Society; and the Billy Rose Theatre Collection of the Library for the Performing Arts at Lincoln Center. In Nebraska, Martha Paulsen at the Stuhr Museum of the Prairie Pioneer, Betsye Paragas at the Omaha Community Playhouse, and Mary-Jo Miller at the Nebraska State Historical Society proved to be Middle Westerners of the best kind—open, friendly, and happy to share.

Thanks to Jordan Person and Nic Rouleau of the New York University Drama School for permitting me to watch their scene from *Two for the Seesaw*. The employees of Jerry Ohlinger's famed movie memorabilia shop were more than helpful. Ron Mandelbum was my heavenly connection to the starry dynamo that is the Photofest archives.

For their conversation and curiosity down the years, I thank Attilla Ertl, Mike Gerber, Peter Greenman, Dylan Hicks, Tim Joyce, Mark Lerner, Bryan Mette, Evan Mueller, Robert Nott, Ed Park, Stella Park, Loree Rackstraw, Tim Riley, John Shaw, Colleen Sheehy, Kathy Zimmer, and the late Peter Dee.

Martha Hunt Huie entered my life unexpectedly and delightfully with a bounty of humor and wisdom. Jonathan Lethem went beyond generosity to help this book find a home, asking nothing in return. A single word from Luc Sante shored me up at a crucial moment.

My agent, Paul Bresnick, took this book personally and represented it that way. I was fortunate to be the beneficiary of his great talent, experience, and belief. My editor, Elizabeth Beier, was never short on enthusiasm, insight, and guidance. Her assistant, Michelle Richter, also earns my enormous thanks, as do the rest of the St. Martin's Press team, who more than earned their pay: production manager Eva Diaz; production editor John Morrone; cover designer Rob Grom; Laura Clark in marketing; John Karle in publicity; and publishers Sally Richardson and Matthew Shear.

The following deserve special thanks: Scott Cawelti, my first and best teacher of film; Ernest Callenbach, former editor of *Film Quarterly,* and the first person outside of Iowa to publish my writing; Ann Martin, his successor in that post, who taught me much; and Nick Thomson, movie friend and lover of noir, Ozu, Jack London, and the Feelies.

Love to Rhoda, Mark, Lori, and Salvador, and to Mike, Hope, and Mya.

Last and deepest thanks go to my mother, to my sister, and especially to my father. He died before this book was finished, but I promised him one day it would be. He was a Henry Fonda fan.

Index

HF stands for Henry Fonda. Kinship terms like (son) are in relation to HF. Married women are listed under their birth names. Films, plays, and TV shows in which HF appeared are designated by genre.